W9-BWZ-426

REASON AND EMOTION
IN PSYCHOTHERAPY

Books and Monographs by Albert Ellis

AN INTRODUCTION TO THE PRINCIPLES OF SCIENTIFIC PSYCHO-
ANALYSIS (*Journal Press*, 1950)

THE FOLKLORE OF SEX (*Charles Boni*, 1951; *Grove Press*, 1961)

SEX, SOCIETY AND THE INDIVIDUAL (with A. P. PILLAY) (*International Journal of Sexology*, 1953)

SEX LIFE OF THE AMERICAN WOMAN AND THE KINSEY REPORT
(*Greenberg: Publisher*, 1954)

THE AMERICAN SEXUAL TRAGEDY (*Twayne: Publisher*, 1954; *Lyle
Stuart*, 1959, 1962)

NEW APPROACHES TO PSYCHOTHERAPY TECHNIQUES (*Journal of
Clinical Psychology*, 1955)

THE PSYCHOLOGY OF SEX OFFENDERS (with RALPH BRANCALE)
(*Charles C. Thomas*, 1956)

HOW TO LIVE WITH A NEUROTIC (*Crown: Publisher*, 1957)

SEX WITHOUT GUILT (*Lyle Stuart*, 1958; *Hillman Books*, 1959)

WHAT IS PSYCHOTHERAPY? (*American Academy of Psychotherapists*,
1959)

THE PLACE OF VALUES IN THE PRACTICE OF PSYCHOTHERAPY
(*American Academy of Psychotherapists*, 1959)

THE ART AND SCIENCE OF LOVE (*Lyle Stuart*, 1960)

ENCYCLOPEDIA OF SEXUAL BEHAVIOR (with ALBERT ABAR-
BANEL) (*Hawthorn Books*, 1961)

CREATIVE MARRIAGE (with ROBERT A. HARPER) (*Lyle Stuart*, 1961)

A GUIDE TO RATIONAL LIVING (with ROBERT A. HARPER) (*Prentice-
Hall*, 1961)

REASON AND EMOTION IN PSYCHOTHERAPY (*Lyle Stuart*, 1962)

Reason
and Emotion
in Psychotherapy

by Albert Ellis, Ph. D.

THE CITADEL PRESS   SECAUCUS, N. J.

Austin Community College
Learning Resources Center

Copyright © 1962 by The Institute for Rational Living, Inc.
All rights reserved
Published by Citadel Press
A division of Lyle Stuart Inc.
120 Enterprise Avenue, Secaucus, N.J. 07094
In Canada: Musson Book Company
A division of General Publishing Co. Limited
Don Mills, Ontario
Manufactured in the United States of America
ISBN 0-8065-0909-0

10 9 8 7 6 5 4

TABLE OF CONTENTS

ACKNOWLEDGMENTS

Thanks are acknowledged to the following journals for permission to reprint some of the material in this book: *American Psychologist, Annals of the American Academy of Psychotherapists, Journal of Clinical Psychology, Journal of Counseling Psychology, Journal of Consulting Psychology, Journal of General Psychology, Journal of Psychology, Marriage and Family Living, Psychological Reports,* and *Quarterly Review of Surgery, Obstetrics and Gynecology.* Thanks are also acknowledged to Prentice-Hall, Inc. for permission to reprint some material from S. W. Standal and R. J. Corsini, *Critical Incidents in Psychotherapy,* and to Lyle Stuart for permission to reprint some material from Paul Krassner, *Impolite Interviews.*

The manuscript of this book was read by Dr. Roger J. Callahan, Dr. Magda Denes, Dr. Robert A. Harper, Dr. John W. Hudson, Dr. Madeleine Mason Lloyd, Dr. Stephen H. Sherman, Brookings Tatum, and Dr. Edwin E. Wagner, all of whom made valuable suggestions, but none of whom are to be held responsible for the views expressed herein.

Foreword

In view of my close association and collaboration with Dr. Albert Ellis, I may seem like the last person who should be writing a testimonial introduction to this book. But it is precisely because I am intimately acquainted with the author and his psychotherapeutic method that I feel most comfortable in calling certain important matters to the reader's attention.

I first of all heartily recommend that every reader of this volume give his careful attention to all its material. There is unfortunately a tendency for sophisticated and professional individuals (as Dr. Ellis points out) to shrug off the practices of rational-emotive psychotherapy as superficial, undynamic, and erroneous. This, quite frankly, tended to be my own first reaction several years ago, when I first conversed with the author about his therapeutic ideas. But I have since been able to see that my original "resistances" originated in my strong conditioning by the psychoanalytically-oriented culture in which I and my fellow psychotherapists have long been rather dogmatically immersed.

It has become increasingly clear to me in the last few years that many of the assumptions with which I and most other psychologists, psychiatrists, and other professional people have been indoctrinated are simply that—assumptions. They have been and still are being presented to us as facts, truths, axioms. But they are still assumptions; and are in numerous instances, I now see, *false* suppositions about how human beings function and how they may be most effectively treated when they function in a troubled manner.

I would therefore suggest that whatever may be your reactions to the theories and procedures advocated by Dr. Ellis in this book, you use his ideas as a challenge to some of your own preconceptions about human behavior and the treatment of behavioral disorders. Even if you never become convinced

1

of the effectiveness of rational-emotive psychotherapy, you will find many of the questions that an honest perusal of this book raises in your mind decidedly worth investigating. Too many psychologists, psychiatrists, social workers, and other professionals develop what Dr. Esther Menaker has called "hardening of the categories." The least that an open-minded reading of *Reason and Emotion in Psychotherapy* can provide is a decalcification of the reader's professional thinking.

Finally, I would suggest that you *try out,* in your actual practice and your daily observations of yourself and others, some of the ideas about human behavior and psychotherapy that Dr. Ellis expounds in this book. On the basis of my own experience, I have become most convinced of the soundness of many of his principles and practices.

In spite of my original doubts about rational-emotive psychotherapy, I honestly tried its methods in my own clinical practice and found that they really worked. What is more, they worked more effectively than other therapeutic techniques I had formerly employed (and continue, in some instances, to use).

I strongly believe that some of the ideas that Dr. Ellis has to offer are as importantly corrective of the prejudice and bigotry of *this* generation of psychotherapists and behavioral scientists as were Dr. Sigmund Freud's ideas for his generation. This statement may be simply a reflection of my own positive irrational proclivities for Albert Ellis and rational-emotive psychotherapy. But I do believe that professional persons who follow my prescription of reading this book carefully, using it as a basis to question some of their own assumptions, and trying out certain of its recommendations, will see that my judgment of its revolutionary import is not totally amiss.

ROBERT A. HARPER, PH.D.
Washington, D. C.

The Origins of Rational-Emotive Psychotherapy

Rational-emotive psychotherapy (often called, for short, rational therapy or RT) was born the hard way. My original training as a psychotherapist had been in the field of marriage, family, and sex counseling: where treatment largely consists of helping individuals with specific marital and sexual problems by authoritatively giving them salient information about how to handle each other, how to copulate effectively, how to rear their children, and so on. This kind of therapy seemed to work fairly—and sometimes surprisingly—well. But it had its obvious limitations, since it quickly became clear to me that in most instances disturbed marriages (or premarital relationships) were a product of disturbed spouses; and that if people were truly to be helped to live happily with each other they would first have to be shown how they could live peacefully with themselves.

So I embarked on a course of intensive psychoanalytic training. I had been highly conversant with all of Freud's main works, and with many of those of his chief followers, ever since my early years in college (when I had practically lived in the old Russell Sage Library at 22nd Street and Lexington Avenue, a block away from the downtown branch of the City College of New York, where I was then a student).

Although, from the very start, I had many reservations about Freud's theory of personality (since, even at the age of seventeen, it was not too difficult for me to see that the man was brilliantly *creating* clinical interpretations to make them fit the procrustean bed of his enormously one-sided Oedipal theories), I somehow, perhaps by sheer wishful thinking, retained my belief in the efficacy of orthodox psychoanalytic technique.

I believed, in other words, that though nonanalytic methods of psychotherapy were often helpful and much less time-consuming than classical analytic methods, the latter were indubitably deeper, more penetrating, and hence considerably more curative. So I very willingly underwent an orthodox psychoanalysis myself, with a highly respectable training analyst of the Horney group, who had been a Freudian analyst for twenty-five years prior to his affiliation with the Horney school, and who also had sympathetic leanings toward some of the main Jungian teachings. For all his theoretical eclecticism, however, his analytic technique was almost entirely Freudian: with the result that I spent the next three years on the sofa, with my analyst for the most part sitting silently behind me, while I engaged in free association, brought forth hundreds of dreams to be interpreted, and endlessly discussed the transference connections between my childhood relations with my mother, father, sister, and brother, on the one hand, and my present sex, love, family, professional, and analytic relations on the other.

Both I and my analyst considered my analysis to have been successfully completed; and at his suggestion I went on to complete several control cases: that is, to work, under the supervision of a training analyst, with my own patients, with whom I consistently employed the sofa, free association, extensive dream analysis, and resolution of the transference neurosis. During this period, although I saw some marriage and family counseling clients with whom I did not attempt psychoanalysis, I routinely put all my regular psychotherapy patients on the sofa and proceeded with them in a decidedly orthodox psychoanalytic way.

Unfortunately, the miracle of depth therapy, which I had confidently expected to achieve through this analytic procedure, never quite materialized. I think that I can confidently say that I was a good young psychoanalyst at this time. Certainly, my patients thought so and kept referring their friends and associates to me. And my therapeutic results were, as far as I could see, at least as good as those of other New York analysts.

Most of my patients stayed in treatment for a considerable

period of time (instead of leaving early in the game, as many psychoanalytic patients do); and about 60 per cent of my neurotic patients showed distinct or considerable improvement as a result of being analyzed (Ellis, 1957b). These results, as Glover (1940), Phillips (1956), and other investigators have shown, are better than average for classical psychoanalytic treatment.

I soon had honestly to admit to myself, however, that something was wrong. First of all, on my patients' side, serious resistance to the psychoanalytic method was frequently encountered. Free association, in the true sense of the term, was most difficult for many of my patients to learn; and some of them never really learned to do it effectively. Where some analysands dreamed profusely and had no trouble relating their dreams to me, others rarely dreamed and often forgot what they did dream.

Long, unhelpful silences (sometimes for practically the entire analytic session) would frequently occur, while I (in accordance with classical technique) sat idly by with a limply held pencil. Quite consistently, although I did my best to hold them with their backs rooted to the sofa, patients would want to jump up and pace across the room, or sit up and look at me, or do everything but stare reflectively at the ceiling. Ever so often, they would bitterly turn on me, complain that I wasn't doing anything to help them, and say that that was just about all they could stand of this kind of nonsense. I, of course, dutifully and cleverly interpreted that they were, by their refusal to go along peaceably with the analytic rules, resisting the transference relationship and resisting getting better. Often, I convinced them of just that; but I myself more and more wondered.

I also wondered about my own role in the therapeutic process. Interpreting my patients' free associations and dreams, and particularly connecting their present problems with their past memories, I at first found to be great fun. "Detectiving" I privately called it; and I often thought how lucky I was to be able to be paid for engaging in delightful brain-picking.

Being an old hand at creative writing, I found this kind of true-life detectiving even more enjoyable than figuring out surprise endings to my own or others' stories. When I would convince a patient that he really was angry today not because his boss cursed him or his wife gave him a hard time in bed, but because he actually hated his father or his mother, and was unconsciously getting back at him or her by his present outbursts, and when my patient would excitedly agree: "Yes, that's right! I see it all so clearly now!" I would feel wonderfully pleased and would be absolutely certain that, now that I had supplied him with this brightly shining key to his basic problems, this patient would unquestionably get better in short order.

I soon found, alas, that I had to honestly admit to myself (and sometimes to the patient as well) that I was usually dead wrong about this. For the same individual who just yesterday had screamed in triumph, as he wildly pounded my desk and almost unmoored my lovely alabaster lamp, "You're right! You're absolutely right! I do hate my father. I hate, hate, hate him very much, and have always hated him, even though I never wanted to admit it before, to myself or anyone else. Yes, you're perfectly right!"—this very individual, after his powerfully abreactive insight, and his jubilation over his finally being able to see why he couldn't get up in the morning and go to work, would come in the very next day, and the day after, and the week and the month after, and *still* not be able to get out of bed to go to the office.

Then he would pitifully, desperately ask: "How come? Why is it, Doctor Ellis, that I saw it all so clearly yesterday, and I still see it so clearly today, and I now admit that I really hate the old bastard, and I still can't get out of bed, still haven't changed a bit in my behavior? Why? Why is it?" And I (strictly, still, in the light of psychoanalytic theory, though wondering more and more about the validity of that very therapeutic theory) would be forced to reply: "Yes, I know. You have had some significant insight, and I'm sure it will help you yet. But I guess that you don't *really* see it clearly enough; or there's something else, some other significant insight, that you still don't see, though you probably are approaching seeing it; and if we just keep on patiently, until yo*u really* see what's troubling you, then you'll be able to get up and go to work in the morning or do anything else which you are now neurotically unable to do."

Usually, again, the patient was reassured (or at least temporarily stopped in his tracks) by these words. But not—no, never entirely—I. I still wondered, wondered. . . .

Other points of classical psychoanalytic technique I also inwardly questioned. Why, when I seemed to know perfectly well what was troubling a patient, did I have to wait passively, perhaps for a few weeks, perhaps for months, until he, by his own interpretive initiative, showed that he was fully "ready" to accept my own insight? Why, when patients bitterly struggled to continue to associate freely, and ended up by saying only a few words in an entire session, was it improper for me to help them with several pointed questions or remarks? Why did I, invariably, have to insist on creating a highly charged transference relationship, including a transference neurosis, between myself and the patient, when some patients honestly seemed to care hardly a fig, one way or the other, about me, but merely were interested in a fairly rapid means of solving their problems with themselves or others?

The more I wondered, the more skeptical of the efficiency and the efficacy of classical analytic technique I became. Little by little, I found myself quietly slipping over into nonclassical, neo-Freudian types of analysis; and then into what is usually called psychoanalytically-oriented psychotherapy. In the course of my slipping, I tried, I think, most of the major analytic methods: including Ferenczi's love-giving, Rank's relationship, Horney's present history emphasis, and Sullivan's interpersonal relationship techniques. All of them I found quite interesting, usually stimulating to me, and frequently insight-producing to my patients. I still had to admit, however, that although most of these patients started feeling better, and some of them behaved more effectively in their own lives, they rarely if ever were getting better in what I considered to be the only true sense of this term: namely, the steady experiencing of minimal anxiety and hostility.

As I gradually slipped from "deep" analysis, with its three to five times a week on the sofa emphasis, to once or twice a week, face-to-face psychoanalytically-oriented psychotherapy, my therapeutic results began to pick up. Much to my surprise, this more "superficial" method actually started to produce not only quicker but apparently deeper and more lasting effects. In psychoanalytically-oriented therapy, while many of the fundamental theories of Freud, Ferenczi, Abraham, Jones, Fenichel, and other leading psychoanalysts are utilized (and the neo-Freudian or neo-Adlerian theories of Horney, Rank, Reich, Fromm, Fromm-Reichman, Sullivan, and others sometimes are used as well), the longer-winded methods of free association and involved dream analysis are usually dispensed with or abbreviated, and instead a much more active and quickly interpretive therapeutic method is employed.

Thus, where a classical Freudian analyst may take a year or two to show his patient that he is still overly-attached to his parents and that this over-attachment causes considerable neurotic behavior on his part today, a psychoanalytically-oriented therapist may convey the same interpretation to a patient after just a few sessions, and may keep very actively relating the patient's past history (which he derives from direct and incisive questions) to his present neurotic performances.

From about 1952 to the beginning of 1955, I consequently became one of the most active-directive psychoanalytically-oriented psychotherapists in the field. And I must say that my activity soon began to bear better results. Where, in practicing classical analysis, I had helped about 50 per cent of my total patients (which included psychotics and borderline psychotics) and 60 per cent of my neurotic patients to significantly improve their lot, with active-directive analytically-oriented therapy I was able to help about 63 per cent of my total patients and 70 per cent of my neurotic patients distinctly or considerably to improve.

Moreover, where the patients treated with classical analytic techniques stayed in therapy for an average of about 100 sessions (with a good many having literally hundreds of sessions), those treated with more active analytically-oriented methods stayed for an average of 35 sessions. From what I could see, the analytically-oriented actively treated patients were getting better results in a shorter length of time than were those treated with the "deeper" classical technique.

Still, however, I was not satisfied with the results I was getting. For, again, a great many patients improved considerably in a fairly short length of time, and felt much better after getting certain seemingly crucial insights. But few of them were *really* cured, in the sense of being minimally assailed with anxiety or hostility. And, as before, patient after patient would say to me: "Yes, I see exactly what bothers me now and why I am bothered by it; but I nevertheless *still* am bothered. Now what can I do about that?" I still would be reduced to answering: "Well, I'm not so sure that you *really* see it entirely." Or: "Yes, I'll agree that you have intellectual insight into this thing that has been bothering you so long; but you still don't have *emotional* insight." Whereupon the patient would often say: "I agree. I guess I don't *really* see the thing entirely. I *don't* have emotional insight. Now how do I get it?"

Like all the other psychotherapists I knew, I would be stumped. I would half-heartedly say: "Well, there just must be something blocking you from *really* getting emotional insight. Now let's see what it is." Or—that old and tried refuge of thwarted therapists!—"Maybe you really don't *want* to get better. Maybe you *want* to keep punishing yourself by keeping your disturbance." All of which, again, often seemed to quiet the patient; but it hardly satisfied me.

The more I began to question the efficacy of psychoanalytically-oriented therapy (and, for that matter, of *all* kinds of therapy that I had ever heard of or utilized), the more convinced I became that something essential was lacking in its theory and practice. Finally, by a process of clinical trial and error, I began to see clearly what part of this something was.

The main tenet of psychoanalysis is essentially the same as that of the psychological theory of behavioristic learning theory, which in turn stems largely from Pavlovian conditioned response theory. This theory holds that, just as Pavlov's dogs had their unconditioned hunger drives thoroughly conditioned to the ringing of a bell by the simple process of the experimenter's ringing this bell in close association with the presentation of food (so that the dogs began to salivate as soon as they heard the bell, before the food was even presented to them), a human being is conditioned early in his life to fear something (such as his father's anger) by threatening or punishing him every time he acts in a certain disapproved manner (for example, masturbates or lusts after his mother).

Since, according to this theory, the individual (like Pavlov's dogs) is *taught* to fear something (such as parental disapproval), and since he was taught to do so when he was very young and didn't even realize what he was learning, the fairly obvious solution to his problem is to show him, in the course of psychoanalytic therapy, exactly what originally transpired. Knowing, therefore, that he has been taught to fear, and also realizing that he is *not* now a child and that he *no longer* needs to fear this same thing (such as, again, parental disapproval), this individual's conditioned fear (or neurosis) presumably will vanish. His insight into the early conditioning process, in other words, will somehow nullify the effects of this process and give him the freedom to recondition himself.

This seemed to me, in my early years as a therapist, a most plausible theory. I became one of those psychologists who thought that a rapprochement between Freudian (or at least neo-Freudian) psychoanalysis and behavioristic learning theory was close at hand, and that everything possible should be done to aid this rapprochement.

Espousal of learning theory helped my therapeutic efforts in at least one significant respect. I began to see that insight alone was not likely to lead an individual to overcome his deepseated fears and hostilities; he *also* needed a large degree of fear- and hostility-combatting *action*.

I got this idea by extrapolating from Pavlov's *de*conditioning experiments. For when the great Russian psychologist wanted to decondition the same dogs that he had conditioned by ringing a bell just before he fed them every day, he merely kept ringing the same bell, time after time, but *not* feeding them after it rang. After a while, the dogs learned to extinguish their conditioned response—that is, they no longer salivated at the sound of the bell alone.

This kind of deconditioning gave me [and apparently a good many other psychotherapists, such as Salter (1949) and Wolpe (1958)], the idea that if disturbed human beings are continually forced to do the thing they are afraid of (such as be in the same room with an animal or ride in a subway train) they will soon come to see that this thing is *not* as fearful as they erroneously think it to be, and their fear will thereby become deconditioned or extinguished.

So I began to try, as a therapist, not only to show my patients the origins of their fears, and to get them to see that they need no longer fear these things (such as parental rejection) no matter how much they *once* may have appropriately feared them; but also, and just as importantly, I tried to encourage, persuade, and impel them to *do* the things they were afraid of (such as *risking* actual rejection by their parents or others) in order more concretely to *see* that these things were not actually fearsome. Instead of a truly psychoanalytically-oriented psychotherapist, I thereby started to become a much more eclectic, exhortative-persuasive, activity-directive therapist. And I found that this type of therapy, although it still had its definite limitations, was distinctly more successful with most patients than my previous psychoanalytic methods.

Still, however, I kept running into many exasperating situations, known alas to therapists of all hues and stripes, where the patients simply refused to do virtually anything to help themselves, even after they had obviously acquired a remarkably large degree of insight into their disturbances.

One of my notable therapeutic failures, for example, was with a girl who refused to go out of her way to meet new boyfriends, even though she desperately wanted to marry. She knew perfectly well, after scores of sessions of therapy with me and two other highly reputable analysts, that she had been specifically taught to be afraid of strangers (by her overly fearful parents and relatives); that she was terribly afraid of rejection, because she was always told that she was uglier and less lively than her younger married sister; that she was petrified about assuming the responsibilities of marriage which she was certain (largely, again, because of family indoctrinations) that she would not be able to live up to successfully; and that she was over-attached to her father, and didn't want to leave his safe side for the lesser safety of marriage. In spite of all this self-understanding, she still utterly refused to meet new boyfriends and found every possible flimsy excuse to stay at home.

The question which I kept asking myself, as I tried to solve the mystery of the inactivity of this fairly typical patient, was: "Granted that she *once* was taught to be terribly afraid of rejection and responsibility in love and marriage, why should this 33 year old, quite attractive, intelligent girl *still* be just as fearful, even though she has suffered greatly from her fears, has succeeded at several other significant areas of her life, and has had years of classical analysis, psychoanalytically-oriented therapy, and now activity-directive eclectic therapy? How is it possible that she has learned so little, in this sex-love area, and still insists on defeating her own ends *knowing*, now, exactly what she is doing?"

My first answer to this question was in terms of Pavlovian-type conditioning and the normal laws of human inertia. "If," I said to myself, "this patient has been so strongly conditioned to be fearful during her childhood and adolescence, and if she is a human being who normally finds it easier to repeat an old action rather than to learn a new one, why should she *not* remain fearful forever?"

But no, this did not quite make sense: since there *was* a good reason why fear, no matter how strongly it may originally be conditioned, should at least eventually vanish in seriously troubled patients such as this one: namely, lack of pleasurable reinforcement and concomitant amassing of highly unpleasurable punishment. For, according to Pavlovian and behaviorist learning theory, the dog originally becomes conditioned to the sound of the bell when it is rung just before he is fed because (*a*) he naturally or unconditionedly *likes* meat and (*b*) he is reinforced or rewarded by this meat every time he hears the bell. It is not, therefore, the meat *itself* which induces him to respond to the bell which is rung in conjunction with it, but the *rewardingness* of the meat to the dog.

Similarly when the deconditioning experiment is done, and the bell is rung continually without any meat being presented to the dog, it is not the absence of the meat, *per se*, which disturbs the dog and induces it to respond no longer to the bell, but the lack of reward or reinforcement which is attendant upon the absence of the meat.

Presumably, then, human beings should act pretty much the same way as Pavlov's dogs reacted in conditioning and deconditioning experiences. If they are conditioned, early in their lives, to fear or avoid something (such as rejection by their parents), they should theoretically be gradually reconditioned or deconditioned when they find, as the years go by, that the thing they were conditioned to fear really is *not* so terrible. This should especially be true of people with psychological insight: who, once they can consciously tell themselves, "I learned to fear rejection during childhood, but I can see that there is really nothing to fear *now*," should presumably overcome their fear in short order and no longer have to be beset by it.

Unfortunately, cures of intense fears and hostilities rarely occur in this manner. Whether or not people acquire considerable insight into the early origins of their disturbances, they seldom automatically extinguish their fears, even though life experiences continue to show them (*a*) that there really *is* nothing to be afraid of, and (*b*) that as they remain afraid they will acquire and maintain seriously punishing and handicapping neurotic symptoms. In spite of the enormous dysfunctional influences of their early-acquired fears, they still persist in maintaining most inconvenient behavioral consequences of these fears.

Noting this, and noting the dogged way in which so many of my patients kept holding on to their self-sabotaging fears and hostilities, I continued to ask myself: "Why? Why do highly intelligent human beings, including those with considerable psychological insight, desperately hold on to their irrational ideas about themselves and others? Why do they illogically and intensely continue to blame themselves (thus creating anxiety, guilt, and depression) and unforgivingly blame others (thus creating grandiosity, hostility, and resentment) even when they get such poor results from these two kinds of blaming?"

Finally, in 1954, I began to put all my psychological and philosophical knowledge together in a somewhat different way than I had previously done and started to come up with what seemed to be a good part of the answer to these important questions. Human beings, I began to see, are not the same as Pavlovian dogs or other lower animals; and their emotional disturbances are quite different from the experimental neuroses and other emotional upsets which we produce in the laboratory in rats, guinea pigs, dogs, sheep, and other animals. For human beings have one attribute which none of the other living beings that we know have in any well-developed form: language and the symbol-producing facility that goes with language (Cassirer, 1953; Whorf, 1956). They are able to communicate with others and (perhaps more importantly, as far as neurosis and psychosis are concerned) with themselves in a manner that is infinitely more complex and variegated than is the signaling of other animals.

This makes all the difference in the world, I was soon able to see. For, whereas the Pavlovian dog is obviously able to signal himself on some rudimentary level, once the bell is rung in juxtaposition with the meat that he enjoys eating, and to convince himself that the sound of the bell equals eating time (and, in the extinguishing process, that the sound of the bell *without* the presentation of food equals non-eating time), his self-signaling tends to be very limited and largely to be at the mercy of *outside* circumstances.

It is relatively easy for the experimenter, therefore, to show the dog that under condition *b* (presentation of the bell without the food) it is wise for him to stop salivating. It is less easy, but still possible, for the experimenter to show the dog that under condition *a* (presentation of food with a noxious stimulus, such as a painful electric shock) it is wise for him to avoid eating, while under condition *b* (presentation of food without any noxious stimulus) it is better for him to resume eating again. This is presumably because the dog's self-signaling processes are fairly rudimentary or primary and he doesn't have what Pavlov called the complex or secondary signaling processes which man, alone of all the animals, seems to have. Consequently, it is easy for him to make the simple equations: food plus electric shock equals *avoid eating*; and food minus electric shock equals *eat*.

As soon, however, as man's complex or secondary self-signaling processes arise, a new factor comes into play that may enormously change the simple going-toward or avoidance equations made by lower animals. This factor may be called self-consciousness or thinking *about* thinking.

Thus, the Pavlovian dog may signal himself: "This meat is good," and he may go toward it or salivate in connection with it. Or he may signal himself: "This meat plus this electric shock is bad," and he may avoid the meat plus the shock. He probably never, however, signals himself, as a human being may well do: "I am aware (conscious) that I am thinking that this meat is good" or "I can see (understand) that I am telling myself that this meat plus the electric shock is bad and I'd better stay away from it."

The dog perceives and to some degree thinks about things outside himself (the meat and the electric shock) and even about himself (his own preferences for the meat or annoyance at being shocked). But he does not, to our knowledge, think about his thinking or perceive his own mental processes. Consequently, he has little ability to *define* external stimuli as good or bad and is largely limited to his concrete pleasant or noxious *sensations* about these stimuli.

The dog, in other words, seems to be telling himself (or, more accurately, signaling himself, since he does not have our kind of language) something along the line of: "Because this food *tastes* good, I like it and shall keep going toward it," and "Because this food plus this electric shock *feels* bad, I dislike it and shall keep avoiding it." He regulates his behavior largely because his *sensations* are reinforced (rewarded) or punished.

A human being, on the other hand, can be rewarded or punished by his sensations, and can accordingly draw conclusions about going toward or avoiding certain situations; but, more importantly, he can *also* be rewarded or punished by all kinds of symbolic, non-sensate processes, such as smiles, critical phrases, medals, demerits, etc., which have little or no connection with his sensing processes. And he can also be rewarded or punished by his *own* thinking, even when this thinking is largely divorced from outside reinforcements and penalties.

A man, for example, may force himself to volunteer for service in the armed forces, which he may ardently dislike and consider very dangerous (especially in wartime), because he feels that, even though his friends or associates will not literally harm him in any way if he refuses to enlist (that is, they will not boycott him, fire him from his job, or actually punish him with any noxious stimuli), they will *think* he is unpatriotic and will (silently and covertly) *feel* that he is not as good as are enlisted men. Although, in a case like this, there are actually very few and minor disadvantages (and probably several major advantages) for this man's staying out of the armed forces, he will *define* or *create* several huge "penalties" for his doing so, and will either drive himself to enlist or refrain from enlisting but force himself to be exceptionally guilty and self-hating about his not enlisting.

Similarly, although a woman's parents may be living thousands of miles away from her and have little or no contact with her, or although they may actually be deceased, she may force her-

self to be terribly guilty and unhappy over some of her behavior (or even contemplated behavior), such as her having
premarital sex relations, because if her parents *were* at hand
they probably *would* disapprove of her actions (or thoughts),
even though they quite probably would take no overt actions
against her performing these acts (or thinking these thoughts).

Here, especially, we have a clearcut case in which an act
(fornication) has no actual disadvantages (assuming that the
woman and her current friends and associates disagree with
her parents and do approve of the act), and probably has considerable advantages; and yet this woman fearfully refrains from
the act (or performs it with intense guilt) because she essentially *defines* it (or her absent or dead parents' reaction to it)
as reprehensible.

Dogs, in other words, fear *real* noxious stimuli, while human
beings fear *imagined* or *defined* as well as real unpleasant
stimuli. To some degree, it is true, lower animals can imagine
or define the obnoxiousness of a situation. Thus, as Skinner
(1953) has shown, pigeons and other animals can become
"superstitious" and can fear a certain corner of a cage (or of
similar cages) because they were *once* punished in that corner,
even though they thereafter receive no punishment in this
situation. Even in these instances, however, the pigeon *once*
had to be concretely punished; and it now avoids the situation
in which it was punished because of overgeneralization, rather
than by pure definition.

Humans, however, merely have to be *told* that it is horrible
or awful for others to disapprove of them; and they easily,
without any real noxious evidence to back this propaganda, can
come to believe what they are told; and, through this very
belief, *make* disapproval thoroughly unpleasant to themselves.

Still another way of expressing the main point I am trying
to make here is to say that lower animals can easily be conditioned to fear physically punishing effects, and through their
physical fears also learn (in the case of some intelligent animals,
such as dogs) to fear others' gestures and words (as a dog first
fears being punished for doing something and then learns to

dread a scowling look from his master when he does this same thing, even though he is not always directly punished for doing it).

Man, in addition to being deterred by physical punishment and by the words and gestures of others that signify that such punishment is likely to follow, also deters himself by (*a*) heeding the negative words and gestures of others even when these are *not* accompanied by any kind of direct physical punishment, and by (*b*) heeding his *own* negative words and gestures *about* the possible negative words and gestures of others (or of some hypothetical gods). Man, therefore, often becomes fearful of *purely* verbal or other signaling processes; while lower animals never seem to be able to become similarly fearful. And human neuroses, in consequence, are qualitatively different from animal neuroses in some respects, even though they may overlap with animal disturbances in certain other respects.

To return to my patients. I began clearly to see, during the year 1954, that they not only learned, from their parents and other people and means of mass communication in our society, to fear words, thoughts, and gestures of others (in addition to fearing sensory punishments that might be inflicted on them by these others), but that they also were able, because of their facility with language (or their ability to talk to others *and* themselves), to fear their *own* self-signalings and self-talk.

With these uniquely human abilities to fear others' and their own gestures and verbal communications, the patients were beautifully able to *imagine* or *define* fears that actually had no basis in physical or sensory punishment. In fact, virtually all their neurotic fears were defined fears: that is, anxieties that were originally defined to them by others and then later carried on as their *own* definitions. More specifically, they were first *told* that it was terrible, horrible, and awful if they were unloved or disapproved; and they then kept *telling themselves* that being rejected or unapproved was frightful. This twice-*told* tale, in the great majority of instances, constituted their neuroses.

What both the Freudians and the behaviorist-conditioning psychologists are misleadingly doing, I clearly began to see, is to leave out a great deal of the *telling* or *language* aspects of human neurosis. Not entirely, of course: for they both tacitly, if not too explicitly, admit that children are told, in one way or another, by their parents and other early teachers, that they are worthless and hopeless if they say or do the wrong things (especially, lust after their mothers or hate their fathers); and that they thereby acquire too strong consciences or (to use a Freudian term) superegos and therefore become disturbed.

While admitting, however, that philosophies of life that are language-inculcated have *some* neurosis-producing power, the classical psychoanalysts and the conditionists also stress the supposedly nonverbal or subcortical early influences on the child and often seem to think that these "nonverbal" influences are even more important factors in creating emotional disturbance than are language indoctrinations. In this, I am quite convinced, they are wrong: as the limitations of the kind of therapy they espouse partially seem to indicate.

More to the point, however, even when Freudians and conditionists seem fully to admit the enormous influence of verbal indoctrinations in the *creation* of neurosis [as, for example, Dollard and Miller (1950) clearly admit], they almost all sadly fail as scientists and clinicians when it comes to admitting the exceptionally important influence of verbal self-indoctrinations in the *maintenance* of emotional disturbance. And this, as I saw when I did both classical psychoanalysis and psychoanalytically-oriented psychotherapy, has even direr consequences for their therapeutic effectiveness.

For, as Bernheim (1887), Coué (1923), and many other psychological practitioners have seen for at least the last 75 years, man is not only a highly suggestible but an unusually *auto*suggestible animal. And probably the main reason, I would insist, why he *continues* to believe most of the arrant nonsense with which he is indoctrinated during his childhood is not merely the influence of human laws of mental inertia (which quite possibly serve to induce lower animals to keep repeating the same dysfunctional mistake over and over again), but because he very actively and energetically keeps verbally reindoctrinating himself with his early-acquired hogwash.

Thus, a child in our culture not only becomes guilty about lusting after his mother because he is quite forcefully taught that anyone who behaves in that manner is thoroughly blameworthy; but he also *remains* forever guilty about this kind of lusting because (*a*) he *keeps* hearing and reading about its assumed heinousness, and (*b*) he *continues* to tell himself, every time he has an incestuous thought, "Oh, my God! I *am* a blackguard for thinking this horrible way." Even if *a* were no longer true—if this child grew up and went to live in a community where incest was thought to be a perfectly fine and proper act—the chances are that, for many years of his life and perhaps to the end of his days, *b* would still hold true, and he would keep thinking of himself as a worthless lout every time he had an incestuous idea.

This is what I continued to see more and more clearly, as I worked my way from psychoanalytically-oriented toward rational-emotive psychotherapy: that my patients were not *merely* indoctrinated with irrational, mistaken ideas of their own worthlessness when they were very young, but that they then inertly or automatically kept hanging on to these early ideas during their adulthood. Much more to the point: they (as *human* beings normally will) most actively-directively *kept* reindoctrinating themselves with the original hogwash, over and over again, and thereby creatively *made* it live on and on and become an integral part of their basic philosophies of life.

This energetic, forcible hanging on to their early-acquired irrationalities was usually something that they did unwittingly, unawarely, or unconsciously—though not always, since sometimes they quite consciously kept repeating to themselves the "truth" of the nonsense they had originally imbibed from their associates and their society. But consciously or unconsciously, wittingly or unwittingly, they definitely *were* making themselves, literally forcing themselves, to continue believing in many unrealistic, purely definitional notions; and *that* was why they not only remained neurotic in spite of the great disadvantages of so being, but why they also so effectively resisted my (or any other therapist's) best efforts, and also resisted their own efforts, to give up their neuroses.

I had finally, then, at least to my own satisfaction, solved the great mystery of why so many millions of human beings not only originally became emotionally disturbed, but why they persistently, in the face of so much self-handicapping, remained so. The very facility with language which enabled them to be essentially human—to talk to others and to talk to themselves —also enabled them to abuse this facility by talking utter nonsense to themselves: to *define* things as terrible when, at worst, these things were inconvenient and annoying.

In particular, their talking and their self-talking abilities permitted people to forget that their real needs, or necessities for human survival, were invariably of a physical or sensory nature —that is, consisted of such demands as the need for sufficient food, fluids, shelter, health, and freedom from physical pain —and permitted them illegitimately to translate their psychological *desires*—such as the desires for love, approval, success, and leisure—into *definitional needs*. Then, once they defined their desires or preferences as necessities, or accepted the false definitions of their parents or others in this connection, their self-talking abilities beautifully enabled them to *continue* to define their "needs" in this nonsensical manner, even though they had no supporting evidence to back their definitions.

Still more precisely: I discovered clinically, when I realized how important talk and self-talk was to neurotics and psychotics, that a disturbed individual almost invariably takes his preference to be loved or approved by others (which is hardly insane, since there usually *are* concrete advantages to others' approving him) and arbitrarily defines and keeps defining this preference as a dire need. Thereby, he inevitably becomes anxious, guilty, depressed, or otherwise self-hating: since there is absolutely no way, in this highly realistic world in which we live, that he can thereafter *guarantee* that he *will* be devotedly loved or approved by others.

By the same token, a disturbed person almost invariably takes his preference for ruling others, or getting something for nothing, or living in a perfectly just world (which again are perfectly legitimate desires, if only one could possibly achieve them) and *demands* that others and the universe accede to his desires. Thereby, he inevitably becomes hostile, angry, resentful, and grandiose. Without human talk and self-talk, *some* degree of anxiety and hostility might well exist; but never, I realized, the extreme and intense degrees of these feelings which constitute emotional disturbance.

Once I had clearly begun to see that neurotic behavior is not merely externally conditioned or indoctrinated at an early age, but that it is also internally reindoctrinated or autosuggested by the individual to himself, over and over again, until it becomes an integral part of his presently held (and still continually self-reiterated) philosophy of life, my work with my patients took on a radically new slant.

Where I had previously tried to show them how they had originally become disturbed and what they most actively now do to counter their early-acquired upsets, I saw that I had been exceptionally vague in these regards: and that, still misled by Freudian-oriented theories, I had been stressing psychodynamic rather than philosophic causation, and had been emphasizing what to undo rather than what to un*say* and un*think*. I had been neglecting (along with virtually all other therapists of the day) the precise, simple declarative and exclamatory sentences which the patients once told themselves in creating their disturbances and which, even more importantly, they were *still* specifically telling themselves literally every day in the week to maintain these same disturbances.

Let me give a case illustration. I had, at this period of my psychotherapeutic practice, a 37 year old female patient whom I had been seeing for two years and who had made considerable progress, but who remained on a kind of therapeutic plateau after making this progress. When she first came to therapy she had been fighting continually with her husband, getting along poorly at her rather menial office job, and paranoidly believing that the whole world was against her. It quickly became clear, in the course of the first few weeks of therapy, that her parents (both of whom were rather paranoid themselves) had literally taught her to be suspicious of others and to demand a good living from the world, whether or not she worked for this living. They had also convinced her that unless she catered to their whims and did almost everything in the precise manner of which they approved, she was ungrateful and incompetent.

With this kind of upbringing, it was hardly surprising that my patient thought that her husband never really did anything for her and that, at the same time, she herself was essentially worthless and undeserving of having any good in life. She was shown, in the course of psychoanalytic-eclectic therapy, that she had been thoroughly indoctrinated with feelings of her own inadequacy by her parents (and by the general culture in which she lived). She was specifically helped to see that she was demanding from her husband the kind of unequivocal accept- ance that she had *not* got from her father; and that, after railing at him for not loving her enough, she usually became terribly guilty, just as she had become years before when she hated and resisted her parents when she thought they were expecting too much from her.

Not only was this patient shown the original sources of her hostility toward her husband and her continual self-depreciation, but she was also encouraged to actively decondition herself in these respects. Thus, she was given the "homework" assign- ments of (*a*) trying to understand her husband's point of view and to act toward him as if he were *not* her father, but an independent person in his own right, and of (*b*) attempting to do her best in her work at the office, and risking the possi- bility that she might still fail and might have to face the fact that she wasn't the best worker in the world and that some of the complaints about her work were justified.

The patient, in a reasonably earnest manner, did try to employ her newly found insights and to do her psychothera- peutic "homework"; and, during the first six months of therapy, she did significantly improve, so that she fought much less with her husband and got her first merit raise for doing better on her job. Still, however, she retained the underlying beliefs that she really was a worthless individual and that almost everyone with whom she came into contact recognized this fact and soon began to take undue advantage of her. No amount of analyzing her present difficulties, or of tracing them back to their correlates in her past, seemed to free her of this set of basic beliefs.

Feeling, somehow, that the case was not hopeless, and that there must be *some* method of showing this patient that her self-deprecatory and paranoid beliefs were ill-founded, I persisted in trying for a therapeutic breakthrough. And suddenly, as I myself began to see things rather differently, this long-sought breakthrough occurred.

The following dialogue with the patient gives an idea of what happened. Like the other excerpts from actual sessions included in this book, it is slightly abridged, grammatically clarified, and cleared of all identifying data. Verbatim transcripts, though giving more of a flavor of what happens in therapy, have been found to be unwieldy, discursive, and (unless carefully annotated) somewhat unclear. A subsequent *Casebook of Rational-Emotive Psychotherapy* will include verbatim transcripts, with considerable more annotation than there is space for in the present volume.

"So you still think," I said to the patient (for perhaps the hundredth time), "that you're no damned good and that no one could possibly fully accept you and be on your side?"

"Yes, I have to be honest and admit that I do. I know it's silly, as you keep showing me that it is, to believe this. But I still believe it; and nothing seems to shake my belief."

"Not even the fact that you've been doing so much better, for over a year now, with your husband, your associates at the office, and some of your friends?"

"No, not even that. I know I'm doing better, of course, and I'm sure it's because of what's gone on here in these sessions. And I'm pleased and grateful to you. But I still feel basically the same way—that there's something really rotten about me, something I can't do anything about, and that the others are able to see. And I don't know what to do about this feeling."

"But this 'feeling,' as you call it, is only your *belief*—do you see that?"

"How can my feeling just be a belief? I really—uh—*feel* it. That's all I can describe it as, a feeling."

"Yes, but you feel it *because* you believe it. If you believed, for example, really believed you were a fine person, in spite of all the mistakes you have made and may still make in life, and in spite of anyone else, such as your parents, thinking that you were not so fine; if you really *believed* this, would you then feel fundamentally rotten?"

"—Uh. Hmm. No, I guess you're right; I guess I then wouldn't feel that way."

"All right. So your feeling that you are rotten or no good is really a belief, a very solid even if not too well articulated belief, that you are just no good, even though you are now doing well and your husband and your business associates have been showing, more than ever before, that they like you well enough."

"Well, let's suppose you are right, and it is a belief behind, and—uh—causing my feelings. How can I rid myself of this belief?"

"How can you *sustain* it?"

"Oh, very well, I'm sure. For I do sustain it. I have for years, according to you."

"Yes, but what's the *evidence* for sustaining it? How can you *prove* that you're really rotten, no good?"

"Do I have to prove it to myself? Can't I just accept it without proving it?"

"Exactly! That's exactly what you're doing, and have doubtlessly been doing for years—accepting this belief, this perfectly groundless belief in your own 'rottenness,' without any proof whatever, without any evidence behind it."

"But how *can* I keep accepting it if, as you say, there *is* no proof behind it?"

"You can keep accepting it because—" At this point I was somewhat stumped myself, but felt that if I persisted in talking it out with this patient, and avoided the old psychoanalytic clichés, which had so far produced no real answer to this often-raised question, I might possibly stumble on some answer for my *own,* as well as my patient's, satisfaction. So I stubbornly went on: "—because, well, you're human."

"Human? What has that got to do with it?"

"Well—" I still had no real answer, but somehow felt that one was lurking right around the corner of the collaborative thinking of the patient and myself. "That's just the way humans are, I guess. They *do* doggedly hold to groundless beliefs when they haven't got an iota of evidence with which to back up these beliefs. Millions of people, for example, believe wholeheartedly and dogmatically in the existence of god when, as Hume, Kant, and many other first-rate philosophers have shown, they can't possibly ever prove (or, for that matter, disprove) his existence. But that hardly stops them from fervently believing."

"You think, then, that I believe in the 'truth' of my own rottenness, just about in the same way that these people believe in the 'truth' of god, without any evidence whatever to back our beliefs?"

"*Don't* you? And aren't they—the theory of god and of your own rottenness—really the same kind of definitional concepts?"

"Definitional?"

"Yes. You start with an axiom or hypothesis, such as: 'Unless I do perfectly well in life, I am worthless.' Or, in your case, more specifically: 'In order to be good, I must be a fine, self-sacrificing daughter, wife, and mother.' Then you look at the facts, and quickly see that you are not doing perfectly well in life—that you are not the finest, most self-sacrificing daughter, wife, and mother who ever lived. Then you conclude: 'Therefore, I am no good—in fact, I am rotten and worthless.'"

"Well, doesn't that conclusion follow from the facts?"

"No, not at all! It follows almost entirely from your definitional premises. And, in a sense, there are no facts at all in your syllogism, since all your 'evidence' is highly biased by these premises."

"But isn't it a fact that I am *not* a fine, self-sacrificing daughter, wife, and mother?"

"No, not necessarily. For, actually, you may well be as good a daughter to your parents as most women are; in fact, you may be considerably better than most in this respect. But your premise says that in order to be good, you must be practically *perfect*. And, in the light of this premise, even the fact of how good a daughter you are will inevitably be distorted, and you will be almost bound to conclude that you are a 'poor' daughter when, in actual fact, you may be a better than average one."

"So there are no real facts at all in my syllogism?"

"No, there aren't. But even if there were—even, for example, if you were not even an average daughter or wife—your syllogism would still be entirely tautological: since it merely 'proves' what you originally postulated in your premise; namely, that if you are not perfect, you are worthless. Consequently, your so-called worthlessness or rottenness, is entirely definitional and has no existence in fact."

"Are all disturbances, such as mine, the same way?"

"Yes, come to think of it—" And, suddenly, I *did* come to think of it myself, as I was talking with this patient. "—all human disturbances seem to be of the same definitional nature. We *assume* that it is horrible if something is so—if, especially, we are imperfect or someone else is not acting in the angelic way that we think he *should* act. Then, after making this assumption, we literally *look* for the 'facts' to prove our premise. And invariably, of course, we find these 'facts'—find that we *are* or someone else *is* behaving very badly. Then we 'logically' conclude that we were right in the first place, and that the 'bad' behavior we found conclusively 'proves' our original assumption. But the only real or at least unbiased 'facts' in this 'logical' chain we are thereby constructing are our own starting premises —the sentences we tell ourselves to begin with."

"Would you say, then," my patient asked, "that I literally tell myself certain unvalidated sentences, and that my disturbance stems directly from these, my own, sentences?"

"Yes," I replied with sudden enthusiasm. "You give me an idea, there. I had not quite thought of it that way before, although I guess I really had, without putting it in just those

terms, since I said to you just a moment ago that it is the
sentences we tell ourselves to begin with that start the ball of
definitional premises, semi-definitional 'facts,' and false conclusions rolling. But, anyway, whether it's your idea or mine,
it seems to be true: that every human being who gets disturbed
really is telling himself a chain of false sentences—since that is
the way that humans seem almost invariably to think, in words,
phrases, and sentences. And it is these sentences which really
are, which *constitute* his neuroses."

"Can you be more precise? What are my *own* exact sentences,
for instance?"

"Well, let's see. I'm sure we can quickly work them out. You
start by listening, of course, to the sentences of others, mainly
of your parents. And their sentences are, as we have gone over
many times here, "Look, dear, unless you love us dearly, in an
utterly self-sacrificing way, you're no good, and people will
find out that you're no good, and they won't love you, and
that would be terrible, terrible, terrible."

"And I listen to these sentences of my parents, told to me
over and over again, and make them mine—is that it?"

"Yes, you make them yours. And not only their precise, overt
sentences, of course, but their gestures, voice intonations, critical looks, and so on. These also have significant meaning for
you: since you *turn them*, in your own head, into phrases and
sentences. Thus, when your mother says, "Don't do that, dear!"
in an angry or demanding tone of voice, you translate it into,
"Don't do that, dear—or I won't love you if you do, and everyone else will think you're no good and won't love you, and that
would be terrible!'"

"So when my parents tell me I'm no good, by word or by
gesture, I quickly say to myself: 'They're right. If I don't love
them dearly and don't sacrifice myself to them, I'm no good,
and everyone will see I'm no good, and nobody will accept me,
and that will be awful!'"

"Right. And it is these phrases or sentences of yours that
create your *feeling* of awfulness—*create* your guilt and your
neurosis."

"But how? What exactly *is* there about my own sentences that creates my awful feeling? What is the false part of these sentences?"

"The last part, usually. For the first part, very often, may be true. The first part, remember, is something along the lines of: 'If I don't completely love my parents and sacrifice myself for them, many people or some people, including my parents, will probably think that I'm a bad daughter—that I'm no good.' And this part of your sentences may very well be true."

"Many people, including my parents, *may* really think that I'm no good for acting this way—is that what you mean?"

"Yes. They actually may. So your *observation* that if you are not a perfect daughter various people, especially your parents, won't approve of you, and will consider you worthless, is probably a perfectly sound and valid observation. But that isn't what does you the damage. It's the rest of your phrases and sentences that do the damage."

"You mean the part where I say 'Because many people may not approve me for being an imperfect daughter, I *am* no good?' "

"Exactly. If many people, even all people, think that you're not a perfect daughter, and that you *should* be a perfect daughter, that may well be their true belief or feeling—but what has it really got to do with what *you* have to believe? How does being an imperfect daughter *make* you, except in *their* eyes, worthless? Why, even if it is true that you are such an imperfect child to your parents, is it *terrible* that you are imperfect? And why is it *awful* if many people will not approve of you if you are a poor daughter?"

"*I* don't have to believe I'm awful just because *they* believe it? I can accept myself as being imperfect, even if it is true that I am, without thinking that this is awful?"

"Yes. Unless your *definition* of 'awful' and 'worthless' becomes the same as *their* definition. And that, of course, is exactly what's happening when you get upset about your parents' and others' view of you. You are then *making* their definition of you *your* definition. You are *taking* their sentences and making them your own. And it is this highly creative, *self*-defining act on your part which manufactures your disturbance."

"I have the theoretical choice, then, of taking their definition of me as worthless, because I am an imperfect daughter, and accepting it or rejecting it. And if I accept it, I make their definition mine, and I upset myself."

"Yes, you illogically upset yourself."

"But why illogically, necessarily? Can't they be right about my being an imperfect daughter making me worthless?"

"No—only, again, by definition. Because, obviously, not every set of parents who have an imperfect daughter considers her worthless. *Some* parents feel that their daughter is quite worthwhile, even when she does not completely sacrifice herself for them. Your parents obviously don't think so and make or define your worth in terms of how much you do for them. They are, of course, entitled to define you in such a way. But their concept of you *is* definition; and it is only tautologically valid."

"You mean there is no absolute way of proving, if they consider me worthless for not being sufficiently self-sacrificing, that I actually am worthless?"

"Right. Even if everyone in the world agreed with them that your being insufficiently self-sacrificing equaled your being worthless, that would still be everyone's definition; and you still would not *have* to accept it. But of course, as we have just noted, it is highly improbable that everyone in the world would agree with them—which proves all the more how subjective their definition of your worth is."

"And even if they and everyone else agreed that I *was* worthless for being imperfectly interested in their welfare, that would still not mean that I would have to accept this definition?"

"No, certainly not. For even if they were right about your being worthless *to them* when you were not utterly self-sacrificing—and it is of course their prerogative to value you little when you are not doing what they would want you to do—there is no connection whatever, unless you *think* there is one, between your value to them and your value to yourself. *You* can be perfectly good, to and for yourself, even though they think you perfectly bad to and for them."

"That sounds all very well and fine. But let's get back to my specific sentences and see how it works out there."

"Yes, you're quite right. Because it's those specific sentences that you have to change to get better. As we said before, your main sentences to yourself are: 'Because they think I am worthless for not being utterly self-sacrificing to them, they are right. It *would* be terrible if they continue to think this of me and don't thoroughly approve of me. So I'd better be more self-sacrificing—or else hate myself if I am not.'"

"And I have got to change those sentences to—?"

"Well, quite obviously you have got to change them to: 'Maybe they are right about *their* thinking I am worthless if I am not a much more self-sacrificing daughter, but what has that really got to do with *my* estimation of myself? *Would* it really be terrible if they continue to think this way about me? *Do* I need their approval that much? *Should* I have to keep hating myself if I am not more self-sacrificing?'"

"And by changing these sentences, my own versions of and belief in *their* sentences, I can definitely change my feelings of guilt and worthlessness and get better?"

"Why don't you try it and see?"

This patient did keep looking at her own sentences and did try to change them. And within several weeks of the foregoing conversation, she improved far more significantly than she had done in the previous two years I had been seeing her. "I really seem to have got it now!" she reported two months later. "Whenever I find myself getting guilty or upset, I immediately tell myself that there *must* be some silly sentence that I am saying to myself to cause this upset; and almost immediately, usually within literally a few minutes of my starting to look for it, I find this sentence. And, just as you have been showing me, the sentence invariably takes the form of 'Isn't it terrible that—' or 'Wouldn't it be awful if—' And when I closely look at and question these sentences, and ask myself '*How* is it really terrible

that—?' or 'Why would it actually be awful if—?' I always find
that it isn't terrible or wouldn't be awful, and I get over being
upset very quickly. In fact, as you predicted a few weeks ago,
as I keep questioning and challenging my own sentences, I
begin to find that they stop coming up again and again, as they
used to do before. Only occasionally, now, do I start to tell
myself that something would be terrible or awful if it occurred,
or something else is frightful because it has occurred. And on
those relatively few occasions, as I just said, I can quickly go
after the 'terribleness' or the 'awfulness' that I am dreaming up,
and factually or logically re-evaluate it and abolish it. I can
hardly believe it, but I seem to be getting to the point, after
so many years of worrying over practically everything and
thinking I was a slob no matter what I did, of now finding that
nothing is so terrible or awful, and I now seem to be recognizing
this *in advance* rather than *after* I have seriously upset myself.
Boy, what a change that is in my life! I am really getting to be,
with these new attitudes, an entirely different sort of person
than I was."

True to her words, this woman's behavior mirrored her new
attitudes. She acted much better with her husband and child
and enjoyed her family relationship in a manner that she had
never thought she would be able to do. She quit her old job
and got a considerably better paying and more satisfying one.
She not only stopped being concerned about her parents'
opinion of her, but started calmly to help them to get over some
of their own negative ideas toward themselves, each other, and
the rest of the world. And, best of all, she really stopped caring,
except for limited practical purposes, what other people thought
of her, lost her paranoid ideas about their being against her,
and began to consider herself worthwhile even when she made
clearcut errors and when others brought these to her attention
in a disapproving manner.

As these remarkable changes occurred in this patient, and I
began to get somewhat similar (though not always as excellent)
results with several other patients, the principles of rational-

emotive psychotherapy began to take clearer form; and, by the beginning of 1955, the basic theory and practice of RT was fairly well formulated.

Since that time, much more clinical experience has been had by me and some of my associates who soon began to employ RT techniques; and the original principles have been corrected, expanded, and reworked in many significant respects. RT theory is by no means static and continues to grow—as any good theory doubtlessly should. Struck with the proselytizing bug, I also began to write a good many papers and give a number of talks on RT, mainly to professional audiences; so that now a number of other therapists espouse the system or have incorporated parts of it into their own psychotherapeutic methods.

Much opposition to RT has also been expressed during the past few years, sometimes by those who do not seem to understand fully what it is, and who accuse rational therapists of believing in and doing all kinds of things in which they are not in the least interested. Others, who better understand RT, oppose it because they say that its theories sound plausible and that perhaps they work clinically, but that there is no experimental or other scientific evidence to support them.

To satisfy this latter group of critics, many of whose points are entirely justified and should be answered with attested fact rather than more theory, I have been gathering a mass of experimental, physiological, and other scientific evidence and will eventually present this as at least partial validation of the basic RT theories. There has proven to be, however, so much of this confirmatory material available, that it will take some time yet to collate it and to present it in a series of theoretical-scientific volumes.

In the meantime, many clinicians who admittedly do not understand RT and who would very much like to do so have kept asking for a book that would summarize and go beyond the papers on the subject that have already been published in the professional literature. It is mainly for these readers that the present book has been written. In this book, I have made

an attempt to gather some of the most important papers and
talks on RT that I have written and delivered during the past
five years and to present them in a fairly integrated way.

The materials in the present volume, then, are *not* intended
to be an adequate substitute for those which will ultimately
appear in a series of more definitive volumes on RT. The pages
of this book only briefly outline the theory of rational-emotive
psychotherapy and make no attempt to bolster it scientifically.
They do try to present the clinician with some of the main
clinical applications of the theory and to enable him (on partial
faith, if you will) to try these applications on some of his own
counselees or patients. By so doing, he may get some indication
of the potential validity of RT. But it must of course always be
remembered, in this connection, that no matter how well a
theory of therapy works in practice, and no matter how many
improved or "cured" patients insist that they have been benefited by it, the theory itself may still be of unproven efficacy,
since something quite different in the patient-therapist relationship (or in some outside aspect of the patient's life) may have
been the real curative agent.

In any event, rational-emotive psychotherapy has, in even the
few brief years of its existence, so far proven to be a highly
intriguing and seemingly practical theory and method. It is
hoped that the publication of this introductory manual will bring
it to the attention of many more individuals than those who
are now conversant with its approach and that it will spur discussion and experimentation that will help develop its principles
and its applications.

2

The Theory of Rational-Emotive Psychotherapy*

Many of the principles incorporated in the theory of rational-emotive psychotherapy are not new; some of them, in fact, were originally stated several thousand years ago, especially by the Greek and Roman Stoic philosophers (such as Epictetus and Marcus Aurelius) and by some of the ancient Taoist and Buddhist thinkers (see Suzuki, 1956, and Watts, 1959, 1960). What probably is new is the application to psychotherapy of viewpoints that were first propounded in radically different contexts.

One of the most gratifying aspects, indeed, of formulating and using many of the concepts that are an integral part of rational therapy is the constant discovery that, although most of these concepts have been independently constructed from my recent experience with patients, I have found that they have also been previously or concurrently formulated by many philosophers, psychologists, and other social thinkers who have had no experience with psychotherapy, as well as by a number of other modern therapists who were trained in widely differing psychoanalytic and nonpsychoanalytic schools—including Adkins (1959), Adler (1927, 1929), Alexander and French (1946), Berne (1957), Cameron (1950), Dejerine and Gaukler (1913), Diaz-Guerrera (1959), Dollard and Miller (1950), Dubois (1907), Eysenck (1961), Frank (1961), Grimes (1961), Guze (1959), Herzberg (1945), Johnson (1946), Kelly (1955), Levine (1942), Low (1952), Lynn (1957), Meyer (1948), Phillips (1956),

---

* Material in this and the following two chapters has been adapted and expanded from "Rational Psychotherapy," a paper originally presented at the American Psychological Association annual meeting, August 31, 1956, and subsequently published in the *J. Gen. Psychol.*, 1958, 59, 35-49.

Robbins (1955, 1956), Rotter (1954), Salter (1949), Shand (1961), Stekel (1950), Thorne (1950, 1961), Wolberg (1954), and Wolpe (1958, 1961a).

Few of these therapists seem to have had any direct contact with my own views before writing their own papers or books, and few of them seem to have been strongly influenced by each other. Most of them, out of their own practice, seem independently to have formulated quite unorthodox and what I would call surprisingly rational theories of psychotherapy. This, to me, is quite heartening. And I continue to be pleasantly surprised when I discover unusually close agreements between my own views on personality and therapy and those of other hard-thinking psychologists—such as Magda Arnold (1960), many of whose positions are amazingly close to my own, although she is a fine physiological psychologist and a fairly uncompromising Catholic, while I am a clinician, a social psychologist, and a confirmed nonbeliever. This kind of coincidence does not, of course, conclusively prove that RT views are correct; but it does perhaps gain for them a little additional credence.

The central theme of RT is that man is a uniquely rational, as well as a uniquely irrational, animal; that his emotional or psychological disturbances are largely a result of his thinking illogically or irrationally; and that he can rid himself of most of his emotional or mental unhappiness, ineffectuality, and disturbance if he learns to maximize his rational and minimize his irrational thinking. It is the task of the psychotherapist to work with individuals who are needlessly unhappy and troubled, or who are weighted down with intense anxiety or hostility, and to show them (*a*) that their difficulties largely result from distorted perception and illogical thinking, and (*b*) that there is a relatively simple, though work-requiring, method of reordering their perceptions and reorganizing their thinking so as to remove the basic cause of their difficulties.

It is my contention, in other words, that all effective psychotherapists, whether or not they realize what they are doing, teach or induce their patients to reperceive or rethink their life events and philosophies and thereby to change their unrealistic and illogical thought, emotion, and behavior (Ellis, 1959; Stark, 1961).

Most of the commonly used psychotherapeutic techniques of enabling patients to become more rational, however, are relatively indirect and inefficient.

Thus, there is no question that therapeutic methods, such as abreaction, catharsis, dream analysis, free association, interpretation of resistance, and transference analysis, have often been successfully employed, and that they somehow manage to convince the patient that he is mistakenly and illogically perceiving reality and that, if he is to overcome his disturbance, he'd better perceive it differently (Arnold, 1960). The question is: Are these relatively indirect, semi-logical techniques of trying to help the patient change his thinking particularly efficient? I doubt it.

I would contend, instead, that the more emotional and less persuasive methods of psychotherapy are, when employed with most disturbed persons, relatively ineffectual and wasteful. On the other hand, the more direct, persuasive, suggestive, active, and logical techniques of therapy are more effective at undermining and extirpating the basic causes (as distinct from the outward symptoms) of the emotional difficulties of most—though by no means necessarily *all*—individuals who come for psychological help.

My views on the efficacy of rational methods of psychotherapy are highly heretical compared to those held by most modern thinkers. Freud (1950), for example, declaimed against rational-persuasive techniques in this wise: "At no point in one's analytic work does one suffer the suspicion that one is 'talking to the winds' more than when one is trying to persuade a female patient to abandon her wish for a penis on the ground of its being unrealizable, or to convince a male patient that a passive attitude toward another man does not always signify castration and that in many relations in life it is indispensable."

Deutsch and Murphy (1955) insist that making of unconscious events conscious "cannot be accomplished by rational discussion." Whitehorn (1955) asserts that because disturbed people have egos that are so badly bruised that they have difficulty in hearing what people say to them, there is "an enormous overrating of the propositional, logical meaning of verbal communication" and that psychotherapy does not consist of probing into a patient's mind to find the errors of its operations and then informing him about them.

Kelly (1955) states that "verbal rationalization does not necessarily facilitate psychological anticipatory processes nor does it necessarily make a person a better neighbor to live next door to." These are but a few comments typical of a whole host of therapists who are skeptical of the value of any rational approach to therapy.

Nonetheless, I shall uphold the thesis in this volume that not only is rational-emotive therapy unusually effective, but that it is *more* effective than *most* other kinds of therapy with *most* patients. Although there as yet are no controlled therapeutic experiments to bolster this view (as someday I expect that there will be), my own experience, as well as that of several of my associates, tend to show that whereas about 65 per cent of patients tend to improve significantly or considerably under most forms of psychotherapy, about 90 per cent of the patients treated for 10 or more sessions with RT tend to show distinct or considerable improvement (Ellis, 1957b). Similar high rates of improvement or "cure" have been reported by several other active-directive and rational-persuasive therapists, including Berne (1957), Phillips (1956), Rosen (1953), Thorne (1957), and Wolpe (1958).

In any event, RT is a somewhat unusual technique of therapy. As such, it should preferably have a rationale or theory behind it. I shall therefore now attempt to state the general theory behind its practice.

The theoretical foundations of RT are based on the assumption that human thinking and emotion are *not* two disparate or different processes, but that they significantly overlap and are in some respects, for all practical purposes, essentially the same thing. Like the other two basic life processes, sensing and moving, they are integrally interrelated and never can be seen wholly apart from each other.

In other words: none of the four fundamental life operations —sensing, moving, emoting, and thinking—is experienced in isolation. If an individual senses something (e.g., sees a stick), he also tends, at the very same time, to do something about it (pick it up, kick it, or throw it away), to have some feelings about it (like it or dislike it). and to think about it (remember seeing it previously or imagine what he can do with it). Similarly, if he acts, emotes, or thinks, he *also* consciously or unconsciously involves himself in the other behavior processes.

Instead, then, of saying that "Smith thinks about this problem," we should more accurately say that "Smith senses-moves-feels-THINKS about this problem." However, in view of the fact that Smith's activity in regard to the problem may be *largely* focused upon solving it and only *incidentally* on seeing, acting, and emoting about it, we may legitimately shortcut our description of his behavior and merely say that he thinks about it.

As in the case of thinking and the sensori-motor processes, we may define emotion as a complex mode of behavior which is integrally related to the other sensing and response processes. As Stanley Cobb (1950) states: "My suggestion is that we use the term 'emotion' to mean the same thing as (1) an introspectively given affect state, usually mediated by acts of interpretation; (2) the whole set of internal physiological changes, which help (ideally) the return to normal equilibrium between the organism and its environment, and (3) the various patterns of overt behavior, stimulated by the environment and implying constant interactions with it, which are expressive of the stirred-up physiological state (2) and also the more or less agitated psychological state (1)."

Emotion, then, has no *single* cause or result, but can be said to have three main origins and pathways: (a) through the sensori-motor processes; (b) through biophysical stimulation mediated through the tissues of the autonomic nervous system and the hypothalamus and other subcortical centers; and (c) through the cognitive or thinking processes. We may also, if we wish, add a fourth pathway and say that emotion may arise through the experiencing and recirculating of previous emotional processes (as when recollection of a past feeling of anger triggers off a renewed surge of hostility).

Emotion appears to occur, under normal circumstances, because of psychophysical, heredenvironmental factors. In the first place, the cells of the body, including those of the central and autonomic nervous systems, are (because of many previous hereditary and environmental influences) in a certain state of excitability and self-stimulation at any given time. A stimulus of a certain intensity then impinges upon the emotional centers and excites or damps their pathways. This stimulus can be directly applied—e.g., by electrical stimulation or drugs transmitted to the nerve cells themselves—or it can be indirectly applied, through affecting the sensori-motor and cerebral processes, which in turn are connected with and influence the emotional centers.

If one wishes to control one's emotional feelings, one can theoretically do so in four major ways: (*a*) by electrical or biochemical means (e.g., electroshock treatment, barbiturates, or tranquilizing or energizing drugs); (*b*) by using one's sensori-motor system (e.g., doing movement exercises or using Yoga breathing techniques); (*c*) by employing one's existing emotional states and prejudices (e.g., changing oneself out of love for a parent or therapist); and (*d*) by using one's cerebral processes (e.g., reflecting, thinking, or telling oneself to calm down or become excited).

All these means of influencing one's emotions are significantly interrelated. Thus, doing movement exercises will also tend to give one pleasurable feelings, make one think about certain things, and perhaps create internal biochemical conditions that will affect one's nerve cells: so that, instead of having a single effect on one's emotions, such exercises may well have a multiple-cumulative effect.

As this book is specifically concerned with rational-emotive psychotherapy, which is largely mediated through cerebral processes, it will say little about biophysical, sensori-motor, and other so-called "non-verbal" (though actually non-*spoken*) techniques of therapy. This is not because these techniques are minor or unimportant. In many instances, particularly when employed with individuals whom we normally call psychotic, they are quite valuable. Their working procedures, however, have been adequately outlined in many other works on therapy; while the details of rational or cognitive psychotherapeutic methods have been delineated, at least in recent years, with surprising infrequency. Therefore, this book will one-sidedly emphasize the rational techniques, while admitting the possible efficacy of other legitimate means of affecting disordered human emotions.

To return to our main theme: emotion is caused and controlled in several major ways; and one of these ways is by thinking. Much of what we call emotion is nothing more nor less than a certain kind—a biased, prejudiced, or strongly evaluative kind—of thought. Considerable empirical and theoretical evidence in favor of the proposition that human emotion is intrinsically an attitudinal and cognitive process has recently been amassed, but will not be reviewed here because of space limitations. Some of this evidence has been incisively presented in an excellent book, *Emotions and Reason*, by the philosopher, V. J. McGill, which should be required reading for all psychotherapists. To quote briefly from Professor McGill: "It is as difficult to separate emotions and knowing, as it would be to separate motivation and learning . . . Emotions . . . include a cognitive component, and an expectation or readiness to act; their rationality and adaptive value depends on the adequacy of these two components in a given situation . . . Foreseeing that an object promises good or ill and knowing, or not, how to deal with it, determines the attitude toward it, and also the feeling" (McGill, 1954).

Independently of McGill, Bousfield and Orbison (1952) also reviewed the physiological evidence regarding the origin of emotion and found that, in direct contradiction to previous impressions, emotional processes by no means originate solely in subcortical or hypothalamic centers of the brain. Instead, they report, "it would seem reasonable to suppose that the cortex, and especially the frontal lobes, is somehow involved in the inhibition, instigation and sustaining of emotional reactions." Even more recently, Arnheim (1958) has done a comprehensive review of emotion and feeling in psychology and art, in which he concludes: "Academic psychology is driven to call certain mental states 'emotions' because it is accustomed to distributing all psychological phenomena into the three compartments of cognition, motivation, and emotion instead of realizing that every mental state has cognitive, motivational, and emotional components, and cannot be defined properly by any one of the three . . . The excitement of emotion is dominant only in rare extremes and even then nothing but an unspecific byproduct of what the person perceives, knows, understands, and desires."

Rokeach (1960) is still more explicit about the overlapping of reason and emotion:

In everyday discourse we often precede what we are about to say with the phrase "I think . . ." "I believe . . ." or "I feel . . ." We pause to wonder whether such phrases refer to underlying states or processes which are really distinguishable from each other. After all, we can often interchange these phrases without basically affecting what we mean to say. "I think segregation is wrong," "I believe segregation is wrong," and "I feel segregation is wrong" all say pretty much the same thing. The fact that these phrases are often (although not always) interchangeable suggests to us the assumption that every emotion has its cognitive counterpart, and every cognition its emotional counterpart.

The most recent comprehensive theory—and in many ways the most convincing theory—of emotion that has been published is the monumental two-volume study of the subject by Magda Arnold (1960). After considering all prior major views, and masterfully reviewing the experimental and physiological evidence that has been amassed during the last century, Dr. Arnold concludes that "emotion is a complex process which starts when something is perceived and appraised. The appraisal arouses a tendency toward or away from the thing that is felt as emotion and urges to action . . . We can like or dislike only something we know. We must see or hear or touch something, remember having done so or imagine it, before we can decide that it is good or bad for us. Sensation must be completed by some form of appraisal before it can lead to action. Most things can be evaluated only when they are compared with similar things in the past and their effect on us. What is sensed must be appraised in its context, in the light of experience; accordingly, our evaluation in many cases will have to draw upon memory . . .

"Human beings are motivated by an appraisal that is both a sense judgment and an intellectual or reflective judgment. The final decision for action is a choice that either implements the original emotion or goes against it. In man, the choice of goal-directed action is essentially a rational wanting, an inclination toward what is reflectively appraised as good (pleasurable, useful, or valuable). These rational action tendencies organize the human personality under the guidance of the self-ideal."

Being even more specific, Dr. Arnold writes:

Emotion seems to include not only the appraisal of how this thing or person will affect me but also a definite pull toward or away from it. In fact, does not the emotional *quale* consist precisely in that unreasoning involuntary attraction or repulsion?

If I merely know things or persons as they are apart from me, there is no emotion. If I know them and judge them theoretically and abstractly to be good for me, there may still be no emotion. But If I think something is good for me *here and now*, and *feel myself drawn toward it*, sometimes even against my better judgment, then my experience is, properly speaking, nonrational; it is other than just cold reason; it is an addition to knowledge; it is *emotional*. . . .

What we call *appraisal* or *estimate* is close to such a sense judgment. In emotional experience such appraisal is always direct, immediate; it is a *sense judgment* and includes a reflective judgment only as a secondary evaluation. Perhaps an example will illustrate the difference. When the outfielder "judges" a fly ball, he simply senses where he is going and where the ball is going and gauges his movements so that he will meet the ball. If he stopped to reflect, he would never stay in the game. We ourselves are constantly making judgments of this sort without paying much attention to them. Now the judgment that the ball is too far or too close or just right for catching is no different from the judgment we make in appraising an object as good or bad, pleasurable or dangerous for us. Such sense judgments are direct, immediate, nonreflective, nonintellectual, automatic, "instinctive," "intuitive" . . .

Summing up our discussion, we can now define emotion as *the felt tendency toward anything intuitively appraised as good (beneficial), or away from anything intuitively appraised as bad (harmful). This attraction or aversion is accompanied by a pattern of physiological changes organized toward approach or withdrawal.*

Dr. Arnold's theory of emotion is remarkably close to a view which I evolved in 1954, just as I was becoming a rational-emotive psychotherapist, and which I wrote up in a paper entitled, "An Operational Reformulation of Some of the Basic Principles of Psychoanalysis" (1956a). In a section of this paper on evaluating, emoting, and desiring, I noted:

An individual *evaluates* (attitudinizes, becomes biased) when he perceives something as being "good" or "bad," "pleasant" or "unpleasant," "beneficial" or "harmful" and when, as a result of his perceptions, he responds positively or negatively to this thing. Evaluating is a fundamental characteristic of human organisms and seems to work in a kind of closed circuit with a feedback mechanism: since perception biases response and then response tends to bias subsequent perception. Also: prior perceptions appear to bias subsequent perceptions, and prior responses to bias subsequent responses.

Evaluating always seems to involve both perceiving and responding, not merely one or the other. It also appears to be a fundamental, virtually definitional, property of humans: since if they did not have some way of favoring or reacting positively to "good" or "beneficial" stimuli and of disfavoring or reacting negatively to "bad" or "harmful" stimuli, they could hardly survive.

An individual *emotes* when he evaluates something strongly—when he clearly perceives it as being "good" or "bad," "beneficial" or "harmful," and strongly responds to it in a negative or positive manner. Emoting usually, probably always, involves some kind of bodily sensations which, when perceived by the emoting individual, may then reinforce the original emotion. Emotions may therefore simply be evaluations which have a strong bodily component, while so-called nonemotional attitudes may be evaluations with a relatively weak bodily component.

If the word "evaluating," which I employed in the above paragraphs, is replaced by the word "appraisal," which Dr. Arnold favors, our views are almost identical. She, however, has gone far beyond my original brief formulation and has very legitimately divided emotions into (a) intuitive, immediate, or unreflective appraisals, which lead to what I prefer to call "feelings," and (b) longer-range, reflective appraisals, which lead to what I prefer to call "emotions," "sustained emotions," "attitudes," or "sentiments." Her emphasis on the immediacy and nonreflectiveness of our common feelings—such as feelings of anger and fear—is, I believe, essentially correct; and yet, as she herself admits, the terms "immediate" and "unreflective" must be viewed as relative rather than as absolutistic means of differentiating quick-triggered feelings from sustained emotions.

Thus, the outfielder is able to sense where he is going and where the ball he is fielding is going because he has (a) prior experiences with ball-catching; (b) some memory of his prior trials and errors; and (c) a general philosophy of running, waiting, putting up his glove, etc., which he has acquired from his prior experiences, his memory of these experiences, and his *thinking about* or *reflecting on* his experiences and memories. Consequently, even though he almost instantaneously goes through certain sensory movements to field a fly ball, he still thinks (or talks to himself) about what he is doing. Otherwise, with the best sensory apparatus in the world, he might run too fast or too slow, fail to put his glove up at the right time, or even walk off the field and not try to catch the ball at all.

Similarly, the person who "immediately" feels angry when someone insults him must have had prior experiences, memories, and philosophies in relation to responding to insults before he can "instantaneously" make a counter-insulting remark or punch his defamer in the jaw. The "here and now" that Dr. Arnold talks about is therefore inextricably related to one's past (and future), and is much more stretchable than at first blush appears.

Nonetheless, Dr. Arnold seems to be correct about the difference between (relatively) immediate and unreflective feelings and sustained and reflective emotions or attitudes. Both fleeting and sustained emotional responses have in common the element of "What does this event that I am responding to mean *to me*?" And both include action tendencies toward or away from appraised objects. But sustained emotions seem to be much *more* reflective than immediate or impulsive emotional reactions; and are consequently *more* philosophically oriented. Thus, almost anyone will respond immediately with some degree of anger to an insult or an injury, because almost all humans will appraise such a stimulus as being bad *to them*. But those individuals with a bellicose, when-you-say-that-partner-smile!, philosophy of life will tend to remain angry much longer, and to do more about their anger, than those with a meek-shall-inherit-the-earth philosophy.

Immediate or unreflective anger depends to *some* degree on one's world-view—since a sufficiently meek individual may not even become angry in the first place, let alone sustaining his anger in the second place. But sustained or reflective anger would appear to depend much more strongly on one's philosophic attitudes and to be less intensely related to one's almost instinctive self-preservative tendencies. As Branden (1962) has noted: "Man's value-judgments are not innate. Having no innate knowledge of what is true or false, man can have no innate knowledge of what is good or evil. His values, and his emotions, are the product of the conclusions he has drawn or accepted, that is: of his *basic* premises."

The emotions that are discussed in this book, and that are an intrinsic part of what we usually call "emotional disturbance," are almost always in the sustained, reflective class. They are the result of what Magda Arnold (and other psychologists) call "attitudes" and "sentiments" and have relatively little of an immediate sensory and much of a reflective philosophic component. Stated otherwise: sustained human emotions are the result of relatively reflective appraisals. Where we are quite capable of *un*reflectively or immediately noting that an apple tastes bad or that a ball is hurtling directly at us, and hence instantaneously feeling disgust or fear, we are also capable of *reflectively* noting that most blotchy apples taste bitter or that we *may* get hit by a ball if we stand too close to two boys who are having a catch. In which latter cases, we may feel disgusted by merely *thinking* about rotten apples or by *imagining* our getting hit by a ball.

Emotion, then, does not exist in its own right, as a special and almost mystical sort of entity; it is, rather, an essential part of an entire sensing-moving-thinking-emoting complex. What we usually label as thinking is a relatively calm and dispassionate appraisal (or organized perception) of a given situation, an objective comparison of many of the elements in this situation, and a coming to some conclusion as a result of this comparing or discriminating process. And what we usually label as emoting, as I pointed out in my earlier article (Ellis, 1956a) is a relatively uncalm, passionate, and strong evaluating of some person or object.

Thus, if we calmly compare John's characteristics to Jim's, we may perceive that John excels at math, chess, and debating, and that Jim excels at racing, handball, and weight-lifting. We may then *thoughtfully* conclude that John is probably brighter than Jim.

If, however, we personally have had pleasant prior experiences with Jim and unpleasant ones with John, we may close our eyes to some of the facts of the situation and may conclude that because Jim is a clever handball player and John sometimes loses at debating, Jim is brighter than John. We would then be *emotionally* or *prejudicedly* judging Jim to be more intelligent than John.

Emotional people may thus be said to be doing a *kind* of thinking that is different from that of nonemotional people: a prejudiced kind of thinking which is so strongly influenced by prior experience that it sometimes becomes limited, vague, and ineffective. Relatively calm, thinking individuals use the maximum information available to them—e.g., that John is good at math, chess, and debating. Relatively excited, emotional individuals use only part of the available information—e.g., that Jim is clever at handball. Emotional persons are always essentially answering the question "Is Jim good for *us?*" when they sometimes mistakenly think they are asking the question "Is Jim good for *anyone?*"

Another way of stating this is to say that there is a kind of continuum, from almost totally unreflective personalized appraisal (which leads to immediate sensory-feeling) to more reflective but still personalized appraisal (which leads to sustained emotion or attitude), and finally to still more reflective but impersonal appraisal (which leads to calm thinking). Thus, we can meet Jim and immediately and almost unreflectively feel that he is a great fellow (because we quickly note that he has some trait that we like). Or we may more reflectively note that Jim is kindly disposed *toward us,* while John does not like *us* that much; and we may therefore feel an enduring emotion of friendship for Jim rather than for John. Or, finally, we may still more reflectively note that John, even though he doesn't particularly like *us,* is good at math, chess, and debating, while Jim, even though he does like *us,* is only clever at handball. We may therefore conclude that John is probably brighter (that is, a better companion for most people who like intelligent discussions) than is Jim, even though we still favor (are emotionally fonder of) Jim.

A good deal—though not necessarily all—of what we call emotion, therefore, would seem to be a kind of appraisal or thinking that (*a*) is strongly slanted or biased by previous perceptions or experiences; that (*b*) is highly personalized; that (*c*) is often accompanied by gross bodily reactions; and (*d*) that is likely to induce the emoting individual to take some kind of positive or negative action. What we usually call thinking would seem to be a more tranquil, less personalized, less somatically involved (or, at least, perceived), and less activity-directed mode of discriminating.

It would also appear that among human adults reared in a social culture which includes a well-formulated language, thinking and emoting usually accompany each other, act in a circular cause-and-effect relationship, and in certain (though hardly all) respects are essentially the *same thing.* One's thinking often *becomes* one's emotion; and emoting, under some circumstances, *becomes* one's thought.

Does this mean that emotion *never* exists without thought? Not necessarily. For a moment or two it may. If a car comes right at you, you may spontaneously, immediately become fearful, without even having time to say to yourself: "Oh, how terrible that this car is about to hit me!" Perhaps, however, you do, with split-second rapidity, start thinking or saying this sentence to yourself; and perhaps this thought or internalized speech *is* your emotion of fright.

In any event, assuming that you don't, at the very beginning, have any conscious or unconscious thought accompanying your emotion, it appears to be almost impossible to *sustain* an emotional outburst without bolstering it by repeated ideas. For unless you keep telling yourself something on the order of "Oh, my heavens! How terrible it would have been if that car had hit me!" your fright over almost being hit by the car will soon die. And unless you keep telling yourself, when you are punched on the jaw by someone, "That fellow who punched me on the jaw is a villain! I hope he gets his just desserts!" the pain of being punched will soon die and your anger at this fellow will die with the pain.

Assuming, then, that thought does not *always* accompany emotion, it would appear that sustained emotion normally *is* associated with thinking and that sustained feeling, in fact, unless it consists of physical pain or some other specific sensation, is the direct result of sustained thinking. We say "normally" here because it is theoretically possible for feelings in your emotional circuits, once they have been made to reverberate by some physical or psychological stimulus, to keep reverberating under their own power. It is also possible for drugs or electrical impulses to keep directly acting on your nerve cells and thereby to keep you emotionally aroused. Usually, however, these types of continued direct stimulation of the emotion-producing centers seem to be limited to highly pathological (or experimental) conditions and are rare.

Assuming that thinking frequently, if not always, accompanies feeling, and assuming that most everyday thinking is done in the form of words, phrases, and sentences (rather than mathematical signs, dream symbols, or other kinds of nonverbal cues), it would appear that much of our emoting takes the form of self-talk or internalized sentences. If this is so, then for all practical purpose the phrases and sentences that we keep telling ourselves frequently *are* or *become* our thoughts and emotions.

Take, for example, a young male who wants to ask a girl for a dance. He will often start talking to himself along the following lines: "She's very beautiful . . . And I would like to ask her to dance with me . . . But she may refuse me . . . However, what have I got to lose? . . . I won't be any the worse off, if she does refuse me, than I am now, when I haven't asked her . . . And she may, of course, accept rather than refuse me— which will be great . . . So I might as well take the chance and ask her to dance." By telling himself these kinds of sentences, this man is thinking or planning in relation to the girl; and, for all practical purposes, his internalized sentences *are* his thinking.

If this same individual, however, becomes highly emotional, he may say certain different sentences to himself: "She's very beautiful . . . And I would like to ask her to dance with me . . . But she may refuse me . . . *And that would be awful!* . . . Or she may dance with me . . . And I may show her that I am a poor dancer . . . And then she might not like me and might even insult me . . . *Wouldn't that be frightful!*"

Or this same individual may say to himself: ". . . She may dance with me . . . *And that would be wonderful!* . . . My friends might see me dancing with this beautiful girl and think that I am a great guy for being able to get along so well with her . . . *And that would be fine!*"

By telling himself these kinds of sentences, including the negative evaluation "That would be awful!" or the positive evaluation "That would be fine!," this individual changes his calm thinking into excited emoting. And, for all practical purposes, his evaluative internalized sentences *are* his emotion (even though, technically, what actually seems to happen is that he first tells himself these sentences; then feels physical sensations in his gut; and then, by a feedback mechanism, perceives his own physical sensations, which he finally *interprets* as his "emotion").

It would appear, then, that positive human emotions, such as feelings of love or elation, are often associated with or result from internalized sentences stated in some form or variation of the phrase "This is good for me!" and that negative human emotions, such as feelings of anger or depression, are associated with or result from sentences stated in some form or variation of the phrase "This is bad for me." Without an adult human being's employing, on some conscious or unconscious level, such evaluative sentences, much of his emoting would simply not exist.

A confusion often arises in this connection because we fail to distinguish between our largely sensory appraisals, or *feelings,* and our cognitive-sensory states, or *emotions.* Thus, when you eat a pleasant-tasting food, such as ice cream, your taste buds, sense of smell, and other sensory organs of response are stimulated and you *feel* good, or are pleased. Your sensations, in this event, are never pure: since you may have prior experience with ice cream, and may associate it with all kinds of pleasant (or unpleasant) events. Consequently, there is some general perceptive or cognitive element in your feeling about the ice cream. But, usually, this cognitive element is minimal and your *feelings* about the ice cream are relatively pure and largely consist of unreflective sensory appraisals.

However, if you eat the same kind of ice cream and begin to think, while eating it, "Oh, isn't it lovely that I can enjoy this ice cream, after being without it for so long a time!" or "I am so grateful that So-and-so has brought me this ice cream!" you then tend to go far beyond your original sensory appraisal of the ice cream and to evaluate other conditions and persons in connection with it and your sensations of it. These cognitive-sensory processes that then occur to you lead, normally, to wider or more profound "feelings" about the ice cream (and the conditions or persons connected with it); and these "feelings" we call emotions. Unfortunately, we use the same term, *feelings*, to cover the pleasures and displeasures of (*a*) pure sensations, such as pain or warmth, (*b*) sensory appraisals, such as pleasure at feeling warm, and (*c*) cognitive-sensory evaluations which may or may not be connected with relatively pure sensory states, such as loving people who provide us with warmth.

In speaking of *feelings* and *emotions* in this book, we shall try to restrict the former term largely to relatively pure sensory states and sensory appraisals while using the latter term to include more wide-ranging cognitive-sensory processes.

If what has been hypothesized so far is true, and human emotions are largely a form of thinking or result from thinking, it would appear that one may appreciably control one's emotion by controlling one's thoughts. Or, more concretely, one may control one's emotions by changing the internalized sentences, or self-talk, with which one largely created these emotions in the first place.

This is precisely the view of the rational-emotive therapist: that by showing his patient how human thinking, and the emotions that are often associated with this thinking, can definitely be controlled or changed by parsing the phrases and sentences of which thoughts and emotions essentially consist, he can usually teach this patient to overcome his emotional disturbances. The rational therapist believes that sustained negative emotions—such as intense depression, anxiety, anger, and guilt —are almost always unnecessary to human living, and that they can be eradicated if people learn consistently to think straight and to follow up their straight thinking with effective action. It is his job to show his patients how to think straight and act effectively.

Does this mean that the rational therapist advocates the control or changing of *all* human emotions by the individual's controlling or changing his thinking? Not at all.

Many emotional outbursts, such as fits of anger or fear, seem to be the spontaneous and almost instantaneous results of sensorimotor processes which are either of innate origin or result from early acquired visceral conditioning. Thus, if you make a loud noise behind someone's back or aim a swiftly moving vehicle at him, he will normally experience fear; while if you keep cooking him fine meals or satisfying him sexually, he will normally like or love you. These kinds of fear, love, and other similar emotions seem to be biologically rooted; and it is difficult to see how people could survive very well without *some* emotional propensities of this nature. Anyone, therefore, who would attempt to control all human emotion out of existence would be aiming at a highly dubious goal.

Quite apart from human survival, moreover, many emotional reactions are highly pleasurable and salutary. Most people can somehow manage to exist without loving; without thrilling to art, music, or literature; and without experiencing any great amount of joy, elation, ecstasy, or delight. But who wants to survive under such circumstances? Even life that is replete with a certain amount of sorrow, regret, disappointment, and annoyance may be more interesting and alive than that which is everlastingly (and monotonously) "nice" and "pleasant." An existence devoid of *some* degree of emotion—of *some* amount of striving, seeking, yearning, and desiring, with all the usual risks attendant upon such cognitive-conative-emotional processes—would be deadly dull and inhuman (Ellis and Harper, 1961a).

The real question relevant to human happiness and emotional well-being, then, is not "Would it be wise to do away with all emotion?" but rather "Do we need to live with *intense* and *sustained* negative emotions, such as enduring fear and strong hostility?" The answer to this question seems to be: In large part, no.

Sustained negative emotions (other than those caused by continuing physical pain or discomfort) are invariably the result of stupidity, ignorance, or disturbance; and for the most part they may be, and should be, eliminated by the application of knowledge and straight thinking. For if perpetuated states of emotion generally follow from the individual's conscious or unconscious thinking; and if his thinking is, in turn, mainly a concomitant of his self-verbalizations, then it would follow that he is rarely affected (made sad or glad) by outside things and events; rather: he is affected by his perceptions, attitudes, or internalized sentences *about* outside things and events.

This principle, which I have inducted from many psychotherapeutic sessions with scores of patients during the last several years, was originally discovered and stated by the ancient Stoic philosophers, especially Zeno of Citium (the founder of the school), Chrysippus, Panaetius of Rhodes (who introduced Stoicism into Rome), Cicero, Seneca, Epictetus, and Marcus Aurelius. The truths of Stoicism were perhaps best set forth by Epictetus, who in the first century A.D. wrote in *The Enchiridion*: "Men are disturbed not by things, but by the views which they take of them." Shakespeare, many centuries later, rephrased this thought in *Hamlet*: "There's nothing either good or bad but thinking makes it so."

If sustained emotion, then, is generally backed by self-verbalizations, and if certain negative emotions are highly unpleasant states which add little to human happiness and make the world a poorer place in which to live, wise people should presumably make a conscious effort to change their internalized sentences with which they often create their negative emotions. If, however, they theoretically *can* control their self-defeating thoughts and feelings, and actually rarely do so, we may conclude that they are refraining because (*a*) they are too stupid to think clearly, or (*b*) they are sufficiently intelligent, but just do not know how to think clearly in relation to their emotional states, or (*c*) they are sufficiently intelligent and informed but are too neurotic (or psychotic) to put their intelligence and knowledge to good use. As I have elsewhere stated (Ellis, 1957a), neurosis essentially seems to consist of stupid behavior by a non-stupid person.

The rational-emotive therapist, then, assumes that a neurotic is a potentially capable person who in some way or on some level of his functioning does not realize that (or how) he is defeating his own ends. Or else he is an individual who (in rare cases) has full understanding of or insight into how he is harming himself but who, for some irrational reason, persists in self-sabotaging behavior. In any case, we may say that the neurotic is emotionally disabled because he does not know how to (or does not care to) think more clearly and behave less self-defeatingly.

That neurotic or emotionally disturbed behavior is illogical and irrational would seem to be almost definitional. For if we define neurotic more broadly, and label as disturbed *all* incompetent and ineffectual behavior, we shall be including actions of *truly* stupid and incompetent individuals—for example, those who are mentally deficient or brain-injured. The concept of neurosis only becomes meaningful, therefore, when we assume that the disturbed individual is *not* deficient or impaired physiologically but that he is theoretically capable of behaving in a more mature, more controlled, and more flexible manner than he actually behaves. Neurosis, then, is illogical behavior by a potentially logical individual.

Assuming that emotionally disturbed individuals act in irrational, illogical ways, the questions that are most therapeutically relevant are: (*a*) How do they originally get to be illogical? (*b*) How do they keep perpetuating their irrational thinking? (*c*) How can they be helped to be less illogical, less neurotic?

Unfortunately, most of the good thinking that has been done in regard to therapy during the past 60 years, especially by Sigmund Freud (1924-1950, 1938) and his chief followers (Fenichel, 1945; Menninger, 1958), has concerned itself more with the first of these questions rather than the second and third. The assumption has often been made that if psychotherapists discover and effectively communicate to their patients the main reasons why these patients originally became disturbed, the treated individuals will thereby also discover how their neuroses are being perpetuated and how they can be helped to overcome them. This is a dubious assumption.

Knowing exactly how an individual originally learned to behave illogically by no means necessarily informs us or him precisely how he *maintains* his illogical behavior, nor what he should do to change it. This is particularly true because people are often, perhaps usually, afflicted with *secondary* as well as *primary* neuroses, and the two may significantly differ. Thus, an individual may originally become disturbed because he discovers that he has strong death wishes against his father and (quite illogically) thinks he should be blamed and punished for having these wishes. Consequently, he may develop some neurotic symptom, such as a hatred against dogs—because, let us say, dogs remind him of his father, who is an ardent hunter.

Later on, this individual may grow to love or be indifferent to his father; or his father may die and be no more a problem to him. His hatred of dogs, however, may remain; not because, as some theorists would insist, they still remind him of his old death wishes against his father, but because he now hates himself so violently for *having* the original neurotic symptom—for behaving, to his own way of thinking, so stupidly and illogically in relation to dogs—that every time he thinks of dogs his self-hatred and his fear of failure so severely upset him that he cannot reason clearly and cannot combat his irrational abhorrence.

In terms of self-verbalization, this neurotic individual is first saying to himself: "I hate my father; my father likes dogs; therefore I hate dogs." But he ends up by saying: "I hate dogs; there is no good reason why I should hate dogs; how terrible it is for me to hate dogs without any good reason; therefore *I* am hateful." Even though both these sets of internalized sentences are neuroticizing, they can hardly be said to be the same set of sentences. Consequently, exploring and explaining to this individual—or helping him gain insight into—the origins of his primary neurosis (that is, his first chain of sentences) will not necessarily help him to understand and overcome his perpetuating or secondary neurosis (that is, his second chain of sentences).

Thus, if this neurotic individual is helped, during a therapeutic process, to see that he hates dogs because he is irrationally connecting them with his father, whom he also hates, he may say to himself: "How silly! Although my father appears to me to be 'a dog,' real dogs are not my father. I can easily learn to like dogs, or at least become indifferent to them, even if I never like my father." In this case, he would be cured of his hatred against dogs.

At the same time, however, he may also say to himself: "How silly! Dogs are certainly not the same as my father; and here I can see, now that I have this new psychological insight, that I am over-generalizing and confusing the two. What an idiot I am! I never realized before how stupid I could be! I was right in the first place about my being so hateful—for how can I like myself when I keep behaving so idiotically?" In this instance, even though he has lost his primary neurosis (his unreasonable hostility to dogs) this individual has stoutly held on to his secondary neurosis (his self-hatred for being stupid or neurotic). Indeed, precisely by getting insight into his primary disturbance, he may sometimes actually blame himself more severely and thus exacerbate his secondary disturbance (which is precisely why so many psychoanalytic patients get worse rather than better as their therapy proceeds and their insights become clearer).

Moreover, if this same patient discovers, after years of psychoanalytic treatment, that he hates dogs because his father loved them and his mother taught him to be hostile to his father and to anything associated with his father, he may not even lose his hostility toward dogs (let alone his hostility to himself for hating them). For he may say to himself, after gaining insight: "Mother hated father and taught me to do the same; actually father wasn't such a bad egg after all; it is silly for me to go on hating father." And he may actually stop hating his father any longer.

But he may still hate dogs. For over the years, once he *originally* began to detest dogs (by associating them with his hated father), he doubtless kept *maintaining* his hostility by saying to himself, over and over, something along these lines: "Dogs are no damn good. They smell bad. They bite people. They have to be cared for. They have all sorts of things wrong with them." And, very likely, these *subsequent* rationalizing sentences, quite aside from his associating dogs with his hated father, have *kept* him a dog-hater. And these sentences are *not* likely to be automatically dissipated just because this individual *now* comes to see that his *original* hostility toward dogs was irrational and unjustified.

Lest this illustration appear to be far-fetched, let me say that I have drawn it from an actual case of one of my patients, who did associate dogs with his hated father and who, after coming to hate and be afraid of any sizable dog, had several unpleasant experiences with this kind of animal (doubtless because he was so hostile and fearful).

Although I had relatively little difficulty, in the course of therapy, in tracking down his original hatred of his father, and showing him that he need not continue this hatred any longer, and although he managed to achieve, for the first time in his life, a fairly good relationship with his father, he never did lose his prejudices toward fairly large dogs, and preferred to end therapy without ever working on this problem. Similarly, I have seen a good many other patients who, after achieving a significant degree of insight into the origin of their neurotic symptoms, never overcame these symptoms (even though they made notable progress in other aspects of their lives in the course of therapy).

If the hypotheses so far stated have some validity, the psychotherapist's main goals should include demonstrating to patients that their self-verbalizations not only *have been* but usually *still are* the source of their emotional disturbances. Patients should be shown that their internalized sentences are quite illogical and unrealistic in certain respects and that they have the ability to change their emotions by telling themselves—or, rather, *convincing* themselves of the truth of—more rational and less self-defeating sentences.

More precisely: the effective therapist should continually keep unmasking his patient's past and, especially, his present illogical thinking or self-defeating verbalizations by (*a*) bringing them forcefully to his attention or consciousness; (*b*) showing him how they are causing and maintaining his disturbance and unhappiness, (c) demonstrating exactly what the illogical links in his internalized sentences are, and (d) teaching him how to re-think, challenge, contradict, and re-verbalize these (and other similar sentences) so that his internalized thoughts become more logical and efficient.

Before the end of the therapeutic relationship, moreover, the rational-emotive therapist should not only deal concretely with his patient's specific illogical thinking, but should demonstrate what, *in general*, are the main irrational ideas that human beings are prone to follow and what are the more rational philosophies of living that may usually be substituted instead. Otherwise, the patient who is released from one specific set of illogical notions may well wind up by falling victim to another set.

I am hypothesizing, in other words, that human beings are the kind of animals that, when reared in any society similar to our own, tend to believe several major fallacious ideas; to keep reindoctrinating themselves with these ideas in an unreflective, autosuggestive manner; and consequently to keep actualizing them in overt behavior that is self-defeating or neurotic. Most of these irrational ideas are, as the psychoanalysts have pointed out for several decades, instilled by the individual's parents during his early childhood and are tenaciously clung to because of his attachment to his parents and because the ideas were ingrained, imprinted, or conditioned before later and more rational modes of thinking were given a good chance to gain a foothold. Most of them, however, as the Freudian revisionists have noted, are also instilled by the individual's general culture, and particularly by the mass media in this culture (Ellis, 1961a); Fromm, 1955; Horney, 1937).

What are some of the major illogical ideas or philosophies which, when originally held and later perpetuated by men and women in our civilization, inevitably lead to self-defeat and neurosis? We shall examine some of these in the next chapter.

3

Irrational Ideas Which Cause and Sustain
Emotional Disturbances

In existing society our family and other institutions directly and indirectly indoctrinate all of us so that we grow up to believe many superstitious, senseless ideas. This notion is hardly original to RT: since philosophers have said as much for centuries, and many sociologists and anthropologists have documented it (Ellis, 1961a, 1962b; Frazer, 1959; Hoffer, 1951, 1955; Rokeach, 1960; Rosenfeld, 1962; Tabori, 1959, 1961). In a recent sociological text, for example, Cuber, Harper and Kenkel (1956) incisively discuss "the older non-rational acceptance of value positions" in American society and indicate that many of our most cherished and dogmatically upheld values—such as those of monogamous marriage, freedom, acquisitiveness, democracy, education, monotheistic religion, technology and science—are only *assumed* to be "good" values and are rarely seriously reviewed or questioned by those who keep drumming them into the heads of our children. As La Barre (1955) aptly notes: In our society "a child perforce becomes a Right Thinker before he learns to think at all."

Recent psychoanalytic writers have also highlighted the manner in which societally-inculcated superstitions and prejudices have caused widespread human disturbance. Horney (1939), Fromm (1941, 1947, 1955), Reich (1949), and others have attempted to show how illogical social teachings have been a prime cause of neurosis, and have insisted that nothing but a change in the basic ideational or philosophic outlook of modern men and women will significantly reduce their neurotic trends.

In an attempt to go somewhat beyond these sociological and

psychoanalytic thinkers, and to be more specific about the ideational bases of emotional aberrations, I shall now outline some of the major illogical and irrational ideas which are presently ubiquitous in Western civilization and which would seem inevitably to lead to widespread neurosis. These ideas may be classified in various ways, so that the following listing is not meant to be definitive or non-overlapping, but constitutes one of several classificatory approaches which may be taken to modern irrationalities.

Irrational Idea No. 1: *The idea that it is a dire necessity for an adult human being to be loved or approved by virtually every significant other person in his community.*

Although it has often been claimed, and may well be true, that children *need* love and approval, and although it is doubtless *desirable* for adults to be loved and approved by many of the people with whom they come into intimate contact, it is questionable whether it is absolutely *necessary* for adults to be accepted by virtually every other person in their community whom they deem to be significant to them (Riesman *et al.*, 1953; Lipset and Lowenthal, 1961; Bain, 1962). Believing that one *must* be accepted by significant others is irrational for several reasons:

1. *Demanding* that you be approved by all those whose approval you would *like* to have sets a perfectionistic, unattainable goal: because even if 99 people accept or love you, there will always be the hundredth, the hundred-and-first, and so on, who do not.

2. Even if you win the approval of all the people you consider important, if you *direly need* their acceptance, you will have to keep worrying constantly about how *much* they accept you or whether they *still* approve you. A considerable degree of anxiety, therefore, *must* accompany the dire need to be loved (Loevinger, 1962; Stewart, 1962).

3. It is impossible, no matter what efforts you make, for you always to be lovable. Because of their own intrinsic prejudices, *some* of the people whose approval you value highly will inevitably dislike or be indifferent to you.

4. Assuming that you could, theoretically, win the approbation of virtually everyone you wanted to approve you, you would have to spend so much time and energy doing so that you would have little remaining for other rewarding pursuits.

5. In trying ceaselessly to be approved by others, you invariably have to become ingratiating or obsequious—and thereby give up many of your *own* wants and preferences and become considerably less *self*-directing.

6. If you obsessively-compulsively seek others' approval, which you will have to do if you arbitrarily define being approved as a necessity rather than a preference, you will tend to behave so insecurely and annoyingly toward these others that you will often actually *lose* their approval or respect and thereby defeat your own ends.

7. *Loving,* rather than *being loved,* is an absorbing, creative, self-expressing occupation. But loving tends to be inhibited rather than abetted by the dire need to be loved.

Instead of illogically trying to solve his problems by constantly seeking love and approval, the rational person should more wisely strive for loving, creative, productive living. More specifically:

1. He should not try to eradicate *all* his desires for approval but to extirpate his inordinate, all-consuming love needs.

2. He should honestly try, in many instances, to be approved for practical reasons (such as companionship or vocational advancement) rather than (like a child) seek to be loved "for himself," for his "immortal soul," or for the sake of raising his (false) "self-esteem." He should realize that true self-respect never comes from the approval of others but from liking oneself and following most of one's own interests *whether or not* others approve one's doings.

3. He should, when he is not loved or approved by those he would very much like to have on his side, fully admit that this is annoying and frustrating but refrain from convincing himself that it is horrible and catastrophic.

4. He should neither conform for the sake of conforming nor rebel for the sake of rebelling, and should keep asking himself,

from time to time: "What do *I* really want to do in the course of my relatively short life?" rather than "What do I think *others* would like me to do?"

5. To the extent that it is desirable and practical for him to win the approval of others, he should try to do so in a calm, intelligent, planful way rather than in a frantic, hit-and-miss manner. To this end, he should realize that one of the best ways to win love is sincerely to give it.

Irrational Idea No. 2: *The idea that one should be thoroughly competent, adequate, and achieving in all possible respects if one is to consider oneself worthwhile.*

Many or most people in our society, perhaps more so than the citizens of any other society that has ever existed, believe that if they are not thoroughly competent, adequate, and achieving in all possible respects—and, at the very least, in one major respect—they are worthless and might as well curl up and die. This is an irrational idea for several reasons:

1. No human being can be perfectly competent and masterful in all or most respects; and most people cannot be truly outstanding even in a single major respect. To *try* to be quite successful is sane enough, since there are real advantages (such as monetary rewards or increased pleasure in participation) if one succeeds in a job, a game, or an artistic endeavor. But to *demand* that one *must* succeed is to make oneself a certain prey to anxiety and feelings of personal worthlessness.

2. Although being reasonably successful and achieving has distinct advantages (particularly in our society), compulsive drives for accomplishment usually result in undue stress, hypertension, and forcing oneself beyond one's own physical limitations: with consequent production of several varieties of psychosomatic ills.

3. The individual who *must* succeed in an outstanding way is not merely challenging himself and testing his own powers (which may well be creatively beneficial); but he is invariably comparing himself to and fighting to best *others*. He thereby becomes other- rather than self-directed and sets himself essentially impossible tasks (since, no matter how outstandingly good

he may be in a given field, it is most likely that there will be others who are still better). It is senseless to keep comparing oneself invidiously to other achieving individuals, since one has no control whatever over *their* performances, but only over one's own. One also has no control, in many instances, over one's own achievements and characteristics—cannot, for example, be beautiful when one is homely or a fine concert pianist when one is tone deaf—and it is therefore pointless for one to be over-concerned about these uncontrollable traits.

4. Giving a great emphasis to the philosophy of achievement confuses one's extrinsic value (the value that other people place on one's performance or characteristics) with one's intrinsic value (one's aliveness, or value to oneself) (Hartman, 1959). To *define* one's personal worth in terms of one's extrinsic achievements, and to contend that one *must* excel others in order to be happy, is to subscribe to a thoroughly undemocratic, fascist-like philosophy, which does not essentially differ from the idea that one must be Aryan, or white, or Christian, or a social registerite in order to be a respectable, worthwhile human being.

5. Concentrating on the belief that one must be competent and successful often effectively sidetracks one from a main goal of happy living: namely, experimentally discovering what one's *own* most enjoyable and rewarding interests in life are and courageously (no matter *what* others think) spending a good part of one's brief span of existence engaging in *these* pursuits.

6. Over-concern with achievement normally results in one's acquiring enormous fears of taking chances, of making mistakes, and of failing at certain tasks—all of which fears, in turn, tend to sabotage the very achievement for which one is striving. Inordinate self-consciousness at performing any task, which generally follows from preoccupation with failing at it (and thereby defining oneself as worthless), almost always leads to (*a*) complete disenjoyment of the task and (*b*) propensity to fail miserably at it.

Instead of illogically concentrating on the utter necessity of succeeding at the tasks and problems he faces in life, an individual would be acting far more reasonably if he took the following paths:

1. He should try to *do,* rather than kill himself trying to *do well.* He should focus on enjoying the *process* rather than only the *result* of what he does.

2. When he tries to do well, he should try to do so for his *own* sake rather than to please or to best *others.* He should be artistically and esthetically, rather than merely egotistically, involved in the results of his labors.

3. When, for his own satisfaction, he tries to do well, he should not insist on his always doing *perfectly* well. He should, on most occasions, strive for *his* best rather than *the* best.

4. He should from time to time question his strivings and honestly ask himself whether he is striving for achievement *in itself* or for achievement *for his own satisfaction.*

5. If he wants to do well at any task or problem, he should learn to welcome his mistakes and errors, rather than become horrified at them, and to put them to good account. He should accept the necessity of his practicing, practicing, practicing the things he wants to succeed at; should often force himself to do what he is afraid to fail at doing; and should fully accept the fact that human beings, in general, are limited animals and that he, in particular, has necessary and distinct limitations.

Irrational Idea No. 3: *The idea that certain people are bad, wicked, or villainous and that they should be severely blamed and punished for their villainy.*

Many individuals become upset, angry, and vindictive because they believe that certain people—often especially including themselves—are villains; that because of their villainy they commit immoral acts; and that the only way to prevent them from acting villainously is to blame and punish them (Diggory, 1962). These ideas are invalid and irrational for several important reasons:

1. The idea that certain people are bad or wicked springs from the ancient theological doctrine of free will, which assumes that every person has the freedom to act "rightly" or "wrongly," in relation to some absolute standard of truth and justice or-

dained by "god" or the "natural law"; and that if anyone uses his "free will" to behave "wrongly," he is a wicked "sinner." This doctrine has no scientific foundation, because its key terms—including "absolute truth," "god," "free will," and "natural law" —are purely definitional and can neither be proven nor disproven in empirical, scientific terms.

Moreover, considerable psychoanalytic findings of the last century indicate that if we operationally define "free will" to mean the individual's (relative rather than absolute) ability to make his own choices of conduct instead of his being compelled to act in accordance with various biosocial influences that are continually exerted on him, then we must realistically accept the fact that human beings in our time have surprisingly little (though not necessarily zero) free will. For they are frequently unaware or unconscious of some of their most powerful motives (such as their sex drives or hostilities); and consequently they find themselves compelled to perform many acts which, consciously, they do not want to perform and are, perhaps, quite guilty about performing. Their unconscious drives and desires nullify their "free will" considerably.

2. When people perform acts which they (or others) consider "wrong" or "immoral," they appear to do so, in the final analysis, because they are too stupid, too ignorant, or too emotionally disturbed to refrain from doing so. Although such individuals indubitably *cause* or *are responsible for* harm to others, it is illogical to *blame* them (that is, denigrate them as human beings) for their stupidity, ignorance, or disturbance. It is logical to say: "They did this 'wrong' act; therefore I should do my best to induce them not to commit it again." But it is a *non sequitur* to say: "They did this 'wrong' act; therefore they are perfectly worthless beings who deserve to be severely punished or killed." A "bad" act does not make a "bad" person (as even the Catholic church will usually admit). It is merely evidence of undesirable behavior on the part of the person that, for his sake as well as that of others, it would be highly *preferable* to change.

3. Because of his biosocial makeup (including his heredity

and his training), man is a distinctly *fallible* animal who can only be realistically *expected* to make mistakes and errors. It is therefore unrealistic to expect him *not* to do so and to condemn him for being the way he is and for failing to fulfill one's own perfectionistic expectations of him. The sentence, "He made a serious blunder; I hope he does better next time," is perfectly sane. But the sentence, "He made a serious blunder; he *should* not have made it and *should* do better next time," is perfectly nonsensical. For it really means: "I unrealistically expected him to be an angel instead of a human and not to make any mistakes; and now that he has proven that he is fallibly human, I even more unrealistically demand that he start being a perfect angel in the future."

4. The theory of calling a wrongdoer a villain and blaming or punishing him for his mistaken (and perhaps antisocial) acts is based on the supposition that blame and punishment will usually induce a human being to stop his wrongdoing and to behave much better in the future. Although this supposition has *some* evidence to support it (since children and adults *sometimes* change for the better when they are blamefully criticized or punished), the history of human crime and punishment presents considerable evidence for the opposing thesis: namely, that individuals who are angrily punished for their "sins" frequently do not change for the better but instead become worse. While calm, objective penalization of a person for his mistakes (as an experimenter objectively penalizes a laboratory animal when it goes in the wrong alley of a learning maze) often aids the learning process (Mowrer, 1960a), there is much reason to believe that angry, blameful penalization more often than not either impedes human learning or else facilitates it with so many harmful side effects (especially, neurotic symptoms) on the part of the learner, that the blaming game comes to be hardly worth the candle.

5. On theoretical grounds, we should probably expect that emotionally punishing (rather than objectively reeducating) an individual for his wrongdoings is likely to have poor learning consequences. For if a person commits a mistaken act (of omis-

sion or commission) out of his innate stupidity, blaming him will hardly make him less stupid or more intelligent. If he commits such an act out of ignorance, blamefully bringing it to his attention is not likely to help him be very much less ignorant. And if he commits it out of emotional disturbance, blame will almost certainly serve to make him more disturbed. It is difficult to see, therefore, how angrily or vindictively punishing a person for his wrongdoings is going to be of much service in getting him to tackle the basic objective problem of competence and morality: namely, "Now that I have made a mistake *this* time, how am I best going to correct it *in the future?*"

6. At bottom, blame, hostility, and anger are almost certainly the most essential and serious causes of most human disturbances (Chambers and Lieberman, 1962). If children were not brought up with the philosophy of blaming themselves and others for possible or actual mistakes and wrongdoings, they would have great difficulty becoming anxious, guilty, or depressed (which feelings result from self-blame) or hostile, bigoted, or grandiose (which result from blaming others). If, therefore, we train our children to become neurotic by blaming them and teaching them to blame; and if we then blame them even more severely when their neurotic symptoms compel them to resort to all kinds of mistaken and antisocial behavior; are we not thereby reaching the topmost pinnacle of circular inanity and insanity?

Instead of becoming unduly upset over his own or others' wrongdoings, the rational individual may take the following approach to errors of commission or omission:

1. He should not criticize or blame others for their misdeeds but should realize that they invariably commit such acts out of stupidity, ignorance, or emotional disturbance. He should try to accept people when they are stupid and to help them when they are ignorant or disturbed.

2. When people blame him, he should first ask himself whether he has done anything wrong; and if he has, try to improve his behavior; and, if he hasn't, realize that other people's

criticism is often *their* problem and represents some kind of defensiveness or disturbance on their part.

3. He should try to understand *why* people act the way they do—to make an effort to see things from *their* frame of reference when he thinks they are wrong. If there is any way of stopping others from doing their misdeeds, he should calmly try to stop them). If there is no way of stopping them (as, alas, often is the case!), he should become philosophically resigned to others' wrongdoings by saying to himself: "It's too bad that they keep acting that way. All right: so it's too bad. And it isn't, from my standpoint, necessarily catastrophic!"

4. He should try to realize that his own mistaken acts, like those of others, are usually the result of ignorance or emotional disturbance; and he should never blame himself for being ignorant or disturbed or for doing misdeeds. He should learn to say to himself: "All right: I admittedly *did* treat So-and-so badly or I *did* fail at a job that I normally should be able to succeed at. So I blundered or failed. That's bad: but it's not terrible, it's not horrible, it's not catastrophic. And the main point is not what a no-goodnik I am for failing, but how can I learn from this mistake and manage to fail less badly next time? I've merely proved, once again, that I'm still a fallible human being. Now let's see how I can manage to become a little less fallible."

Irrational Idea No. 4: *The idea that it is awful and catastrophic when things are not the way one would very much like them to be.*

It is simply amazing how many millions of people on this earth are terribly upset and miserable when things are not the way they would like them to be, or when the world is the way the world is. That these people should be distinctly frustrated when they are not getting what they strongly want to get is of course normal. But that they are pronouncedly and enduringly depressed or angry because they are frustrated is quite illogical for many reasons:

1. There is no reason, why things *should* be different from

the way they are, no matter how unfortunate or unfair their present state of existence is. And there are many reasons, especially the facts of reality themselves, why unpleasant situations and events *are* the way they are. *Disliking* nasty people or conditions is perfectly reasonable; but *becoming seriously disturbed* because reality is reality is patently absurd. It would often *be nice* if things were different from the way they are, or if we got what we wanted out of life instead of what we actually get. But the fact that it would be nice if this were so hardly makes it so nor gives us sensible reason to cry when it is *not* so.

2. Getting enduringly or extremely upset over a given set of circumstances will rarely help us to change them for the better. On the contrary, the more upset we make ourselves over the unpleasant facts of life, the more we shall tend to become disorganized and ineffective in our efforts to improve existing conditions.

3. When things are not the way we would like them to be, we should certainly strive, and often mightily strive, to change them. But when it is impossible (for the nonce or forever) to change them—as, alas, it often is—the only sane thing to do is to become philosophically resigned to our fate and accept things the way they are. The fact that children, who have little ability to think philosophically, usually are unable to tolerate any amount of inevitable frustration hardly proves that adults cannot calmly do so. They can—if they will work half as hard at accepting grim reality as they usually work at convincing themselves that they cannot accept it.

4. Although at first blush there may seem to be considerable evidence that the Dollard-Miller hypothesis is sound and that frustration inevitably leads to aggression, a more detailed examination of the evidence will show—as Pastore (1950, 1952) and Arnold (1960) have indicated—that it is not really the frustration itself, but one's subjective and moralistic *attitude* toward this frustration that really causes hostility and aggression. Thus, people who wait 20 minutes in the cold for a bus only to see it finally pass them by are not particularly hostile if (*a*) they discover that the bus is out of order, but are almost

always angry if (*b*) they see that the bus driver sneeringly
passes them by without any good reason. Yet in both instances
they do not get on the bus and are equally frustrated.

Similarly, recent experimentation by Beecher, Livingston,
Melzack, and others (Melzack, 1961) has shown that even physical pain is experienced and reacted to not only in relation to
the intensity of the painful stimulus but largely in relation to
the subjective, individual, attitudinal prejudices of the person
who is stimulated. No matter, therefore, how badly you may be
frustrated or deprived of something that you badly want, you
normally *need* not make yourself terribly unhappy about this
deprivation if you do not *define* your preference as a dire
necessity.

Instead of becoming or remaining illogically upset over the
frustrating circumstances of life, or over the real or imagined
injustices of the world, a rational human being may adopt the
following attitudes:

1. He can determine whether seemingly frustrating or painful circumstances are truly annoying in their own right or
whether he is imagining or highly exaggerating their irritating
qualities. If certain circumstances are intrinsically unpleasant,
he should do his best to face them calmly and to work at im-
proving them. If it is somehow impossible, for the present, for
him to change or eradicate existing poor conditions, he should
philosophically accept or resign himself to their existence.

2. More specifically, he should perceive his own tendency to
catastrophize about inevitable unfortunate situations—to tell himself: "Oh, my Lord! How terrible this situation is; I positively
cannot stand it!"—and should question and challenge this catastrophizing, and change his internalized sentences to: "It's too
bad that conditions are this frustrating. But they won't kill me;
and I surely *can* stand living in this unfortunate but hardly
catastrophic way."

3. Whenever possible, he should try to make the most of
frustrating situations: to learn by them, accept them as challenges, integrate them usefully into his life.

4. When plagued by unpleasant physical sensations, such as

headaches, he should do his best to eliminate them; and when they are not eradicable, should try to practice some measure of sensation-neglect and distraction. Thus, he can focus on other, more pleasant aspects of life (such as reading or playing ping-pong) until his unpleasant sensations go away. He should accept inevitable annoyances and irritations and see that he does not exaggerate them by making himself annoyed at being annoyed (and thereby doubling or quadrupling his original irritation) (Ellis, 1957a).

Irrational Idea No. 5: *The idea that human unhappiness is externally caused and that people have little or no ability to control their sorrows and disturbances.*

Most people in our society seem to believe that other people and events make them unhappy and that if these outside forces were different they would not be miserable. They think that they cannot possibly help being upset when certain dreadful circumstances occur, and that they have no control over themselves or their emotions in these circumstances. This idea is invalid on several counts:

1. Other people and events can actually do little to harm you other than physically assaulting you or (directly or indirectly) depriving you of certain tangible satisfactions (such as money or food). But, in our present society, people rarely do physically or economically assault you; and almost all their "onslaughts" consist of psychological attacks which have little or no power to harm you unless you erroneously *believe* that they are harmful. It is impossible for you to be harmed by purely verbal or gestural attacks unless *you* specifically *let* yourself—or actually *make* yourself—be harmed. It is never the words or gestures of others that hurt you—but *your* attitudes toward, *your* reactions to these symbols.

2. Whenever you say "*it* hurts me, when my friends are unkind," or "I can't stand *it*, when things go wrong," you are saying nonsense. *It* in these sentences refers to nothing meaningful and is purely definitional in content. What you really mean is "*I* disturb *myself* by telling myself that it is horrible when my

friends are unkind" or "*I* tell *myself* that it is perfectly frightful to have things go wrong and that I can't stand this kind of situation." Although the *it* in "it hurts me" or "I can't stand it" seems to refer to some external event that is uncontrollably impinging on you, at most *it* is just a somewhat annoying act ɔr event which becomes horrible because you *make* it so and which, in its own right, has little or no actual effect on you.

3. Although millions of civilized people stoutly believe that they cannot control their emotions and that unhappiness is therefore forced upon them no matter what they do, this idea is quite false. The truth is that it is *difficult* for most people in our society to change or control their emotions, largely because they rarely attempt to do so and get so little practice at doing this. Or, when they occasionally do try to control their emotions, they do so in a slipshod, hasty, and imprecise way. If these people stopped looking on their emotions as ethereal, almost inhuman processes, and realistically viewed them as being largely composed of perceptions, thoughts, evaluations, and internalized sentences, they would find it quite possible to work calmly and concertedly at changing them.

It is true that, once one has told oneself for a long period of time that one really *should* get upset about certain annoyances or dangers, one will then form the habit of becoming so upset about these things that it will be most difficult, if not impossible, for one to remain calm. But it is also true (if generally unacknowledged by Americans) that once one tells oneself, again for a long enough period of time, that one need *not* upset oneself about these same kinds of annoyances or dangers, one will then find it difficult to get over-excited about them and will find it easy to remain calm when they occur. With few exceptions, to parapharase Shakespeare, there's nothing so upsetting in life but thinking makes it so.

Instead of erroneously believing that his emotions are invariably beyond his control, the informed and intelligent individual will acknowledge that unhappiness largely (though not entirely) comes from within and is created by the unhappy person himself. This informed individual will, in relation to his own negative and self-destructive emotions, take the following tacks:

1. Whenever he finds himself becoming intensely upset (as distinguished from his becoming moderately regretful about some loss or irritated by some frustration), he will quickly acknowledge that *he* is creating his own negative emotions by reacting unthinkingly to some situation or person. He will not allow himself to be deluded by the "fact" that his acute anxieties or hostilities are "naturally" caused or are his existential lot as a human being or are created by external conditions; but he will forthrightly face the fact that *he* is their prime motivator and that because *he* produced them he, too, can eradicate them.

2. After objectively observing his acute unhappy emotions, he will *think about* and trace them back to his own illogical sentences with which he is creating them. He will then logically parse and forcefully question and challenge these emotion-creating sentences until he becomes convinced of their inner contradictions and finds them no longer tenable. By radically analyzing and changing his self-verbalizations in this manner, he will effectively change and counteract the self-destructive emotions and actions to which they have been leading.

Thus, if the individual intensely fears coming into contact with cripples, he will assume that it is not the cripples who actually frighten him but his own internalized sentences about the "frightfulness" of cripples. He will calmly observe these sentences (e.g., "Cripples are in an undesirable situation because they need help; and if I needed help like they do, that would be terrible.") Then he will logically parse these sentences (e.g., ask himself: "How does the last part of this sentence, that if I needed help like cripples do it would be terrible, logically follow from the first part of the sentence, that cripples are in an undesirable situation?") Then he will forcefully challenge his sentences (e.g., by showing himself, over and over again: "Even though it certainly would be *undesirable* if I were a cripple and needed help, it would *not* be *terrible* or catastrophic; and it would surely not prove that I was worthless.")

Finally, he will consider and contradict the *general* false philosophies behind his specific fears of coming into contact with cripples and reminding himself that he, too, might become a "horrible" cripple and thereby be in a "terribly frightful" situation. Thus, he will show himself that (*a*) coming into contact with cripples (or other unfortunates) can *never* magically make him crippled; that (*b*) practically *nothing* that is highly undesirable (such as being crippled) is truly terrible or catastrophic; that (*c*) he can *almost always,* if he has a reasonably sane philosophy of life, overcome physical handicaps and other adversities, as long as he is alive and as long as he keeps thinking, planning, and acting about any unfortunate situations in which he may find himself; *et cetera.*

Irrational Idea No. 6. *The idea that if something is or may be dangerous or fearsome one should be terribly concerned about it and should keep dwelling on the possibility of its occurring.*

Most people in our society stubbornly seem to believe that if they are in danger, or if some fearsome event may possibly befall them, they should keep worrying about this actual or potential danger. This is an irrational belief for many reasons:

1. Although it is often wise to think prophylactically about a dangerous possibility, to plan to avert it, and to do something practical to stave it off or to meet it successfully if it does occur, what you normally feel as "anxiety," "worry," or "intense fear" is rarely of a prophylactic or constructive nature, and more often than not seriously impedes your being able to do something effective about preventing or meeting any real danger. In the first place, if you become terribly worried or over-concerned about some possible hazard, you usually become so excited and edgy that you are actually *prevented* from objectively observing whether this "hazard" is real or exaggerated.

Thus, if you are horribly afraid that a group of boys who are throwing a ball to each other are going to hit you with it and knock you unconscious, you will probably be in no position to notice whether the ball they are throwing is a hard and dangerous instrument (such as a baseball or a golf ball) or whether it is a soft and harmless object (such as a light plastic or rubber ball). Worry or over-concern therefore frequently leads to fantasies about the "harmfulness" in a given situation that actually have no basis in fact.

2. Intense anxiety about the possibility of an actual danger's occurring will frequently prevent your being able to meet this danger effectively when and if it does occur. Thus, if you know that the boys in the street are throwing around a hard and dangerous ball, and you are petrified lest you or someone you love be hit and harmed by this ball, you may become so upset about this real danger that, instead of calmly explaining to the boys how dangerous it is to be using this ball and inducing them to use a lighter one, you may antagonize them by nervously yelling at them, calling the police, or otherwise bothering them so that they then deliberately keep using the hard ball.

3. Worrying intensely over the possibility of some dire event's happening will not only not prevent it from occurring in most cases, but will often contribute to bringing it about. Over-concern about your getting in a car accident may actually make you so nervous that you then drive into another car or a lamp post when, if you were calmer, you might have easily avoided getting into this kind of accident.

4. Over-concern about a dangerous situation usually leads to your exaggerating the chances of its actually occurring. Thus, if you are terribly frightened about taking an airplane trip, you will probably imagine that there is an excellent possibility of your plane's getting into a serious accident when, actually, there is about one in one hundred thousand chances of its doing so. Even though your worry, in such an instance, has *some* real grounds for existing, it by no means has the unrealistically exaggerated grounds that you, by your over-concern, create.

5. Some dreaded events—such as your ultimately becoming seriously ill or dying—are inevitable and nothing, including your worrying about them, can possibly prevent them from occurring. By worrying about these inevitable events, therefore, you do not in any manner, shape, or form, decrease the chances of

their occurring; and you not only thereby manage to obtain the disadvantages of the dreaded events themselves, but create for yourself the additional, and often much more crippling, disadvantages of being upset about these events long before they actually occur. Thus, if you have good reason to believe that you will actually die, say, a few years hence, your anxiety about your impending death will not only fail to stave off this event, but it will make a misery of your remaining days which you very well might, if you accepted the inevitability of your dying, manage to enjoy.

6. Many dangerous and normally dreaded events—such as the possibility of your becoming diabetic if you happen to be born into a family that has a high incidence of this disease—would not actually be so handicapping if they did occur as your worries about their occurrence often will make them appear to be. You *can* live fairly comfortably (though admittedly inconveniently) with diabetes (or, for that matter, with tuberculosis, many forms of cancer, and various other unfortunate ailments) if you are actually stricken with this disease. Catastrophizing about the possible results of such an affliction is therefore pointless, even when there is a good chance that you may soon acquire it.

Instead of defeating his own ends by being exaggeratedly fearful, a rational human being should take quite a different set of attitudes toward the possible dangers and handicaps that may occur in his life:

1. He should realize that most of his worries are caused not by external dangers that may occur but by his telling himself, "Wouldn't it be terrible if this danger occurred?" or "It would be frightful if this event exists and I cannot cope adequately with it." He should learn, instead, to examine his catastrophizing internalized sentences and to change them for the saner and more realistic philosophy: "It would be an awful nuisance or a bad thing if this danger occurred; but it would *not* be terrible, and I *could* cope with this nuisance or bad thing."

2. He should keep showing himself how his irrational fears do not help him ward off dangers, often actually increase or augment these dangers, and usually are more debilitating and

defeating than are the so-called fearsome events of which he is making himself so afraid.

3. He should realize that many or most of his fears are disguised forms of the fear of what others think of him and he should continually question and challenge this kind of fear and see how silly it generally is. He should question the appropriateness of most of his present anxieties, even though some of them may have been appropriate in the past—when he was smaller and younger and had more really to be afraid of.

4. He should frequently do the things he is most afraid of doing—such as speaking in public, expressing his views to a superior, or standing up for his own rights—in order to prove to himself that there *is* nothing intrinsically frightful about these things.

5. He should not be alarmed when previously-conquered fears temporarily arise again, but should work at eradicating them once more, by honestly facing and thinking about them, until they have little or no tendency to return to smite him.

Irrational Idea No. 7: *The idea that it is easier to avoid than to face certain life difficulties and self-responsibilities.*

Many people feel that it is much easier to do only the things that come "easily" or "naturally" or that are intrinsically enjoyable, and to avoid certain life difficulties and self-responsibilities. These people's ideas are fallacious in several significant respects:

1. The idea that there is an easy way out of life's difficulties only considers the ease of avoidance at the exact moment of decision, and fails to consider the many problems and annoyances engendered by avoidance. Thus, if you find it difficult to ask a girl for a kiss (or to try to kiss her without asking!) and you decide not to face her rejection, you will, at the moment of making your negative decision, sigh with relief and feel better about getting away from the problem. But you will, as soon as that moment of relief passes, probably give yourself a continuing rough time because you have missed possible satisfaction, have never discovered what she does think of you, have gained no practice in asking or in kissing, etc. Your "pleasure"

of the moment may therefore well result in hours, days, or even years of subsequent unhappiness.

2. Although the effort you take in avoiding a decision or a difficulty seems, often, to be inconsequential and easy to perform, it is actually deceptively long and hard. For you may spend literally many hours of self-debate, self-torture, and ingenious plotting and scheming before you can arrange *not* to commit yourself to a difficult but potentially rewarding task; and the discomfort you thus create for yourself may be ten times as great as the discomfort that you imagine would exist if you actually committed yourself to this task.

3. Self-confidence, in the last analysis, arises only through doing something, and virtually never through avoidance. We are confident that we can do a thing in the future (and enjoy doing it) because, essentially, we have already succeeded in doing some aspects of it in the past and present. If, therefore, you spend a good part of your life avoiding difficult problems and responsibilities, you may possibly gain an "easier" life but you will almost certainly concomitantly acquire a less self-confident existence.

4. It is somehow assumed by millions of people that an easy, evasive, or less responsible life is also an exceptionally rewarding one. This, as Magda Arnold (1960) and Nina Bull (1960) have recently emphasized, is a very dubious assumption. Human beings seem to be "happiest" not when they are sitting passively around doing little or nothing, and perhaps not even when they are (for relatively few moments at a time) highly excited and intensely emotionally involved in something. Rather, they seem to get along best when they are goal-oriented in the sense of being committed to and working steadily and relatively calmly at some long-range, fairly difficult project (whether it be in the field of art, science, business, or anything else).

If this is true, then a life of ease and avoidance of responsibility may often be temporarily satisfying—especially on periods of *vacation* from a more active kind of life—but it is rarely continually rewarding. Life, at bottom, is acting, moving, experiencing, creating; and human beings miss enormous amounts

of high-level satisfaction when they focus on avoiding challenging and difficult problems of living.

Instead of trying to avoid many of life's difficulties, challenges,
and responsibilities, the rational individual might well follow
these kinds of procedures:

1. He should uncomplainingly do the things that are necessary for him to perform, no matter how much he dislikes doing
them, while figuring out intelligent methods of avoiding the *unnecessary* painful aspects of living. He can discipline himself
to do necessary tasks by logically convincing himself that they
are necessary, and by then literally forcing himself to do them
and get them out of the way as quickly as possible.

2. If he refuses to face certain life problems and responsibilities, he should never accept as fact the notion that he is
"naturally" or "biologically" indolent, but should assume that
behind virtually every such refusal is a chain of his own sentences indicating either needless anxiety or rebellion. And he
should ruthlessly reveal and logically parse these sentences, until
he changes them for saner and more activity-propelling ones.

3. He should avoid trying to lean over backward to be *too*
self-disciplined or to do things the *too*-hard way (usually out
of guilt and self-punishment). But he should try to aid his
normal self-disciplining activities; if necessary, by adopting
planned schedules of work, giving himself reasonable sub-goals,
and working in terms of intermediate rewards.

4. He should fully face the fact that *living* is exactly what
the name implies, and that *resting* and *avoiding* are often legitimate intervals in a full life, but become deadly if they occupy
the major part of that "life." He should philosophically accept
the fact that the more responsible, challenging, and problem-
solving his existence is, the more, especially in its long-range
aspects, he is truly likely to enjoy it.

Irrational Idea No. 8: *The idea that one should be dependent
on others and needs someone stronger than oneself on whom
to rely.*

Although we theoretically endorse freedom and independence
in our society, many of us appear to believe that we should be

dependent on others and that we need someone stronger than
ourselves on whom to rely. This is an irrational notion for several
reasons:

1. Although it is true that all of us are *somewhat* dependent
on others in this complex society (since we could hardly buy
food, ride on trains, clothe ourselves, or do a hundred other
necessary acts without considerable collaborative division of
labor), there is no reason why we should *maximize* this dependency and literally demand that others make our choices
and do our thinking for us. Let us by all means be socially
cooperative; but as little as possible *subservient.*

2. The more you rely on others, the more you are bound, in
the first or last analysis, to give up many things that *you* want
to do in life and to go along, out of dire need for their help,
with things that *they* want you to do. Dependency, by definition,
is inversely related to individualism and independence; and you
cannot very well be *you* and be sorely dependent on others at
one and the same time.

3. The more you rely on others to guide you and help you
do various things, the less you will tend to do these things for
yourself, and in consequence to learn by doing them. This
means that the more dependent you are, the still more dependent you tend to become. Moreover, if you depend on others in
order to feel safe—for then you cannot make mistakes yourself or
be blamed if you do make them—you essentially lose rather than
gain basic security: since the only real security that you can have
in life is that of knowing that, no matter how many mistakes you
make, you are still not worthless, but merely a fallible human
being. Dependency leads, in a vicious circle, to less and less
self-confidence and greater anxiety. Being dependent constitutes
a never-ending quest for a never-findable (by *that* means) sense
of self-esteem and security.

4. By depending on others, you put yourself to a considerable
degree at *their* mercy, and hence at the mercy of outside forces
which you often cannot possibly control. If you depend on
yourself to make decisions and to carry out actions, you can
at least work with and rely on your own thinking and behavior.

But if you depend on others, you never know when they will cease being dependable, move to another part of the world, or die.

Instead of striving to be dependent on other individuals (or upon hypothetical abstractions, such as the State or God), the rational individual should do his best to stand on his own two feet and to do his own thinking and acting. Some of the more concrete goals that he may strive for in this respect are these:

1. He should accept the fact that he is and will always be, in some essential respects, alone in this world—and that it is not necessarily a terrible thing to stand by oneself and be responsible for one's own decisions. However friendly and collaborative he may be with others, when the chips are down only *he* knows his own basic wants and urgings; and only he can fundamentally face his own living problems.

2. He should see most clearly that it is never terrible and awful to fail to achieve certain goals; that humans mainly learn by failing; and that his failures have nothing intrinsically to do with his personal worth as a human being. He should consequently keep striving for whatever he wants in life, even though the chances of obtaining it are often poor; and should adopt the philosophy that it is better to take risks and to commit possible errors of his own choosing, than to sell his soul for the unnecessary "aid" of others.

3. He should not defensively and rebelliously refuse *all* help from others, to prove how "strong" he is and how he can *completely* stand on his own two feet; but should at times frankly seek and accept others' aid—when it is really needed.

Irrational Idea No. 9: *The idea that one's past history is an all-important determiner of one's present behavior and that because something once strongly affected one's life, it should indefinitely have a similar effect.*

Many people in our civilization appear to believe and to act on the proposition that because something once affected their life significantly, or was once appropriate to their existence, it should remain so forever. There are several elements of irrationality in this belief:

1. If you allow yourself to be unduly influenced by your past history, you are committing the logical error of over-generalization: that is, you are assuming that because a thing is true in *some* circumstances it is equally true in *all* circumstances. It may well have been true, for example, that you were not able effectively to stand up for your rights against your parents or other adults in the past, and that therefore it was necessary for you to be subservient or ingratiating to them in order to preserve some vestige of peace and get some of the things you badly wanted. But that does not mean that it is *now*, perhaps twenty years or more later, necessary to be similarly subservient or ingratiating to others to protect yourself or get what you want.

2. If you are too strongly under the sway of past events, you will usually employ superficial or "easy" solutions to your problems which were once useful but may now be relatively inefficient. Normally, there are several alternate solutions to any problem, and they have various degrees of efficiency or thoroughness. The more you are influenced by those solutions that you successfully employed in the past, the less likely you will be to cast around for better possible alternate solutions to your present problems.

3. The so-called influence of the past can be employed as a powerful excuse not to change your ways in the present. Thus, if you are afraid of what other people think of you and you know, especially as you go for therapeutic help, that you have to do some powerful thinking and acting against your fear in order to eradicate it, it becomes one of the easiest excuses in the world for you to say that you are so strongly influenced or conditioned by the past that you cannot possibly think and act in a concerted manner to overcome your neurosis. This using of the past as an excuse for not trying to solve your problems in the present often leads to the most vicious cycle of emotional disturbance.

By the same token, if you rebelliously want to cut off your nose to spite your face, you can easily refuse to do something that you would now really like to do (such as go to college) because your parents or someone else insisted that you do this thing for their sake in the past. By continuing, in this manner, to remain emotionally rooted to the past, you can get the great "satisfaction" of defeating *those* "blackguards."

4. Over-emphasizing the great significance of your formative years tends to encourage you to take the true sentence, "Because I learned in my early life to do things in a neurotic manner, it is now *very difficult* for me to change," and illegitimately to substitute the ending, ". . . it is *impossible* for me to change, so I might as well give up and remain hopelessly neurotic."

Instead of overweighting the importance of his past and acting in accordance with what psychoanalysts call his transference relationships, the rational individual can assume the following kinds of attitudes:

1. He can accept the fact that the past is important and that he is bound to be significantly influenced by his past experiences in many ways. But he should also acknowledge that *his present is his past of tomorrow* and that, by working at changing this present, he can make his morrow significantly different from, and presumably more satisfactory than, today.

2. Instead of automatically continuing to do things, in the present, because he *once* did them, he can stop and *think* about repeating his past acts. When he is strongly held by some past influence that he believes is pernicious, he can persistently and forcefully fight it on both a verbal and an active level: by depropagandizing himself about the importance of following prior actions and by forcing himself to change his behavior in suitable instances. Thus, if he is afraid to eat chicken because his mother taught him, early in his life, that it was a harmful food, he can keep challenging his mother's (and his own internalized) philosophy about chicken until he begins to undermine it and he can keep forcing himself to eat chicken, until he proves to himself, in action, that it is not a harmful food.

3. Instead of spitefully rebelling against *most* or *all* past influences, he should objectively assess, question, challenge, and rebel against only those historically acquired notions that are clearly harming him in the present.

Irrational Idea No. 10: *The idea that one should become quite upset over other people's problems and disturbances.*

Many people seem to feel that what other people do or believe is most important to their existences, and that they should therefore become distinctly upset over the problems and disturbances of others. This notion is erroneous in several respects:

1. Other people's problems frequently have little or nothing to do with us and there is no reason why we *must* become unduly upset when they are different from us or are behaving in a manner that we consider to be mistaken. If Mrs. Jones is harsh to her children, that may well be unfortunate for her and her family; and if there is something that we can effectively do to help her change her ways, or to protect her children from her, that is fine. But she is not necessarily a criminal *because* we disagree with her actions—in fact, it is even possible that she is right and we are wrong about the advisability of her acting in the way she does. And even if she is a criminal (if she maims or kills her children, for example), there is no point in our upsetting ourselves terribly over her behavior, even though it may be wise if we firmly bring her acts to the attention of the proper authorities.

2. Even when others are so disturbed that they do things which annoy or injure us, most of our annoyance stems not from their behavior but by the injustice-collecting idea that *we* take toward this behavior. Thus, if someone is impolite to us, his impoliteness rarely does us much actual harm. But we tell ourselves: "What gall he has! How *could* he have done this to me?" And it is much more *our* non-acceptance of reality in our own sentences, rather than *his* impoliteness, which really is upsetting.

3. When we get upset over others' behavior, we imply that we have considerable power over them, and that our becoming upset will somehow magically change their behavior for the better. But, of course, it won't. Although we do have enormous power to control and change ourselves (which, alas, we rarely use) we actually have little power to change others. And the

more angry and upset we become over their behavior—thereby rewarding them with considerable attention—the less likely we are to induce them to change.

4. Even when we do induce others to change by becoming upset over their actions, we pay a sorry price for our self-created disturbance. Certainly, there must be, and there invariably are, *other*, less self-defeating ways in which we can calmly go about trying to get others to correct their wrongdoings. But, for the most part, our getting terribly disturbed about others' behavior helps neither them nor ourselves.

5. Upsetting ourselves over the way others behave will often only help to sidetrack us from what should be our main concern: namely, the way *we* behave and the things *we* do. Letting ourselves dwell on the horror of their behavior can often be used as a fine excuse for not tackling our own problems and not cultivating our own gardens.

Instead of being upset when other people act in a negative manner or do things that we would like to see left undone, we would do much better if we adopted the following kinds of attitudes in this connection:

1. We should ask ourselves whether the behavior of others is actually worth getting excited about, either from their standpoint or our own, and should be considerably concerned about them only when we care sufficiently for them, when we think that they can be helped to change, and when we think that we are able to be of real help to them by being concerned.

2. When those for whom we definitely care are behaving badly, we should still not become unduly upset about their behavior, but instead calmly and objectively attempt to show them the errors of their ways and lovingly help them over their handicaps and hurdles.

3. If we cannot possibly eliminate the self-defeating or annoying behavior of others, we should at least attempt not to become annoyed at the idea of their being annoying and should, instead, resign ourselves to making the best of a bad situation.

Irrational Idea No. 11: *The idea that there is invariably a right, precise, and perfect solution to human problems and that it is catastrophic if this perfect solution is not found.*

Millions of modern men and women believe that they must have perfect, certain solutions to the problems that beset them and that if they have to live in a world of imperfection and uncertainty they cannot happily survive. This kind of quest for certainty, absolute control, and perfect truth is highly irrational on several counts:

1. As far as we can tell, there is no certainty, perfection, nor absolute truth in the world. As Hans Reichenbach (1953) and many other recent philosophers have convincingly shown, whether we like it or not we live in a world of probability and chance, and we can be certain of nothing external to ourselves. Since this is the way things are, and since the quest for certainty can only raise false expectations and consequent anxiety in connection with these expectations, the only sane thing to do is to accept (grim or pleasant) reality and never idiotically to tell oneself that one *must* know it fully, or *has* to control it completely, or *ought* to have perfect solutions to all its problems.

2. The disasters that people imagine will ensue if they do not arrive at and stick to a single "correct" solution to their problems, or if they cannot perfectly control the external world, have no objective existence but are only made "disastrous" by their thinking them so. If you absolutely insist that it will be catastrophic if you do not completely solve your basic problems immediately, then, *by your very insistence,* you will bring on some catastrophe (such as an acute state of panic or a hopeless state of inefficiency) when, as inevitably will happen, this perfect and immediate solution is not at hand.

3. Perfectionism normally limits your possible solutions to a problem and induces you to solve it much less "perfectly" than you otherwise would if you were not perfectionistic. Thus, if there are many possible ways of learning to play the piano, and you insist that you *must* learn to play by taking lessons for a few weeks with a particular teacher, the chances are that you will never learn to play at all or will learn to play pretty badly.

Instead of insisting that there *must be* a perfect, quick solution to a given life problem and that he *has to* have a certain, absolute control over the exigencies of his world, a rational human being would do much better to go about his problem-solving in these ways:

1. When faced with a significant life problem, he should first make an effort to think of several possible solutions and to choose, from these alternatives, the one that is most practical and feasible, rather than the one that is "perfect." He should not perfectionistically consider every *possible* side of every *possible* alternative—since, in practice, he would never get around to making any decisions whatever on this basis—but should gracefully accept the necessity of compromise and be prepared to make his decisions in a reasonable amount of time, after giving the various alternatives a reasonable amount of consideration.

2. He should accept the fact that extreme plans or decisions are often (though not always) likely to be inadequate or un-workable and should give due consideration to moderate views and mean estimates that lie somewhere between the extremes of the decision-making he is contemplating.

3. He should fully acknowledge that to err is to be human, and that there is every likelihood of his making, especially at first, wrong or mediocre decisions; and that his doing so has nothing to do with his essential worth as a human being. Knowing that humans generally learn by trial and error, he should be willing and eager to experiment, to try various plans to see if they will work, and to keep seeking and pragmatically testing possible new solutions to problems.

4

The Essence of Rational Therapy

It is the central theme of this volume that the kinds of basic irrational ideas listed in the previous chapter, and the many corollaries to which they normally lead, are the basic causes of most emotional disturbances. For once a human being believes the kind of nonsense included in these notions, he will inevitably tend to become inhibited, hostile, defensive, guilty, anxious, ineffective, inert, uncontrolled, or unhappy. If, on the other hand, he could become thoroughly released from all these fundamental kinds of illogical thinking, it would be exceptionally difficult for him to become intensely emotionally upset, or at least to sustain his disturbance for any extended period.

Does this mean that all the other so-called basic causes of neurosis, such as the Oedipus complex or severe maternal rejection in childhood, are invalid and that the Freudian and other psychodynamic thinkers of the last sixty years have been barking up the wrong tree? Not necessarily. It only means, if the main hypotheses of this book are correct, that these psychodynamic thinkers have been emphasizing secondary causes or results of emotional disturbances rather than truly prime causes.

Let us take, for example, an individual who acquires, when he is young, a full-blown Oedipus complex: that is to say, he lusts after his mother, hates his father, is guilty about his sex desires for his mother, and is afraid his father is going to castrate him. This person, when he is a child, will certainly be disturbed. But, if he is reared so that he acquires none of the basic illogical ideas we have been discussing in the last chapter, it will be impossible for him to *remain* disturbed.

For we must remember that this individual's disturbance, when he is a child, does not consist of the *facts* of his Oedipal attachment to his mother but of his *attitudes*—his guilt and his fear—about these facts. He is not guilty, moreover, *because* he lusts after his mother, but because *he thinks it is criminal* for him to lust after her. And he is not fearful *because* his father disapproves his sexual attachment to his mother, but because *he thinks it is horrible* to be disapproved by his father.

It may be very "natural"—meaning *quite common*—for a child to think himself a criminal when he lusts after his mother; but there is no evidence that he is born with this idea or that he *has* to acquire it. In fact, considerable autobiographical and clinical evidence regarding individuals reared even in our own very anti-incestuous society shows that many boys are able to lust after their mothers quite consciously and openly without becoming guilty about their lusting or terribly fearful of their father's opposition.

So it should be clear that Oedipal *attachments* do *not* have to result in Oedipal *complexes*. Even if, in a given case, a boy does become disturbed about his sexual feelings for his mother, he does not, as the Freudians stoutly and erroneously contend, have to remain neurotic in his adult life. For if he is reared (as, alas, he rarely is in our society) to be a truly rational person, he will not, as an adult, be too concerned if his parents or others do not approve all his actions, since he will be more interested in *his own* self-respect than in *their* approval. He will not believe that his lust for his mother (even should it continue to his adolescent and adult years) is wicked or villainous, but will accept it as a normal part of being a fallible human whose sex desires may easily be indiscriminate. He will realize that the actual danger of his father castrating him is exceptionally slight, and will have no fears on that account. And he will not feel that because he was *once* afraid of his Oedipal attachment he need *forever* remain so.

If this individual, when he is adult, still believes that it would be improper for him to have sex relations with his mother, instead of castigating himself for even thinking of having such relations, he will merely resolve not to carry his desires into practice and will stick determinedly to his resolve. If (by any chance) he weakens and actually has incestuous relations, he will again refuse to castigate himself mercilessly for being weak but will keep showing himself how self-defeating his behavior is and will actively work and practice at changing it.

Under these circumstances, if this individual has a truly logical and rational approach to life in general, he will take an equally sane approach to Oedipal feelings in particular. How, then, can he possibly *remain* disturbed about any Oedipal attachment that he may have?

Take, by way of further illustration, the case of a person who, as a child, is continually criticized by his parents, who consequently feels himself loathesome and inadequate, who refuses to take chances at trying and possibly failing at difficult tasks, and who comes to hate himself more because he knows that he is evasive and cowardly. Such a person, during his childhood, would of course be seriously neurotic. But how would it be possible for him to *sustain* his neurosis if he began to think, later in life, in a truly logical manner?

For if this person does begin to be consistently rational, he will quickly stop being overconcerned about what others think of him and will begin to care primarily about what *he* wants to do in life and what *he* thinks of himself. Consequently, he will stop avoiding difficult tasks and, instead of blaming himself for making mistakes, he will say to himself something like: "Now this is not the right way to do things; let me stop and figure out a better way." Or: "There's no doubt that I made a mistake this time; now let me see how I can benefit from making it, so that my next performance will be improved."

This person, if he is thinking straight in the present, will not blame his defeats on external events, but will realize that he himself is causing them by his inadequate or incompetent behavior. He will not believe that it is easier to avoid than to face difficult life problems, but will see that the so-called easy way is invariably the harder and more idiotic procedure. He will not think that he needs someone greater or stronger than himself on whom to rely, but will independently buckle down to hard tasks without outside help. He will not feel, because he once defeated himself by avoiding doing things the hard way, that he must always continue to act in this self-defeating manner.

How, with this kind of logical thinking, could an originally disturbed person possibly maintain and continually revivify his neurosis? He just couldn't. Similarly, the spoiled brat, the worry-wart, the egomaniac, the autistic stay-at-home—all these disturbed individuals would have the devil of a time indefinitely prolonging their neuroses if they did not continue to believe utter nonsense: namely, the kinds of basic irrational postulates listed in the previous chapter.

Will not the individual's experiences during his early childhood frequently *make* him think illogically, and thereby cause his neurosis? No, not exactly. For even during his childhood, the human being has to *accept* the ideas that are pounded into his head, and *need* not (at least technically speaking) automatically take them over.

Thus, it is statistically probable that the great majority of children, if taught that they are monstrous if they do not behave well, will get the idea that this is true, and will come to despise themselves for their misdeeds. But all children *need* not accept this belief; and a few, at least, do not seem to do so. These few, apparently, can and do challenge the notion that they are worthless, and somehow manage to grow up thinking of themselves as being worthwhile, even though their parents or others teach them the contrary.

Moreover, even when young children tend to accept their parent-inculcated irrational thinking, they are quite able, in many instances, to challenge and contradict these views during their adolescence and adulthood, and to think otherwise—just as they are able to give up the religious views of their parents at this time. It is certainly *difficult* for an adolescent or young adult to disbelieve the nonsense about himself (or about religion) that his parents raise him to believe; but it is not impossible for him to do so. Childhood training, then, is an exceptionally strong influence in causing an individual to think illogically or neurotically. But it is not a fatal or irrevocable influence.

Neurosis, in sum, seems to originate in and be perpetuated by some fundamentally unsound, irrational ideas. The individual comes to believe in unrealistic, impossible, often perfectionistic goals—especially the goals that he should be approved by everyone who is important to him, should do many things perfectly, and should never be frustrated in any of his major desires. Then, in spite of considerable contradictory evidence, he refuses to surrender his original illogical beliefs.

Why do so many millions of intelligent, well-educated, potentially rational people act in such an illogical, neurotic manner today? A full answer to this question can only—and will eventually—be given in a volume of its own. Part of this answer is summarized in the final chapter of the present book. Suffice it to say here that even the most intelligent and capable persons in our society tend *also* to be, because of their biological inheritance, amazingly suggestible, unthinking, overgeneralizing, and strongly bound to the low-level kinds of ideation which it is so easy for them to become addicted to as children; and, perhaps more importantly, we bring up our citizens so that, instead of counteracting their normal biological tendencies toward irrationality, we deliberately and forcefully encourage them to keep thinking in childish, nonsensical ways.

By innate predisposition, therefore, as well as by powerful social propaganda (especially that promulgated by our families, schools, churches, and governmental institutions), even the brightest human beings often tend to become and to remain neurotic—that is, to behave stupidly and self-defeatingly when they are potentially able to behave more sanely and constructively.

Some of the neurotic's basic philosophies, such as the idea that he should be approved or loved by all the significant people in his life, are not entirely inappropriate to his childhood state; but they are decidedly inappropriate to adulthood. Since most of his irrational ideas are specifically taught him by his parents and other social agencies, and since these same irrational notions are held by the great majority of others in his community, we must acknowledge that the neurotic individual we are considering tends to be *statistically* normal. In many respects, he has what may be called a cultural or philosophic rather than a psychiatric disturbance (Paul Meehl and William Schofield, personal communications).

Ours, in other words, is a generally neuroticizing civilization, in which most people are more or less emotionally disturbed because they are brought up to believe, and then to internalize and to keep reinfecting themselves with, arrant nonsense which must inevitably lead them to become ineffective, self-defeating, and unhappy. Nonetheless, it is not absolutely *necessary* that human beings believe the irrational notions which, in point of fact, most of them seem to believe today; and the task of psychotherapy is to get them to disbelieve their illogical ideas, to change their self-sabotaging attitudes.

This, precisely, is the task the rational-emotive therapist sets himself. Like other therapists, he frequently resorts to some of the usual techniques of therapy which I have outlined elsewhere (Ellis, 1955a, 1955b)—including the techniques of relationship, expressive-emotive, supportive, and insight-interpretative therapy. But he views these techniques, as they are commonly employed, largely as preliminary strategies, designed to gain rapport with the patient, to let him express himself fully, to show him that he has the ability to change, and to demonstrate how he originally became disturbed.

Most therapeutic techniques, in other words, wittingly or unwittingly show the patient *that* he is illogical and how he *originally* became so. But they usually fail to show him how he is presently *maintaining* his illogical thinking and precisely what he must do to change it and replace it with more rational philosophies of life. And where most therapists rather passively or indirectly show the patient that he is behaving illogically, the rational therapist goes beyond this point to make a forthright, unequivocal *attack* on his general and specific irrational ideas and to try to *induce* him to adopt more rational views.

Rational-emotive psychotherapy makes a concerted attack on

the disturbed person's illogical positions in two main ways: (*a*) The therapist serves as a frank counter-propagandist who directly contradicts and denies the self-defeating propaganda and superstitions which the patient has originally learned and which he is now self-instilling. (*b*) The therapist encourages, persuades, cajoles, and occasionally even insists that the patient engage in some activity (such as his doing something he is afraid of doing) which itself will serve as a forceful counter-propaganda agency against the nonsense he believes.

Both these main therapeutic activities are consciously performed with one main goal in mind: namely, that of finally inducing the patient to internalize a rational philosophy of life just as he originally learned and internalized the irrational views of his parents and his community.

The rational therapist, then, assumes that the patient somehow imbibed irrational modes of thinking and that, through his illogical thoughts, he literally *made* himself disturbed. It is the therapist's function not merely to show the patient that he has these low-level thinking processes but to persuade him to change and substitute for them more efficient cognitions.

If, because the patient is exceptionally upset when he comes to therapy, he must first be approached in a cautious, supportive, permissive, and warm manner, and must sometimes be allowed to ventilate his feeling in free association, abreaction, role playing, and other expressive techniques, that may be a necessary part of effective therapy. But the rational therapist does not delude himself that these relationship-building and expressive-emotive methods are likely to really get to the core of the patient's illogical thinking and induce him to cogitate more rationally.

Occasionally, this is true: since the patient may, through experiencing relationship and emotive-expressive aspects of therapy, come to see that he *is* acting illogically; and he may therefore resolve to change and actually work at doing so. More often than not, however, his illogical thinking will be so ingrained from constant self-repetitions and will be so inculcated in motor pathways (or habit patterns) by the time he comes for therapy, that simply showing him, even by direct interpretation, *that* he is illogical will not greatly help. He will often, for example, say to the therapist: "All right: now I understand that I have castration fears and that they are illogical. But I *still* feel afraid of my father."

The therapist, therefore, must usually keep pounding away, time and time again, at the illogical ideas which underlie that patient's fears and hostilities. He must show the patient that he is afraid, really, not of his father, but of being blamed, of being disapproved, of being unloved, of being imperfect, of being a failure. And he must convincingly demonstrate to the patient how and why such fears (for some of the reasons explained in the previous chapter) *are* irrational and *must* lead to dreadful results.

If the therapist, moreover, merely tackles the individual's castration fears, and shows how ridiculous *they* are, what is to prevent this person's showing up, a year or two later, with some *other* illogical fear—such as the horror of his being sexually impotent? But if the therapist tackles the patient's *basic* irrational thinking processes, which underlie *all* kinds of fear that he may have, it is going to be most difficult for this patient to turn up with a new neurotic symptom some months or years hence. For once an individual truly surrenders ideas of perfectionism, of the horror of failing at something, of the dire need to be approved by others, of the world's owing him a living, and so on, what else is there for him to be fearful of or disturbed about?

To give some idea of precisely how the rational therapist works, a good many excerpts from therapeutic sessions will be given in some of the remaining chapters of this book. Before this is done, however, it might be well to outline an illustrative case.

Mervin Snodds, a 23 year old male, came into his therapeutic session a few weeks after he had begun therapy and said that he was very depressed but did not know why. A little questioning showed that this severely neurotic patient, whose main presenting problem was that he had been doing too much drinking during the last two years, had been putting off the inventory-keeping he was required to do as part of his job as an apprentice glass-staining artist. "I know," he reported, "that I should do the inventory before it keeps piling up to enormous proportions, but I just keep putting it off and off. To be honest, I guess it's because I resent doing it so much."

"But why do you resent it so much?"

"It's boring. I just don't like it."

"So it's boring. That's a good reason for *disliking* this work, but is it an equally good reason for *resenting* it?"

"Aren't the two the same thing?"

"By no means. Dislike equals the sentence, 'I don't enjoy doing this thing and therefore I don't want to do it.' And that's a perfectly sane sentence in most instances. But resentment is the sentence, '*Because* I dislike doing this thing, I shouldn't *have* to do it.' And that's invariably a very crazy sentence."

"Why is it so crazy to resent something that you don't like to do?"

"For several reasons. First of all, from a purely logical standpoint, it just makes no sense at all to say to yourself, 'Because I dislike doing this thing, I shouldn't *have* to do it.' The second part of this sentence just doesn't follow in any way from the first part. For the full sentence that you are saying actually goes something like this: 'Because *I* dislike doing this thing, *other people* and the *universe* should be so considerate of me that they should never make me do what I dislike.' But, of course, this sentence doesn't make any sense: for why *should* other people and the universe be that considerate of you? It might be nice if they were. But why the devil *should* they be? In order for your sentence to be true, the entire universe, and all the people in it, would really have to revolve around and be uniquely considerate of you."

"Am I really asking that much? It seems to me that all I'm asking, in my present job, is that I don't have to do the inventory-keeping. Is that too much to ask?"

"Yes, from what you've told me, it certainly is. For the inventory-keeping *is* an integral part of your job, isn't it? You *do* have to do it, in order to keep working at your present place, don't you?"

"Yes. I guess I do."

"And you do, from what you told me previously, want to keep working at this place, for your own reasons, do you not?"

"Yes. As I told you before, in my field I must have an apprenticeship for at least a year. And they agreed to take me on as an apprentice, if I'd work pretty long hours and do the work—"

"—including the inventory-keeping?—"

"Yes, including the inventory-keeping. If I did that and worked long hours, they'd take me on for the year I'd need toward the apprenticeship."

"All right, then. Because *you* wanted to learn the art of glass-staining and *you* can only learn it by having a year's apprenticeship, *you* decided to take on this job, with all its onerous aspects, especially including the inventory-keeping. You had, in other words, a logical choice between graciously accepting this job, in spite of the onerous parts of it, or giving up trying to be a glass-stainer. But then, after presumably taking the first of these alternatives, you're now resentful because you can't get the second alternative without this onerous first part."

"Oh, but it isn't the work itself that I resent, in toto; but just the inventory-keeping part."

"But that still doesn't make sense. For the work, in toto, *includes* the inventory-keeping; and your choice of accepting the work in toto obviously includes accepting this part of it, too. So, again, instead of selecting one of two logical alternatives—doing the onerous work, including the inventory-keeping, or giving up trying to be a glass-stainer—you are resentfully and grandiosely refusing the first of these and yet insisting that you should not *have to* give up the second one, too. You are thereby actually insisting, as I said before, that the universe and the people in it should really revolve around *your* wishes rather than be what it and they actually are."

"It sounds, the way you're putting it, like I really haven't got a leg to stand on logically. But what about the fact that my boss *could,* if he wanted to be really fair to me—since I do quite a bit of work for him at a very low rate of pay—get someone else to do the inventory-keeping? After all, he knows perfectly well how I feel about it; and it is *not* work that is necessary for my glass-staining apprenticeship."

"True. Your boss *could* arrange matters differently and *could* let you off from this work that you so abhor. And let's even assume, for the moment, that he is wrong about *not* arranging things more this way and that any decent kind of boss would let you, say, do more glass-staining and less inventory-keeping work."

"Oh, that would be fine! Then I wouldn't gripe at all."

"No, probably you wouldn't. But even assuming that your boss *is* completely in the wrong about this inventory-keeping matter, your resenting him for *being* wrong still makes no sense."

"Oh? How come?"

"Because, no matter how wrong he is, every human being has the right to be wrong—and you're not giving him that right."

"But why does every human being have the right to be wrong?"

"Simply because he *is* human; and, because he is human, is fallible and error-prone. If your boss, for example, is wrong about making you do this inventory work—and let's still assume that he is dead wrong about it—then his wrongdoing would obviously result from some combination of his being stupid, ignorant, or emotionally disturbed; and he, as a fallible human being, has every right to be stupid, ignorant, or disturbed—even though it would be much better, perhaps, if he weren't."

"He has a right, you say, to be as nutty or as vicious as he may be—even though I and others might very much like him to be less nutty or vicious?"

"Correct. And if you are blaming him for being the way he is, then you are denying his right to be human and you are expecting him—which is certainly silly, you'll have to admit! —to be superhuman or angelic."

"You really think that that's what I'm doing?"

"Well, isn't it? Besides, look again at how illogical you are by being resentful. Whether your boss is right or wrong about this inventory deal, resenting him for being, in your eyes, wrong is hardly going to make him be any the righter, is it? And your resentment, surely, is not going to do *you* any good or make you feel better. Then what good is it—your resentment—doing?"

"No good, I guess. If I take the attitude that—well, it's too bad that inventory-keeping is part of my job, and that my boss sees it this way, but that's the way it is, and there's no point in resenting the way it is, I guess I'd feel a lot better about it, wouldn't I?"

"Yes, *wouldn't* you? On still another count, too, your resentful attitude doesn't make sense."

"On what ground is that?"

"The ground that no matter how annoying the inventory-keeping may be, there's no point in your making it still *more* irksome by your continually telling yourself how *awful* it is. As we consistently note in rational therapy, you're not merely being annoyed by the inventory-keeping job itself, but you're making yourself annoyed *at* being annoyed—and you're thereby creating at least two annoyances for the price of one. And the second, the one of your own creation, may well be much more deadly than the first, the one that is being created by the circumstances of your job."

"Because I'm refusing to gracefully *accept* the inherent annoyingness of doing the inventory, I'm giving myself an even harder time than *it* is giving me—is that right?"

"Quite right. Where the inventory-keeping is a real pain in the neck to you, you are a much bigger pain in the neck to yourself."

"Yeah. And since I have to do this kind of clerical work anyway, since I know darned well that the boss is not going to take it away from me, I would be doing myself much more good if I calmly and quickly got it out of the way, instead of making this terrible to-do about it."

"Right again. Can you see, then, the several points at which your resentment is thoroughly illogical in this situation, even though your dissatisfaction with doing the bookkeeping procedure may well be justified?"

"Let's see, now. First, I make a decision to take the job, in spite of its disadvantages, because I really want to be an apprentice, and then I try to go against my own decision by refusing to accept these disadvantages that I had first presumably accepted."

"Yes, that's illogical point number one."

"Then, second, I go to work for a human being, my boss, and then I refuse to accept him as human, and insist that he be a goddam angel."

"Exactly. That's illogical point number two."

"Third—let's see—I get quite wrapped up in my resentment, and give myself a start on an ulcer, when it's not likely at all to get my boss to change his mind or to do me any good."

"Right."

"And fourth. Now, what was the fourth? I don't seem to remember."

"Fourth: you make yourself annoyed at being annoyed and put off doing work that you'll have to do, sooner or later, anyway, and with your annoyed-at-being-annoyed attitude, almost certainly make that work become considerably *more* onerous than it otherwise doubtless would be."

"Oh, yes. To my real annoyance I add to and imagine up a fake annoyance. And I make an unpleasant job more unpleasant than ever."

"Yes. Now can you see, not just in this case, but in every case of this kind, how your resenting someone is highly irrational?"

"Hm. I think so. But how can I stop being resentful? Just by seeing that it doesn't pay for me to be so?"

"No, not exactly. That's too vague. And too easy. More concretely, you must track down the exact sentences which you are saying to yourself to cause your resentment; and then question and challenge these sentences, until you specifically see how silly they are and are prepared to substitute much saner sentences for them."

At this point, I helped this patient to see that he must be telling himself sentences like these in order to be upsetting himself: "My boss makes me do inventory-keeping. . .

I do not like to do this. . . There is no reason why I have to do it. . . He is therefore a blackguard for making me do this kind of boring, unartistic work. So I'll fool him and avoid doing it. . . And then I'll be happier."

But these sentences were so palpably foolish that Mervin could not really believe them, so he began to finish them off with sentences like this: "I'm not really fooling my boss, because he sees what I'm doing. So I'm not solving my problem this way . . . I really should stop this nonsense, therefore, and get the inventory-keeping done. . . . But I'll be damned if I'll do it for him! . . . However, if I don't do it, I'll be fired. . . . But I still don't want to do it for him! . . . I guess I've got to, though. . . . Oh, why must I always be persecuted like this? . . . And why must I keep getting myself into such a mess? . . . I guess I'm just no good. . . . And people are against me. . . . Especially that son-of-a-bitch boss of mine. . . . Oh, what's the use?"

Employing these illogical kinds of sentences, Mervin soon became depressed, avoided doing the inventory-keeping, and then became still more resentful and depressed. Instead, I pointed out to him, he could tell himself quite different sentences, on this order: "Keeping inventory is a bore. . . . But it is presently an essential part of my job. . . . And I also may learn something useful by it. . . . Therefore, I'd better go about this task as best I may and thereby get what *I* want out of the job, and later what *I* want out of the profession of glass-staining."

I also emphasized that whenever Mervin found himself intensely angry, guilty, or depressed, he was thinking illogically and should immediately question himself as to what was the irrational element in his thinking, and set about replacing it with a more logical element or chain of sentences. I used his current dilemma—that of avoiding inventory-keeping—as an illustration of his general neurosis, which largely took the form of severe alcoholic tendencies. He was shown that his alcoholic trends, too, resulted from his trying to do things the easy way and from his resentment against people, such as his boss, who kept making him toe the line and blocking his easy-way-out patterns of response.

Several previous incidents of irrational thinking leading to emotional upheaval in Mervin's life were then reviewed, and some general principles of rational thought were discussed. Thus, the general principle of blame was raised and he was shown precisely why it is illogical for one person to blame anyone else (or himself) for anything.

The general principle of inevitability was brought up, and Mervin was shown that when a frustrating or unpleasant event is inevitable, it is only reasonable to accept it uncomplainingly instead of dwelling on its unpleasant aspects. The general principle of hostility was discussed, and he was shown that liking oneself and trying to do what one is truly interested in doing in life is far more important than being obsessed with others' behavior and resentfully trying to get back to them.

In this manner, by attempting to teach Mervin some of the general rules of rational living, I tried to go beyond his immediate problem and to help provide him with a generalized mode of thinking or problem-solving that would enable him to deal effectively with almost any future similar situation that might arise.

After 47 sessions of rational therapy, spread out over a two year period, Mervin was able to solve his work problems, to finish his apprenticeship, and to go on to high-level activity in his profession. More importantly, he cut out almost all drinking and restricted himself to a half dozen glasses of beer a week. His hostilities toward his bosses and his other associates became minimal, and for the first time in his life he became "popular." Today, three and a half years after the close of therapy, he is maintaining his gains and is reasonably unescapist and un-hostile.

The rational therapist, then, is a frank propagandist who believes wholeheartedly in a most rigorous application of the rules of logic, of straight thinking, and of scientific method to everyday life. He ruthlessly uncovers the most important elements of irrational thinking in his patient's experience and energetically urges this patient into more reasonable channels of behaving. In so doing, the rational therapist does not ignore or eradicate the patient's emotions. On the contrary, he considers them most seriously and helps change them, when they are disordered and self-defeating, through the same means by which they commonly arise in the first place—that is, by thinking and acting. Through exerting consistent interpretive and philosophic pressure on the patient to change his thinking and his actions, the rational therapist gives him a specific impetus toward achieving mental health without which it is not impossible, but quite unlikely, that he will move very far.

Man is a uniquely suggestible as well as a uniquely rational animal. Other animals are to some degree suggestible and reasoning, but man's better equipped cerebral cortex, which makes possible his ability to talk to himself and others, gives him unusual opportunities to talk himself into *and* out of many difficulties.

The rational therapist hold that although man's possession of a high degree of suggestibility and negative emotionality (such as anxiety, guilt, and hostility) may possibly have been adequate or advantageous for his primitive survival, he can get along with himself and others much better today when he becomes more rational and less suggestible. Perhaps it would be more realistic to say that since suggestibility seems to be an almost ineradicable trait of human beings, we should not aim at destroying but at modifying it so that man becomes more *intelligently* suggestible.

In other words: people act in certain ways because they *believe* that they should or must act in these ways. If they are irrationally suggestible, they believe that they should act in intensely emotional, self-defeating ways; and if they are more rationally suggestible, they believe that they should act in less negatively emotional, less neurotic ways. In either event, the deeds in which they believe they tend to actualize. As Kelly (1955) has noted, an individual's difficulty frequently "arises out of the intrinsic meaning of his personal constructs rather than out of the general form which they have assumed. A person who believes that punishment expunges guilt is likely to punish himself."

The main problem of effective living, then, would seem to be not that of eradicating people's beliefs, but of changing them so that they become more closely rooted to information and to reason. This can be done, says the rational therapist, by getting people to examine, to question, to think about their beliefs, and thereby to develop a more consistent, fact-based, and workable set of constructs than they now may possess.

Rational-emotive psychotherapy is by no means entirely new, since some of its main principles were propounded by Dubois (1907) and many pre-Freudian therapists. Unfortunately, these therapists for the most part did not understand the unconscious roots of emotional disturbance, and it was Freud's great contribution to stress these roots. But although Freud, in his first book with Josef Breuer (*Studies on Hysteria*, 1895), was willing to go along with the notion that "a great number of hysterical phenomena, probably more than we suspect today, are ideogenic," he later often talked about emotional processes in such a vague way as to imply that they exist in their own right, quite divorced from thinking.

Because he came to believe that neurosis originates in and is perpetuated by unconscious "emotional" processes, and because he (and his leading followers) never defined the term "emotional" very accurately, Freud held that neurotic symptoms only could be thoroughly understood and eradicated through an intense emotional relationship, or transference relationship, between the patient and the therapist. He and his psychoanalytic followers have used cognitive, or interpretive, therapeutic techniques to a considerable degree. But they still mainly stress the importance of the transference encounter in therapy.

In this emphasis, the psychoanalysts are at least partly correct, since many borderline and psychotic individuals (whom Freud himself often mistakenly thought were hysterical neurotics) are so excitable and disorganized when they come for therapy that they can only be approached by highly emotionalized, supportive or abreactive methods.

Even these severely disturbed patients, however, are often surprisingly and quickly responsive to logical analysis of their problems and to philosophic reeducation if this is adequately and persuasively done with them. And the run-of-the-mill, less disturbed neurotics who come to therapy are usually quite reactive to rational therapeutic approaches and have little or no need of an intensely emotionalized transference relationship (including a transference neurosis) with the therapist.

That cognitive and rational processes can be most important in understanding and changing human behavior has become increasingly acknowledged in recent years. Thus, Robbins (1955) notes that "cure is change; cure is the development of rational consciousness." Sarnoff and Katz (1954), in listing four major modes of changing human attitudes, put first the attacking of the cognitive object and frame of reference in which it is perceived, or the rational approach. Cohen, Stotland and Wolfe (1955) point out that, in addition to the usual physical and emotional needs of the human organism, "a need for cognition may exist, and . . . it may be a measurable characteristic of the organism, and . . . it may operate independently of other needs."

Bruner, Goodnow and Austin (1956) note that "the past few years have witnessed a notable increase in interest in and investigation of the cognitive processes. . . . Partly, it has resulted from a recognition of the complex processes that mediate between the classical 'stimuli' and 'responses' out of which stimulus-response learning theories hoped to fashion a psychology that would bypass anything smacking of the 'mental.' The impeccable peripheralism of such theories could not last long. As 'S-R' theories came to be modified to take into account the subtle events that may occur between the input of a physical stimulus and the emission of an observable response, the old image of the 'stimulus-response bond' began to dissolve, its place being taken by a mediation model. As Edward Tolman so felicitously put it some years ago, in place of a telephone switchboard connecting stimuli and responses it might be more profitable to think of a map room where stimuli were sorted out and arranged before every response occurred, and one might do well to have a closer look at these intervening 'cognitive maps.' "

Mowrer (1960a) even more strongly makes the point that the old S-R behaviorism has to be replaced by neobehaviorism which includes a liberalized view of perception. He notes that "the relevance of *cognitive* as well as *affective* processes is being recognized in systematic theory; and the solution to the problem of response selection and initiation hinges, quite specifically it seems, upon the reality of *imagery* (or *memory*), which is a cognitive phenomenon, pure and simple."

Even the Freudians have in recent years given much attention to "ego psychology," which is a distinct emphasis on the cognitive processes and how they make and can unmake human emotional disturbance. Freud himself noted, in *The Future of an Illusion* (1927): "We may insist as much as we like that the human intellect is weak. . . . But nevertheless there is something peculiar about this weakness. The voice of the intellect is a soft one, but it does not rest until it has gained a hearing. Ultimately, after endlessly repeated rebuffs, it succeeds." Modern psychoanalysts, such as Hartmann, Kris, and Loewenstein (1947, 1949), French (1952-1960), and Menninger (1958), have gone far beyond Freud, and beyond Anna Freud's (1937) pioneering work in ego psychology, and have helped make psychoanalytic technique radically different from its early ways and means.

In the field of modern psychology, Bartlett (1958), Berlyne (1960), Brown (1960), Brunswik (1952), Church (1961), Hovland and Janis (1959), Johnson (1955), Piaget (1952, 1954), in addition to the above-mentioned Bruner, Goodnow, and Austin (1956), have pioneered in the study of cognitive processes in recent years; and Leon Festinger (1957) has devised a theory of cognitive dissonance to explain much human normal and abnormal behavior. The work of these thinkers and experimentalists has sparked literally scores of recent studies that are adding to our knowledge in this area and showing how tremendously important cognitive and rational processes are in human affairs. As Arnold (1960) has appropriately noted in

this connection, the emphasis of the orthodox Freudians on unconscious thinking and emotional affect may well have been an
excellent corrective against the one-sided mentalistic views of
the nineteenth century. But the fact remains that "in deliberate
actions (and they comprise the large majority of our daily
activities) we must depend on a judgment that is not intuitive
to arouse an impulse to do something that may or may not be
pleasant. Whatever may be the explanation for such rational
judgments and deliberate actions, it is such judgments and
actions that distinguish man from the brute."

It may also be glancingly noted that preoccupation with
language and the cognitive processes has been most prevalent
in recent years in many semi-psychological areas of knowledge,
such as communication theory (Shannon, 1949; Wiener, 1948);
the theory of games and economic behavior (Marschak, 1950;
von Neumann and Morgenstern, 1944); philosophy (Ayer,
1947; Morris, 1946); and literature and semantics (Burke, 1950,
1954; Korzybski, 1933, 1951). In fact, it is difficult to think of
any major social science where an absorbing interest in the
cognitive-rational processes has not become pronounced in the
last two decades.

Friedman (1955) contends that Pavlovian conditioning consists largely of laws of unconscious biological learning and does
not by any means cover the whole field of human adaptability.
Rather, there also exists "learning at a conscious level with little
involvement of dominant biological activities" and this cognitive
type of learning "may well follow principles that are quite
different from those found by Pavlov." Fromm (1950) insists
that "to help man discern truth from falsehood in himself is the
basic aim of psychoanalysis, a therapeutic method which is an
empirical application of the statement, 'The truth shall make
you free.'" Flew (in Feigl and Scriven, 1956) contends "that
the fundamental concepts of psychoanalysis are distinctly human
because they can only be applied to creatures possessed of our
unique capacity to employ a developed language; that these are
precisely the notions which rational agents employ to give account of their own conduct and that of other rational agents *qua*

rational agents; that their place in psychoanalysis necessarily makes this a peculiarly rational enterprise . . ."

Modern anthropological thinking, as Voget (1960) shows in an important recent paper, has also swung away from the concepts of the early 1900's which emphasized man's dependency upon and subservience to cultural processes or to his own unconscious emotions. Today, says Voget:

> It is apparent that judgment in human action is admitted and the individual no longer is conceived to be a habituated social unit or subject wholly to unconscious feeling states. The trend moved cautiously in the direction of Grace de Laguna's (1949) assertion that:
> ". . . Man's rationality is not a higher faculty added to, or imposed upon, his animal nature. On the contrary, it pervades his whole being and manifests itself in all that he does well as in what he believes and thinks. Men may rationalize more often than they think objectively, but it is only because they are fundamentally rational beings that they are capable of rationalizing or feel the need of it. Man is rational in all his acts and attitudes, however unreasonable these may be; he is rational also in his feelings and aspirations, in his unconscious desires and motivations as well as in his conscious purposes, and his rationality shows itself in the very symbolism of his dreams. Men could not act and feel as they do if they could not form concepts and make judgments, but neither could they make use of concepts and engage in the ideal activity of thinking if they had not developed their innate capacity for the 'idealized' modes of behavior and feeling characteristic of human beings."

By direct statement and by implication, then, modern thinkers are tending to recognize the fact that logic and reason can, and in a sense must, play a most important role in overcoming human neurosis. Eventually, they may be able to catch up with Epictetus in this respect, who wrote—some nineteen centuries ago—that "the chief concern of a wise and good man is his own reason."

5

Requisite Conditions for Basic Personality Change *

Are there any necessary and sufficient conditions which an emotionally disturbed individual *must* undergo if he is to overcome his disturbance and achieve a basic change in his personality? Yes and no—depending upon whether our definition of the word *conditions* is narrow or broad.

Carl Rogers (1957), in a notable paper on this subject, stuck his scientific neck out by listing six conditions that, he hypothesized, must exist and continue to exist over a period of time if personality change is to be effected. I shall now stick out my own scientific neck by contending that none of his postulated conditions are necessary (even though they may all be desirable) for personality change to occur.

For purposes of discussion, I shall accept Rogers' definition of "constructive personality change" as consisting of "change in the personality structure of the individual, at both surface and deeper levels, in a direction which clinicians would agree means greater integration, less internal conflict, more energy utilizable for effective living; change in behavior away from behaviors regarded as immature and toward behaviors regarded as mature." In my own terms, which I believe are a little more specific, I would say that constructive personality change occurs when an individual eliminates a significant proportion of his needless,

* This chapter consists of an expanded version of a paper read at the workshop on psychotherapy of the American Academy of Psychotherapists, held in Madison, Wisconsin, August 9, 1958, and subsequently published in *J. Consult. Psychol.*, 1959, 23, 538-540.

unrealistically based self-defeating reactions (especially intense, prolonged, or repeated feelings of anxiety and hostility) which he may consciously experience or whose subsurface existence may lead him to behave in an ineffective or inappropriate manner (Ellis, 1957a, 1958a).

According to Rogers, the six necessary and sufficient conditions for constructive personality change are as follows: 1. Two persons are in psychological contact. 2. The first (the client or patient) is in a state of incongruence, being vulnerable or anxious. 3. The second person, the therapist, is congruent or integrated in the relationship. 4. The therapist experiences unconditional positive regard for the patient. 5. The therapist experiences an empathic understanding of the patient's internal frame of reference and endeavors to communicate this experience to the patient. 6. The communication to the patient of the therapist's empathic understanding and unconditional positive regard is to a minimal degree achieved.

Let us now examine each of these six conditions to see if it is really necessary for basic personality change.

Two persons, says Rogers, must be in psychological contact. This proposition, I am afraid, stems from a kind of therapeutic presumptuousness, since it ignores thousands, perhaps millions, of significant personality changes that have occurred when a single individual (*a*) encountered external experiences and learned sufficiently by them to restructure his philosophy and behavior patterns of living, or (*b*) without being in any actual relationship with another, heard a lecture, read a book, or listened to a sermon that helped him make basic changes in his own personality.

I am reminded, in this connection, of many individuals I have read about, and a few to whom I have talked, who narrowly escaped death and who were significantly changed persons for the rest of their lives. I am also reminded of several people I have known who read books, ranging from Mary Baker Eddy's idiotic mish-mash, *Science and Health, with Key to the Scriptures,* to my own *How to Live with a Neurotic* or my collaborative effort with Dr. Robert A. Harper, *A Guide to Rational*

Living, who immediately thereafter significantly changed their unconstructive behavior toward others and themselves.

I am not saying, now, that having dangerous life experiences or reading inspirational books is likely to be the most *effective* or *frequent* means of personality reconstruction. Obviously not —or psychotherapists would quickly go out of business! But to claim, as Rogers does, that these non-relationship methods of personality change *never* work is to belie considerable evidence to the contrary.

Rogers secondly contends that for personality change to occur the patient must be in a state of incongruence, being vulnerable or anxious. Incongruence he later defines as "a discrepancy between the actual experience of the organism and the self picture of the individual insofar as it represents that experience." Here again, although he may well be correct in assuming that *most* people who undergo basic personality changes are in a state of incongruence before they reconstruct their behavior patterns, he fails to consider the exceptions to this general rule.

I have met several individuals who were far above the average in being congruent and basically unanxious and yet who, as I said above, improved their personalities significantly by life experiences or reading. I have also seen a few psychologists, psychiatrists, and social workers who were distinctly congruent individuals and who came to therapy largely for training purposes or because they had some practical problem with which they wanted help. Most of these patients were able to benefit considerably by their therapy and to make significant constructive personality changes—that is, to become *more* congruent and *less* anxious. I often feel, in fact, that such relatively congruent individuals tend to make the *most* constructive personality changes when they come to therapy—largely because they are best able to benefit from the therapist's placing before them alternative philosophies of life and modes of adjustment which they had simply never seriously considered before.

It should be remembered, in this connection, that there are often *two* main reasons why an individual comes to and stays in therapy: (*a*) he wants to be healed, and (*b*) he wants to grow. Once he has been healed—that is, induced to surrender most of his intense and crippling anxiety or hostility—he still can significantly grow as a human being—that is, reëvaluate and minimize some of his less intense and less crippling negative emotions, and learn to take greater risks, feel more spontaneously, love more adequately, etc. Frequently I find that group therapy, in particular, is an excellent medium for individuals who have largely been healed in a prior (individual and/or group) therapeutic process, but who still would like to know more about themselves in relation to others, and to grow experientially and esthetically. And I find that relatively healed individuals, who are what Carl Rogers would call congruent persons, can still grow and make basic personality changes in themselves in some form of therapy.

The third requisite for constructive personality change, says Rogers, is "that the therapist should be, within the confines of this relationship, a congruent, genuine integrated person. It means that within the relationship he is freely and deeply himself, with his actual experience accurately represented by his awareness of himself. It is the opposite of presenting a facade, either knowingly or unknowingly." Here, once again, I feel that Rogers is stating a highly *desirable* but hardly a *necessary* condition.

Like most therapists, I (rightly or wrongly!) consider myself a congruent, genuine, integrated person who, within my relationships with my patients, am freely and deeply myself. I therefore cannot be expected to quote a case of my own where, in spite of my own lack of congruence, my patient got better. I can say, however, that I have seen patients of other therapists whom I personally knew to be among the most emotionally disturbed and least congruent individuals I have ever met. And *some* of these patients—not all or most, alas, but *some*—were considerably helped by their relationship with their disturbed and incongruent therapists.

In saying this, let me hasten to add that I am definitely *not* one of those who believes that a therapist is most helpful to his patient when he, the therapist, is or has been a victim of severe disturbance himself, since then he is supposedly best able to empathize with and understand his patients. On the contrary, I believe that the therapist who is least disturbed is most likely to serve as the best model for, and be able to accept without hostility, his severely disturbed patients; and I am consequently in favor of discouraging highly incongruent therapists from practicing. I distinctly agree, therefore, with Rogers' contention that congruence on the part of the therapist is very desirable. That such congruence is in all cases necessary, however, I would dispute.

Rogers next lists as a necessary condition for personality change the therapist's experiencing unconditional positive regard for the patient—by which he means "a caring for the client, but not in a possessive way or in such a way as simply to satisfy the therapist's own needs." Here, with almost nauseating repetition, I must insist that Rogers has again turned a desideratum of therapy into a necessity.

I have recently been in close contact with several ex-patients of a small, and I think highly unsavory, group of therapists who do not have any real positive regard for their patients, but who deliberately try to regulate the lives and philosophies of these patients for the satisfaction of the therapists' own desires. In all cases but one, I would say that the ex-patients of this group whom I have seen were not benefited appreciably by therapy and were sometimes harmed. But in one instance I have had to admit that the patient was distinctly benefited and underwent significant constructive personality change—though not as much as I would have liked to see him undergo—as a result of this ineffective and in some ways pernicious form of therapy. I have also seen many other ex-patients of other therapists who, I am quite certain, were emtionally exploited by their therapists; and some of them, surprisingly enough, were considerably helped by this kind of an exploitative relationship.

The fifth condition for constructive personality change, says Rogers, "is that the therapist is experiencing an accurate, empathic understanding of the client's awareness of his own experience. To sense the client's private world as if it were your own, but without ever losing the 'as if' quality—this is empathy, and this seems essential to therapy." This contention I again must dispute, although I think it is perhaps the most plausible of Rogers' conditions.

That the therapist should normally *understand* his patient's world and *see* the patient's behavior from this patient's *own* frame of reference is highly desirable. That the therapist should literally *feel* his patient's disturbances or *believe in* his irrationalities is, in my opinion, usually harmful rather than helpful to this patient. Indeed, it is precisely the therapist's ability to comprehend the patient's immature behavior *without* getting involved in or believing in it that enables him to induce the patient to stop believing in or feeling that this behavior is necessary.

Even, however, when we strictly limit the term *empathy* to its dictionary definition—"apprehension of the state of mind of another person without feeling (as in sympathy) what the other feels" (English and English, 1958), it is still doubtful that this state is *always* a necessary condition for effective therapy. I have had, for example, many patients whose problems I have been able to view from their own frame of reference and whom I have shown exactly how and why they have been defeating themselves and what alternate modes of thinking and behaving they could employ to help themselves. Some of these patients have then dogmatically and arbitrarily indoctrinated their friends or relatives with the new philosophies of living I have helped them acquire, without their ever truly understanding or empathizing with the private world of these associates. Yet, somewhat to my surprise, they have occasionally helped their friends and relatives to achieve significant personality changes with this non-empathic, dogmatic technique of indoctrination.

Similarly, some of the greatest bigots of all time, such as Savonarola, Rasputin, and Adolf Hitler, who because of their own severe emotional disturbances had a minimum of empathy with their fellow men, frequently induced profound personality changes in their adherents, and at least in a few of these instances the changes that occurred were constructive. This does not contradict the proposition that to empathize with another's private

world *usually* helps him become less defensive and more congruent; but it throws much doubt on the hypothesis that em-
·pathically-motivated therapy is the *only* kind that is ever effective.

Rogers' final condition for constructive personality change is
"that the client perceives, to a minimal degree, the acceptance
and empathy which the therapist experiences for him." This
proposition I have disproved several times in my own therapeutic practice. On these occasions, I have seen paranoid patients
who, whether or not I was properly empathizing with their own
frames of reference, persistently insisted that I was not. Yet, as
I kept showing them how *their* attitudes and actions, including
their anger at me, were illogical and self-defeating, they finally
began to accept *my* frame of reference and to make significant
constructive personality changes in themselves. Then, *after* they
had surrendered some of their false perceptions, they were able
to see, in most instances, that I might not have been as un-
empathic as they previously thought I was.

In one instance, one of my paranoid patients kept insisting,
to the end of therapy, that I did not understand her viewpoints
and was quite wrong about my perceptions of her. She did
admit, however, that my attitudes and value systems made a
lot of sense and that she could see that she'd better adopt some
of them if she was going to help herself. She did adopt some
of these attitudes and became more understanding of other people and considerably less paranoid. To this day, even though
she is making a much better adjustment to life, she still feels
that I do not really understand her.

In the light of the foregoing considerations, it may perhaps
be legitimately hypothesized that *very few* individuals significantly restructure their personalities when Rogers' six conditions
are all unmet; but it is most dubious that *none* do. Similarly, it
is equally dubious that no patients make fundamental constructive improvements unless, as Freud (1924-1950) contends, they
undergo and resolve a transference neurosis during therapy; or,
as Rank (1945) insists, unless they first have a highly permissive
and then a strictly limited relationship with the therapist; or as

Reich (1949) claims, unless they loosen their character armor by having it forcefully attacked by the therapist's psychological and physical uncoverings; or as Reik (1948) notes, unless they are effectively listened to by the therapist's "third ear"; or, unless as Sullivan (1953) opines, they undergo an intensive analysis of the security operations they employ with the therapist and with significant others in their environment. All these suggested therapeutic techniques may be highly desirable; but where is the evidence that any of them is *necessary?*

Are there, then, any other conditions that are absolutely necessary for constructive personality change to take place? At first blush, I am tempted to say yes; but on second thought, I am forced to restrain myself and say no, or at least probably no.

My personal inclination, after working for the last several years with rational-emotive psychotherapy, is to say that yes, there is one absolutely necessary condition for real or basic personality change to occur—and that is that somehow, through some professional or non-professional channel, and through some kind of experience with himself, with others, or with things and events, the afflicted individual must learn to recognize his irrational, inconsistent, and unrealistic perceptions and thoughts, and change these for more logical, more reasonable philosophies of life. Without this kind of fundamental change in his ideologies and philosophic assumptions, I am tempted to say, no deep-seated personality changes will occur.

On further contemplation, I nobly refrain from making this claim, which would so well fit in with my own therapeutic theories, for one major and two minor reasons. The minor reasons are these:

1. Some people *seem* to make significant changes in their personalities without concomitantly acquiring notably new philosophies of living. It could be said, of course, that they really, unconsciously, *do* acquire such new philosophies. But this would be difficult to prove objectively.

2. Some individuals appear to change for the better when environmental conditions are modified, even though they retain their old childish views. Thus, a person who irrationally hates

himself because he is poor may hate himself considerably less if he inherits a fortune. It could be said that the security he receives from inheriting this money really *does* make him change his childish, irrational views, and that therefore he has had a philosophic as well as a behavioral change. But again: there would be difficulty in objectively validating this contention. It could also be alleged that this individual *really* hasn't made a constructive personality change if he can now be secure only when he is rich. But how, except by a rather tautological definition, could this allegation be proven?

Which brings me to the major and I think decisive reason for my not contending that for constructive personality change to occur, the individual must somehow basically change his thinking or his value system. Granted that this statement may be true —and I am sure that many therapists would agree that it is—it is largely tautological. For all I am really saying when I make such a statement is that poor personality integration consists of an individual's having unrealistic, self-defeating ideological assumptions and that to change his personality integration for the better he must somehow surrender or change these assumptions.

Although descriptively meaningful, this statement boils down to the sentence: in order to change his personality the individual must change his personality. Or: in order to get better he must get better. This proves very little about the "necessary" conditions for personality change.

Again: rational psychotherapy significantly differs from virtually all other theories and techniques in that, according to its precepts, it is desirable not merely for the therapist to uncover, understand, and accept the patient's illogical and unrealistic assumptions which cause him to remain immature and ineffective, but it is usually also required that he forthrightly and unequivocally *attack* and *invalidate* these assumptions. Is this desideratum of psychotherapy necessary?

Most probably not: since *some* patients and non-patients (although relatively few, I believe) seem to have significantly improved in spite of their not having the benefit of a competent rational therapist to help them understand how they acquired, how they are currently sustaining, and how they can and should forthrightly attack and annihilate their basic irrational attitudes and assumptions.

The conclusion seems inescapable, therefore, that although basic constructive personality change—as opposed to temporary symptom removal—seems to require fundamental modifications in the ideologies and value systems of the disturbed individual, there is probably *no* single condition which is absolutely necessary for the inducement of such changed attitudes and behavior patterns.

Many conditions, such as those listed by Freud, Rank, Reich, Reik, Rogers, Sullivan, and other outstanding theorists, or such as are listed in this book, are highly desirable; but all that seems to be necessary is that the individual *somehow* come up against significant life experiences, *or* learn about others' experiences, *or* sit down and think for himself, *or* enter a relationship with a therapist who is *preferably* congruent, accepting, empathic, rational, forceful, etc. Either/or, rather than this-and-that, seems to be the only realistic description of necessary conditions for basic personality change that can be made at the present time.

The basic contention of this book, then, is not that RT is the *only* effective method of therapy. It is, rather, that of all the scores of methods that are variously advocated and employed, RT is probably one of the *most effective* techniques that has yet been invented. Certainly, in my twenty years as a counselor and psychotherapist, it is far and away the best method that I have found; and an increasing number of my professional colleagues are finding it unusually efficient in their own practices. Even when it is only partially employed, along with other basic therapeutic methods, it often produces fine results. And when it is consistently and thoroughly used, the results seem to be still better.

6

Rational Therapy versus Rationalism*

One of the most difficult aspects of rational-emotive psycho-therapy has been that of giving it a suitable name. When I first developed the theory and practice of RT, I thought of, and quickly discarded, many possible names. Thus, I thought of calling it logical therapy, persuasive therapy, objective therapy, realistic therapy, etc. But most of these names seemed to give too narrow descriptions of what its theory and practice actually was; and other designations, such as realistic therapy, seemed to be sufficiently broad, but to be overly-vague or indiscriminate. Thus, to call a mode of therapy realistic or reality-centered is to impinge upon the domain of virtually every other kind of therapy—for what psychotherapeutic technique does *not* try to adjust patients to reality?

In asking myself what the *distinctive* aspect of my thera-peutic method was, I finally hit upon the term *rational*: for that, more than anything else, was what I seemed to be doing—demonstrating to patients exactly what the irrational or illogical aspects of their thinking was, and inducing them to think or talk to themselves (or reorient their internalized sentences) in a decidedly more rational manner. So when I gave my first paper on RT back in 1956 I entitled it "Rational Psychotherapy," and felt that this rather accurately and distinctively described what I was doing.

Unfortunately, even though I carefully explained in this paper that human emotions are largely derived from human thinking processes, and that I was mainly concerned with changing my

* This chapter is an expanded version of "Rationalism and its Therapeutic Applications." In Albert Ellis, Ed., *The Place of Value in the Practice of Psychotherapy*. New York: American Academy of Psychotherapists, 1959.

patients' emotional disturbances by changing their thinking, I soon ran into great difficulties with other psychologists, psychiatrists, and psychiatric social workers. For they took my terms *rational* and *thinking* much too literally, arbitrarily divorced these terms in their own minds from sensing, moving, and emotional processes, and therefore insisted that in doing rational therapy I was only superficially getting at my patient's thinking, and was not really affecting their deep-down, highly emotionalized behavior. What these professionals *believed* or *said* I was doing with my patients had, of course, very little correlation to the therapy I was actually practicing. But nothing, apparently, that I could tell them about my work dented the prejudices that crept into their mind as soon as they heard me use the terms *cognitive* and *rational*. So we, these other psychotherapists and I, were just not communicating too well.

To make matters still worse, another group of therapists, whenever I used the term *rational psychotherapy*, immediately began to think in terms of the philosophy which is often called rational*ism*, and to confuse my position with that of the orthodox adherents of this philosophic view. Again, a severe blockage in communication ensued, since I am definitely not a rationalist, in any orthodox philosophic sense of this word. Once more, I began to be accused of believing all kinds of notions which I heartily do *not* believe, and of employing these ideas in rational psychotherapy.

Finally, to confuse matters still more, I learned, after I had been using the term *rational therapy* for well over a year, that there were at least two other kinds of therapists who were employing exactly the same term, and that my work had little in common with either of these other therapeutic groups. The first of these groups consisted of some Catholic-oriented therapists who, following the "rational" position of St. Thomas Aquinas, helped their patients to be logically consistent, usually within the strict framework of Thomistic premises. The second group, going to quite opposite extremes, consisted of Marxist-oriented therapists, such as Behr (1953), who seemed to be unusually rational in their approach—until they came up against some of the basic premises of communism, when they suddenly became just as presuppositional (though in a different manner) as the Catholic Thomists.

Considering all these difficulties in using the term *rational psychotherapy*, I gave much thought to modifying the term so that it would mean more of what I wanted it to mean, and also distinguish what I and my colleagues were doing more accurately from what other therapists were doing under similar or different titles. I finally hit upon the term *rational-emotive psychotherapy*, which I now use in the long-hand version (reserving the terms *rational therapy* and *RT* for short-hand forms).

The term *rational-emotive* probably describes what I do better than most other terms would, because it has the connotation of a form of therapy that is at least *doubly* oriented. Thus it clearly emphasizes the cognitive-persuasive-didactic-reasoning method of showing a patient what his basic irrational philosophies are, and then of demonstrating how these illogical or groundless or definitional premises must lead to emotionally disturbed behavior and must be concertedly attacked and changed if this behavior is to be improved. And, at the same time, it also indicates that the primary aim of the therapy is to change the patient's most intensely and deeply held emotions as well as, and along with, his thinking. In fact, the term implies, as the theory of rational-emotive psychotherapy holds, that human thinking and emotions *are*, in some of their essences, the same thing, and that by changing the former one *does* change the latter.

The double-barreled approach to therapy that is implied in the term *rational-emotive psychotherapy* also indicates that the therapy itself is something more than didactic or passive, and that it strongly emphasizes and insists upon, in addition to verbal discussion, action, work, effort, and practice. Which is exactly what RT does: it employs logical parsing and rational persuasion *for* the inducing of the patient to *act* and *work* against his neurotic attitudes and habit patterns.

The rational-emotive therapist does not merely demonstrate to his patient that he *is* indoctrinating himself with silly premises and is acting on these groundless suppositions. He also does his best to convince this patient that he must *fight*, in practice as well as in theory, against his self-indoctrinations *and* the poor behavior patterns to which they are continually leading him. And unless the therapist somehow induces the patient to un*do* (as well as to un*think*) his self-defeating indoctrinations, no thoroughgoing reversal of the neurotic process is expected to occur.

In any event, RT is not to be construed as a form of rational-*ism*—and certainly not of any orthodox or classical kind of philosophic rationalism. In philosophy, rationalism is basically an idealistic and anti-empirical mode of viewing the world: since it holds that reason, or the intellect, rather than the senses is the true source of knowledge. The classical rationalist is therefore a believer in absolutism, since for him reason is the prime and absolute authority in determing what is true and what course of action one should take in life (Rand, 1961).

The modern rationalist, such as the member of various non-religious rationalist groups in America and Great Britain, tends to have views quite different from those of the classical rationalist, and is much closer in his theoretical orientation to the philosophic position of the rational-emotive therapist. This philosophic position, briefly summarized, includes the following points:

1. Reason and logic do not contain or convey scientific evidence or truth in their own right, but are most valuable tools for the sifting of truth from falsehood (Bakan, 1956; Ryle, 1957).

2. Science is intrinsically empirical; and scientific knowledge must, at least in principle, be confirmable by some form of human experience (Ayer, 1947). However, theorizing that is limited only to generalizations inducted from empirical evidence is often not the best form of theory making; and the hypothetico-deductive method, including the employment of rational curves, may be more productive for advancing scientific research than a pure adherence to inductive methods of reasoning (Hilgard, 1956).

3. Rationalism is a tenable philosophic position insofar as the term means opposition to all forms of supernaturalism, spirit-

ualism, mysticism, revelation, dogmatism, authoritarianism, and antiscientism.

4. Although man cannot live by reason alone, he can considerably aid his existence and lessen his disturbance by thinking clearly, logically, consistently, and realistically. Most human ills are originated, sustained, or significantly aggrandized by irrational ideas and can be appreciably ameliorated by one's acquiring a rational attitude toward or philosophy of life (Dreikurs, 1950, 1955; McGill, 1954; Grimes, 1961; Branden, 1962). A scientific system of human ethics is difficult but probably not impossible to construct; and to the degree that man develops rational ethics, he will be able to live more peacefully and creatively with himself and his fellows (Bronowski, 1956; Rapoport, 1957).

The rational therapist believes, in other words, that scientific truths must be logically possible and confirmable by some kind of experience, and his theories are based on both facts and reason. But he also strongly believes in the power of human ideas—of mind not over but in integral partnership with matter. In regard to the universe, he takes a hard-headed empiricist position. In regard to man and his ability to live effectively with himself and others, he takes a rather "idealistic," individualistic, hedonist-stoical position.

Philosophically, the rational-emotive therapist is also quite in sympathy with most of the goals for living of the modern existentialists, such as Buber (1955), Sartre (1957), and Tillich (1953). An excellent list of the main existentialist themes for living has recently been made by Braaten (1961); and, with some relatively minor modifications, these main themes are also dear to the heart of the psychotherapist who practices rational analysis. They include: "(1) Man, you are free, define yourself; (2) Cultivate your own individuality; (3) Live in dialogue with your fellow man; (4) Your own experiencing is the highest authority; (5) Be fully present in the immediacy of the moment; (6) There is no truth except in action; (7) You can transcend yourself in spurts; (8) Live your potentialities creatively; (9) In choosing yourself, you choose man; and (10) You must learn to accept certain limits in life."

Rational emotive-therapy, then, does not espouse any classic or pure rationalist position, but a rational-humanist view of life and the world. The RT approach especially emphasizes the idea that human emotion does not exist as a thing in itself, has no primacy over human behavior, cannot for the most part be clearly differentiated from ideation, and is largely controllable by thinking processes.

As opposed to the theory that man is hopelessly enslaved by his base primitive emotions—which was perpetrated centuries ago by the Judeo-Christian clergy and which has recently been perpetuated by the orthodox Freudian clergy—the rational therapist believes that so-called emotions or motivations of adult human beings who are reared in a civilized community largely consist of attitudes, perceptual biases, beliefs, assumptions, and ideas which are acquired by biosocial learning and which therefore can be reviewed, questioned, challenged, reconstructed, and changed with sufficient effort and practice on the part of the emoting individual.

On the important issue of free will versus determinism, the rational therapist takes a flexible, somewhat middle-of-the-road position. Although he is more than willing to acknowledge that human events, as well as the workings of the universe, are largely controlled by causal factors which are far beyond any single individual's will or efforts (Skinner, 1953), he nonetheless takes the stand that the human being is a unique kind of animal who has the possibility, if he exerts considerable time and effort in the present, of changing and controlling his future behavior (Adkins, 1959; Hartmann, 1961). As Wolfensberger (1961) has aptly noted: "The view that the better part of human behavior is quite determined is not necessarily opposed to the proposition that man *can* exercise his freedom upon occasion, or that some men are more free than others."

The aspect of rational-emotive psychotherapy that best epitomizes the attitude its practitioners take toward the ability of the individual existentially to determine a good part (though hardly all) of his own behavior, and either to create or re-create his own emotional experience, is best epitomized in the A-B-C theory of human personality which is an integral part of RT. An illustration of the use of this theory is shown in the following dialogue that I had with a patient who said that he was terribly unhappy because, the day before our session, he had played golf with a group of men and they obviously hadn't liked him.

Therapist: You think you were unhappy because these men didn't like you?

Patient: I certainly was!

T: But you weren't unhappy for the reason you think you were.

P: I wasn't? But I was!

T: No, I insist: you only think you were unhappy for that reason.

P: Well, why was I unhappy then?

T: It's very simple—as simple as A, B, C, I might say. A, in this case, is the fact that these men didn't like you. Let's assume that you observed their attitude correctly and were not merely imagining they didn't like you.

P: I assure you that they didn't. I could see that very clearly.

T: Very well, let's assume they didn't like you and call that A. Now, C is your unhappiness—which we'll definitely have to assume is a fact, since you felt it.

P: Damn right I did!

T: All right, then: A is the fact that the men didn't like you, C is your unhappiness. You see A and C and you assume that A, their not liking you, caused your unhappiness, C. But it didn't.

P: It didn't? What did, then?

T: B did.

P: What's B?

T: B is *what you said to yourself* while you were playing golf with those men.

P: What I said to myself? But I didn't say anything.

T: You did. You couldn't possibly be unhappy if you didn't. The only thing that could possibly make you unhappy that occurs from without is a brick falling on your head, or some such equivalent. But no brick fell. Obviously, therefore, you must have *told yourself* something to make you unhappy.

P: But I tell you . . . Honestly, I didn't say anything.

T: You did. You must have. Now think back to your being with these men; think what you said to yourself; and tell me what it was.

P: Well . . . I . . .

T: Yes?

P: Well, I guess I did say something.

T: I'm sure you did. Now what did you tell yourself when you were with those men?

P: I . . . Well, I told myself that it was awful that they didn't like me, and why didn't they like me, and how could they not like me, and . . . you know, things like that.

T: Exactly! And that, what you told yourself, was B. And it's *always* B that makes you unhappy in situations like this. Except as I said before, when A is a brick falling on your head. *That,* or any physical object, might cause you real pain. But any mental or emotional onslaught against you—any word, gesture, attitude, or feeling directed against you—can hurt you only if *you* let it. And your letting such a word, gesture, attitude, or feeling hurt you, your *telling yourself* that it's awful, horrible, terrible—that's B. And that's what *you* do to *you.*

P: What shall I do then?

T: I'll tell you exactly what to do. I want you to play golf, if you can, with those same men again. But this time, instead of trying to get them to love you or think you're a grand guy or anything like that, I want you to do one simple thing.

P: What is that?

T: I want you merely to *observe,* when you're with them and they don't love you, to observe what you say to you. That's all: merely watch your own silent sentences. Do you think you can do that?

P: I don't see why not. Just watch my own sentences, what I say to me?

T: Yes, just that.

When the patient came in for his next session, I asked him if he had done his homework and he said that he had. "And what did you find?" I asked. "It was utterly appalling," he replied, "utterly appalling. All I heard myself tell myself was self-pity; nothing but self-pity."

"Exactly," I said. "That's what you keep telling yourself—nothing but self-pity. No wonder you're unhappy!"

I then showed this patient, in regard to this and many other instances in his life, how to observe, as soon as he began to feel angry, hurt, guilty, tense, anxious, or depressed, exactly what he had been telling himself, just prior to experiencing this kind of negative feeling. Secondly, I induced him to start tracing back his internal verbalizations to their philosophic sources. Thus, in the instance illustrated, the philosophic ideas behind his being hurt by his golfing associates not liking him were: (1) It was absolutely necessary that he *must* be loved; (2) Because he was a nice fellow and a fair golfer, he *deserved* to be approved by others; and (3) It was unfair, terrible, and awful that he was *not* approved or loved.

Thirdly, when he had observed or inferred the philosophic beliefs behind his being hurt (or, more accurately, behind his hurting himself), I taught this patient to challenge, question, and attack the irrationality of these beliefs. Thus, he was to ask himself "*Why* must I (or anyone else) be loved?" "*Why* do I (or anyone) *deserve* to be approved merely because I'm a nice fellow and a fair golfer?" "*Why* is it unfair, terrible, and awful that I am *not* loved or approved by this particular group of golfers?"

Finally, this patient was taught to *change* his irrational philosophies: to keep telling and convincing himself that it was *not* necessary (though it may have been desirable) for him to be loved; that he did *not* deserve to be approved by others, simply because he behaved well with them and *wanted* their approval; and that not being approved or loved by others might well be inconvenient, but that it was hardly terrible or catastrophic.

In this manner, the patient was shown how to observe, track down, question, and change some of the fundamental irrational ideas behind his unnecessary emotional disturbances; and eventually he came truly to disbelieve the nonsense he had held for many years and to believe much more realistic, effective philosophies instead. In particular, he came to see that it was not terribly important (even though it was desirable) that other people like or love him; and as he did come to see this, his main neurotic symptoms, which included extreme shyness and lack of self-confidence, vanished. Today, several years later, he can enjoy playing golf no matter what his companions think of him or his game, and he is able to do many other similar things with quiet assurance instead of with his old state of near-panic.

The A-B-C theory of personality and of emotional disturbance can be used—as will be shown in several later case presentations in this book—with virtually all kinds of individuals, from mild neurotics to severe psychotics. It can also be used, at times, with young children as well as adults—as Dr. Roger Callahan of Detroit has recently been effectively employing it. In my own case, I only occasionally see young children (since I feel that helping their parents become sane and rational is usually more efficient than seeing the children themselves), but I have experimented successfully with RT with a few youngsters.

In one case I saw an eight year old child and decided to try some rational therapeutic techniques with him, just to see how effective they might be. This child, a bright but very disturbed boy, stuttered quite badly and was not only upset because of the stuttering but because his friends and relatives kept teasing him about it.

I was able to show the boy that it really wasn't very important if others teased him and that he need not—at point B—upset himself about their teasing by telling himself how awful it was that they were teasing. I quoted him the same nursery rhyme that I often quote my adult patients—"Stick and stones/ May break your bones/ But names will never hurt you"—and I insisted that he need not be hurt by the teasing of others and that he could stop upsetting himself if he recognized that these others had their own problems and that their words really didn't matter that much.

Some of the things that this boy said to me after the third

session I had with him were amazing; they showed clearly how he had really understood what I had said and that he was beginning to see that no, he need not be upset by the words and gestures of others, and that it really *didn't* matter that much when he was teased.

By the end of the fourth session, my young patient was not only much less disturbed about being teased, but was stuttering considerably less, and he has continued to make remarkable improvement, even though I have seen him only occasionally. Apparently, bright eight-year-olds can also benefit from RT and the A-B-C theory of emotional disturbance—sometimes, in fact, more than their more difficult and prejudiced elders.

I have also tried rational methods with young adolescents in several instances and I have frequently been able to show them that, whether they like it or not, their parents are disturbed individuals; that they don't have to take these parents too seriously (particularly when the parents are highly negative toward the children); and that they don't *have* to get upset (or upset themselves) just because their parents are disturbed.

Here again, I show these adolescents that it is not what happens to them at point A (their parents' negativism) which really hurts them, but their own catastrophizing and rebellious sentences which they tell themselves at point B: "How could they do that to me?" "How terribly unfair they are!" "I can't stand their horrible treatment of me!" When I get them to change their own thoughts and internalized sentences, these youngsters are able to live more peacefully with some of the most difficult and disturbed parents.

Rational-emotive psychotherapy, then, for all its emphasis on logic, reason, and objectivity, is also a highly personal, individualistic, and "idealistic" way of looking at oneself and the external world. It fully accepts human beings as fallible, limited, biologically rooted animals. But it also accepts them as unique, symbol-producing and thought-creating persons who have unusual potentials, in most instances, to build or rebuild their own emotions and behavior. Philosophically, it is therefore far from being classically rationalistic; but it takes some of the best elements of ancient and modern rationalism and tries to mate them with similarly workable elements of humanism, existentialism, and realism.

7

Sin and Psychotherapy*

One of the most challenging and lucid of recent thinkers on the subject of psychotherapy has been the eminent psychologist, O. Hobart Mowrer. Vigorously condemning the Freudian attitudes regarding the id, ego, and superego, Professor Mowrer has for the last decade upheld the thesis that if the psychotherapist in any way gives his patients the notion that they are not responsible for their sins, he will only encourage them to keep sinning; and that they cannot become emotionally undisturbed, since at bottom disturbance is a moral problem, unless they assume full responsibility for their misdeeds—and, what is more, *stop* their sinning.

In a recent symposium in which I participated with Dr. Mowrer, he made some excellent points with which I heartily agree (Mowrer, 1960b): namely, that psychotherapy must largely be concerned with the patient's sense of morality or wrongdoing; that classical Freudianism is mistaken in its implication that giving an individual insight into or understanding of his immoral or antisocial behavior will usually suffice to enable him to change that behavior; that if any Hell exists for human beings it is the Hell of neurosis and psychosis; that man is pre-eminently a social creature who psychologically maims himself to the degree that he needlessly harms others; that the only basic solution to the problem of emotional disturbance is the correction or cessation of the disturbed person's immoral actions; and that the effective psychotherapist must not only give his patient insight into the

* This chapter is an expanded version of two previously published articles: "There is No Place for the Concept of Sin in Psychotherapy" (*J. Consult. Psychol.*, 1960, 7, 188-192) and "Mowrer on 'Sin'" (*Amer. Psychologist*, 1960, 15, 713).

origins of his mistaken and self-defeating behavior but must also provide him with a highly active program of working at the eradication of this behavior.

On the surface, then, it would appear that I am in close agreement with Mowrer's concepts of sin and psychotherapy. This, however, is not true: since one of the central theses of rational-emotive psychotherapy is that there is no place whatever for the concept of sin in psychotherapy and that to introduce this concept in any manner, shape, or form is highly pernicious and antitherapeutic. The rational therapist holds, on the contrary, that no human being should ever be blamed for anything he does; and it is the therapist's main and most important function to help rid his patients of every possible vestige of their blaming themselves, blaming others, or blaming fate and the universe.

My pronounced differences with all those who would advocate making patients more guilty than they are, in order presumably to get them to change their antisocial and self-defeating conduct, can perhaps best be demonstrated by my insistence on a more precise and reasonably operational definition of the terms "sin" and "guilt" than is usually given by those who uphold this concept.

In their recent *Comprehensive Dictionary of Psychological and Psychoanalytical Terms,* English and English (1958) give a psychological definition of "sin" as follows: "Conduct that violates what the offender believes to be a supernaturally ordained moral code." They define a "sense of guilt" in this wise: "Realization that one has violated ethical or moral or religious principles, together with a regretful feeling of lessened personal worth on that account." English and English do not give any definition of "blame" but Webster's *New World Dictionary* defines it as: 1. "a blaming; accusation; condemnation; censure. 2. responsibility for a fault or wrong."

The beauty of these definitions, if one pays close attention to them, is that they include the two prime requisites for the individual's feeling a sense of sin, or guilt, or self-blame: (*a*) I have done the wrong thing and am responsible for doing it; and (*b*) I am a blackguard, a sinner, a no-goodnik, a valueless person, a louse, for having done this wrong deed. This, as I have shown my patients for the last several years, and as I and my co-author, Dr. Robert A. Harper, have noted in several recent publications on rational-emotive psychotherapy (Ellis, 1957b; Ellis and Harper, 1961a, 1961b), is the double-headed essence of the feeling of sin, guilt, and blame: not merely the fact that the individual has made a mistake, an error, or a wrong move (which we may objectively call "wrongdoing") but the highly insidious, and I am convinced quite erroneous, belief or assumption that he is worthless, no good, valueless as a person for having done wrong.

I fully accept Hobart Mowrer's implication that there is such a thing as human wrongdoing or immoral behavior. I do not, as a psychologist, believe that we can have any absolute, final, or God-given standards of morals or ethics.

However, I do believe that, as citizens of a social community, we must have *some* standards of right and wrong. My own feeling is that these standards are best based on what I call long-range or socialized hedonism—that is, the philosophy that one should primarily strive for one's own satisfactions while, at the same time, keeping in mind that one will achieve one's own best good, in most instances, by giving up immediate gratifications for future gains and by being courteous to and considerate of others, so that they will not sabotage one's own ends. I am also, however, ready to accept almost any other rationally planned, majortiy-approved standard of morality that is not arbitrarily imposed by an authoritarian clique of actual men or assumed gods.

With Mowrer and almost all ethicists and religionists, then, I accept it as fact that some standard of morality is necessary as long as humans live in social groups. But I still completely reject the notion that such a standard is only or best sustained by inculcating in individuals a sense of sin or guilt. I hold, on the contrary, that the more sinful and guilty a person tends to feel, the less chance there is that he will be a happy, healthy, or law-abiding citizen.

The problem of all human morality, it must never be forgotten, is not the problem of appeasing some hypothetical deity or punishing the individual for his supposed sins. It is the very simple problem, which a concept of sin and atonement invariably obfuscates, of teaching a person (*a*) not to commit an antisocial act in the first place, and (*b*) if he does happen to commit it, not to repeat it in the second, third, and ultimate place. This problem, I contend, can consistently and fully be solved only if the potential or actual wrongdoer has the philosophy of life epitomized by the internalized sentences: (*a*) "If I do this act it will be wrong," and (*b*) "Therefore, how do I *not* do this act?" Or: (*a*) "This deed I have committed is wrong, erroneous, and mistaken." (*b*) "Now, how do I *not* commit it again?"

If, most objectively, and without any sense of self-blame, self-censure, or self-guilt, any human being would thoroughly believe in and continually internalize these sentences, I think it would be almost impossible for him to commit or keep committing immoral acts. If, however, he does not have this objective philosophy of wrongdoing, I do not see how it is possible for him to prevent himself from being immoral, on the one hand, or for him to be moral and emotionally healthy, on the other. For the main alternatives to the objective philosophy of nonblaming morality which I have just outlined are the following:

1. The individual can say to himself: (*a*) "If I do this act it will be wrong," and (*b*) "If I do this wrong act, I will be a sinner, a blackguard." If this is what the individual says to himself, and firmly believes, he will then perhaps be moral in his behavior, but only at the expense of having severe feelings of worthlessness—of deeply feeling that he is a sinner. But such feelings of worthlessness, I submit, are the essence of human disturbance: since disturbance basically consists of intense anxiety (that is, the feelings following from the internalized sentence, "I am worthless and therefore I cannot live comfortably and safely in a world filled with much more worthwhile persons") or sustained hostility (that is, the feeling often following from the sentence, "He is more worthwhile than I, and I cannot live comfortably and compete with him, and therefore I hate him").

So, at best, if a human being remains moral mainly because

he would feel guilty and worthless if he did not so remain, he will most probably never be able to rid himself of his underlying feelings of worthlessness and his fear of these feelings showing through if he did, by some chance, prove to be fallible and did behave immorally. We have, then, a moral individual who keeps himself so only by plaguing himself with feelings of sin or worthlessness. And since none of us are angels, and all must at some time make mistakes and commit immoral acts, we actually have a moral individual who actively (as well as potentially) hates himself. Or we would have, as Mowrer might well put it if he were more precise about what a sense of sin actually is and what it does to human beings, an individual who perpetually keeps himself on the verge of or actually in the Hell of neurosis or psychosis.

2. The self-blaming or guilty individual can say to himself, as I contend that most of the time he does in actual practice: (a) "If I do this act it will be wrong," and (b) "If I am wrong I will be a sinner." And then, quite logically taking off from this wholly irrational and groundless conclusion, he will obsessively-compulsively keep saying to himself, as I have seen patient after patient say, "Oh, what a terrible sinner I will be (or already am). Oh, what a terrible person! How I deserve to be punished!" And so on, and so forth.

In saying this nonsense, and thereby equating his potential or actual act of wrongdoing with a concomitant feeling of utter worthlessness, this individual will never be able to focus on the simple question, "How do I *not* do this wrong act?" or "How do I not repeat it now that I have done it?" He will, instead, keep focusing senselessly on "What a horrible sinner, what a blackguard I am!" Which means, in most instances, that he will—ironically enough—actually be diverted into doing the wrong act or repeating it if he has already done it. His sense of sin will tend literally to drive him away from not doing wrong and toward "sinning." Or, in other words, he will become a compulsive wrongdoer.

To make matters still worse, the individual who blames himself for acting badly (or, sometimes, for even *thinking* about

acting badly) will usually feel (as blamers normally do) that
he should be punished for his poor behavior. His internalized
sentences therefore will tend to go somewhat as follows: "I
committed a horrible crime. I am therefore a terrible sinner
and must atone for my sins, must punish myself for this crime.
But if I keep doing badly, keep committing these kinds of
crimes, I will certainly be caught or will have to keep being
anxious about the danger of being caught. My being caught
and punished or my being anxious about being caught will
itself be a hard, punishing thing. Therefore, maybe it would
be better if I kept committing crimes like this, in order to
punish myself, and thereby atone for my sins."

In other words, the individual who construes his misdeeds
as sins will often compulsively drive himself to more misdeeds
in order, sooner or later, to bring punishment for these sins on
his own head.

3. The self-blaming person (or, synonymously, the person with
a pronounced sense of sin) may say to himself the usual sequence:
(*a*) "If I do this act it will be wrong," and (*b*) "If I am wrong,
I am a worthless sinner." Then, being no angel and being
impelled, at times, to commit wrong deeds, and being prepared
to condemn himself mercilessly (because of his sense of sin) for
his deeds, he will either refuse to admit that he has done the
wrong thing or admit that he has done it but insist that it is
not wrong. That is to say, the wrongdoer who has an acute
sense of sin will either repress thoughts about his wrongdoing
or psychopathically insist that he is right and the world is wrong.

Any way one looks at the problem of morality, therefore, the
individual who sanely starts out by saying (*a*) "It is wrong to
do this act" and then who insanely continues (*b*) "I am a sinner
or a blackguard for doing (or even for thinking about doing)
it" can only be expected to achieve one or more of four most
unfortunate results: (1) a deepseated feeling of personal worthlessness; (2) an obsessive-compulsive occupation with a consequent potential re-performance of the wrong act for which he
is blaming himself; (3) denial or repression of the fact that his
immoral act was actually committed by him; and (4) psycho-

pathic insistence that the act was committed but was not really wrong.

To make matters infinitely worse, the individual who has a sense of sin, guilt, or self-blame inevitably cannot help blaming others for their potential or actual wrongdoings—and he therefore becomes angry or hostile to these others. And he cannot help blaming fate, circumstances, or the universe for wrongly or unjustly frustrating him in the attainment of many of his desires—and he consequently becomes self-pitying and angry at the world.

In the final analysis, then, blaming, in all its insidious ramifications, is the essence of virtually all emotional disturbances; and, as I tell my patients on many occasions, if I can induce them never, under any circumstances, to blame or punish anyone, including and especially themselves, it will be virtually impossible for them ever to become seriously upset. This does not mean that no child or adult should ever be objectively or dispassionately penalized for his errors or wrongdoings (as, for example, psychologists often penalize laboratory rats by shocking them when they enter the wrong passage of a maze); but merely that no one should ever be *blamefully* punished for his mistakes or crimes.

There are several other reasons why, almost invariably, giving an individual a sense of sin or of self-worthlessness in connection with his wrongdoing will not make for less immorality or greater happiness or mental health. Let me briefly mention some of these reasons.

For one thing, guilt and self-blame induce the individual to bow nauseatingly low to some arbitrary external authority, which in the last analysis is always some hypothetical deity; and such worship renders him proportionately less self-sufficient and self-confident. Secondly, the concept of guilt inevitably leads to the unsupportable sister concept of self-sacrifice for and dependency upon others—which is the antithesis of true mental health. Thirdly, guilty individuals tend to focus incessantly on past delinquencies and crimes rather than on present and future constructive behavior. Fourthly, it is psychophysically impossible for a person to concentrate adequately on changing his moral actions for the better when he is obsessively focused upon blaming himself for his past and present misdeeds. Fifthly, the states of anxiety created in an individual by his self-blaming tendencies induce concomitant breakdown states in which he cannot think clearly of anything, least of all constructive changes in himself.

The full measure of the harmfulness of self-blaming is perhaps best seen in regard to its interference with the reestablishment of mental health once it has set the wheels of emotional disturbance in working order. The vicious circle usually goes somewhat as follows. Jim Jones, who is a fairly normal, fallible human being, first demands that he be perfect and infallible, because he very falsely equates making mistakes with being incompetent and equates being incompetent with being worthless (that is, blameworthy). Naturally, he does not achieve perfection or infallibility; and, in fact, just because he is so over-concerned about being error-less, and focuses on *how* rather than on *what* he is doing, he tends to make many more mistakes than he otherwise would make if he did not blame himself and consider himself worthless for being error-prone.

So Jim Jones excoriates himself severely for his mistakes and develops some kind of neurotic symptom—such as severe anxiety or hostility against those he thinks are less incompetent than he. Once he develops this symptom, Jim soon begins to notice that he is afflicted with it, and then he blames himself severely for having the symptom—for being neurotic. This second-level self-blaming of course causes him to be still more neurotic.

Thus, where he was originally anxious about his potential incompetence, and then became more anxious because his original anxiety drove him to become actually incompetent, he now goes one step further, and becomes anxious about being anxious. In the process—naturally!—he tends to become still more incompetent, since he is even less than ever focused on problem-solving and more than ever concentrated on what a terrible person he is for being such a poor problem-solver.

Finally, after he has become anxious (that is, self-blaming) about (*a*) the possibility of being incompetent, (*b*) actual incompetence, stemming from (*a*), and (*c*) his anxiety or acute panic state resulting from both (*a*) and (*b*), Jim sees that he is terribly disturbed and goes for psychotherapeutic aid. But here again he is smitten down by his self-blaming tendencies and tends to sabotage his therapeutic efforts in several significant ways:

1. The more the therapist helps him see what he is doing to himself—that is, the more insight he is helped to acquire into how he is blaming himself—the more he tends to blame himself for being so stupid or incompetent or sick. Otherwise stated, the more he sees how he is blaming himself, the more he may, especially at the beginning of therapy, blame himself *for* blaming himself. He thereby may actually become considerably worse before he starts to get better.

2. As soon as he sees that therapy requires that he do something in order to get better—which it always does, since it is no magic formula for self-improvement without effort on the part of the patient—he frequently starts worrying about whether he is going to be able (meaning, competent enough) to do what he has to do to help himself. His internalized sentences may therefore run something along these lines: "My therapist is showing me that I have to see what I am doing to create my disturbances, and to challenge and contradict my own negative thinking in this connection. From what I can see, he is perfectly right. But wouldn't it be awful if I tried to do this kind of challenging of my own nonsense and failed! Wouldn't it be terrible if I proved to him and myself that I *couldn't* do what I have to do! Perhaps, since it would be so awful to try and to fail, I'd better not even try, and in that way at least save face."

In telling himself these kinds of sentences, the patient often gives himself an excuse to give up trying to cure himself early in the game; and he either continues therapy in a half-hearted and ineffective manner, or he gives it up entirely by convincing himself that "Well, maybe it works with other people, but obviously not with me. I guess I'm just hopeless."

3. If the patient continues in therapy for a while, and if he

begins surely but fairly slowly to improve (as is usually the case, since he has become so habituated for so many years to mistaken patterns of thinking and acting), he then often starts to tell himself: "How disgusting! Here I've been going for therapy for quite a while now and I'm *still* not better. Why, considering how I blew up the other day, I'm probably just as bad as I was when I started! How stupid! Obviously, I'm not really trying at all—in which case I'm idiotically wasting my time and money in therapy—or I'm trying and I just haven't got what it takes to get better. Other people I know have made much greater strides in equal or lesser periods of time. I guess I really *am* no good!"

4. Sometimes the patient is sorely disappointed with his own progress in therapy but, realizing that if he frankly admits that he has not been working too hard or consistently to help himself, he will mercilessly blame himself, he fails to face his own avoidance of the problem and bitterly starts resenting his therapist for not helping him enough. Knowing little but a basic philosophy of blame, he cannot conceive that neither he nor his therapist could be reprehensible (though either or both of them might be responsible) for his lack of progress; so he is faced with the choice of hating one of the two—and in this instance picks the therapist, and either quits therapy completely (telling himself that *all* therapists are no damn good) or keeps shopping around for another, and perhaps another, and perhaps still another therapist. In any event, he refuses to admit that probably *he* is responsible—though not blameworthy—for his lack of progress, and that he'd therefore better get back to the task of therapy with more effort and much less blaming.

The vicious circle, in instances like these, is now complete. First the individual upsets himself by his self-excoriating philosophy; then he blames himself (or others) for his becoming so upset; then, if he goes for therapeutic help, he again blames himself (or others) for his not immediately becoming completely cured. Under such triply self-blaming blows, it is virtually certain that he will not only become, but often forever remain, exceptionally disturbed.

It should be quite patent, then, that giving an individual a sense of sin, guilt, or self-blame for his misdeeds is enormously disadvantageous. This is not to say that blame *never* helps human beings to correct their mistaken or criminal behavior. It certainly seems to work with many children and with some adults. But often it is highly ineffective—as shown by the fact that after thousands of years of censuring, ridiculing, jailing, killing, and otherwise severely blaming and punishing human beings for their immoralities, we still have not greatly reduced the quantity or quality of wrongdoing that goes on in this world.

Even, moreover, when blame is effective, and people do commit significantly fewer misdeeds because of harsh social sanctions which are leveled against them in their formative and later years, it is most dubious whether the game is worth the candle. For the toll, in terms of the immense amounts and intense degrees of anxiety and hostility that ensue, is so great as to call into question almost any amount of morality which is thereby achieved.

The concept of sin (as distinguished from the objective appraisal of wrongdoing) is so humanly inhuman that it would be difficult even to conceive a more pernicious technique for keeping mankind moral. And because any deity-positing religion almost by necessity involves endowing those members who violate the laws of its gods with a distinct concept of blameworthiness or sinfulness, I am inclined to reverse Voltaire's famous dictum and to say that, from a mental health standpoint, if there were a God it would be necessary to uninvent Him.

It is sometimes objected, when rational therapists talk of the distinction between "sin" and "wrongdoing," that they are merely quibbling and that the two are essentially the same. Thus, Mowrer (1960c), in a recent issue of the *American Psychologist*, argues that because "sin" is a stronger word than "wrongdoing" or "irresponsibility" it is better for the neurotic individual to admit his "sins" than to accept his "wrongdoings." Says Mowrer:

> The only way to resolve the paradox of self-hatred and self-punishment is to assume, not that it represents merely an "introjection" of the attitudes of others, but that the self-hatred is realistically

justified and will persist until the individual, by radically altered attitude *and action*, honestly and realistically comes to feel that he now deserves something better. As long as one remains, in old-fashioned religious phraseology, hard-of-heart and unrepentant, just so long will one's conscience hold him in the vise-like grip of "neurotic" rigidity and suffering. But if, at length, an individual confesses his past stupidities and errors and makes what poor attempts he can at restitution, then the superego (like the parents of an earlier day—and society in general) forgives and relaxes its stern hold; and the individual once again is free, "well."

In upholding the concept of individual (if not original) "sin," Mowrer is contending that the neurotic individual must, if he is to get well, accept the following syllogism: (*a*) Sinning is unjustified; (*b*) I have sinned; (*c*) therefore, I must justify my existence by acknowledging my sins, changing my ways, and becoming a non-sinner.

At first blush, this seems like a perfectly valid syllogism. But, as Mowrer himself suggests, it rarely works because "there is some evidence that human beings do not change radically unless they first acknowledge their sins; but we also know how hard it is for one to make such an acknowledgment unless he has *already changed*. In other words, the full realization of deep worthlessness is a severe ego 'insult'; and one must have some new source of strength, it seems, to endure it. This is a mystery (or is it only a mistaken observation?) which traditional theology has tried to resolve in various ways—without complete success. Can we psychologists do better?"

I am sure that psychologists can do better—if they avoid the trap which Mowrer, by insisting on replacing the naturalistic words, "wrongdoing" and "responsibility," with the moralistic word, "sin," has got himself into.

Let us first see what is wrong with Mowrer's syllogism and why, because of the manner in which it is stated, it virtually forces the individual to think that he is "worthless" and consequently to be unable to change his immoral behavior. Mowrer's premise is that sinning is unjustified or that the sinner's "self-hatred is realistically justified." By this statement he appears to mean two important things, only the first of which can be objectively validated: (*a*) the sinner's act is mistaken or wrong (because it is, in some early or final analysis, self- or society-defeating); and (*b*) therefore, the sinner is personally blameworthy or integrally worthless for performing this mistaken or wrong act.

Although (*a*) may be a true observation, (*b*) is an arbitrary value judgment, or moralistic definition, that can never possibly be objectively validated and that, as Epictetus, Hartman (1959), Lewis (1949), Mead (1936), and other writers have shown, is philosophically untenable. No matter how responsible, in a causative sense, an individual may be for his mistaken or wrong behavior, he becomes a villain or a worthless lout only if members of his social group *view* or *define* him as such and if, more importantly, he *accepts* their moralistic views. Where Mowrer, for example, obviously thinks that the average murderer should hate himself, I (for one) believe that he should fully acknowledge and deplore his murderous *act*, but that he should in no way despise him*self* for committing this act.

The paradox, therefore, that Mowrer posits—that the neurotic sinner will not get better until he acknowledges and actively repents his sins and that he will not acknowledge his sins until he gets better—is a direct and "logical" result of explicitly or implicitly including the concept of personal worthlessness in the definition of "sin." Naturally, (as noted previously in this chapter) if someone believes that his acts are sinful—meaning (*a*) that he is wrong (self- or socially-defeating) for perpetrating them, *and* (*b*) that he is blameworthy or worthless for being wrong—he will not *dare* acknowledge that he has sinned; or he will make invalid excuses for so doing; or he will feel so worthless after his acknowledgment that he will hardly have the energy or efficiency to change his wrong or mistaken behavior.

How can the non-moralistic and rational psychologist help his neurotic patients resolve this paradox? Very simply: by taking the objective and "weaker" (that is, unmoralistic) words, such as "wrongdoing" and "irresponsibility," that Mowrer abandons in place of "sin," and putting them into his original syllogism. The syllogism then becomes: (*a*) Wrongdoing is self-

or society-defeating; (*b*) I have made a mistake or committed a wrong act; (*c*) therefore, I'd better stop being self-defeating by acknowledging my wrongdoing and take considerable time and effort to work at not repeating it, so that eventually I'll become a less frequent wrongdoer.

If the neurotic wrongdoer states his syllogism in *this* form, he will never think that he is quite worthless, will never experience any ego "insult," and will easily be able to acknowledge his wrongdoings *before* he has changed and stopped committing them. The artificial problem that was created by his feeling he was a sinner and therefore blaming himself immediately for any wrongdoing that he may have perpetrated is no longer created when a misdeed is viewed as a serious mistake rather than as a heinous crime.

Although I still agree heartily with Hobart Mowrer that the healthy and happy human being should have a clear-cut sense of wrongdoing, and that he should not only try to understand the origin of his antisocial behavior but to do something effective to become more morally oriented, I contend that giving anyone a sense of sin, guilt, or self-blame is the worst possible way to help him be an emotionally sound and adequately socialized individual.

A rational psychotherapist certainly helps show his patients that they have often behaved wrongly, badly, and self-defeatingly by performing antisocial actions, and that if they continue to act in this kind of self-defeating manner they will inevitably continue to defeat their own ends. But he also shows them that this is no reason why they should feel sinful or guilty or self-blaming about the actions for which they may well have been responsible. He helps his patients to temporarily accept themselves as wrongdoers, acknowledge fully their responsibility for their acts, and then focus intently, in their internalized sentences and their overt activities, on the only real problem at hand— which is: How do I *not* repeat this wrong deed next time?

If, in this thoroughly objective, non-guilty manner, we can teach patients (as well as the billions of people in the world who, for better or worse, will never become patients) that even

though human beings can be held quite accountable or responsible for their misdeeds, no one is ever to blame for anything he
does, human morality, I am sure, will be significantly improved
and, for the first time in human history, civilized people will
have a real chance to achieve sound mental health. The concept
of sin is the direct and indirect cause of virtually all neurotic
disturbance. The sooner psychotherapists forthrightly begin to
attack it the better their patients will be.

8

Reason and Personal Worth*

Assuming that a human being can be taught not to blame himself for anything that he does (such as the misdeeds or anti-social acts discussed in the last chapter), should he not fully acknowledge and accept self-blame for some of his serious errors of omission—for example, for his failing to live up to his own potential and for his being lazy and inert instead of as success-ful and achieving as, with some degree of effort, he could be? Yes and no. Meaning: yes, he should fully acknowledge and accept responsibility for his errors of omission; and no, he should never blame himself for these errors, but merely focus, instead, on trying to correct them in the future.

Almost the entire history of Western civilization has been motivated by the dubious proposition that human beings are worthwhile only when they are extrinsically competent, suc-cessful, or achieving, and that they are basically worthless or valueless when they have little or no potential or—especially—when they are falling far below achieving the intellectual, esthetic, industrial, or other potential that they do possess. Al-though the Christian tradition presumably is strongly in favor of the notion that a man is good or worthy to the degree that he is meek, socially oriented, and spiritual, only a small minority of Christians have ever truly followed this view, while the great majority have been far more motivated by achievement and status-seeking.

Only recently, after Kierkegaard, Nietzsche, Heidegger, and other Existentialist pioneers had been propounding a radically

* This chapter is expanded from a talk, "Science and Human Values," presented at the Merrill Palmer Institute, Detroit, February 1, 1960.

new (and essentially quite un-Christian) view for a good many years, have a considerable number of thinkers begun to accept the idea that a human being is good or worthwhile merely because he exists, because he *is*, and not because of any of his extrinsic achievements (Maslow, 1954; May, Angel, and Ellenberger, 1958; Moustakas, 1957). And this new concept, that an individual always has what Robert S. Hartman (1959) calls "intrinsic value," no matter what extrinsic evaluation others may place on him, has far-reaching consequences for human behavior and for psychotherapy.

The concept of human value is a most slippery one and is remarkably easy to be confused about. Although I think that I have basically grasped it for the last several years, I have found that it is exceptionally difficult to teach it to others—largely because there are both biological and social influences which tend to contradict any sensible and consistent notions of personal worth that a human being may figure out for himself. Thus, I used to teach my patients, in the course of my rational-emotive psychotherapy sessions with them, that they were good because they existed: that existence itself is a good thing and that anyone who is alive is worthwhile. Therefore, I held, they could not be as worthless as most of them insisted that they were.

This worked in some cases. But ever so often a bright patient would come along and challenge me. "Granting that I exist," he would say, "how does *that* prove that I am worthwhile?" On second thought, I could see that he was right: it didn't prove anything of the sort. *By definition,* of course, I can say that human existence *equals* human worth; or that aliveness, singularity, I-ness (or whatever you want to call it) *is* and that just because it is, it is worthwhile. But that is still a definition; and definitions, obviously, prove nothing.

I therefore began to take a different tack and to say to my patients: "Granting that I cannot prove that you are worthwhile because you exist, by the same token you cannot prove that you are worthless becuse you do not succeed in life, or fail to attain your potential, or cannot win the love of significant others. Because your concept of worthlessness, like my definition of worth, is *also* a definition. And how can you prove a definition?"

Of course, my patients could not prove that they were worthless; nor can anyone prove this. Because personal worth *and* worthlessness are both premises, or suppositions, or definitions. Exactly like the concepts of God and godlessness, they cannot be scientifically proven. For there is no empirical evidence, at bottom, to which they can be referred.

Even the concept of extrinsic value—or one's worth to people other than oneself—cannot too accurately be pinned down, since it is always a highly relative concept. Thus, if you are a good basketball player other devotees of basketball may value you very highly and think you are a great guy; but devotees of baseball, chess, or philosophy may consider you worthless. Or if you are Jewish, you may be deemed a criminal in Nazi Germany or some other anti-Semitic community; while in modern Israel you would be held to be quite worthwhile. Although extrinsic value can [as Hartman (1959) shows] be measured and rated, it varies widely from evaluator to evaluator.

Further confusion arises since it is so easy to believe that because the evaluations of others often *are* accepted as one's evaluation of oneself, they *must* be so accepted. Thus, as George Herbert Mead has accurately pointed out, a child's evaluation of himself usually arises from his acceptance of reflected appraisals by others; and almost all adults similarly view themselves, though to a somewhat lesser degree, in the light of the approval and esteem (or lack thereof) that they receive from other members of their community. But the fact that this is *usually* so by no means proves that it *has* to be so. Indeed, history is full of examples of outstanding people who liked and respected themselves and had full faith in their own ideas, even though they obtained little or no support from others for most of their lives. And the offices of psychotherapists are full of people who thoroughly dislike and have no faith in themselves, even though they are highly respected in their community and are approved by many relatives, friends, and associates.

In spite, therefore, of the insightful sociological analyses of Mead and the clinical observations of Harry Stack Sullivan

(1947) and his followers, there is hardly any one-to-one relationship between one's extrinsic and one's intrinsic value. It is, of
course, exceptionally *difficult* to value yourself highly when
almost everyone around you thinks otherwise; and it is also
difficult to hate yourself when most others approve of you
highly. But it is obviously possible for your self-evaluation to
be quite different from others' evaluation of you, and there are
literally millions of instances in which a significant discrepancy
in the two evaluations occurs.

Another confusion arises which may well be biologically
rooted, and that is in relation to the concept of self-mastery. As
Alfred Adler (1927, 1929, 1931) and his followers (especially
Ansbacher and Ansbacher, 1956) have shown for the last half
century, and as Robert White (1959) has recently reaffirmed,
the human urge to mastery is very deep-rooted and probably
originates in some kind of biological drive. There may consequently be a normal, innate tendency for a person to feel good
when he has mastered some challenging situation or difficult
problem, and to feel bad when he has had a failure, or especially a series of failures, at tasks which he would like to complete successfully.

The fact, however, that an individual may normally or even
instinctively like *his mastery* of a given situation does not mean
that he has to like *himself* for mastering it, any more than the
fact that he likes ice cream means that he has to like himself
for liking or having the pleasure of eating ice cream. The chances
are that his *self*-evaluation, which tends to be significantly correlated with his mastering or failing at a certain task, is socially
acquired (as Mead has shown) rather than inborn. He is *taught*,
in other words, that he *should* like himself when he succeeds
and that he *should* hate himself when he fails. Or, perhaps
more concretely, he is taught that because *others* dislike or
disapprove him when he fails to master something, he should
accept their evaluation of himself and make it his own.

Even if there *were* a biological tendency for an individual to
like himself when he kept succeeding at various tasks and to
consider himself worthless when he kept failing, there is no

theoretical reason why this tendency could not be socially overcome. Thus, there is certainly a biological tendency for human
beings to walk barefooted rather than with shoes on; and in-
numerable people who are quite used to wearing shoes quickly
take them off and go around in slippers or bare feet when they
are in their own homes. Yet, in spite of our instinctive tendencies to go barefooted, practically all of us who live in urban
areas do manage, for the sake of our arches, to get used to
wearing shoes when we walk on concrete and other hard
surfaces.

Similarly, if there were a biological tendency for humans to
evaluate themselves in direct proportion to their mastery of outside situations, this tendency could almost certainly be overcome if it were shown to lead, in most instances, to unfortunate
results.

Actually, the facts seem to show that there are many people
who are almost thoroughly incompetent, and who master little
or nothing in life; and yet some of these people seem to like
themselves and to be less self-blaming than many far more
competent persons. Every institution, for example, for mentally
deficient individuals includes a number of persons who, although
they have little or no competence at practically anything, and
would have a very low evaluation in the eyes of most persons
of normal intelligence, have considerable self-esteem. These
individuals apparently *accept* themselves, in spite of their clear-
cut limitations; and that is that.

What is more, most people in our society, who would consider that mentally deficient persons have little or no extrinsic
value—that is, would be of no use to *them*—would be horrified
at the suggestion that, therefore, these deficient persons should
be exterminated. Obviously, therefore, they must believe that
mentally deficient and other extrinsically valueless individuals
have some value *to themselves*—have some intrinsic value. And,
of course, they do: since no matter how defective or handicapped an individual may be, as long as he is alive, there is some
possibility that he may become less handicapped; and even if
he doesn't, there is some possibility that he may, albeit in his

own limited manner, learn to enjoy himself and thereby to
have a good life.

The problem of intrinsic worth is further complicated by the
confusion, which most of us seem to be victimized by, between
an individual's value to himself and his happiness or enjoyment.
There is no question that one's happiness may be in some way
measured and striven for. Thus, one may be very happy,
moderately happy, or very unhappy. And the more one intelligently strives to live a sane, unanxious, and unhostile life, the
happier one is likely to be. Moreover, the more achieving one
is, the more one is likely to have more money, friends, worldly
goods, etc., and thereby to enjoy oneself in certain ways that
might well not be available if one were totally unachieving.

Happiness, however, does not equal personal worth; and one
does not become more worthwhile as one becomes happier. A
man, for example, may be in almost continual pain, and therefore not particularly happy. But we cannot say that consequently
he is worthless and should commit suicide. For he may well
consider that his aliveness itself is worth preserving, even though
it is not a particularly happy aliveness. Or he may reason that
even if he is alive and in pain today, he may be alive and happy
tomorrow; and therefore, his life is worth continuing. In almost
all instances, as long as he is still alive and has even the slightest
possibility of someday being happier than he now is, his *potentiality* for leading a satisfactory existence still remains, and he
may yet lead a satisfactory existence.

A man's existing or being, as the Existentialists point out, is
never a static thing, but includes the possibility of his *becoming*
—of his creatively making himself into something different from
what he is at any given moment. The *process* of his becoming,
rather than the *product* of his having already become, may
well be the most important aspect of his existence. Therefore, the
fact that he has *right now* become this or that (e.g., has become
mentally deficient or unhappy) does not mean that he cannot
in the future become something quite different (e.g., brighter
or happier). As long as he is *alive*, he can still remain in process,
have a future, change himself to a better or more satisfying

state. True, he may never actually do this, and may remain, until the end of his days, as handicapped or as unhappy as he happens to be at this moment. But he also may *not*. And as long as his aliveness gives him the slightest *potentiality* of becoming, of changing, of growing, it can hardly be said that he is intrinsically worthless.

Although, then, it is perfectly true that, through working hard and somehow achieving such things as fame or fortune, an individual will usually (though hardly always) increase his own satisfactions, and although it is probably true that there is *some* connection between an individual's being (at least potentially) happy and his having intrinsic value or self-worth, it does not follow that when any person achieves more of what he wants to achieve in life, he automatically raises his own worth. He may well, by his mastery over himself and external people and things, increase his self-confidence to some degree (especially if we operationally define self-confidence as the assurance that one can do and get certain things that one wants to do and get). But self-confidence (except by arbitrary definition) is still not exactly self-worth—as shown by the fact that many people are perfectly confident that they can accomplish great things in life, but still hate themselves; while many other people have little confidence that they can attain notable achievements, but still like themselves.

All that has been said so far in this chapter would seem to lead to the conclusion that if there *is* an objectively definable concept of self-worth or intrinsic personal value, it can only realistically be conceived as the individual's existence, being, aliveness, or becoming—which gives him the possibility or potentiality of being happy. Other definitions of self-worth, such as the concept that it consists of mastery, or social acceptance, or the actual achievement of one's potential for being happy, seem to be illogical in that (*a*) they invariably refer to product rather than living process; (*b*) they are really concerned with one's extrinsic rather than intrinsic value; and (*c*) they lead to moralistic and self-defeating patterns of behavior on the part of those who believe in and follow them (Lichtenberg, 1962).

Convincing oneself, if one is a therapist, that the usual concepts of self-worth are illogical and illegitimate and convincing one's patients of this fact are, unfortunately, two different things. I must say that I have had the devil of a time, in recent years, showing many of my patients that they are not as worthless as they think they are. My present tack, as I started to say in the beginning of this chapter, is to put the onus on them of proving that they *are* valueless—since, scientifically, the onus of proving the validity of a theory should always be on the one who constructs it, rather than (as many religionists and other non-scientists seem to believe) placing the onus of disproving a theory on those who disagree with it.

I therefore often say to my patients: "Look: you insist that you are worthless, valueless, and no damn good. Now give me some evidence to prove your hypothesis." Of course, they can't. They almost immediately come up with some statement as: "Well, I am worthless because I'm no good at anything," or "I have no value because no one could possibly care for me." But, as I soon show them, these are tautological sentences which say nothing but: "I am worthless because I consider myself to be worthless." "Incompetence, unlovability, or what you will," I tell them, "only make you valueless because you *think* they do. Others who think differently can and do consider themselves worthwhile even though they may be ten times more incompetent or unlovable than you."

I then go through a whole battery of reasons with these patients which indicate why it is untenable for them to consider themselves worthless. In addition to those reasons already considered previously in this chapter, I enumerate several more, some adapted from Hartman's brilliant monograph (1959):

1. Evaluating yourself extrinsically depends on your fulfilling an abstract concept of what a human being should be; while evaluating yourself intrinsically, in terms of your personal worth, depends on your fulfilling a singular, unique concept of yourself. It is therefore illegitimate to measure intrinsic or personal value in extrinsic (achievement) terms.

2. The abstract concept on which extrinsic value depends is

denumerably infinite while the singular concept on which intrinsic value depends is nondenumerably infinite. In mathematical terms, therefore, the first cannot be measured in terms of the second, nor vice versa; and nondenumerably infinite concepts cannot be measured at all in conventional degrees of worthwhileness.

3. Human existence, aliveness, or I-ness is a special kind of state which is peculiarly biological, while me-ness or role-taking or trait-possession is a different kind of state of being which is largely social or sociological; and the two cannot be measured (as neurotics with a low sense of personal worth invariably do measure them) by the same kind of scales or value systems.

4. I-ness or aliveness or intrinsicness can be properly perceived in only two positions: existence and nonexistence, life and death. It cannot be scaled and measured as can be the traits or characteristics which a live individual may possess.

To these technical, logical reasons why it is illegitimate for anyone to measure his personal worth or value in the same kind of terms in which he normally measures his extrinsic value, or worth to others, I add a final, and to me more clinically convincing reason why my patients should stop viewing themselves as worthless.

"Let us face it," I tell them. "Assuming that you do measure your intrinsic and extrinsic value by the same kind of scales, and therefore arrive at the conclusion that you are worthless, you must, once this conclusion is reached, thereafter be prey to everlasting feelings of anxiety, guilt, depression, and other kinds of emotional upset. On the other hand, if you do *not* conclude that you are worthless (because, at bottom, your definition of worth is human, personal perfection), you may live with a minimum of anxiety and hostility. Obviously, then, the only sane pragmatic course to follow is to assume that you are *not* valueless."

In other words, I am usually able, with these arguments, to prove to my patients that (*a*) they are only worthless by their own arbitrary definitions; and that (*b*) if they maintain these definitions and keep looking upon themselves as valueless, they will inevitably bring on highly disadvantageous neurotic symptoms, especially anxiety, guilt, and depression. They are then able to conclude, if I am successful in these respects, that they are *not* intrinsically worthless or valueless. But does this combination of two negatives necessarily equal a positive? Does an individual's not being worthless prove that he must be worthwhile?

Yes and no. Assuming that there *is* definitely such a thing as a human's having intrinsic worth or value, then if he is not worthless, he presumably is worthwhile. If both A and not-A exist, and a thing is not not-A, then it presumably, according to the Aristotelian laws of logic, must be A.

But there are two flaws in this kind of thinking. In the first place, as Korzybski (1933) and many of his followers have shown, Aristotelian logic has its own distinct limitations and does not fully cover the laws of thinking. The world does not just consist of A and not-A, but often consists of A_1, A_2, A_3, etc. Secondly, it is always possible that both A and not-A are suppositions or premises that have no actual empirical existence, and that instead of being mutually exclusive, they are both meaningless.

Thus, it can be postulated that if Christ (A) and anti-Christ (not-A) exist, and John Doe is against Christ, then he must be on the side of the anti-Christ. But it can also be held that since there is no empirical evidence supporting the existence of either Christ or anti-Christ, it is meaningless to state that John Doe is on the side of either of these "beings."

Similarly, it may be said that according to the laws of non-Aristotelian logic, the usual concepts of an individual's having intrinsic worth are rather meaningless, since his $worth_1$ (say, when he is in a state of physical well-being and psychological happiness) is quite different from his $worth_2$ (say, when he is miserably tired and has a splitting headache). It may also be said that the concepts of worth *and* worthlessness are premises, suppositions, or definitions which have no possible empirical referent; and that, like the concepts of God and godlessness, they cannot be operationally defined or scientifically proven or disproven.

Philosophically, therefore, even when I prove to my patients that they are only worthless by definition, and that their defining themselves as valueless will necessarily result in their becoming seriously anxious and unhappy, I have not necessarily proven to them that they therefore must be intrinsically worthwhile. Perhaps the best solution to this problem would be for us to realize that, essentially, there *is* no such thing as intrinsic worth or worthlessness, for these are terms of measurement which can be properly attributed only to extrinsic, external things and events.

A man's happiness, efficiency, achievement, or other traits can certainly be measured. But can his existence itself, his being and becoming, be accurately evaluated? Existence and nonexistence, aliveness and nonaliveness, life and death seem to be peculiarly bipolar: either you have them or you don't, and there is no inbetweenness about them.

As Hartman (1959) aptly notes:

Who am I? I am this human on this planet earth. I was born a naked baby and I have to die. That's all. That's the gist of being myself; and being a professor or anything else for that matter is a different thing from being this human, born on this planet earth and having to die. Any extrinsic definition of myself is really not the definition of myself. In order to make the definition of myself I must neither construct myself nor even abstract from myself but simply *be*, namely identify myself with myself. And this is the most difficult and most important task of our moral life.

In a very real sense, the idea of human value and disvalue is something of a misnomer—a misleading question. People of course have extrinsic value or social value—meaning that *others* find them to be bright or stupid, tall or short, useful or useless as an associate, a partner, or a mate. But *to themselves* they do not really have value or worth, at least in the usual intent of these words. They exist or they do not exist. And if one wants to say that because they exist they are "worthwhile," that cannot be gainsaid—but neither can it really be proven, since it is a definition rather than a statement of fact.

If people consider themselves to be "worthwhile," they will tend to feel good about their self-evaluation, and perhaps to be happier and more efficient in their doings. But by considering themselves "worthy" they also bring in the concomitant concept of "worthlessness," and run the danger of creating needless pain and inefficiency. The concept of Heaven normally carries with it the counter-concept of Hell. Instead of having either of these sets of self-values, it might well be better if men and women would spontaneously, unmoralistically, and unself-consciously *be.*

In the course of their being, humans can legitimately try to be happier or more efficient (in the sense of their getting more of the things they want or prefer and less of the things they dislike or detest out of life). But is it legitimate for them to try self-consciously to be *superior to* or *better than* others, at least in the sense of trying to be more *worthwhile* than others?

Otherwise stated: people may efficiently try to *live* better (that is, to better their own performances and get more of what they want out of life); but it is doubtful if they can do themselves any real good by trying to *be* better (that is, to prove their "superiority" over or higher "status" than others). While objectively accepting *others'* extrinsic evaluation of their worth; and while at times striving to change some of their external characteristics (such as their appearance or their job performance) to win the approval or the *practical* love of others; people can still basically *be* or *be themselves* (that is *largely* try to discover what *they* want to do in life and spend *most* of their time and efforts trying to do what *they* want to do).

If personal value or worth is to have any tangible meaning—and quite possibly there *is* no very tangible meaning, apart from vague definition that it can have—it would be better to relate it to one's own being and becoming (that is, one's becoming what one thinks or guesses one would *like* to become) than to the arbitrary, external notions of value that most of us unthinkingly connect it with.

This is what the rational-emotive therapist tries to help his patients to do: to have what Tillich (1953) calls the courage to be: which, operationally defined, would seem to include: (*a*) the desire, rather than the dire need, to be loved or approved by others; (*b*) the consequent willingness to acknowledge the extrinsic value that others place on oneself, and at times, for one's own practical benefit, to act wisely and well to help raise this value, so that one's desire for approval will be fairly well satisfied; (*c*) the determined unwillingness to accept the extrinsic value that others place on oneself as one's full or intrinsic value and the insistence on spending most of one's life discovering what one really wants to do and actively doing what one really wants, even though many others may not approve, as long as one does not literally destroy oneself in the process; (*d*) a concomitant commitment to the process rather than the products of life, with an emphasis on enjoying oneself in the here and now, while at the same time keeping some clear sight of the long-range hedonistic pleasures and absorptions of one's later days; (*e*) a full acceptance of oneself as a creative *I*, rather than only as a passive *me* who must be utterly dependent on the help and approval of significant others (Hamilton, 1962).

To enable the individual to attain these kinds of goals, and to define his intrinsic "worth" (if there really is such a thing) in terms of his being and his becoming, rather than in terms of his achieving or being externally approved, the rational therapist induces the patient to hack vigorously away at his own unchallenged premises about his dire needs to be approved and to achieve in order to be "worthy," and to retranslate these needs into preferences.

Let me illustrate with the case of one of my patients, a 36 year old female psychologist, who came for therapy because she kept waking up around 3 A.M. every morning in a state of panic about what was going to happen on her job the next day, and whether the testing procedure she had devised for the large corporation for which she worked was going to function effectively. After once waking early in the morning, she could not go back to sleep again; and then she would be practically useless on her job during that day. She had had four years of Freudian psychoanalysis several years previously; and although it had helped her understand and resolve some problems in connection with her relationships with her parents, she found that it had not helped her a bit in her continual worry over her work. So she decided to try some rational-emotive therapy.

During the third session with this patient, the following dialogue occurred:

Patient: Please tell me exactly what I have to do. This morning, I was up again at 3:30 A.M. and couldn't get back to sleep at all, but lay in bed sweating and stewing and turning. And, of course, although I somehow managed to drag myself to the office, I really wasn't there, and I was just going through the motions ineffectually. Now how can I stop this—which I've just got to, and soon!

Therapist: Let me go over it once again. It's really quite a simple procedure; and if you will only work at it, especially with your kind of training, I am sure that you can get on to it quickly. But although it's simple, it *does* require work. And, as you know, there's no magic about this therapy business.

P: All right, I'll try to listen carefully, although I'm so distraught these days that I can hardly concentrate on anything for more than a minute or two at a time. My mind just keeps wandering to that damn testing procedure I devised, and that they've put so much money into; and whether it's going to work well or be just a waste of all that time and money. I'm certainly sorry I ever thought of it in the first place!

T: But that's what I'm trying to show you: your very *sorriness* is your sickness. Here you creatively design a new testing procedure, and whether or not it works it's *your* creation, and you should be having great fun out of experimenting with it and seeing if you can perfect it. But you're so intent on its positively, absolutely being a *paying* procedure, and one that your concern will praise you for and tell you how great you are for inventing it, that you completely forget about the you-ness of the procedure and are only obsessively involved with the they-ness of it: with how it's going to appear to *them*.

P: But it's *them* who pay me, isn't it? And if they don't like this procedure, or it just doesn't work at all when it's all set up, I could easily lose my job. After I've worked so hard for so long to get to this best place I've ever had, it could all go down the drain. Isn't *that* something to worry about?

T: No, it isn't. In the first place, you know perfectly well that even if you lost your job and never worked another day in your life, your husband is very well able to support you and your child, and that he wouldn't be at all disturbed about your not working. So it isn't that. You also know that you're the most conscientious person at your firm, and that no matter how badly your testing procedure works out, there is virtually no chance of their letting you go. Besides, even if there *were* a good chance of your losing your job because of the way you're behaving at work—because of your panic state during the day and your not being able to concentrate after staying up half the night berating yourself—would *worrying* about your losing this job help you *not* lose it? Or would it not, as definitely seems to be the case, actually help you lose the job—by keeping you awake more nights and in a greater panic state during the days?

P: All right, you're right, of course. But how do I *stop* myself from worrying in the middle of the night—or any other time?

T: Yes, let's get back to essentials. As I have already explained to you during the first two sessions, you worry only because you tell yourself something just before you start worrying, and because that something that you tell yourself is nonsense. Now point one is that you must admit that you *are* telling yourself something to start your worrying going, and you must begin to look, and I mean really *look*, for the specific nonsense with which you keep reindoctrinating yourself.

P: And that is?

T: And that is a perfectly true followed by a ridiculously false statement. The true statement is: "If my testing procedure doesn't work, and if I keep worrying about things like this as much as I am now doing, I will continue to be unable to concentrate on anything very well during the day, and sooner or later my co-workers will see that I am becoming woefully inefficient, and they will not want me on this job." Perfectly sane, this sentence; nothing crazy about it at all.

P: And the ridiculously false statement that I am saying to myself?

T: The false statement is: "If, because my testing procedure doesn't work and I am functioning inefficiently on my job, my co-workers do not want me or approve of me, then I shall be a worthless person."

P: But wouldn't I be worthless—good for nothing—if I couldn't work properly on this or any other job and no one wanted to associate with me professionally?

T: No. You would then be handicapped or inconvenienced. But your failure as a professional would have nothing to do with your intrinsic worth, or your value to yourself.

P: But what good *would* I be to myself if I couldn't do the kind of work I wanted to do and get the results I wanted to get?

T: You would then be of very great worth to yourself—as long as you were still alive and had any possibility of being happy, of enjoying yourself.

P: But how could I be happy and enjoy myself if I couldn't do what I most want to do?

T: Why couldn't you be? A blind man probably wants to see more than he wants to do anything else in the world. But does that mean that all blind men are desperately unhappy?

P: No, I suppose not. But they're not very happy either, I imagine.

T: No, not about their being blind. But they *can* be happy about many other aspects of life. And many of them, who have a good philosophy, are happy; and many of them, who have a poor philosophy, are not. So you, let us say, would not be able to do the thing you wanted most, if you were unable to perfect your testing procedure and continue to be fully appreciated at your firm. Tough! Look how many other things you could do in life to enjoy yourself. Besides, how does your being useless *to your firm*—which we are still assuming that you would be--prove that you are worthless *to yourself*?

P: But if *I* want to do what my firm also wants me to do, and I am useless to them, aren't I also useless to me?

T: No—not unless you *think* you are. You are frustrated, of course, if you want to set up a good testing procedure and you can't. But need you be desperately unhappy because you are frustrated? And need you deem yourself completely unworthwhile because you can't do one of the main things you want to do in life?

P: No, I guess not. But most people who can't do the main thing they want to do in life *do* feel pretty worthless, don't they?

T: Yes, they probably do. But *need* they? Most intelligent people believe various kinds of superstitions, and thereby more or less sabotage themselves. But do they *have* to?

P: Hmm—.

T: Well, do they *have* to?

P: No, of course they don't.

T: Then why do you? Why do you have to believe perhaps the biggest of all superstitions—that being non-achieving or being frustrated equals your being worthless, undeserving of life or happiness?

P: But how do I *not* believe this, uh, superstition as you call it?

T: How the devil do you keep *believing* it? It's obviously definitional, that you are no damn good when you aren't doing well at work. And this definitional premise obviously does you no good whatever, and causes you, instead, immense pain and harm. Now how, under the circumstances, can you go on *believing* this definitional drivel?

P: That's a good question! How do I?

T: You know. You're just not bothering to probe and find out. Now how does anyone, especially someone who is as well educated psychologically as you, and who can usually think in an intelligent, logical manner, believe utter nonsense?

P: Well, as the Freudians and learning theorists would say, by imbibing the nonsense early in his life, particularly from my parents.

T: Right. But how does one, after *originally* learning that he is no damn good because his parents think that he is when he doesn't do things their way, *keep* believing this balderdash for the rest of his life, even when he no longer has contact with these parents?

P: Well, obviously, I guess by re-suggesting these things to himself after he has once learned them.

T: Right again. By continued autosuggestion, or self-talk, the individual internalizes the parent-inculcated notion that he is worthless unless he is a perfect achiever, and he keeps repeating this idea over and over to himself, without ever stopping to ask: "*Why* am I intrinsically worthless if I fail to please others, or even if I fail to do what I want to do in life? What is the *proof* that my parents' proposition ever was or will be true?"

P: So if I go to work tomorrow morning, even after a poor night's sleep again, and ask myself, "*Why* will I be no good if my testing procedure fails and I do poor work generally and I even lose my job?"—I will, uh, find no sensible answer to this question.

T: Exactly. For there *is* no reason why failure at your work will make you—or anyone else, for that matter—a worthless slob. Only your *thinking* yourself such a slob will really make you one—by definition. What is more, there is no good reason why, if you get over defining yourself as worthless whenever there is even the possibility of your failing at an important task, you have to keep waking up in the middle of the night in a cold sweat as you have recently been doing.

P: Oh? What sentences have I been telling myself to cause *that* condition?

T: Can't you guess or infer them? Try to figure them out, right now.

P: Hmm. I guess I've been saying something like: "Three A.M.! A few more hours and I'll have to get up and go to work again. And that blankety-blank testing procedure, which maybe I should have stayed away from trying to devise in the first place, will be up for appraisal and validation again. And it may not work or may only partly do the job it's supposed to do.

Won't *that* be terrible! What a nincompoop they will think me! God—!"

T: Say, that's very good! I told you that you could get at these sentences yourself, and now with very little training or effort in doing so, you've come up with quite a batch of them. Just keep that up, and soon you'll be out of the neurotic woods.

P: You know, I could really *feel* those sentences, just as I was saying them right now. I could feel myself getting upset, right this minute, as I re-evoked them.

T: And can you also see how silly these sentences are, now that you have brought them to light?

P: You mean, how it really *won't* be terrible if the people I work with think me a nincompoop?

T: Yes.

P: Well, to be honest, I see it a little. But I guess I mainly still believe it—believe that it *will* be.

T: All right, that's the next step—to see that it *won't* be terrible if this rejection of you by your associates actually does occur. You've just been able to take the first important step— to see *what* you're saying to yourself to cause your current disturbance, or at least a large part of it. Now you're ready for the next step: to logically parse, and to question and vigorously challenge what you're saying to yourself.

P: I must convince myself, then, that even though it would be highly *inconvenient* for me to have my associates disapprove of my work, and especially of this new testing procedure I've been devising, it won't be *terrible* if they do disapprove?

T: Exactly. You've got to see that the inconvenience and frustration of being disapproved or even fired from your job have nothing at all to do with your personal worth as a human being. For isn't that *really* what's terrible if you were to lose the respect of your associates—not that your income but that your *prestige* would suffer, and that you would *interpret* this loss of prestige as a black mark against your inner worthiness?

P: Yes, the more I think of it, the more right I think you are. The "terribleness" of the situation is the low esteem that I would have of *myself* if this eventuality occurred.

T: And *need* you have this low estimation of yourself even
if you *do* wake up in the middle of the night sweating, if you
are at a low working ebb the next day, and if you *do* eventually
lose your job because you are not functioning properly or your
testing procedure doesn't work too well?

P: No, I guess not. In fact, uh, yes, I'm really beginning to
see, I think, really beginning to feel not. I *don't* have to hate
myself when I fail to sleep well, work well, or get others to
like me. I don't!

T: Fine. You really are beginning to see this, I'm sure. Now,
how do you feel right now, at *this* moment?

P: Sort of like, well, a weight has been lifted from me, a big
weight that was pressing down on my head.

T: See what happens when you challenge and change your
own sentences! Just a couple of minutes ago, you were saying
to yourself, and unfortunately convincing yourself, "But it *is*
terrible if my associates reject me." And you *felt* pretty awful.
But now you are beginning to ask yourself, "But *is* it really so
terrible? Why *can't* I like me, whether or not others approve of
my work?" And now you're beginning to *feel* much better.

P: Yes, it's amazing. I am! And I can always do this same
sort of thing, this changing of my sentences and changing of
my feelings of awfulness with the sentences?

T: Why not? Is your feeling of awfulness really much more
than the sentences which you compose to create it? Is your
feeling of worthlessness basically different from your self-
depreciating words, phrases, and paragraphs about yourself?

P: It's all as simple as *that?* My God, what was my first analyst
doing all those years that I saw him, if he couldn't even see
and show me this simple thing?

T: Maybe he was telling himself his *own* nonsensical sentences
that helped him obscure what was really going on in your head.
But anyway, that's *his* problem. What are *you* going to do about
your sentences, now that you are beginning to see how intimately
they are connected with your feelings of anxiety and anguish?

P: I guess they need a lot of working on.

T: I guess they do. And not only your original sentences,

mind you, such as "Wouldn't it be terrible if my testing procedure didn't work and they fired me?" But also your secondary
and tertiary sentences that you build on top of these original
ones. Such as: "Isn't it terrible that I now wake up every middle
of the night and lie here and sweat?" And: "Isn't it awful that,
after not being able to sleep last night, and lying like a fool
sweating in bed, I now am so tired that I can't think straight
today?" These additional sentences, or the blame that you heap
on yourself for first being self-blaming and hence neurotic, do
as much, or more, damage as the original sentences. And the
vicious circle goes on and on.

P: It never ends, does it?

T: No, it never ends—until you end it. Blame is the essence
of virtually all emotional disorder. And you, and only you,
can stop your own blaming.

P: Goddam it, I'm determined to. I really am! I think I've
learned more about myself in these three sessions with you than
I did in my whole previous four years of analysis. And what's
even better, I think I can now see how to *use* this knowledge
effectively. And I shall!

This patient did begin to use her new knowledge of
herself and her own self-blaming, and within another month
she was sleeping peacefully each night and only occasionally
during the day giving herself a hard time about how well she
was doing at work. Her testing procedure, although it worked
reasonably well, never did exactly fill the bill as she and her
associates would have liked to see it do; but she took her
partial disappointment (and theirs) in her stride and refused
to devalue herself because of it. She is now (two years later)
working more efficiently than ever before in her life; but, even
more importantly, she is accepting herself as a worthwhile
human being even when she does poorly at the office or at
home. As she said to me at a recent professional meeting where
we met and talked for a few moments:

"Not only do I now see quite clearly that my worth to myself
is not really related to what other people think of me, but I am
able, by believing this and acting on it, to get the same idea over

to my 13-year-old daughter, who is a very bright girl but used to be on the terribly worrying side. And getting *her* to see that she is a valuable person no matter what anyone else, even I and her father, think of her is the most gratifying experience I have ever had in my life. The sessions with you would have been well worth it if they had resulted in nothing else."

I, too, was happy that this patient's new attitudes toward her own worth were being extended, as well, to the emotional education of her daughter. For in the last analysis, the concept that human beings are valuable because they exist and because they may creatively become what they would like to become (no matter *what* other people think they *should* become) is more of an educational than a psychotherapeutic question. It is far better that we rear people with this idea early in their lives than that we painfully attempt to re-educate them in a latter-day psychotherapeutic experience.

After reading the above material on personal worth, Dr. Robert A. Harper of Washington, D. C., agreed with the spirit of the material but thought it was on too high a philosophic plane for the most effective use with many patients. As a more down-to-earth approach for use with many self-depreciating individuals, he suggested the following therapeutic attack:

"Every person who is still voluntarily alive is, regardless of what he may *say* that he believes, *acting* on the assumption that life is worth living. Correspondingly, the belief that life *is* worth living *is* nothing *but* an assumption for every living human. No one has *proof* that life is worth living, for he has never experienced anything but life, has no extrinsic measuring rod, and therefore has no basis of comparing life and non-life. Hence, the person who by his voluntary continuance of living is acting out his belief that life is worth living has nothing more than his subjective impression to go on.

"The silliest of questions, therefore, is the commonly heard one: 'Is life worth living?' It is silly because (*a*) the questioner has already answered the question affirmatively in *action*, or he would be dead; and (*b*) the person to whom the question is asked has never experienced non-living and consequently has no more insight into the whole matter of the 'worth of living' than has the questioner.

"So, since everyone who is still alive is acting on the *assumption* that life is worth living, it follows that the assumer, the individual person, *is* (or at least *thinks* he is) of worth. Since, by continuing to live, I am expressing my belief that life is worth living, then—so long as I continue to hold to this assumption—I *must* be worthwhile. Why? Because the only way *I* can experience life (which I believe to be worthwhile) is through *me*. I am the only channel or container or instrument of getting to this worthwhile process for me—therefore, I, as the only possible channel to life for me, have to be (as long as I continue to live) worthwhile. There is no getting around the fact that by just *being* I am worthwhile—so long as I hold to the belief that *life* is of value.

"Suppose I decide that life is not really worth the candle and that I am not really worthwhile. Then, if I truly believe this, I shall kill myself or arrange for someone else to kill me. But my suicidally negative answer about the worthwhileness of life and me will still be an assumption, an acting out of a belief. I will not have *proved* to myself or others that life is worthless. I shall have simply, by my moribund condition, asserted my *assumption* that life and I are not worthwhile. But, so long as I am alive (and, hence, acting out my belief that life *is* worth something), I'd better (for my own enjoyment and satisfaction) face the inevitable corollary that I—just by being, existing, living —am worthwhile, too.

"As a practitioner of rational-emotive psychotherapy, I have faced this question of life and self-worth with many patients. Some of them have actually been on the verge of committing suicide (rather than just talking about doing so). I have faced them with the attitude: 'Suicide is certainly your privilege, as I see it. I will not in any way try to prevent your exercising this privilege. But there is no proof that either life *or* death is a worthwhile experience. No live person has ever really been dead. And no dead person has ever returned to compare the life and death processes for us. Those of us who are alive, however, can observe that death seems to be a very *final* process insofar as any individual is concerned. So, though I have no intention of stopping you from dying, wouldn't something less finally drastic *within* the confines of the life process be worth assuming or believing in, and wouldn't it be better if you tried this life process more efficiently and intensively *before* you kill yourself?'

"Thus far, maybe only by chance, all my patients have chosen to give life a further try. I say 'maybe only by chance,' but I really believe that suicide is often a rebellious—'I'll-show-the-sons-of-bitches!'—way of acting-out. When the therapist gives the patient a free ticket and says, 'Feel free to take the trip, but it looks like a *very* long ride,' the starch is usually taken out of the patient's rebellion.

"Getting back to the belief that life is at least potentially worthwhile (and, hence, rationally accepting that this very belief *makes* the individual valuable to himself), I find that once patients are convinced that they are worthy just by *being*, they stop feeling so anxious about accomplishment. They, then, no longer think that they must be perfectly achieving in what they do or don't do. This is true because their previous anxiety to achieve, to be loved, to set the world on fire, originated in the underlying feeling (belief) that 'only in this way can I become worthwhile.' Or it originated in the even sicker and perhaps more common self-sentence: 'I am basically and will forever remain no damn good; but, if I behave perfectly, I may fool people into believing that I am worthwhile; while, if I fail to keep fooling them, my life will be dreadful, awful, and intolerable.'

"Until recently, I would ask my patients to prove they were worthless—which they, of course, could not do. But then I had to admit that I could not prove they were worthwhile; and this seemed to me to be too weak a rejoinder to their not being able to prove they were worthless. So neither of us proved *anything*—and the brighter patients would tend to think (and say): 'If you can't prove that I am worthwhile, it may just be your bet that I have value and my bet that I do not. Neither of us really seems to know what he's talking about. So why should I believe you?'

"Now, however, I show my patient that since he is *alive*, he fundamentally is betting that life is worth living and he must therefore admit that the only source of life for him—namely, himself—is valuable so long as he keeps on living. There is no need of his proving *anything* to himself or anybody else. Let him, rather, find out how he, by definition a worthwhile human being, can enjoy life (which we *all* seem to assume can be an enjoyable process) more than he now is. So I say again: let's stop asking silly questions and get on with the question of how to improve the process of living—how to enjoy life more, be happier."

Another way of looking at an individual's worth has been worked out by Dr. Edwin E. Wagner (personal communication), who notes that feelings of worthlessness and depression result when the individual makes a special kind of internalized verbalization—namely, that (a) he is unable, because of his essential inadequacy, to handle his life situations and get what he wants, and (b) he will *always* be inadequate and incompetent and therefore will *never* get what he wants. Or, putting this differently, the individual tells himself not only (a) that he is inadequate, but (b) that he is *hopelessly* inadequate. And, in terms of the world around him, the depressed individual tells himself (a) that conditions are pretty awful, and (b) that they will *always* be awful and will *never* get any better.

Although the (a) sentences in the preceding paragraph may at least in part be true—since the individual *may* be inadequate in the present situation and world conditions *may* be pretty bad—the (b) sentences are unsupported by objective evidence, since there is no proof that the individual is *hopelessly* inadequate or that conditions will *always* be bad. As Ayer (1947) and Stevenson (in Feigl and Sellars, 1949) point out, absolutistic statements, such as that an individual is hopelessly inadequate or that the world will never get any better are largely emotive or unverifiable propositions that constitute personal value judgments of the individual making such statements, and that cannot ultimately be supported (or disproven) by any empirical evidence. One has a perfect right to make such statements, if one chooses to do so; but they say little or nothing about the objective world.

Emotive or absolutistic postulates, however, can have a significant effect on the individuals making such statements. If one *believes* that one is hopelessly inadequate, one will feel depressed—and will not try more adequately to cope with an existing situation. If one does not believe this emotive, unverifiable statement, one probably will try to cope with a difficult world situation—and, very probably, one will often succeed. Assumptions that one is essentially worthless are, at bottom, sentences that have no factual meaning but that may have pernicious results. They are metaphysical postulates that are most likely to lead to much harm and little good. It would seem to be much the better part of both valor and wisdom to refrain from making such unverifiable assumptions.

9

Reason and Unconscious Thinking*

In the old days, before Sigmund Freud and his most ardent
disciples came along to make an involved depth-analysis of
every man's motives, the word "unconscious" simply meant
unremembered or out of immediate awareness. Thus, the well-
known Gothic novelist, Matthew G. Lewis, wrote in the preface
to his novel, *The Monk*, which was published in 1796:

> The first idea of this Romance was suggested by the story of the
> *Santon Barsisa*, related in The Guardian.—The *Bleeding Nun* is a
> tradition still credited in many parts of Germany; and I have been
> told, that the ruins of the castle of *Lauenstein*, which she is supposed
> to haunt, may yet be seen upon the borders of *Thuringa*.—The *Water-
> King*, from the third to the twelfth stanza, is the fragment of an origi-
> nal Danish ballad—and *Belerma and Durandarte* is translated from
> some stanzas to be found in a collection of old Spanish poetry, which
> contains also the popular song of *Gayferos and Melesindra*, mentioned
> in Don Quixote.—I have now made a full avowal of all the plagiarisms
> of which I am aware myself; but I doubt not, many more may be
> found, of which I am at present totally unconscious.

Freud, then, hardly invented the notion of unconscious thinking; he merely expanded and deepened it so that today "unconscious" has largely come to mean that which is deeply and
almost inaccessibly buried in one's psyche and that is the prime
mover of almost all one's important desires. It has also come
to imply a chain of crucial events in one's early life, such as
one's Oedipal attachment to one's mother and father, which
one has long ago deliberately repressed because of the pain
attached to experiencing these events, which now lie at the root

* This chapter is adapted from a talk, "Hidden Problems of Sex and
Violence," given at Cooper Union, New York City, November 30, 1960.

of one's emotional problems, and which must now be painstakingly brought to light by a longwinded psychoanalytic process of free association, dream analysis, and working through the transference relationship with a trained analyst.

An unconscious thought or feeling, in other words, has often come to mean, today, an idea or emotion that (*a*) the person knows about but whose origins are quite unknown and unacceptable to him; or (*b*) the person is unaware of having because he is consciously ashamed to acknowledge its existence. This psychoanalytically-inspired definition of unconscious psychical processes may be all very well as far as it goes—but it does not go far enough to suit my own clinical or theoretical tastes. For I have found in the course of my psychotherapeutic practice of the last two decades that there are many unconscious aspects of human behavior that do not quite come under the heading of seriously repressed or deeply buried feelings and motives. I would contend, instead, that emotional disturbances are largely caused by hidden ideas and feelings—but that the unconscious or unaware ideologies that lead us to behave neurotically are usually by no means as deeply or mysteriously hidden as the classical psychoanalysts stubbornly still believe.

I contend, instead, that what is importantly hidden in most instances where the individual is emotionally disturbed is not the facts of his problems, nor the whys and wherefores of his originally acquiring these problems. Rather, it is the *present* causation of his difficulties that is truly unknown to him; and this causation is *not* deeply hidden but can, in almost all instances, be quickly brought to consciousness. Therefore, I hold, even the most unconscious thoughts can be forthrightly understood, tackled, and the emotional problems that they create solved—providing that the disturbed person and his therapist are not so dogmatically afflicted with so-called depth-centered prejudices that they steadfastly refuse to see the unconscious thinking processes (which Freud early in his writings called the preconscious processes) that are practically right under their noses.

To be more specific, let me cite a case in point. Several years ago I saw a successful young business man who was convinced that he was thoroughly impotent, because he had failed miserably with the last two girls with whom he had attempted sex relations. He had read some psychoanalytic literature and excitedly began to tell me about his early life: particularly about his lustful feelings for his mother when he was eight years of age, his incestuous relations with his young aunt when he was twelve, and his youthful fear of his father's catching him in the act of masturbation. To his surprise, I wasn't too interested in this material from his childhood; and I was even less enthused when he started to tell me about some long, involved sexual dreams.

Seeing how deflated he was—for these psychoanalytically-biased patients frequently become depressed when I cold-bloodedly deprive them of the pleasure of spewing out the gory details of their early love-lives—I explained that I was more interested in one fact that he was ignoring completely: namely, that for the last two decades he had been having a great time sexually, in spite of Oedipus feelings, overt incest, castration fears, etc., and that only very recently, after two consecutive failures, had he evinced any impotence problems.

"How come," I asked this patient, "that all these horrible Freudian complexes that you are parceling out for my edification didn't bollix up your sex life long before this? The way you've been alley-catting around for the last 15 years would put even a Wilhelm Reichian to shame. And yet you seem to be convinced that your lust after your mother at the age of eight totally blighted your life. How come?"

The patient was momentarily stumped. Whereupon I went into my usual rational-emotive approach and began to show him that his early life and parent-transmitted ideologies had little to do, at the moment, with his sex problem. Rather, I insisted, it was his own currently hanging on to and actively reindoctrinating himself with early-inculcated hogwash that was now negatively affecting him.

"What do you mean?" he bewilderedly asked.

"I simply mean," I replied, "that virtually all emotional disturbance is as simple as A-B-C—if you clearly see the A-B-C of what is occurring to you. At point A something happens—the girl you are with, for example, makes a comment about the small size of your sex organs or indicates that she is difficult to satisfy sexually and that perhaps you're not going to make the grade. At point C, you become impotent. Erroneously, then, you believe that A causes C—that her remarks cause you to fail sexually. Or else you believe that quite another kind of A—the fact, for example, that you lusted after your mother at the age of eight and are still guilty about this—causes your impotence at point C. Actually, however, A has very little to do with causing C."

"What does cause C, or my impotence, then?" my patient asked.

"B does," I replied. "And B is what you tell yourself—and in this case the utter nonsense you tell yourself—about A. Thus, instead of saying to yourself, 'OK, so she thinks I have a small sex organ; but I can still use it effectively to satisfy her and myself with,' or instead of telling yourself, 'Well, maybe she is difficult to satisfy sexually, but I can still try. If I succeed, fine; and if I don't that will just be too bad, but not catastrophic,' you are obviously telling yourself something like: 'Oh, my God! How terrible it is that she thinks I have a small set of genitals!' or 'Wouldn't it be positively awful if I were not able to satisfy her sexually and she thought I was no darned good?' And by telling yourself these catastrophizing, utterly false sentences at point B, you bring about, yes, literally bring about, your impotent results at point C."

"But doesn't my early upbringing have anything to do with this at all, even if what you say is true and I am now telling myself the things you say I am?"

"Yes, it has something to do with what you're now telling yourself at B. Because, obviously, you weren't born thinking this catastrophizing nonsense at B, and you must have learned it somewhere. It is not greatly important to know, however, that you originally learned it when you were taught to be guilty about lusting after your mother or having sex relations with your aunt or when you were afraid that your father would castrate you. The main and much more important thing is that you've *continued*, for the last fifteen years or so, to tell yourself the same kind of false statements that you were originally taught to say. And it is your *reiteration* of these statements that *now* keeps them alive and perpetuates the illogical things you are telling yourself at point B."

"But why are these things that I'm telling myself so illogical? *Wasn't* it terrible for me to lust after my mother when I was eight; and *isn't* it now awful when my sex partner makes critical remarks about the size of my sex organs?"

"Absolutely not. It was perfectly normal and natural for you to lust after your mother when you were a child; and even if you did some socially wrong acts, such as having relations with your aunt, it is certainly expectable for children and adults to be fallible and make sex mistakes. To blame yourself unceasingly for making such mistakes is certainly self-defeating and illogical. And although it is undesirable if the girl you are with feels that your sex organs are too small, it is not, as I noted before, necessarily catastrophic; and you can still enjoy yourself with her or with some other girl if you stop telling yourself that her remarks and feelings about you are horrendous."

"Then," asked my patient, "even though the things that happen to me at point A—such as my lusting after my mother or my having a girl make nasty comments on the size of my sex organs —are undesirable, they do not necessarily have to lead to poor results, such as my own impotence, at point C unless I tell myself that these undesirable events are horrible, awful, and unforgivable? Is that right?"

"Yes," I replied, "that's exactly right. And if I can convince you, really convince you, that all your emotional upsets, including this symptom of impotence that you are now so concerned about, result from what you tell yourself at point B, instead of what other people say or think or do at point A, then you will be able to question and challenge your own self-repeated nonsense, and will quickly stop upsetting yourself."

So it actually happened. Within three weeks, my patient began to regain his potency and was soon a better sexual performer than he had ever been. What is perhaps more important, much to his surprise he began to admit that he had had, for many years, many nonsexual problems, especially the problem of being shy and weak in many social and business situations. And along with working on his sex problem, he began to work on the other things he was telling himself to create his social and business shyness, and he improved appreciably. I have spoken to him every once in a while since that time (as he calls me from time to time to refer new patients) and he has maintained his improvement for the last four years and, as far as his impotence is concerned, seems to be completely cured.

The main point of this case is that the patient's sex problem was quite conscious when he came to treatment, since he was thoroughly aware that he had it. Nor were some of the important early origins of his problem hidden from him, as he had worked them out for himself as a result of some of his psychoanalytic reading. But he was quite unconscious of the most important element in his disturbed history: namely, the simple exclamatory sentences—the highly illogical, catastrophizing sentences—that he kept telling himself at point B. And when these hidden sentences were brought to light during the first several sessions of rational-emotive therapy, and he was shown exactly how they were defeating his ends and causing his current impotence, he was able to change these sentences and improve significantly.

I contend that this is the usual case in emotional difficulties. The problem itself is not too often hidden; and the original source of the problem may be either known or be irrelevant to its solution. Thus, to know that your present sex difficulty is traceable to your early Oedipus complex is frequently to have little help in ridding yourself of this difficulty. But if the exact phrases and sentences which you are *now* telling yourself to create and sustain this sex problem are known, its eradication becomes quite feasible.

Let me further illustrate this thesis with a problem of violence. In this particular case, that of a 35 year old housewife, the problem itself was hidden: since this woman came for therapy because she had severe tension headaches and did not realize, at the outset, that she violently hated her role as a housewife and frequently thought of murdering the youngest of her three children. It was only after I forcefully pointed out to her that, on theoretical grounds, she must be violently hating some persons or things if she were getting the physical tensions she was experiencing, that she began to admit to me and herself that she was terribly hostile to her husband, her children, and the world at large. She then gave me a hair-curling story of how she frequently took naps during the day and, when in between a state of sleeping and waking, dreamed of losing her two-year-old daughter on a heavily trafficked street, or scalding her by mistake, or otherwise maiming or killing her.

Significantly enough, this same patient also recollected, after I had induced her to reveal her murderous thoughts about her child, that she had never consciously permitted herself to masturbate when she was a teenager, but that she had often found herself doing so when she was in the same kind of a half-waking, half-sleeping state that she now employed for her sadistic fantasies.

At first blush, this seemed to be another juicy case for the classical psychoanalyst's sofa: since my patient had been severely rejected by her own mother, when she was a child, and had had distinct sexual feelings, with considerable guilt, when her father, to whom she was closely attached, rocked her on his knees and was physically affectionate to her. In my former days as a practicing analyst, I would have had little hesitation in interpreting to her that she identified with her own daughter and wanted to punish this little girl for the sins which she herself had committed during her childhood; and that, instead of being a responsible wife and mother, she wanted to remain a child-wife to her husband, just as she had been something of a child-wife to her father, and she bitterly resented the husband and her housewifely responsibilities when he refused to allow her to play this kind of a childish role.

I did, very mildly, point out these connections between this patient's past history and her present violent resentment of her young daughter. But, being a wiser if not sadder therapist than I was when I practiced classical analysis some years ago, I did not over-emphasize this transference from the patient's past to her present. And, as is so often the case, I found that although the patient was more than willing to accept this kind of interpretation, and agree that she identified with her young daughter and still wanted to be a child-wife to her father-surrogate husband, her newly found insight into these origins of her disturbance did her very little if any good. She still came to me for session after session, saying that she had the same murderous thoughts and fantasies about her daughter.

I then tried a more active-directive RT-type approach with this patient, and attempted to show her that, whatever had happened to her in the past with her mother and father, the real cause of her *present* disturbance was her telling herself, at point B, such sentences as: "It is *still* terrible that I received sex pleasure with my father; and I must atone for my sin by punishing myself and my young daughter and bringing down death and destruction on both our heads." And: "It is horribly unfair that I have to take care of my house, husband, and three children, and not be the irresponsible girl I was when I was a little child and Daddy took good care of me. Things *shouldn't* be this awful way and I'll be damned if I let them continue to be." And again: "My little daughter is a great bother and she *shouldn't* behave the way she does when I have so many things to do and so many enormous responsibilities to take care of. I'll fix her for being such a bother!"

At first, as is often true, my patient was reluctant to admit that she was telling herself these kinds of sentences. But I kept proving to her, time and again, that if she were getting the results she was getting, there was simply no way that she could get them *except* by telling herself this kind of nonsense. Thus, she came to see me one day and said that her headaches had been nonexistent for an entire week, but then, just the night before she saw me, she got a dreadful one again.

"What were you telling yourself," I asked, "just before you began to get this dreadful headache?"

"Nothing," she answered. "Nothing at all."

"That's quite impossible," I said. "First of all, we never tell ourselves nothing, but are ceaselessly thinking—that is, saying internalized sentences to ourselves—about something. Secondly, if you got this tension headache again, you must, on theoretical grounds, have been telling yourself something, since there is no magic, and neurotic symptoms must have *some* cause. Now *what* were you telling yourself?"

"Well I remember, now that you make me think about it, that I was telling myself something before the headache started—for a whole week before it started, in fact."

"And what was that?"

"I kept telling myself—just as you had shown me how to do in these sessions—that it *wasn't* terrible and awful the way my young daughter was acting; that she *should* be a frightful pain in the neck at times; and that it *wasn't* horribly unfair if she made me, by being as young and helpless as she is, assume lots of uninteresting work and responsibility that I frankly can't get enthused about assuming."

"And what happened when you kept telling yourself these kinds of sentences?"

"Well, as I said before, I had the best week I've had in years. In fact, I can't remember any time in my whole life when I've felt so good and so free from nervous or physical tension. It certainly worked like a charm, those sentences!"

"Fine. But then what happened to get you to change them? Where did you go off again?"

"Hmm. Let me see. All day yesterday everything was great. Little Linda, if anything, was a real pain, since she had a difficult day, spilled most of the food I gave her, and howled like hell even when I was patient. But I still kept telling myself that that's the way she is, children are like that, and it's too darned bad but that's the way they are. And it went fine. Then Joe came home at six. And—let me see—"

"Yes, what happened when Joe came home?"

"Hmm. Oh, yes. I remember now! He had had a rough day at work. And, seeing that I was in an unusually good mood, he began to take things out a bit on me. Told me some things, some critical things about my not being such a good cook and stuff like that, that he said he had been saving up for awhile and hadn't dared to open up about before. And, well, before I knew it he was going at it full blast. And I—yes! that's it. Now I really remember. I took his guff for a short time, but then I said to myself: 'Damn it all! Here I behave so well with Linda, who is just a child, and accept all her guff all day; and now Joe, who is certainly old enough to know better, and whom I married just because he wasn't, at least not then, critical, now he gives me worse than the child does. How unfair! And after I've been so good for a whole week. I really don't deserve this!"

"Ah," I said, as my patient's voice rose with excitement and the color of her cheeks rose in unison with the feelings she was now re-living, "so you *did* say something to yourself just before your dreadful headache started!"

"Yes," she sheepishly smiled. "I guess I did. And *how* I did! Now I see what you're talking about. I guess it's always this way: whenever I do well for awhile, then I think that I more than ever deserve to have everything my way, and less than ever deserve to be criticized or disapproved. So at the slightest provocation, at those times, I go into my resentful spell and bring on a tension headache."

"Exactly. You revert, under those circumstances, to your usual philosophy: that it is totally unfair and horrible that you, especially when you have been a good girl for awhile, do not get your own way. And you protest this supposed unfairness and horror with a vengeance. But the vengeance, unfortunately, is directed mostly against yourself."

"How right you are! It's certainly clear to me now. I really must keep after that philosophy of mine, mustn't I?"

And she did, this patient, keep after her own philosophy, and the oft-repeated internalized sentences of which it consisted. A few months later she not only had no more murderous thoughts about her child, but got along better with her husband, her other children, and many other friends and relatives. Her unconscious thoughts of violence were no longer under cover;

and, more importantly, the concrete self-sentences which she used to create her violence were themselves clearly revealed during the rational-emotive therapeutic process and she was able consciously to question and challenge them until she no longer subscribed to their fallacious formulations.

Time and again, in the course of RT, thoughts and feelings that appear to be deeply unconscious are quickly revealed as the patient's arbitrary moralizing, his blaming and punishing himself or others, is brought to light and vigorously challenged. As the patient, because of this rational attack on his moralizing tendencies, begins to acquire a philosophy of non-blaming, and to accept himself and others as "worthwhile" humans because he and they exist and are alive, he loses almost all his incentives for keeping his problems hidden and is freely able to admit and express them openly. The force—which Freud called the super-ego but which can more operationally be defined as arbitrary and vigorous self-blame—which induces him to repress or avoid looking at his own wrongdoings is therapeutically undone, and his dire need to remain unconscious of some of his most significant thoughts, feelings, and actions is evaporated.

Let me give another illustrative case. A few years ago I saw a 31 year old male who had some of the most extreme unconscious tendencies toward sex violence that I have encountered in my fairly long history as a psychotherapist. He was compulsively promiscuous, both before and after his marriage to a charming woman whom he said that he really loved; and his sex compulsivity often took the form of his following a young girl or an older woman on a dark street late at night, rudely and crudely propositioning her and, if she did not immediately give in to his overtures, violently beating her and then running away. Later on, when he began to see how dangerous this procedure was, he modified it by not making any sexual propositions to his victims, but merely sneaking up behind them and beating them without any provocation whatever.

Although this patient, surprisingly enough, was never caught in the course of making a dozen different attacks on women, his wife became suspicious of his bruised condition on a few occasions, and he gave her a partial account of what had been going on. In talking the matter over with her, he agreed to go for classical psychoanalytic treatment; and he remained in this treatment for six years on a three to five times a week basis. His analyst convinced him that he had great unconscious feelings of hostility against his mother, who he thought had favored his older brother over him, and encouraged him to acknowledge and release this pent-up hostility, so that he would not have to take it out on other women.

Accordingly, the patient began to stand up to his mother in no uncertain terms. He told her that he had always hated her for favoring his brother, and finally broke with her completely. At the same time, encouraged by his analyst, he fought violently with his brother, his father, and his business partner; and presumably he thereby released an enormous amount of pent-up aggression.

Unfortunately, this kind of treatment, although highly gratifying to the patient, worked only moderately well. When he came to see me he was still occasionally attacking women on the streets; and, more to the point, he had recently burned down his house, in order to collect on an insurance policy, and had almost killed his six-year-old daughter whom he had allowed to stay in the burning house for a while in order to make the fire appear more authentic. Obviously, this patient still had serious problems of sex and violence; and although ostensibly the reasons for these problems were no longer hidden, but had been psychoanalytically tracked down to his hostility to his mother, the problems still persisted.

I quickly took a different tack with this patient than his previous therapist had taken and attempted to show him, right at the start, that he was not just hostile to women, but to virtually everyone; and that his hostility would never evaporate by his honestly admitting and continuing to release it overtly against his mother or anyone else. He had, I insisted, a general philosophy that kept bolstering his hostility; and that was the grandiose view, which he had derived in childhood and now unconsciously *kept* repeating to himself over and over again, that people (especially those who were close to him) *should* love him above all others, and *should* accede to his reasonable or unreasonable demands. Instead of believing, as any sane person would, that it would be *nice* or *pleasant* if others approved him or did his bidding, he ceaselessly kept convincing himself that it was *necessary* and *mandatory* that they do so, and (as a natural corollary of this silly belief) that they were no-good skunks if they did not always love and help him.

Peculiarly enough, this patient's psychoanalytical therapy had helped him retain and deepen his grandiose and hostile convictions: since his analyst apparently also believed that a person's mother *should* love all her children equally; that she is a no-good bitch if she does not; and that she therefore deserves to be dealt with in a hostile manner. Contrary to this previous psychoanalytic training, I endeavored to show the patient that there *was* no reason why his mother should have loved him—nor any reason, for that matter, why anyone in the world should give him the things or the love he would *like* to have. Although I had considerable difficulty in getting him to see and accept this point, I persisted in revealing and attacking his grandiose philosophy of life. He finally came to me one day and said:

"I'm beginning to see now what you mean by not blaming others for their mistakes and wrongdoings. My mother called me up the other day—the first time in a year that she has dared to do so, after I gave her a real piece of my mind the last time I spoke to her—and she started going on as usual, after at first being nice for a few minutes, about how I wasn't getting anywhere in life, how terrible it was that I was still going for psychotherapy, and all that kind of jazz. I began, as usual, to feel my temperature rising and I was all set to tell her off again.

"But then I said, as you have been teaching me to do, 'What am I telling *myself* to make me get so angry at this poor woman? *She's* not making me mad; *I* am.' And I could see right away that I was telling myself that she shouldn't be the nagging, bitchy type of woman that she is and has always been. So I said to myself: 'All right: *why* shouldn't she be the way she is and has always been?' And of course, just as you keep pointing out,

I couldn't find any good reason why she shouldn't be exactly as she is. For there isn't any such reason! Sure, it would be nice if she were approving, and calm, and everything else. But she isn't. And she's not going to be. And I don't *need* her to be, in order to get along well in the world myself.

"Well, as soon as I clearly saw *that*, all my anger against the old gal of course vanished. I tried, just as an experiment, to work it back up again, to get angry at her all over. But I just couldn't make it. Instead, I was very nice to her—much to her surprise, you can imagine!—and even invited her to my home for Christmas dinner—which I haven't done or even thought of doing for years now. And I felt so *good* about being able to do so. Not for her so much, I think; but for *me*. For now I really see that one doesn't have to agree with people like my mother, and think oneself a louse because *they* think you are; nor does one have to kick them in the teeth to try to disprove their views. There is a third way—that of calmly accepting them the way they are and not giving a fig about their bitchy remarks and attitudes. And that, the third way, is the one I intend to take from now on. And if I do, I am practically certain that I won't be having to attack women, men, or anyone else anymore."

All of which proved to be quite true. Several years have gone by since this patient terminated his therapy; and he has had no inclination whatever during this time to attack females, burn down houses, or do any of the violent sexual and nonsexual deeds he used to commit so often and so compulsively. His reasons for his previous sadistic fantasies and acts—which consisted not of his unconscious hostility toward his mother but of his underlying belief that virtually *everyone* in the world should approve him and do his bidding—no longer are hidden. He has brought his basic philosophies of life out into the open; and what is more significant, has been able logically to analyze, attack, and destroy these self-defeating philosophies. With his new—and much more conscious—value systems, he has no further need to be openly or covertly hostile toward others, and his violence has therefore lost its main supports.

In rational-emotive psychotherapy, then, the negative emotions of the individual are able to be fully revealed and acknowledged because the philosophic sources of these emotions are ruthlessly analyzed and counterattacked, so that they can be replaced with saner, more rewarding philosophies of living. Whereas most conventional forms of therapy only help the disturbed individual to acquire Insight No. 1, RT helps him to acquire and employ Insights No. 2 and 3 as well. Insight No. 1 is the usual kind of understanding that the Freudians make much of: namely, the individual's seeing that his present actions have a prior or antecedent cause. Thus, in the case of the patient just discussed, his first analyst showed him that his early hostility toward his mother was the prior and unconscious cause of some of his present hostility toward women.

Insight No. 2 is a deepened and more concrete extension of Insight No. 1: namely, the understanding that the irrational ideas acquired by the individual in his past life are still existent, and that they largely exist today because he himself keeps re-indoctrinating himself with these ideas—continuing, consciously or unconsciously, to tell himself (to use the case of this woman-attacking patient again) that his mother *is* no good, that she *should* love and approve him, that other people *should* give him his own way, and that they are villains if they don't.

Insight No. 3, which in many ways is even more important than Insights No. 1 and 2, but which also depends upon and is an extension of these first two insights, is the full understanding by the disturbed individual that he simply has got to change his erroneous and illogical thinking (which he derived from the past and is reiterating in the present). Thus, in the case just exposited, I not only had to show the woman-attacking patient that his old hatred of his mother stemmed from a childish philosophy that he *should* be catered to by others and that his present hostility toward his mother and other women resulted from his contemporary self-repetition of this childish view, but I also had to convince him that unless he forcefully challenged and questioned his past and present world-view, he could not possibly prevent himself from being hostile and from compulsively being driven to attack females.

This is usually true; and, unfortunately, is ignored or glossed over by perhaps the majority of modern psychotherapists. Unless the patient, after acquiring Insights No. 1 and 2, fully sees and accepts the fact that *there is no other way* for him to get better than his forcefully and consistently *attacking* his early-acquired and still heartily held irrational ideas, he will definitely not overcome his emotional disturbance. This is why so many individuals, who are seemingly full of insight, and who go for many years of intensive psychotherapy, do not help themselves appreciably. They face and accept Insight No. 1, and perhaps even Insight No. 2; but they do not see or accept Insight No. 3.

Rational-emotive psychotherapy, although it has often been accused of being less intensive and not as "deep" as classical psychoanalysis or other "depth-centered" therapies, is perhaps the deepest form of therapy presently known: because it particularly emphasizes the patient's acquiring Insights No. 1, 2, and 3; and because it insists on homework assignments, desensitizing and deconditioning actions both within and outside of the therapeutic sessions, and on other forms of active work on the part of the patient which help him to reinforce his Insights No. 1 and 2 and to put into actual practice Insight No. 3.

To the usual psychotherapeutic techniques of exploration, ventilation, excavation, and interpretation, the rational therapist adds the more direct techniques of confrontation, confutation, deindoctrination, and reëducation. He thereby frankly faces 'and resolutely tackles the most deep-seated and recalcitrant patterns of emotional disturbance.

10

Active-Directive Psychotherapy*

Most of the major and most highly publicized schools of psychotherapy, especially the classical Freudian school at one end of the scale and the Rogerian nondirective or client-centered school at the other end of the scale, roundly abjure active-directive modes of therapy and enthusiastically favor passive-indirect modes.

Devotees of these nondirective methods hold that patients must be very close to achieving significant insights for themselves before the therapist's interpretation can be effective; that a therapist's authoritarian presentation encourages continued dependency on the patient's part; that directive techniques are highly undemocratic and ethically unjustified; that the patient has enormous potentials for growth within himself and that this potential can be best released if the therapist is nondirective; and that other serious disadvantages ensue when the therapist is highly active or interpretive (Freud, 1924-1950; Rogers, 1951; Snyder, 1953).

On the other hand, psychotherapeutic theory and practice during the last decade have given a much greater emphasis to active-directive therapy than was true in the previous several decades (Ellis, 1955a). Several influential groups, such as the followers of Adler (1927, 1929), Alexander and French (1946), Reich (1949), Thorne (1950), and the hypnotherapists (Kline, 1955; Wolberg, 1948), have heartily advocated direct intervention by the therapists; and a good many modern theorists, such as Eysenck (1961), Herzberg (1945), Hunt (1962), Johnson (1946), Mowrer (1953), Perls, Hefferline, and Goodman (1951),

* This chapter is an expanded version of several comments on cases in Standal, Stanley W. and Corsini, Raymond, J. *Critical Incidents in Psychotherapy.* Engelewood Cliffs, N. J. : Prentice-Hall, 1959.

Phillips (1956), Salter (1949), Salzinger (1959), Shapiro (1962), Shapiro and Ravenette (1959), Staats (1962), Walker (1962), Whitaker and Malone (1953), and Wolpe (1958), have, albeit from widely different frames of reference, upheld active-directive modes of therapy that are radically at odds with some of the main passive-indirect modes.

In rational-emotive psychotherapy a most forthright stand is taken in favor of intensive activity on the part of both the patient and the therapist. And this stand is taken not merely on the pragmatic grounds that it works better than do more passive techniques (particularly with psychotic and borderline psychotic patients), but on theoretical grounds as well.

In the first place, the theory of RT says that what is essentially done in effective psychotherapy is the changing of the patient's attitudes, especially his attitudes toward himself and others. And although changing an individual's attitudes can obviously be done in a variety of ways, including even by highly nondirective techniques (as when the mere reflection and clarification of his thinking by a therapist helps him to see that this thinking *is* illogical and that he'd *better* change it), it is clear that one of the main methods of effecting attitudinal changes is the didactic method. Thus, clergymen, politicians, armed force officers, scientists, and philosophers all try to change the views of their parishioners, pupils, or readers; and quite often, by their highly propagandistic teachings, they do so with startling effectiveness. Not only, moreover, do these kinds of teachers frequently help change the factual views of their audiences; but they also effect significant changes in the emotional allegiances, ethical behavior, or value systems of the members of these same audiences. To contend, therefore, as the Freudian-oriented and nondirective therapists often do, that people's emotional or unconscious or deeply held thoughts and desires are rarely affected by didactic or logical methods of appealing to them is to uphold the veriest hogwash. Hundreds of years of recorded history give thousands of instances of evidence to the contrary. As Victor Hugo [quoted by Reid (1962)] said: There is nothing so powerful as an idea whose time has come.

If—as RT theory contends—people essentially become emotionally disturbed because they unthinkingly accept certain illogical premises or irrational ideas, then there is good reason to believe that they can be somehow persuaded or taught to think more logically and rationally and thereby to undermine their own disturbances (Platonov, 1959). If an individual falsely believes, for example, that just because he has acted a certain way in the past he must continue to act that way in the future, there is no reason why he cannot be actively challenged on this belief and required to uphold it with factual evidence. His therapist can point out to him that (*a*) he has changed various modes of behavior that he once performed in the past; that (*b*) there is no *necessary* connection between present and past acts, even though there is *some* tendency for an individual to repeat his past performances; that (*c*) one's past of tomorrow is one's present of today, and that therefore by changing today's behavior one *does* change one's past; that (*d*) millions of human beings have modified and will continue to modify their past behavior, and there is no reason why the patient cannot be included among these millions; etc.

Irrational premises, in other words, *are* only premises, and they can be shown to be exactly that. And illogical thinking that follows from (valid or invalid) premises *is* illogical, and can be proven to be so. Teachers of history, mathematics, economics, and many other subjects would not hesitate to show their pupils that, and how, they were thinking unclearly. Why, then, should not the psychotherapist (who is essentially, if he is effective, an emotional reëducator) just as forthrightly and persistently show his patients precisely how invalid is their thinking about themselves and others?

According to RT theory, the disturbed individual not only becomes neurotic because his parents (or other early intimates and teachers) propagandize him to believe several untrue propositions (such as the proposition that he *has* to be loved or approved by significant other people in his life) but he also actively repropagandizes himself continually with these same falsehoods. Moreover, if he lives in a society such as our own, he is further propagandized by most of the important mass media to *keep* believing the original nonsense that he learned. Thus, magazine advertisements, TV dramas, best-selling novels, motion pictures, popular songs, and various other popular media ceaselessly drum into his ears the "fact" that it *will* be terrible if he is unpopular or unloved (Ellis, 1961a, 1962b).

Because of this powerful triple-headed propagandistic broadside—that is, from his parents, his autosuggestions, and his general society—the individual's irrational premises about himself and others are most tenaciously rooted, and it is highly unlikely that mild-mannered contradiction of these premises by even the most skilled therapist is going to help him appreciably to eradicate his self-defeating thinking. This is particularly true of severely disturbed patients, who keep talking to themselves for years about their life philosophies and their neurotic symptoms before they get to see a therapist. In the course of this self-discussion, they often construct involved theories, sometimes of a paranoid nature, about why they originally became disturbed and why they are not getting better.

These patients' endlessly-repeated sentences and theories about their illness eventually become gospel, and they become certain that they know all about themselves and their problems. Moreover, they may use their "explanations" of their disturbances as rationalizations for not getting better and may typically blame others, including the therapist, and insist that they could easily get better if these others helped them. But, since they are not being adequately helped, they "normally," in their own eyes, remain disturbed.

To make an effective inroad into this type of repeated, viciously circular thinking on the part of the patient, it is usually necessary for the therapist to take an extremely active role in contradicting their false thinking and in giving them more efficient alternate solutions to their problems. The proponents of the self-actualization theory of personality, such as Kurt Goldstein (1954), A. H. Maslow (1954), and Carl Rogers (1951), while sanely emphasizing the great potential of the human being to make himself well or sick, often fail to realize that this potential exists but is deeply buried under miles of cognitive-emotional silt, and that only with active outside help is it likely to be given leeway to exert itself.

In the case of paranoid patients in particular, they are often so utterly convinced that their particular pattern of behavior is being helpful to them—that it has some distinct gains in contrast to alternate types of behavior—that they stubbornly, albeit erroneously, resist almost any mild-mannered counterpropositions that a therapist may make. In these instances, sometimes a dramatic, most definite, I-refuse-any-longer-to-take-any-nonsense approach on the part of the therapist may finally convince the patient that his own self-propagandizations are illogical and self-defeating, and that he'd better listen to the therapist or else. This does not mean that this kind of dramatic or shock technique is necessary or useful in all cases; but in some instances, especially some of those involving stubbornly paranoid patients, I am convinced that most vigorous, dramatic counterproposals by the therapist are almost the only ways of getting results.

Even with considerably less disturbed patients, their problems are generally of many years standing by the time they come for therapy, and they have been intensively emotionally brainwashed by others and themselves during these years. Moreover, as therapy itself progresses, they tend forcefully to convince themselves that they cannot really help themselves or that it is easier for them to remain sick. Consequently, passive measures by the therapist will only play into their neurotic premises and their illogical deductions from these premises; while active counterproposals will usually help jolt them out of their emotional ruts. Self-discouragement is probably one of the most frequent symptoms of all kinds of psychological illness; and active encouragement, persuasion, and upward pushing on the part of the therapist is usually required to counteract some of the pernicious effects of self-sabotaging.

Classical psychoanalysts and nondirective therapists have used the fact of the patient's normal resistance to change as one of the main excuses for not making any head-on attack against his existing security system. If such an attack is made, they insist, the patient will soon feel so uncomfortable that he will become defensive or upset, and may even leave therapy. Although this possibility certainly exists, and at times actually occurs, I have found it to be grossly exaggerated; and it has always been surprising to me how seriously therapists tend to take so-called resistance and how easily they are intimidated by it.

Much of what is called the patient's "resistance," especially as this term is used in the psychoanalytic literature, is, I am convinced, largely the result of his quite healthy reactions to the therapist's poor technique. The patient comes to therapy asking for help; the therapist, because of his own prejudices, maintains a passive attitude and refuses to give any substantial help; so the patient, quite naturally I believe, "resists" the therapist and often ends up by quitting the relationship.

This is not to say that some amount of genuine resistance is not to be expected in therapy: since the patient has normally been disturbed for a considerable period before coming for aid and cannot be expected to change his behavior simply because the therapist explains why he has been acting in a given manner or asks him to act differently. Particularly in those cases in which the patient has repressed or is loath to admit certain underlying feelings of anxiety or hostility, we must expect resistance to insight and action to occur. Moreover, as pointed out in the closing chapter of this book, a considerable amount of resistance may even be biologically rooted, and hence most difficult to overcome.

All right, then; so the patient often resists. School children and college students also resist learning new things, changing their behavior. But is this any reason why teachers should stop trying to get them to learn and to change? The therapist's job, more often than not, is to accept resistance for what it is worth—namely, a highly expectable disinclination to give up a well-trodden road for a relatively unexplored one—and to keep hacking away at it, often by a sheer process of attrition, until it is overcome. To be bulldozed by it, and cravenly retreat in the face of its "hopelessness," is certainly to take a nontherapeutic, and often an antitherapeutic, attitude.

One of the main aspects of neurosis, in fact, is that the disturbed individual, when he sees that a difficulty exists and that he may not succeed at some task or venture, easily and quickly gives up and retreats to safer ground. If the therapist passively and inactively takes the same kind of tack, and gives up in his task of overcoming the patient's resistance, using the convenient alibi that this is just a "too resistant" individual who is unsuitable to therapy, he thereby sets an unusually poor—and, possibly, quite neurotic—example for the patient, who naturally is going to be encouraged to continue his own passive resistant tactics. If, on the other hand, the therapist keeps actively, hopefully blasting away at the patient's defenses, he thereby acts as a good example and may finally, by his own undefeatist behavior, convince the patient that he really *can* get better.

In my own recent use of rational therapeutic techniques, I have rarely found a case in which, no matter how stiff the patient's resistance originally was, I could not, by one method of attack or another, eventually overcome it. Naturally, this procedure of actively assailing the patient's resistances has its own dangers, especially that of his leaving therapy. I find in actual practice, however, that few of my patients do leave for this reason and that still fewer experience the pernicious effects, such as psychotic breaks, which the professional literature so cavalierly assumes that they will experience if their defenses are directly assaulted.

What is commonly forgotten in this connection is that the therapist is, almost by definition, supposed to be emotionally stronger and healthier than the patient. If this is true, then he should be able to take the *risk* of attacking the patient's defenses —and possibly being counterattacked or rebuffed for doing so. Moreover, if he is adequately trained, there should be relatively few instances in which, in the long run, the therapist's strength and knowledge cannot overcome the patient's irrational resistances. If the therapist is unduly intimidated by these resistances, then it may well be that he is not sufficiently stable and healthy to do effective psychotherapy and that he'd better stick to some nontherapeutic specialty.

Nondirectiveness or passivity on the part of a therapist may encourage some patients to take advantage of their therapist endlessly and to avoid facing their basic problems—which invariably have to be *worked* at in order for them to get better. The more passive the therapist is, the less this kind of patient is forced to change. Consequently, they happily stay in therapy for years, so that they can falsely tell themselves, "Well, I'm doing everything I can to get better. Look how religiously I keep going to therapy," when actually, of course, they are doing everything they can to avoid overcoming their disturbances.

In one of the cases in Standal and Corsini's *Critical Incidents in Psychotherapy* (1959), the therapist, after rather passively going along with an obstreperous patient for a period of time, finally loses his temper at one point and tells him to "go plumb to hell." Whereupon, the patient for the first time really seems to respect the therapist and begins to make considerable progress. I personally do not feel that the therapist's losing his temper with his patient is ever a very good thing (since it indicates to the patient that *he* himself is justified in losing his temper on various occasions). But I do feel that the therapist's calmly but firmly telling a patient to go plumb to hell, or some reasonable equivalent, is sometimes productive of therapeutic change when more passive acceptance of the patient's nonsense has miserably failed.

In one instance, when I was seeing a schizophrenic girl who had had no less than 15 years of previous therapy with several competent therapists and who, when I saw her, was still exceptionally disturbed, I took all the patient could give for several months. And she gave plenty! She would call me up literally in the middle of the night; would refuse to leave the therapeutic session when her time had expired; would yell at me in a loud tone of voice, so that any other waiting patients would hear; would phone me while other patients were being seen and would refuse to make the call brief, so that I finally would have to hang up on her; and would do all kinds of other negative, hostile acts. I absorbed all this hostility and obtained a fine degree of rapport with her; but still, from time to time, she would be overtly hostile.

One day, when she was refusing to leave my office when her session had expired, I deliberately raised my voice and said: "Now, look here: I've taken enough of your nonsense as far as not getting out of here on time is concerned. I've spoken to you nicely about this several times before, but apparently it hasn't done any good. Now I'm telling you once and for all: if you don't get out of here *pronto* whenever I signal that the session has come to an end, you can take yourself straight to another therapist. And that goes for those telephone calls and other annoyances of yours, too. If I ever so much as receive one single unnecessary call from you again, especially when I tell you that I am busy and cannot speak to you at the time, that's the end of our relationship. And I mean it! I've taken enough of your nonsense, and it seems to me that I've been pretty nice to you in the meantime. But enough is enough! Either, hereafter, you are going to show some respect for me and my way of working, or you can go to the devil and get another therapist. And, if you want, I'll be glad to recommend you to one right now."

My patient, with a terribly shocked look, immediately became conciliatory and apologetically left. Thereafter, for a period of several months, I had no trouble with her. During this period, she also improved considerably, for the first time in her long history of psychotherapy. She then began to slip slowly back into her previous negative behavior toward me; and, after taking this for a few sessions, I again let her have it, right between the ears, and told her that I would refuse to see her again if she did not immediately change her ways. She quickly became much more considerate; I had little trouble with her thereafter, and she made even more improvements.

On two other occasions, with male patients, I told each one, after I had seen him only a few sessions: "Now let's stop this nonsense. You're giving me an obvious pack of lies and evasions, and at that rate we'll get absolutely no place. If you want to go on kidding yourself, and refraining from trying to get better, that's your business. But my business is helping people get better, and I don't intend to waste any time with those who keep giving me a lot of trouble. Now either you quit or stew in your own damned neuroses for the rest of your life. Which shall it be?" In both of these instances, my patients made significant changes in their attitudes toward me, toward therapy, and toward themselves.

I feel, therefore, that a wise and courageous therapist, instead of passively accepting negativism and inertia from his patients, will often use well-timed and well-aimed language, and at times even harsh language, to help them or jolt them out of their nastiness and lethargy. I find the use of well-chosen expletives, especially with certain patients, often useful in this connection.

If a patient says to me, "You know, I just didn't feel like doing the homework assignment you gave me, and I didn't like you for giving it to me, so I just forgot about it," I rarely nondirectively reflect back to him: "So you didn't like the assignment and hated me for giving it to you?" And I often fail to say, in an approved psychoanalytic manner: "What is there about the assignment and about me that you didn't like?"

Rather, I am likely to say: "So you didn't feel like doing the assignment. Tough! Well you're goddam well going to have to do it if you want to overcome the nonsense you keep telling yourself. And you didn't like me for giving you the assignment. Well, I don't give a shit whether you like me or not. We're here not to have a lovey-dovey relationship—and thereby to gratify you for the moment so that you don't *have* to work to get better —but to convince you that unless you get off your ass and do that assignment I gave you, and many equivalent assignments, you're going to keep stewing in your own neurotic juices forever. Now when are you going to cut out the crap and *do* something to help yourself?"

With this kind of a highly active-directive, *unpampering* approach, I often find that I can push negativistic and inert people into self-healing action when a passive, nondirective technique would merely encourage them to continue their defeatist and defeating tendencies forever.

I also find, in the course of rational-emotive psychotherapeutic encounters, that persistent activity by the therapist often pays off. This is again to be expected on theoretical grounds: since if an individual's disturbances largely consist of the irrational sentences he has originally been indoctrinated with in his childhood and that he has kept telling himself ever since that time, it is only to be expected that such persistently ingrained indoctrinations will require a considerable amount of, shall we say, persistent "*out*graining." This seems to be true of most learned habits: once they are distinctly overlearned, then, even though they lead to unfortunate results, it is difficult to unlearn them and to learn different habits; and the habituated individual must usually persist and persist in the unlearning and relearning process.

The rational therapist, consequently, frequently keeps questioning, challenging, and reindoctrinating his patients, until they are ready to give up their dysfunctional behavior patterns —at long last!—and replace them with more functional philosophies and behaviors. If the therapist fails to persist, the patient often runs back into his old hiding places, and refuses ever to be smoked out of his neurosis.

In one case of a difficult patient, I was seeing a highly intelligent young woman teacher who had urinary and defecatory symptoms which seemed to be closely related to her sexual problems, but she was loath to discuss sexual issues and, in spite of some probing on my part, she remained exceptionally vague about her sex life. She particularly insisted that she had never masturbated nor had any guilt in relation to masturbation. I was most doubtful about this, but could not get any additional information with repeated questioning.

Feeling that the patient was definitely resisting, I determined to make an even more concerted frontal attack on her masturbatory feelings and actions. In spite of her insistence that she had never masturbated, I forced the issue and asked her if she knew what masturbation consisted of in females. She looked confused, so I said:

"Masturbation in females is not usually like it is commonly supposed to be in so-called dirty jokes or conversational innuendo. Do you know how it's actually done?"

She became quite flustered and finally blurted out: "Well, I've never used a candle, or anything like that."

"No doubt you haven't," I persisted, "but masturbation in females very rarely consists of using a candle or anything like that. What it does consist of is utilizing some kind of friction, such as manual friction, on the external sex organs or the clitoris. Have you ever done anything like that? I'm sure you must have, since almost all girls do at one time or another. Maybe you pressed your thighs together, or rubbed against desks, or did things along that line. Can't you remember now?"

My patient suddenly blushed furiously and became completely mute for almost ten minutes. After that, slowly, and at my continued insistence, she indicated that she had been masturbating for years. It was then easy to show her that she had known all along what she had been doing, but had refused to acknowledge this fact by pretending that masturbation consisted only of inserting objects into the vagina. This meant that she must have been exceptionally guilty about continuing to masturbate; and her guilt was, at least in part, causing her defecatory and urinary symptoms. The patient quickly acknowledged this and slowly began to improve, whereas previously we had been able to effect virtually no improvement.

In many other cases treated with RT, I have found that persistence has paid off. When patients have insisted that they are not guilty, or angry, or tense, I have kept confronting them, with evidence from their own behavior, that they probably are upset; and in most instances they have soon begun to admit that they are disturbed, but insist that they do not know why, or that they are not telling themselves anything to make themselves disturbed. I keep even more forcefully contending that they *do* know why and that they *are* telling themselves upsetting sentences. Again, the more I persist, the more they usually come to admit that I am correct, and that they *can* help themselves much more than they first thought they could.

Another most important mode of activity that frequently is used in rational-emotive psychotherapy is the therapist's giving the patient definite homework assignments. Sometimes these assignments are relatively vague; sometimes highly specific.

As an example of the giving of a common vague or general assignment, we may take the instance of the 27-year old male who was sent to therapy by his fiancée, who claimed that he didn't relate at all to their mutual friends, but would sit reading a newspaper or work on some accounting problem when they were visiting or being visited. After seeing this boy for only two sessions, it became perfectly clear that he was unusually inhibited and that he had been so ever since his early childhood. His mother had been exceptionally critical of everything he ever did; and his father had perfunctorily accepted his school successes (which were notable) but had not really shown any interest in him. As a result of being terribly hurt by his horrified view of the reactions (or lack of reactions) of his parents, he had begun to distrust everyone and to relate in an entirely superficial manner.

On theoretical grounds, this patient was shown that he must be continually telling himself sentences such as: "If I get too close to people, they may reject me, as my mother and father have done; and that would be terrible!" and: "If I make myself relatively inaccessible to people and they *still* accept me, then I'll feel safe with them, and be able to open up more to them in the future."

The patient could not see, as yet, that he actually was telling himself these kinds of sentences, but was willing to admit that he very well might be. He was therefore given the homework assignment of (*a*) looking for his own specific self-defeating sentences whenever he found himself in any kind of a social retreat, and (*b*) deliberately forcing himself, at these times of retreat, to enter into closer relations with other people, to stop reading his newspaper, to say anything he had on his mind no matter how stupid it might seem to be.

After two weeks of this assignment, the patient came into his next session of therapy and reported: "I did what you told me to do."

"Yes? And what happened?"

"Quite a lot! I found it much more difficult than I thought it would be to put what you said into effect. Really difficult!"

"But you did so, nevertheless?"

"Oh, yes. I kept doing, forcing myself to do so. Much more difficult than I expected, it was!"

"What was difficult, exactly?"

"First of all, seeing those sentences. The ones you said I was telling myself. I just couldn't see them at all at first. I seemed to be saying absolutely nothing to myself. But every time, just as you said, I found myself retreating from people, I said to myself: 'Now, even though you can't see it, there must be some sentences. What are they?' And I finally found them. And there were many of them! And they all seemed to say the same thing."

"What thing?"

"That I, uh, was going to be rejected."

"If you spoke up and participated with others, you mean?"

"Yes, if I related to them I was going to be rejected. And wouldn't that be perfectly awful if I was to be rejected. And there was no reason for me, uh, to take that, uh, sort of thing, and be rejected in that awful manner."

"So you might as well shut up and not take the risk?"

"Yes, so I might as well shut my trap and stay off in my corner, away from the others."

"So you did see it?"

"Oh, yes! I certainly saw it. Many times, during the week."

"And did you do the second part of the homework assignment?"

"The forcing myself to speak up and express myself?"

"Yes, that part."

"That was worse. That was really hard. Much harder than I thought it would be. But I did it."

"And—?"

"Oh, not bad at all. I spoke up several times; more than I've ever done before. Some people were very surprised. Phyllis was very surprised, too. But I spoke up. And, you know something?"

"What?"

"I even enjoyed it some of the times!"

"You enjoyed expressing yourself?"

"Yes. The Slotts were there one day, at Phyllis's place. And they were talking about the United Nations and political things that I really don't know very much about, because I think, you know, that I've actually avoided finding much about that sort of thing in the past, knowing that I would be afraid to talk about it. Well, anyway, they were talking about this recent stuff that's been in the papers, and I had an idea about it that I thought I'd like to bring up, but I could see that, as I used to do, I was going to keep my mouth shut and say nothing, for fear of their all looking at me as if I was crazy and didn't know what I was talking about. But I said to myself, instead, 'Here's my chance to take the plunge, and do more of my homework!' And I spoke up and said my little piece, and they all looked at me, and I don't even know how it exactly went over, though nobody seemed to disagree very much. But, anyway, *I* knew that I had expressed myself for once, and that was the thing."

"And how did you feel after expressing yourself like that?"

"Remarkable! I don't remember when I last felt this way. I felt, uh, just remarkable—good, that is. It was really something to feel! But it was so *hard*. I almost didn't make it. And a couple of other times during the week I had to force myself again. But I did. And I was glad!"

"So your homework assignments paid off?"

"They did; they really did."

Within the next few weeks, this patient, largely as a result of doing his homework assignments, became somewhat less inhibited socially and was able to express himself more freely than he had ever been able to do before. It is quite doubtful whether, without this kind of homework assignment, he would have made so much progress so quickly.

In another instance, I gave a more specific assignment to a

20-year old female who had recently married and who was having considerable difficulty being affectionate to her mother-in-law. Her own mother and father had never been overtly affectionate to her, and she had always referred to them, from early childhood, as Jack and Barbara, rather than Pop and Mom. But her mother-in-law, whom she liked and wanted to be friendly with, was a very affectionate woman, who winced every time the patient called her Mrs. Steen or Marion, and obviously wanted to be called Mom.

The patient's problem was that she did not *feel* like calling her mother-in-law "Mom," and felt that she would be hypocritical if she did so just to remain on good terms with her. I showed her, however, that she was refusing to see things from the mother-in-law's frame of reference, and that she was moralistically viewing the woman as being childish. If she objectively and unblamefully accepted her mother-in-law, I convinced her, she would be helping herself, her husband, and her in-laws, and getting the results that she herself wanted; and with this kind of unmoralistic attitude, she would have no difficulty in calling her mother-in-law "Mom" instead of "Mrs. Steen."

The patient theoretically accepted this view, but still had great difficulty thinking of and addressing her mother-in-law as "Mom." Whereupon, I gave her the specific assignment of calling the woman on the phone every day for a two-week period, and beginning the conversation with "Hi, Mom," and forcing herself to get two or three more "Moms" into the talk before it was over. She reluctantly said she would try this assignment, even though she still felt uncomfortable and somewhat hypocritical about it.

After this experiment had progressed for a week, I saw the patient, and asked her how she was doing in her psychotherapeutic homework.

"Oh, yes," she said, "I meant to tell you about that. After talking to my mother-in-law for only three days, as you had directed me to do, I found that calling her 'Mom' was really easy. In fact, I kind of got to like the sound of the word. And, do you know what? I actually started using it with my own mother, too! And *she* seems to like it!"

"So now you have two 'Moms' for the price of one!"

"Yes. And, just as you predicted, I really *feel* closer to my mother-in-law. And to my mother, as well! It didn't take long at all, did it?"

"No, it certainly didn't. The feeling of closeness pretty quickly followed the action of saying the word. That's what Stendhal pointed out about love, well over a century ago: that if you act *as if* you are in love with another, you very likely soon *will be*. That's what happens to many of our feelings—that *after* we act on them, we begin to feel them quite deeply."

"It worked out just like that in my case. And I'm very glad that it did, and that I kept doing my homework conscientiously. I never thought I'd go back to school through psychotherapy, but that's the way it's seemed to work out."

"Which is probably just the way it should, considering that effective psychotherapy and reëducation are practically synonymous."

These are typical instances of the many in which highly active-directive methods, including general or specific homework assignments, are used in rational-emotive psychotherapy. While other schools of therapy, such as the Gestalt school, employ somewhat similar techniques, RT does so on theoretical grounds which are an integral part of its basic rationale.

If verbal *and* sensory-motor indoctrinations significantly teach human beings to think irrationally and to feel disturbed, then the same kind of double-barreled reindoctrinations should be most helpful in reorganizing their thinking and emoting. Vigorous verbal re-thinking will usually lead to changed motor behavior; and forcefully re-patterned sensory-motor activity will usually lead to changed ideation. But the quickest and most deep-rooted behavioral modifications will usually follow from a *combined* verbal and sensory-motor attack on the old, dysfunctional ways of thinking-doing (Israeli, 1962; Martí-Ibáñez, 1960; Permyak, 1962).

11

A Rational Approach to Marital Problems*

The first part of this book has been concerned with expounding some of the general theory and practice of rational-emotive psychotherapy. This second part will be devoted to the application of the RT method to several different kinds of patients, including those with marital and premarital problems, psychosexual disturbances, homosexual neurosis, psychopathy, and borderline schizophrenia.

One of the main advantages of RT is that it is applicable not only to a wide range of typical psychotherapy cases, but that it is beautifully designed for counseling with individuals who do not believe that they are emotionally disturbed but who know that they are not functioning adequately in some specific area of life, such as in their marriages or on their jobs, and who are willing to be counseled in this area. Very possible, most of these troubled individuals should come for intensive psychotherapy rather than for "counseling," but the fact is that they do not. It therefore behooves the counselor, and especially the marriage counselor, to be enough of a trained and experienced therapist to be able to deal adequately with the individuals who come to him for help (Ellis, 1956b; Harper, 1953). If he learns and practices the essentials of RT, he will be well prepared in this regard.

Most couples who come for marriage counseling are victims of what has been fairly aptly called neurotic interaction in marriage (Eisenstein, 1956). Since neurotics, as has been previously

* This chapter is adapted and expanded from the articles, "Neurotic Interaction Between Marital Partners" (*J. Counseling Psychol.*, 1958, 5, 24-28) and "Marriage Counseling with Demasculinizing Wives and Demasculinized Husbands," *Marriage & Family Living*, 1960, 22, 13-21.

pointed out in this book, are individuals who are not intrinsically stupid and inept—but who *needlessly* suffer from intense and sustained anxiety, hostility, guilt, or depression—neurotic inter- action in marriage arises when a theoretically capable husband and wife actually behave in an irrational, marriage-defeating way with each other. If, again, the theses of RT are correct, then marital neurotic interaction arises from unrealistic and irrational ideas, beliefs, or value systems on the part of one or both of the marriage partners; and it is these beliefs and value systems which must be concertedly attacked if neurotic inter- action is to cease.

More concretely, let us briefly look at some of the main neuroticizing ideas which have been outlined in Chapter 3 and see how they apply to marriage. We previously noted that one of the main irrational beliefs that people use to upset themselves with is the notion that it is a dire necessity for an adult human being to be approved or loved by almost all the significant other people he encounters; that it is most important what others think of him instead of what he thinks of himself; and that it is better if he depends on others than on himself. Applied to mar- riage, this means the the neurotic individual firmly believes that, no matter how he behaves, his mate, just because she *is* his mate, *should* love him; that if she doesn't respect him, life is a horror; and that her main role as a wife is to help, aid, succor *him*, rather than to be an individual in her own right.

When *both* marriage partners believe this nonsense—believe that they *must* be loved, respected, and catered to by the other— they are not only asking for what is rarely accorded an individ- ual in this grimly realistic world, but are asking for unmitigated devotion from another individual who, precisely because he demands this kind of devotion himself, is the *least* likely candi- date to give it. Under such circumstances, a major marital holo- caust is almost certain to occur.

The second major irrational belief which most neurotics in our society seem to hold is that a human being should or must be perfectly competent, adequate, talented, and intelligent and is utterly worthless if he is incompetent in any significant way.

When married, these neurotics tend to feel that, as mates and as sex partners, they should be utterly successful and achieving. The wife therefore berates herself because she is not a perfect housewife, mother, and bedmate; and the husband despises himself because he is not an unexcelled provider and sex athlete. Then, becoming depressed because of their supposed inadequacies, both husband and wife either compulsively strive for perfection or hopelessly give up the battle and actually *make themselves into* poor spouses and lovers. Either of these maladjusted choices of behavior usually incenses the other mate; and another marital holocaust ensues.

A third irrational assumption of the majority of neurotics is that they should severely blame themselves and others for mistakes and wrongdoings; and that punishing themselves or others will help prevent future mistakes. Married neurotics, in consequence, tend to get upset by their mates' errors and stupidities; spend considerable time and energy trying to reform their spouses; and vainly try to help these spouses by sharply pointing out to them the error of their ways.

Because, as we previously noted, emotionally disturbed human beings already have the tendency to blame themselves for their imperfections; because even healthy men and women tend to resist doing the so-called right thing when they are roundly berated for doing the so-called wrong one; and because criticized humans tend to focus compulsively on their wrongdoings rather than calmly face the problems of how they may *change* their behavior—for many reasons such as these, one partner's blaming another for this other's imperfections does immense harm in just about one hundred per cent of the cases. Even counselors— who quite obviously are on their client's side—rarely can get away with blaming an individual; and spouses—who were often wed in the first place mainly because the bride or groom felt that he or she would *not* be criticized by this spouse—can virtually never do anything but the gravest harm to their relationship by criticizing their mates. But this is precisely what most neurotics are driven to do by their basically false philosophies of living.

A fourth idiotic assumption which underlies and causes emotional disturbance is the notion that it is terrible, horrible, and catastrophic when things are not the way one would like them to be; that others should make things easier for one, help with life's difficulties; and that one should not have to put off present pleasures for future gains. In their marriages, neurotics who consciously or unconsciously espouse this I-cannot-stand-frustration system of values invariably get into serious difficulties. For marriage, of course, *is* an exceptionally frustrating situation in many instances, involving considerable boredom, sacrifice, pleasure postponement, doing what one's mate wants to do, and so on.

Neurotic individuals, consequently, bitterly resent their marriages and their mates on numberless occasions; and, sooner or later, they clearly show this resentment. Then, neurotically feeling that *they* are not loved or are being frustrated in *their* desires, the spouses of these neurotics get in a few or a few hundred counter-licks themselves, and the battle is on again. The ultimate result can only be a hellish marriage—or a divorce.

A fifth and final irrational belief which we shall consider here is the mythical supposition that most human unhappiness is externally caused or forced on one by outside people and events and that one has virtually no control over one's emotions and cannot help feeling badly on many occasions. Actually, of course, virtually all human unhappiness is *self*-caused and results from silly assumptions, and internalized sentences stemming from these assumptions, such as some of the beliefs we have just been outlining. But once a married individual is convinced that his own unhappiness is externally caused, he inevitably blames his mate, and his or her behavior, for his own misery; and, once again, he is in a marital stew. For the mate, especially if she is herself neurotic, will contend (*a*) that she does *not* cause his unhappiness, and that (*b*) he, instead, causes hers. Of such silly beliefs, again, are the stuff of separations made.

It is my staunch contention, then, that a seriously neurotic individual possesses, almost by definition, a set of basic postulates which are distinctly unrealistic, biased, and illogical. Consequently, such an individual will find it almost impossible to be happy in a realistic, everyday, down-to-earth relationship such as modern marriage usually is. Moreover, being unhappy, this mate will inevitably jump on his or her partner—who, if reasonably well adjusted, will tend to become fed up with the relationship and to want to escape from it; and, if reasonably neurotic, will return the spouse's resentful sallies in kind, thus leading to neurotic interaction in marriage (Fink, 1962).

No matter, therefore, how irrational the beliefs of one spouse may be, it takes a double neurosis to make for true neurotic marital interaction. Suppose, for example, a husband believes that he must be inordinately loved by his wife, no matter how he behaves toward her; that he must be competent in all possible respects; that he should blame others, especially his wife, for errors and mistakes; that he must never be frustrated; and that all his unhappiness is caused by his wife's behavior and other outside events.

If the spouse of this severely neurotic husband had virtually no similar illogical beliefs of her own, she would quickly see that her husband was seriously disturbed, would not take his hostility toward herself with any resentment, and would either accept him the way he was, or would calmly try to see that he got professional help, or would quietly conclude that she did not want to remain married to such a disturbed individual and would divorce him. She would *not*, however, neurotically react to her husband herself, thus causing a mighty conflagration instead of a nasty, but still limited, flame.

If what has thus far been said in this chapter is reasonably accurate, then the solution to the problem of treating neurotic interaction in marriage would appear to be fairly obvious. If neurotics have basically irrational assumptions or value systems, and if these assumptions lead them to interact self-defeatingly with their mates, then the marriage counselor's function is to tackle not the problem of the marriage, nor of the neurotic interaction that exists between the marital partners, but of the irrational ideas or beliefs that *cause* this neurosis *à deux*.

My own marriage counseling is part and parcel of the general technique of rational-emotive psychotherapy. It largely consists of showing each of the marital partners who is neurotically interacting (*a*) that he has some basic irrational assumptions; (*b*) precisely what these assumptions are; (*c*) how they originally arose; (*d*) how they currently are being sustained by continual unconscious self-indoctrination; and (*e*) how they can be replaced with much more rational, less self-defeating philosophies.

More concretely, each spouse is shown that his disturbed behavior can arise only from underlying unrealistic beliefs; that these beliefs may have originally been learned from early familial and other environmental influences but that they are now being maintained by internal verbalizations; that his marriage partner, in consequence, is never the real cause of his problems; that he himself is actually now creating and perpetuating these problems; and that only by learning carefully to observe, to question, to think about, and to reformulate his basic assumptions can he hope to understand his mate and himself and to stop being unilaterally and interactionally neurotic.

Let me cite an illustrative case. A husband and wife who had been married for seven years recently came for counseling because the wife was terribly disturbed about the husband's alleged affairs with other women and the husband was "fed up" with his wife's complaints and general unhappiness and thought it was useless going on. It was quickly evident that the wife was an extremely neurotic individual who believed that she had to be inordinately loved and protected; who hated herself thoroughly for her incompetency; who severely blamed everyone, especially her husband, who did not love her unstintingly; and who felt that all her unhappiness was caused by her husband's lack of affection.

The husband, at the same time, was a moderately disturbed individual who believed that his wife should be blamed for her mistakes, particularly the mistake of thinking he was having affairs with other women, when he was not, and who also believed that it was unfair for his wife to criticize and sexually frustrate him when he was doing his best, under difficult circumstances, to help her.

In this case, the somewhat unorthodox procedure of seeing both husband and wife together at all counseling sessions was employed—largely because I have found this method to be time-saving, in that the main difficulties between the mates are quickly arrived at, and because I feel that the witnessing of one mate's emotional reëducation by the other spouse may serve as a model and incentive for the second spouse's philosophic reformulations. The husband-wife-therapist group, in this sense, becomes something of a small-scale attempt at group therapy.

In any event, because the husband, in this case, was less seriously disturbed than the wife, his illogical assumptions were first brought to his attention and worked upon. He was shown that, in general, blame is an irrational feeling because it does neither the blamer nor his victim any good; and that, in particular, although many of his complaints about his wife's unrealistic jealousy and other disturbances might well have been justified, his criticizing her for this kind of behavior could only serve to make her worse rather than better—thus bringing more of the same kind of jealous behavior down on his own head.

He was also shown that his assumption that his wife *should not* excoriate or sexually frustrate him was erroneous: since why *should* not disturbed individuals act precisely in this kind of critical or frustrating manner? He was led to see that even though his wife's actions were mistaken, two wrongs do not make a right—and his reaction to her behavior was equally mistaken, in that instead of getting the results he wanted, it was only helping make things worse. If he really wanted to help his wife—as he kept saying that he did—then it would be much wiser if he, for the nonce, *expected* her to act badly, stopped inciting himself to fury when she did so, and spent at least several weeks returning her anger and discontent with kindness and acceptance—thereby giving her leeway to tackle her own disturbances.

The husband, albeit with some backsliding at times, soon

began to respond to this realistic approach to his wife's problems; and, in the meantime, her irrational assumptions were
tackled by the therapist. She was shown how and why she
originally acquired her dire need to be inordinately loved and
protected—mainly because she reacted badly to her mother's
failing to give her the love she required as a child—and how
necessarily self-defeating it was for her, as an adult, to continue
to reinfect herself with the belief that she *still* needed everyone's
love. Her general philosophy of blaming herself and others was
ruthlessly revealed to her and forthrightly attacked. She, like
her husband, was shown just how such a philosophy is bound
to alienate others, rather than win their approval or get them
to do things in a different and presumably better manner.

Finally, this wife's notion that her unhappiness was caused
by her husband's lack of affection was particularly brought to
her conscious awareness and exposed to the merciless light of
rationality. She was shown, over and over again, how her unhappiness could come only from within, from her own attitudes
toward external events such as her husband's lack of love, and
that it could be expunged only by her facing her own integral
part in creating it.

As the husband in this case started accepting his wife's neurosis more philosophically, she herself was more easily able to
see, just because he was not goading and blaming her, that
she was the creator of her own jealousies, self-hatred, and
childish dependency. She began to observe in detail the sentences she kept telling herself to make herself unhappy.

On one occasion, when the counselor was explaining to the
husband how he kept goading his wife to admit she was wrong,
ostensibly to help her think straight but actually to show how
superior to her he was, she interrupted to say:

"Yes, and I can see that I do exactly the same thing, too. I
go out of my way to find things wrong with him, or to accuse
him of going with other women, because I really feel that I'm
so stupid and worthless and I want to drag him down even
below me."

This, in the light of the wife's previous defensiveness about her jealousies, was real progress. After a total of 23 joint sessions of counseling, the fate of the marriage of this couple was no longer in doubt and they decided to go ahead with child-bearing and rearing, which they had previously avoided because of their mutual uncertainties. They also helped themselves with several other problems which were not necessarily related to their marriage but which had previously proven serious obstacles to happy, unanxious living.

One of the fairly common problems of modern-day marriage can serve as another illustration of how rational-emotive psychotherapy can be effectively employed in cases of marriage counseling. This is the problem of the demasculinization of the husband by his castrating wife.

Definitions are in order when one uses such terms as *castrating wives* and *demasculinized husbands;* so let me, before discussing the counseling of individuals in these categories, do a little defining and do so in fairly classic clinical terms. A while ago I saw a man and woman who had been married 12 years and who, according to their initial story, were thoroughly disgusted with each other, but who wanted to keep their marriage intact because they had four children and could not manage economically if they separated. The husband contended that his wife did nothing but nag him continually and try to dominate him in every possible way; and the wife bitterly noted that her husband was a weakling who refused to assume responsibility for anything, including rearing their children, unless she continually kept after him.

The husband, 45 years of age, ran a small service station, was respected by his fellow townsmen, and had a considerable number of old and trusted friends. At home, however, he drank heavily, ignored the children, rarely attempted to have sex relations with his wife, and refused point-blank to enter into any serious discussions about household affairs. He never encouraged or opposed his wife's plans, but would be passively uncooperative whenever she tried to do anything domestically or socially. On several occasions, especially when he was heavily under the influence of alcohol, he had attempted to kiss and fondle girls below the age of ten; but he steadfastly denied this, even though he had more than once been caught in the act by his wife.

The wife, 39 years old, not only ran the entire household and took complete charge of the children; but, in addition, she made more money than her husband by raising race horses, rarely wore anything but blue jeans or a riding outfit, and fairly openly carried on with a succession of other men right under her husband's nose. By her own admission, she spent much of her time with her husband trying to correct what she considered his irresponsible ways, telling him that he "was just like his father, who had never amounted to anything."

This, then, would seem to be a fairly classical case of a so-called demasculinizing or castrating woman and a demasculinized or castrated man. Such a classic instance has deliberately been chosen for presentation here because I want to uphold the contention that, actually, there *is* no such entity as a demasculinizing woman *per se;* and if it can be proven with this extreme kind of case that the wife really was not, in her *own* right, demasculinizing, then a good brief can be made for the position that *no* wife, in, of, and by herself, really is.

My objection to the concept of demasculinizing is mainly on theoretical grounds (although the theory which opposes this concept was, of course, derived in the last analysis from empirical and clinical evidence). The theoretical construct from which stems my opposition to the concept of so-called demasculinizing or castrating wives is the A-B-C theory of personality and emotional disturbance which has been previously presented in this book. This theory, which is closely related to certain phenomenological and Existential approaches to human behavior (Combs and Snygg, 1960), holds that it is rarely the stimulus, A, which gives rise to a human emotional reaction, C. Rather, it is almost always B—the individual's beliefs regarding, attitudes toward, or interpretation of A—which actually lead to his reaction, C. Thus, as I frequently explain to my marriage counseling clients, it is rarely their spouses' actions at A which cause them to become anxious, angry, or otherwise upset at C.

Instead, it is their *own* irrational *interpretations* of their mates' actions at A which really create their disturbances at C.

Applied to demasculinization, the A-B-C construct of emotional disturbance holds that it is impossible for any woman, at point A, to demasculinize any man, at point C, unless she quite literally emasculates him. What actually "demasculinizes" any male who is psychologically castrated is his own beliefs at B—namely, his beliefs that it is terrible, awful, and horrible for his wife (or any other woman) to criticize, nag, reject, or otherwise disapprove of him. No matter how castrating a woman may *try* to be, her efforts will utterly fail unless her spouse takes her would-be castrating words, gestures, and attitudes *seriously*—unless he *uses* her views to destroy *himself*.

Is it possible for any man, no matter how strong or self-approving he may be, to stand up against the continual barrage of a would-be demasculinizing woman? It certainly is. For no matter *what* his wife is saying or doing, other than resorting to concrete punishment (such as refusing to feed him) or physical violence (such as hitting him with the proverbial rolling pin), her words and deeds can be effective only if he quite falsely believes that (*a*) they are terrible, and (*b*) he is worthless because these words are true.

If a husband entirely refuses to believe this and believes, instead, that his wife must be seriously prejudiced and quite possibly emotionally disturbed for berating him, and that even if she is correct, he is merely mistaken, but never worthless, for acting in a manner such as to incur her wrath—he cannot possibly lose any masculinity or (to use a more objective and less invidiously sex-slanted term) any ego-strength.

To be still more specific, let us take the case of the husband and wife which was outlined a few paragraphs back. The wife's negative and would-be castrating words and deeds at point A consisted of her continually castigating her husband for his irresponsible ways, her completely running the home, making more money than her husband, adopting so-called masculine attire, and cuckolding her husband with a succession of lovers. Shouldn't, then, her behavior at point A *naturally* make her husband, at point B, believe that her criticism was terrible and that he was a worthless fool? This is exactly the question which the husband asked me, when I first saw him for marriage counseling; and to it I replied, "No, absolutely not."

I then proceeded to show this husband, in the course of the next several sessions, that his wife's carping and criticism were not terrible, awful, and frightful. Objectively viewed, they were, to be sure, undesirable, annoying, and self- and family-defeating. O.K.: so the wife's critical onslaughts were undesirable. The problem presented, then, was how to try to *change* her negative words and actions—and *not* how to do his best to upset himself about them. If the husband, I insisted, would calm down and face his wife's behavior as *a problem to tackle* rather than a "horror" to cry or get angry about, it was quite likely that he might be able to do something to help solve this problem,

Moreover, as I very directly and actively pointed out to the husband, even if his wife's behavior might well be said, from almost any marital or conventional standard, to be undesirable and destructive, this was still no good reason for him to *blame* her for her behavior and to recoil from it in a fearful or rebellious manner.

Obviously, if she, who was an intelligent and capable woman, was consistently acting in a destructive way, she must be pretty disturbed and unrealistic—even granted that he wasn't the best husband in the world and granted that, in a sense, she had some objective reason for her negativism. By her would-be demasculinizing tactics, this wife was hardly getting the result she kept saying she most wanted—namely, the assumption of greater responsibility by her husband. She was repetitively resorting to what G. V. Hamilton (1925) aptly called persistent nonadjustive behavior, and consequently was neurotic.

If, I pointed out to the husband, his wife were considerably disturbed and her nagging and carping were largely a product of her disturbance, why should *he* take her critical attitudes so seriously? Why should he not, instead, make due allowances for his wife's castration tendencies, understand where they arose, and stop telling himself, at point B, how horrible and terrible they were—thus creating actual *self*-emasculation at point C?

I kept working with this husband in this wise for several sessions, until he was finally able to see that his getting angry about his wife's nagging was no more justifiable than his getting angry at a child or a mentally deficient adult who is mischievous or even vicious. *Disliking* the behavior of a child or mentally deficient or disturbed adult is certainly legitimate; but hating this individual because he theoretically *should be* older or wiser or less disturbed, but *actually is not,* is being unrealistic and grandiose.

"Haven't I the right," asked this husband at one point during the third counseling session, "to get irritated by my wife's nagging and resent her for it?"

"You are positing, in your question," I replied, "two statements, one of which is quite sane and the other quite irrational and insane. The first statement is that you have a right—or, more accurately, a normal human tendency—to get irritated or annoyed by, or to dislike, your wife's nagging. And that is perfectly true, since there is no reason why you should not, as a human being, dislike almost anything you feel like disliking —even your wife's best characteristics."

"So my disliking her nagging is normal, then?"

"Yes, quite normal—not merely in the sense that almost everyone dislikes nagging (for the fact that most people do a thing hardly proves that it is "good" or "well adjusted" for you to do it)—but normal in the sense that it is not self-defeating. Disliking nagging wives, or Martinis, or what you will is often largely a matter of taste or preference; and you are fully entitled to your tastes and preferences, however bizarre they may seem to be to most others, as long as you keep within the law and do not needlessly harm others by catering to them."

"Then what's the insane part of my question?"

"The implied second statement—that is, that *because* you dislike something (in this case, your wife's nagging), *therefore* it should not, must not, ought not to exist. A child or an unrealistic adult (who is essentially a big child) believes that because he doesn't like it to rain it *shouldn't* rain. But why *shouldn't* it? What he really means, if we translate his statement into sane terms, is that because he doesn't like it to rain, *it would be nice* if it didn't. But if it does rain, as well it may, then that's just too bad, and there's little he can do about it."

"You seem to be saying that I can legitimately dislike my wife's nagging, but that if I hate or resent her for doing this nagging, I am telling myself, insanely, 'Because I dislike it, she shouldn't do it,' instead of, sanely, 'Because I dislike it, it would be nice if she didn't do it.'"

"Yes, that's exactly what I'm saying: that you're translating your perfectly rational *desire* to have your wife stop nagging into a sick *need* and a grandiose *command* that she do so. Your anxiety, when your sick need is not satisfied, is really caused by your own internalized sentence, 'She must stop nagging because I can't *stand* it,' and your anger, when your grandiose command is not satisfied, is caused by your own illogical sentence, 'She *should* stop nagging because I dislike it; and she is no darn good because she doesn't do what I like.'"

"According to you, then, I'd be much better off, and wouldn't get anxious and angry, if I change my sentences and tell myself that 'I dislike her nagging, but I *can* stand it,' and 'It would be nice if she stopped nagging, because I dislike it, but she probably won't stop for that reason, so I'll just have to put up with it for the time being.'"

"Exactly. Your anxiety *is* your belief that you can't stand your wife's nagging and are weak and worthless because you can't stand it; and your anger *is* your belief that she *should* not nag you, instead of the sane belief that it would be nice if she didn't. If you change these beliefs, you soon change the negative feelings or emotions to which they lead."

"So it is my own sentences that do all the damage?"

"Yes, you literally and figuratively are self-sentencing—are self-condemned by your own inner signaling or intracommunication."

At the same time that I was attacking, in this manner, the husband's resentment against his wife, I also went to work on his guilt. For his wife's accusations, of course, were hardly entirely unfounded; and he *had* been, from the beginning of their marriage, a not-overly-responsible husband. I showed him, in this respect, that his irresponsibility stemmed not, as he thought it did, from his inability to do well or to live without making mistakes, at point A, but from his self-blaming attitudes, at point B, *about* his not doing well or making such mistakes.

Thus, whereas the husband believed, when he first came for counseling, that he just wasn't *able* to handle children and, therefore, had quickly given up all attempts to learn to control and guide his own children, I was able to show him that it was his irrational belief about the *awfulness* of making mistakes with his children that actually drove him away from assuming any responsibility for their upbringing. When he finally began to see that it *wasn't* horrible for him to make mistakes or to fail at something that he tried, he became much less defensive about assuming responsibilities at home—and also started to think about enlarging his business facilities.

In any event, perhaps my main therapeutic point with this husband was convincing him that he didn't *have* to be demasculinized even though his wife, for neurotic reasons of her own, was attempting to castrate him. He alone, I insisted, had real control over his own ego-strength; and if he stopped taking the words and deeds of others, especially his poor, disturbed wife, too seriously, he could build instead of destroy his own self-confidence.

Once he became convinced of this point, my client began to look upon himself differently, to try things he never had tried before, to stand up against his wife's onslaughts, and even, for the first time in months, to attempt marital sex relations. Simultaneously, he was able to see clearly that his interest in little girls stemmed from (*a*) his hostility to his wife (who was most incensed by this particular kind of behavior), and (*b*) his fear of trying to have sex relations with another adult woman after he had been so severely browbeaten—or, rather, had *let* himself be browbeaten—by his wife. His interest in little girls then vanished in direct proportion to his becoming less intimidatable.

At the same time I was seeing this husband, I was having once-weekly sessions with his wife. I thought, at first, that she would be more difficult to re-orientate than he; actually, I had somewhat less difficulty in showing her the A-B-C's of her own self-defeating behavior. In just seven sessions—in comparison to the 33 I ultimately spent with the husband—I demonstrated that her would-be castrating tendencies did not stem, as she thought, from point A—her husband's irresponsibility and her honest desire to see him become more responsible—but from point B—her own catastrophizing and wailing about point A.

In the wife's case, too, I had to enable her to see that it was not *terrible*, but simply quite unpleasant, for her husband to behave as he did; and that once she took his irresponsibility as *a problem to work at* instead of a heinous crime, something might well be done about it. With amazing rapidity, she then stopped most of her nagging. At first, she continued her affairs with other men; but later, as her husband improved sexually, she stopped having these affairs.

I cannot truthfully say, in this case, that I was able to patch up these people's marriage to such an extent that they lived blissfully ever after. To my knowledge they are still married, and they are much more content with themselves and each other than they ever previously were. But, partly because of some basic incompatibilities of interests which should have been, but definitely were not, considered before they married, they will never get along ideally. The main point of this case presentation, however, is that the wife is no longer a would-be castrator; and even if she were, the husband would now refuse, point-blank, to be demasculinized.

I insist, then: there are no truly or directly demasculinizing women. There are many males, unfortunately, who *think* they can be castrated psychologically by their wives or sweethearts and who, because they think they can be, actually are. But these males, in a very real sense, are always *self*-castrated rather than demasculinized by any woman. If there is any female who truly might be called castrating it is a man's mother: for she often gives him the original attitudes, prejudices, and interpretations which, later on in life, he employs at point B to make himself give over-serious heed to point A—the so-called demasculinizing wife. Even in regard to the originally castrating mother, however, we must make two important qualifications.

In the first place, a man's basic set of beliefs, assumptions, or philosophic attitudes toward and interpretations of life are by no means entirely inculcated by his mother, but also by his father, his other relatives, his siblings, his teachers, his books, his peers—by his whole social culture. It is really this culture, rather than his mother alone, which basically encourages him to become demasculinized or to believe, irrationally, that he *must* be hurt and castrated by the words and gestures of others.

In the second place, even if a man's mother or his culture as a whole indoctrinates him with the belief that he cannot control his own psychological destiny and that he must be vulnerable to the insults and castration-tendencies of others, this does not mean that he *has* to believe this for the rest of his life. He can, even without psychotherapeutic aid, contradict, question, and challenge the basic ideologies with which he was reared and, through such questioning, become invulnerable to *any* attempts at psychological castration. Since he *can* become thus released, the individual, by the time he reaches adulthood, is never really demasculinized or weakened by others; in the last analysis, he *allows* these others to wreak "their" damage and, thereby, castrates himself. When a human being is truly rational and realistic, any possibility of demasculinization, angrily pushed by the female or defensively accepted by the male, becomes highly remote.

12

A Rational-Emotive Approach to Premarital Counseling*

Just as rational-emotive psychotherapy is highly useful when used in marriage counseling cases, so is it an efficient method of treatment with many premarital counseling cases. For, like the individual who comes with a marital problem, the person who seeks help because of his premarital difficulties is, in the great majority of cases, in need of some kind of intensive psychotherapy. It is not merely his girlfriend or fiancée who is behaving badly; nor is it only the complicated premarital situation which drives him to seek help. Almost always, it is *he* who has distinct difficulty in relating to his prospective mate or in handling the situation in which they are entangled.

Although, then, I see a few clients for premarital counseling who have simple questions to be answered, which can sometimes be resolved in one or two sessions, the vast majority come for deeper and more complicated reasons. Their main presenting questions are: "Is my fiancée the right person for me?" "Should I be having premarital sex relations?" "How can I find a suitable mate?" "How can I overcome my sexual incompetence or my homosexual leanings before I marry?" These and similar questions usually involve deep-seated personality characteristics or longstanding emotional problems of the counselees.

When put in more dynamic terms, the real questions most individuals who come for premarital counseling are asking themselves are: "Wouldn't it be terrible if I were sexually or

* This chapter is an expanded presentation of the talk, "A Rational Approach to Premarital Counseling," given at the annual meeting of the National Council on Family Relations at Columbia University, August 26, 1960, and published in *Psychological Reports*, 1961, 8, 333-338.

amatively rejected? or made a mistake in my sex-love choice? or acted wrongly or wickedly in my premarital affairs?" And: "Isn't it horribly unfair that the girl or fellow in whom I am interested is unkind? or not sufficiently understanding? or overly-demanding? or too selfish?"

Stated differently: the majority of premarital counselees are needlessly anxious and/or angry. They are woefully afraid of rejection, incompetence, or wrongdoing during courtship or marriage; and they are exceptionally angry or hostile because general or specific members of the other sex do not behave exactly as they would like them to behave. Since, according to the principles of rational-emotive psychotherapy, feelings of anxiety and resentment are for the most part needlessly self-created and inevitably do the individual who experiences them more harm than good, my psychotherapeutic approach to most premarital counselees is to show them, as quickly as possible, how to rid themselves of their fear and hostility and thereby to be able to solve their present and future courtship and marital difficulties.

The main theoretical construct and technique which I employ, in extirpating an unmarried person's shame and anger in relation to himself and his would-be mate, is the same A-B-C theory of personality previously expounded in this book. Let us see how this construct has been specifically applied to some pre-marital cases.

Let us take, first of all, premarital anxiety—which is often the main presenting symptom of young people who come for counseling before marriage. I have recently been seeing a girl of 25 who, in spite of her keen desire to marry and have a family, has never been out on a date with a boy. She is reasonably goodlooking and very well educated and has had a good many opportunities to go with boys, because her entire family is concerned about her being dateless and will arrange dates for her on a moment's notice. But she always has found some excuse not to make appointments with boys; or else has made dates and then cancelled them at the last minute. At the very few social affairs she has attended, she has latched on to her mother or some girlfriend and has literally never left her side and never allowed herself to be alone with a male.

Although it is easy to give this girl's problem an impressive "psychodynamic" classification and to say that she is pregenitally fixated or has a severe symbiotic attachment to her mother, such labels, even if partially accurate, are incredibly unhelpful in getting her over her problem. Instead, she was simply told that her phobic reaction to males, at point C, could not possibly be caused by some noxious event or stimulus at point A (such as her once being rejected by a boy in whom she was interested); but that her own catastrophizing sentences at point B must be the real, current cause of her extreme fear of dating boys.

"What," I asked this client, "are you telling yourself at point B that makes you react so fearfully at point C?"

At first, as is the case of many of my psychotherapy patients and marriage counseling clients, she insisted that she wasn't telling herself anything at point B; or that, if she were, she couldn't say what it was. I insisted on theoretical grounds, however, that she must be telling herself some nonsense in order to produce the sorry results she was getting in her emotional tone and her behavior; and I kept questioning her in this regard. My persistent questioning soon paid off. She found that she was telling herself that it would be perfectly awful if she went with boys and, like her two older sisters before her, got sexually seduced before marriage but, unlike these sisters, didn't actually marry her seducer.

These internalized sentences, in their turn, were subheadings under the client's general philosophy, which held that marriage rather than sex is the only real good in life and that any girl who fails to achieve the marital state is thoroughly incompetent and worthless. Perversely enough, as happens in so many instances of neurosis, by overemphasizing the necessity of her marrying, this girl literally drove herself into a state of panic which effectively prevented her from achieving the goal she most desired.

What was to be done to help this client? In my old psychoanalytic days I would have encouraged her to transfer her love and marital needs toward me, and then, interspersed with a considerable amount of free associational and dream analysis rituals, I would have tried to show her that because I accepted her, she could well accept herself, and then presumably feel free to go off and marry some other male. Maybe, after a few hundred hours of analysis, this would have worked; or maybe she would have become just as symbiotically attached to me as she now was to her mother and would have finally, at the age of 65, realized that I was not going to marry her and been pensioned off to a home for ex-analysands which I once fondly thought of organizing.

Not being willing any longer to risk this dubiously fortuitous outcome of therapy, I very directly took this girl's major and minor irrational philosophies of life and ruthlessly beat them— the philosophies, mind you, not the girl—over the head until, after three months of counseling, she decided to give them up. More specifically, I vigorously attacked her idiotic notions that premarital sex relations are wicked and shameful; that marriage is the only good state of female existence; and that anyone who fails to attain a major goal, such as that of achieving a good relationship with a member of the other sex, is completely inept and valueless as a human being. I helped this girl to see, instead, that sex-love relations can be fine in themselves, quite apart from marriage; that marriage may be a highly *preferable*, but that it is hardly a *necessary*, goal for a female; and that failing in a given purpose is a normal part of human living and proves nothing whatever about one's essential worth.

In miracles or any other supernatural influences I passionately disbelieve. But the changes that took place in this client concomitant with her changing her sex-love and general philosophies of life were almost miraculous. It needed relatively little urging on my part to get her to make several dates with young males. She thoroughly enjoyed petting to orgasm with some of these partners. A few months later she entered into a full sex-love relationship with one of them. And she is now engaged to be married to her lover. Moreover, although we rarely talked about some of the other important aspects of her life, she has also gone back to college, which she had left in despair because of her poor social life there, and is intent on becoming a nursery school teacher.

Let us consider another case of premarital counseling along rational psychotherapeutic lines. A 28-year old male came for counseling because he kept becoming angry at his fiancée, ostensibly because she continually "unmanned" him by criticizing him in public. On questioning, he also admitted that he had never been fully potent with a female and had acute fears of whether he would succeed sexually with his fiancée after they were married. According to psychoanalytic interpretation—which I would have cheerfully (and wrongheadedly) made years ago—he was really not afraid of his fiancée unmanning him in public, but of his unmanning himself when he finally got into bed with his bride; and her so-called attacks on him were actually a projection of his own castration fears.

So I would have interpreted in my dear dead psychoanalytic youth. Fortunately, however, I had the good sense to call in this client's fiancée and — surprise, surprise! — I quickly discovered that she was a querulous, negativistic woman and that she did, figuratively speaking, often castrate my client in public. Whereupon I set about doing two non-psychoanalytic and highly directive things: First I talked the fiancée herself into becoming a counselee, even though at first she contended that there was nothing wrong with her, and that the entire problem was the result of her boyfriend's inconsiderateness and ineptness. When I got her into psychotherapy—to the tune of 48 sessions of individual and a year of group therapy—I set about showing her that her anger, at point C, stemmed not from her boyfriend's inept behavior, at point A, but from her own prejudiced and grandiose interpretation of this behavior at point B.

I showed this woman, in other words, that she kept saying to herself: (*a*) "John is doing these inept and inconsiderate things in public," and (*b*) "He *shouldn't* be acting that way and is a no-good son-of-a-gun for doing so." Instead, I pointed out, she would do much better if she told herself: (*a*) "John is doing these things, which I consider to be inept and inconsider-

ate in public," and (*b*) If I am correct, which I may not be, then
it *would be much nicer* if he could be induced to stop acting
this way; and I should be trying everything in my power to help
him see what he is doing (without blaming him for doing it) so
that he changes his actions for the better."

When I convinced this client—and again let me say that she
ran me a little bit ragged for awhile, but a good larynx and
rational-emotive methodology finally triumphed—that no one is
ever to blame for anything, and that people's errors and mistakes
are to be accepted and condoned rather than excoriated if we
are truly to be of help to them, she not only stopped berating
her boyfriend in public but became a generally kinder and less
disturbed individual in her own right.

Meanwhile, to flashback to my original client in this duo,
whom we left gnashing his teeth at his fiancée and shivering
about the spectre of his sexual impotence, he proved to be a
relatively easy convert to the cause of rational thinking. After
16 sessions of highly directive counseling he was able to see
that, whatever the verbal harshness of his intended bride, her
words—at point A—could hurt and anger him—at point C—only
if he kept telling himself sufficient nonsense about these words
at point B.

Instead of what he had been telling himself at point B—
namely, "That bitch is de-balling me by her horrible public
criticism and she has no right to do that to poor weakly me"—
he was induced to question the rationality of these internal
verbalizations. After actively challenging his own unthinking
assumptions—particularly the assumptions (*a*) that his fiancée's
critical words *were* necessarily hurtful; (*b*) that she *should not*
keep repeating her criticism of him; and (*c*) that he *was* too
weak to hear this criticism and not be able to take it in his
stride—this client began to believe in and tell himself a radically
different philosophy of sex-love relationships, namely: "There
goes my poor darling again, making cracks at me because of
her own disturbance. Now let me see if any of her points about
me are correct; and, if so, let me try to change myself in those
respects. But let me also try, insofar as she is mistaken about

her estimates of me, to help her with her own problems, so that she doesn't need to keep being nasty to me in public."

When this change in the client's internalized sentences was made, he improved in his ability to take his fiancée's criticism; and his hostility toward her largely vanished. He was then also able to face the matter of his own impotence—which proved to be, as it so often does, a result of his worrying so greatly over the possibility of his failing that he actually tended to fail. When he was able to acquire a new sexual and general philosophy about failing, he became more than adequately potent.

In his new philosophy, instead of saying to himself: "If I fail sexually, it will be terrible and I will be totally unmanned," he began to say: "It is highly desirable, though not necessary, that I succeed in being potent; and in the event that I am impotent for the present, there are various extravaginal ways of satisfying my partner; so what's the great hassle?" Losing his acute fear of sexual failure, he mainly succeeded; and losing his terrible fear of his fiancée's publicly criticizing him, he helped her to be much less critical.

The main aspects of RT which are usually applied to premarital counseling, then, include the counselee being taught that it is *not* horrible for him to fail in his sex-love ventures; that there is no reason why his love partner *should* act the way he would like her to act; and that any intense unhappiness that he may experience in his premarital (or, later, marital) affairs almost invariably stems from his *own* self-repeated nonsense rather than from his partner's attitudes or actions. Rational-emotive therapy, in these respects, directly forces the client to accept reality, particularly in his relations with his sex-love partner.

This is one of the chief advantages of RT, when it is applied to premarital and marital counseling cases: that it is reality-rather than fantasy-centered. Whereas some forms of therapy take engaged or married couples far away from reality, and encourage them to concentrate exclusively on their own psychological navels while they are undergoing treatment, and whereas in consequence these types of therapy tend to pull the engaged

or married pair *away* from each other, rational-emotive psychotherapy tries to induce them to confront themselves *and* reality.

Thus, RT places the individual, as some of the Existentialists
would say, squarely in the world, and does not arbitrarily remove him from other people or other things. And it encourages
him to understand that relationships such as marriage *are* exceptionally down-to-earth and (often) difficult; and that there
is no point in his ignoring their harsh aspects or trying to run
away from these aspects into a world of fantasy. In the last
analysis, he must live in some kind of reality; and he can only
know and realize himself in this reality when, to a somewhat
(though not totally) maximum degree he takes risks, experiments, commits himself.

But such a commitment, RT tells the individual, even though
it has risks of pain, frustration, and problems, can never lead
to *his* being worthless or hopeless if and when he fails. If he
makes the mistake of marrying the wrong girl or not marrying
the right one, or of staying with a wife he would better have
left or leaving one he might well better have remained with,
that is sorrowful, regrettable, and unfortunate—but it is not
terrible and catastrophic. In such an endeavor he has failed;
but he is not, with a capital F, a Failure. He is still a living,
ongoing human being; and he can try and try again, until he
finally finds what he wants, or something reasonably close to
what he wants, in sex-love or marital relationships.

RT, then, gives the individual a fully realistic view of marriage
and the fact that he'd better stop blaming his fiancée or wife
and buckle down to cultivating his *own* marital garden in a
more efficient manner. But it also gives him the "idealistic"
philosophy that, win or lose, he is still largely the master of his
own fate and the captain of his own soul, and that he can
utilize his losing experiences to his own future advantage. It
encourages him to be an individual *in* the world in general
and the world of marriage in particular: to assume full responsibility for his own actions and reactions, but to accept outside
reality in its own right, and not super-romantically to ignore,
avoid, or deny it.

13

The Treatment of Frigidity and Impotence*

There are many reasons why women become frigid and men become impotent in our society, not the least of which is an overpowering sense of guilt on the part of the sexually incapacitated female or male (Ellis, 1952, 1961b; Hirsch, 1957; Hitschmann and Bergler, 1949; Kinsey, Pomeroy, Martin and Gebhard, 1953). Thus, I have presented elsewhere considerable evidence to the effect that people in our Western world are usually overwhelmed with antisexual attitudes, with which we indoctrinate them almost literally from birth; and that consequently they are inordinately guilty about letting themselves go and fully enjoying themselves sexually. Varying degrees of frigidity and impotence naturally result (Ellis, 1958b, 1962b).

Be that as it may, another phenomenon has come to exist in contemporary society that is different from and in many ways more pernicious than the sexual guilt which was so prevalent in previous days, and upon the basis of which Freud constructed a considerable part of his psychoanalytic theory. This phenomenon is that of intense shame—which overlaps with guilt in some significant respects, but which is also somewhat different. Whereas when he feels guilty, an individual believes that he has acted wrongly or wickedly in the eyes of some God, fate, or social value system, when he feels ashamed or inadequate, he is more likely to believe that he has acted ineptly or weakly in his own eyes and in those of the people with whom he has immediate contact.

As Piers and Singer (1953) and several other psychological

* This chapter is expanded from "Guilt, Shame and Frigidity," *Quart. Rev. Surg., Obset. & Gynecol.*, 1959, 16, 259-261; and Chapter 11, pp. 232-236 of *The Art and Science of Love* (New York: Lyle Stuart, 1960).

and sociological thinkers have recently pointed out, shame and its concomitant feelings of inadequacy (as distinguished from guilt and its concomitant feelings of sinfulness) are likely to be particularly enhanced in a society, such as our own, which stresses success rather than goodness, achievement rather than sainthood.

As a result of our having so many millions of shame-inculcated individuals in this country, I have been seeing, in my private practice of psychotherapy and marriage counseling, one person after another who, in spite of having had adequate sex education, is frigid or impotent. These sexually inadequate people are often highly sophisticated people who do not consider sex wicked and who have little or no guilt about engaging in premarital or marital relations. Indeed, most of them want very much to experience full sex satisfaction and will do anything in their power to experience it.

This goes for women, these days, as much as for men. Whereas, in previous years, it was frequently husbands who came to see me to complain that their wives weren't too interested in sex relations, today it is just as likely to be the wives who complain that *they* want bigger and better orgasms and are not, alas, achieving them. The husbands still come to complain—but largely about their own impotence rather than their wives' sexual inadequacies.

One of the major reasons, ironically, why both men and women in our society are not achieving full sex satisfaction is because they are often so over-determined to achieve it. Because of their upbringing, they are so ashamed if they do not reach the greatest heights of expressive sexuality that they tragically sabotage their own desires. That is to say, instead of focusing clearly on the real problem at hand—which, baldly stated, is "How can I think of something sexually exciting enough and how can I concentrate on movements that are sufficiently stimulating to bring me to fulfillment?"—these people are focusing on quite a different problem—namely, "Oh, what an idiot and an incompetent person I am for not being able to copulate without any difficulty." Stated differently: sexually inadequate people are usually obsessed with the notion of *how* rather than *what* they are doing when they are having sex relations (Eichenlaub, 1962; Ellis, 1962b).

The physiological and endocrinological aspects of impotence and frigidity are not to be ignored (Ellis, 1960; Kleegman, 1959; Kupperman, 1959; Walker and Strauss, 1952). It would nonetheless appear that most men and women who come for help because they are sexually inadequate are physiologically and endocrinologically normal and that there is little that can be done for them by prescribing sex hormones. Sex desire and fulfillment is largely mediated through the central nervous system and the cerebral cortex; and in order for arousal and satisfaction to be maximal, there must be a concerted focusing on specific sexual ideation.

If, instead of concentrating on sexually arousing stimuli, a person keeps telling himself that it would be terrible if he were sexually incompetent; that this would prove that he was worthless and inferior; that he simply must be able to get as many and as powerful orgasms as other people get; that when he comes to climax, bells should ring and lights should flash—if this is the kind of nonsense that a person keeps repeating to himself, it can only be expected that he will rarely achieve a high degree of excitement and fruition.

Another form that sex shame currently takes in our society is equally inhibiting—that is, as an inhibitor of varied coital and extracoital technique. Today, fewer college-educated and middle-class individuals are desisting from trying various coital positions or types of noncoital sex play which once were erroneously called "perversions." Having little sex guilt, in the old-fashioned sense, they do not deem these aspects of sex wicked.

At the same time, however, literally millions of Americans are employing extravaginal methods only as "preliminary" or "love play" techniques and are not using them, when necessary, up to and including the achievement of orgasm. Their reasons for so restricting themselves are again bound up with shame: that is, they feel that they "should" be able to achieve full satisfaction through "natural" coital means, and should not require digital manipulation of the genitals, oral-genital relations, or other techniques of coming to climax.

If people do require noncoital methods of achieving orgasm —as many of them quite normally do—they feel that there is something "wrong" with them, that they are sexually "inferior" or "incompetent." This feeling, of course, is perfectly illogical and is almost entirely a consequence of their arbitrary notions of what is "shameful." To compound the problem here, where many wives feel that they are abnormal because they cannot come to orgasm in the course of penile-vaginal copulation, many of their husbands also believe that they are inferior when they cannot give their wives orgasms except through noncoital methods. Both partners thereby shamefully—and most mistakenly— interfere with their own sex satisfactions.

As a case in point, I saw a 25 year old wife who had never achieved an orgasm with her husband and was ready to divorce him because of her shame about her own and his sexual ineptness. Without even attempting at first to uncover any of her "deep" unconscious feelings of guilt, anxiety, or hostility, I merely forcefully explained to this woman how she was forestalling her own orgasms.

"From what you tell me," I said, "it seems clear that you are almost constantly telling yourself: 'Oh, how horrible I am because I never get an orgasm during intercourse! and 'How can an incompetent person like me ever get a full climax?' and 'If I can't make it with this husband, who treats me so well, how will I possibly be able to be successfully married to anyone else?' and so forth."

"I'm sure you're right. That's just what I do keep telling myself."

"But how can you *possibly* focus on your sex pleasure when you are agitatedly focusing on this kind of self-blaming? In order to feel sexually aroused, you must *think* of sexually-arousing things. And you are thinking of the most *un*arousing thing imaginable—that is, of your own unworthiness as a woman."

"But how can I consider myself to be a worthy woman if I am bad sexually?"

"How can you *not?* In the first place, as you told me before, your husband is not complaining at all, since *he* is being well satisfied by your mutual sex activity. And in the second place, even if he were complaining, it would merely mean that *he* has certain arbitrary prejudices—that he, for example, *insists* on your having an orgasm during intercourse, instead of telling himself that it would be nice if you did have one—and that he is just as disturbed, for having these prejudices, as you are for having yours. At the worst, in any event, you would prove to be a relatively poor sex partner to your husband. But that would hardly make you a worthless *woman.*"

"You mean I might then be good for some other man—or good for myself, even though my husband would find me no good in bed?"

"Exactly. But you really seem to think that *you're* no good if you aren't a perfectly lovely sex partner to your husband. And that's only your *definition* of yourself, and has no relation to external facts."

I insisted, in session after session, that this patient was a worthwhile human being in her own right, no matter how poor she might be as a sex partner. I also kept pointing out that if she focused on sexually exciting stimuli, instead of on how worthless she was for not having orgasms, she could almost certainly bring herself to have fully satisfying climaxes.

She at first resisted my suggestions, but after eight sessions of fairly repetitive rational-emotive psychotherapy, I began to convince her. She tried, really for the first time, to let herself go in the course of her marital relations, and got so she could enjoy intercourse, even though she didn't have an orgasm while it was going on. She finally became sufficiently released to try mutual oral-genital relations with her husband and found that she was unusually aroused by this method, but that it was so exciting that she could not focus adequately on her own climax. When her husband was independently practicing cunnilinctus, however, she was able to focus quite well and soon experienced explosive orgasm.

After some practice, this patient was able to focus properly on sexual enjoyment during the act of coitus itself. As she reported during one of the closing psychotherapy sessions:

"I had considerable difficulty at first, because I found myself thinking, 'Will it happen this time? Will it happen this time?' And, of course, just as you explained to me, it didn't happen when I kept thinking that. Then I finally said to myself, 'All right, if it doesn't happen this time, so what? If I *never* get an orgasm this way it won't be too bad, either. But let me try to get it.' And I could feel myself, as I thought that it wouldn't be too bad, really, if it never happened at all, getting much more relaxed about the whole thing than I ever was before.

"Then I was able, without too much difficulty really, to focus on my own pleasure. Not even on Jim's, for a change, but just on my own. And I found that it started coming, almost immediately, and I kept focusing on the pleasant feeling I was getting, the sex feeling that is, and how I wanted to keep that feeling going. And before I knew it, after only about five minutes of active intercourse, there it was, and it was thrilling as all hell. Other times, we had tried for a half hour or more and nothing had happened. But this time, wow!"

At the last session I had with this patient, when we were talking about other aspects of her life (since sex was no longer a problem), she smilingly informed me that her husband had been away on a business trip for a few days and when he came home they had spent almost the entire night having sex relations in many different positions and ways. "And would you believe it?" she said, "I'm sure that I had about a hundred orgasms during the night!"

As an example of how rational-emotive therapy was employed with a male with serious sex problems, we may take the case of a 25 year old patient whom I saw because he kept either losing his erection as soon as he started to have intercourse with his wife or ejaculating within a few seconds after penetration. It was quickly apparent in his case that this patient did have a somewhat classical Oedipus complex—which I by no means see in most of my patients today, but which from time to time does turn up—and that he always had felt guilty in having sex relations with any female partner because his mother, who was still young and attractive, had literally taught him that sex was for procreative purposes and that "more worthwhile" people enjoyed themselves with "higher and better" pursuits.

Consequently, this patient had had only two or three abortive attempts at intercourse before marriage and had married a rather unattractive physician, a few years older than himself, who was a highly intellectual and (according to his mother's and his own standards) "more worthwhile" sort of person. He had been potent with his wife until she became pregnant with their first and so far only child; and since that time, though the child was now two years of age, he had never been completely sexually adequate.

It was easy to see why this patient was afraid to be potent—or, to risk a pun, was scared unstiff—and it was not difficult to get him to accept the interpretation that his impotency originally stemmed from his indoctrinations concerning incest and his conscious belief that sex for the sake of fun was improper. Unfortunately, however, his acceptance of these interpretations had no particular effect on his sexual competence.

The patient was then shown that, while his *primary* disturbance may well have been connected with his relations with his mother and his antisexual beliefs thus engendered, his *secondary* (and for the moment *more* important) disturbance was connected with his feelings of shame, of incompetence, of failure. That is to say, his society (and, in his particular case, his father more than his mother) had taught him to believe wholeheartedly that the worst possible thing in the world, and in many ways even worse than enjoying himself sexually, was being a weakling, a nincompoop, a failure.

Consequently, when he first started to become incapable of sustaining an adequate erection, instead of asking himelf the simple questions: "*Why* am I failing sexually?" and "What can I do *not* to keep failing?" he kept telling himelf, over and over, "See what a failure I am! This proves what I've always suspected: that I'm weak and no good! Oh, my God: how awful it is for me to be so incompetent and unmanly!" By repeating these kinds of catastrophizing sentences the patient (of course!) kept focusing and refocusing on sexual failure rather than success, and he could not possibly overcome his disability.

It must again be remembered, in this connection, that both male and female sexual arousal and incitation to orgasm are mainly mediated through impulses from the cerebral cortex of the brain and are basically cognitive in origin. And when we focus upon nonsexual notions—such as the idea that it is awful or catastrophic when we are not becoming sufficiently erect or are prematurely achieving a climax—it is literally impossible for us to focus, simultaneously, on sexually exciting ideas. The result, in the male, is often inability to obtain or maintain erection.

I have not found a single case, recently, of male inadequacy in which, no matter what the *original* cause of the problem, the afflicted individual was not *secondarily* telling himself how horrible it was to be impotent, convincing himself that he was a terrible failure and that, as such, he would doubtless continue to be inadequate. So with this patient. He kept, once his first symptoms arose, ceaselessly watching himself, expecting sexual weakness to occur, worrying about his weakness, and continually giving himself a difficult time. When he was shown exactly what he was doing and what nonsensical catastrophizing sentences he was telling himself to sustain his erectile and ejaculatory difficulties, and when he was induced to start *contradicting* the nonsense that he kept telling himself, he quickly began to improve.

Thus, this patient began to see that it was *not* terrible—but only expectable—for him to be sexually inadequate, considering his upbringing. He was led to admit to himself that he was *not* an incompetent or a failure just because he had a sex problem. And he was forced, generally, to question his entire concept of masculinity and failure and to see that *doing, trying, working at* things are more important than necessarily *succeeding at* or doing them *perfectly*. Once he began to surrender his philosophy of the necessity of achieving absolute success and perfection, he was able to watch his sexual behavior more objectively and to focus on sexually exciting stimuli.

At the same time (though this seemed less necessary with this patient since he had already, by himelf, worked through some of his originally mother-inculcated puritanism), I also tackled his basic beliefs that sex was wicked outside of procreation and that incestuous desires toward one's own mother were horrible to contemplate.

On two levels, then, by attacking (a) his original antisexual philosophy that first led to his sex problem, and (b) his secondary philosophy of success and perfectionism that encouraged him to retain, sustain, and aggravate his original symptoms, I directed this patient to more rational modes of thinking about himself and his sexuality.

Whereas, when I used to do psychoanalysis, I mainly would have concentrated on the first of these points, I now, with the use of rational-emotive therapy, mainly concentrate on the second point and find this kind of focusing to be much more efficient. Almost invariably, I find this technique to be effective in cases of male and female psychosexual disability.

I also note that, although I see many people every year who specifically come to me with severe sexual problems, I rarely see one who has what I would call a pure sexual disturbance. With few exceptions, my patients have *general* emotional difficulties, which stem from their poor, illogical, and self-defeating *general* philosophies of life. Their sex symptoms almost always are derivatives of these idiotic general creeds or assumptions; and when their basic beliefs, of which they are unconscious in the sense of not knowing how important they are to their lives, are forthrightly brought to their attention, ruthlessly revealed and analyzed to show how ridiculous these are, and consistently attacked, discouraged, and rooted out, their sex problems do not automatically vanish but are at least much more susceptible to specific reëducating instructions.

In regard to the treatment of frigidity and impotence, therefore, rational-emotive psychotherapy is (as usual) no palliative, superficial, or symptom-removing technique. Rather, it is an intensive, theory-rooted form of therapy that goes right to the main philosophic roots of the individual's presenting disorder and that aims at fundamental attitudinal changes rather than any cursory "cures."

14

The Treatment of Fixed Homosexuality*

More bosh has probably been written about homosexuality than about virtually any other "abnormal" aspect of human behavior. Thus, it has commonly been believed that anyone who engages in sex activity with members of his or her own sex is a homosexual, and as such is severely perverted or disturbed. This is nonsense: since, as Kinsey and his associates (1948, 1953) and many other investigators and clinicians have shown, perhaps 40 per cent of normal males and a considerably less but still significant per cent of females have some homosexual incidents at some period in their lives; and few of these individuals become fixed, confirmed, or practically exclusive homosexuals for life.

At the same time, it is commonly believed, especially by homosexuals themselves, that exclusively homosexual persons are born the way they are, and that they are not essentially neurotic or psychotic, except insofar as they become disturbed by being persecuted for their aberration. Several authorities state or imply that it is practically useless to treat homosexuals by any form of psychotherapy (Baker, 1959; Bell, 1959; Hooker, 1957; Mercer, 1959; Wolfenden Report, 1957). None of these statements is supported by impressive objective evidence; but all of them are quite widely believed by professional and lay people.

It is also widely believed that homosexuals are, on the whole, distinctly more creative individuals than are nonhomosexuals;

* This chapter is an expanded version of "A Homosexual Treated with Rational Psychotherapy," *J. Clin. Psychol.*, 1959, 15, 338-343, and "Homosexuality and Creativity," *J. Clin. Psychol.*, 1959, 15, 376-379.

but no facts supporting this belief are available. When asked to speak on the topic of homosexuality and creativity at one of the Cooper Union forums a few years ago, it occurred to me that, rather than speculating about the subject, I might well be true to my Ph.D. and my clinical training by doing a little research to discover just what the relationship is between homosexuality and creativeness.

Research with homosexuals is particularly hazardous because the researcher rarely gets an opportunity to know his subjects very well, he often has to employ a nontypical group, and he rarely is able to obtain a control group of nonhomosexuals who can be properly compared to his homosexual subjects. Happily, however, I have been working in circumstances in which some of these major limitations of research with homosexuals can be ameliorated or eliminated. During the past several years, I have seen about 130 patients who have had severe homosexual problems; and I have also intensively treated a much greater number of heterosexual patients, many of whom have had little or no homosexual tendency and were exceptionally heterosexual in their orientation.

It occurred to me, therefore, when I was considering what I would say about homosexuals and creativity in my Cooper Union talk that I might find some distinctly factual and highly interesting material on this subject by comparing the creativeness of 66 homosexual and 150 quite heterosexual patients that I had intensively seen for from 10 to 350 sessions of psychotherapy.

Although it is true that the individuals thus investigated were all psychotherapy patients, and consequently not necessarily typical of the American population, it is also true, as I have pointed out in previous publications (Ellis 1955c, 1956c, 1962b), that fixed homosexuals in our society are almost invariably neurotic or psychotic; that, therefore, no so-called *normal* group of homosexuals is to be found anywhere; and that the only legitimate control group with which a homosexual group can be matched probably is one which also consists of emotionally disturbed individuals. It was a most fortunate coincidence that

I could find, among my therapy patients, a group of exceptionally heterosexual individuals who, in terms of age, sex, and
educational status, were closely matched with the individuals
with severe homosexual problems whom I also had seen for
therapy.

Since the 66 homosexuals used in this study were not a homo-
geneous group, it was thought advisable to divide them, for
purposes of comparison, into three subgroups. The first subgroup, including 9 males and 10 females, consisted of individuals
with a strong homosexual component, including a history of
overt homosexuality, but who also had a reasonably strong
heterosexual component and who were consequently more or
less bisexual. The second subgroup, including 23 males and 10
females, consisted of individuals who were exclusively or predominantly homosexual up to the time they came for therapy
but who, while being homosexual, maintained their own sex
role—that is, the males normally behaved as males do in our
society and the females as females do. The third subgroup,
including 10 males and four females, consisted of individuals
who were exclusively or predominantly homosexual up to the
time they came for psychotherapy, but who maintained sex
role inversion—that is, the males adopted a female (or "fairy")
role whenever it was convenient for them to do so and the
females played a masculine or "butch"-type role.

Although brief descriptions of these three groups may be
somewhat misleading and not entirely accurate, it would not
be too inaccurate if we label the members of the first group of
homosexuals as *bisexuals,* the second group as *homosexuals,* and
the third group as *inverts.*

The first question to be investigated in this study was: How
did the highly heterosexual patients compare in creativity to
the three groups of homosexual patients? For the purpose of
these comparisons, each of the patients was rated by the therapist as to whether he or she was (*a*) highly creative, (*b*)
moderately creative, or (*c*) very little creative. Creativity itself
was defined in terms of originality and inventiveness—or, as
English and English define it in their *Dictionary of Psychological*

and Psychoanalytical Terms (1958), the ability "to find new solutions to a problem or new modes of artistic expression."

It was found that, in the case of the highly heterosexual patients, 26 per cent were highly creative, 31 per cent moderately creative, and 43 per cent little creative. Of the bisexual patients, 11 per cent were highly creative, 52 per cent moderately creative, and 37 per cent little creative. Of the homosexual patients, 9 per cent were highly creative, 39 per cent moderately creative, and 53 per cent were little creative. Finally, of the homosexual inverts, zero per cent were highly creative, 14 per cent moderately creative, and 86 per cent noncreative.

These findings indicate that there was a distinct decline in creativity from the most heterosexual to the most homosexual patients studied, with the bisexual patients being somewhat in between. When the highly heterosexual patients were compared to the predominantly homosexual and inverted patients, 43 per cent of the former as against 63 per cent of the latter were found to show little or no creativity. When tested for statistical significance by use of Chi-square analysis, this difference proved to be highly significant.

It was further found that whereas 61 per cent of the highly heterosexual patients seemed to become more creative, or to turn their creative potential into an actual reality, as psychotherapy progressed, and 63 per cent of the bisexuals similarly became more creative with therapy, only 54 per cent of the predominant homosexuals and 53 per cent of the inverts increased their creativity during therapy.

It would seem reasonably clear from these findings, therefore, that not only do homosexual patients tend to be less creative than bisexuals and heterosexuals but that they also benefit less from psychotherapy in terms of increased creativeness. In an attempt to determine why the homosexual patients were significantly less creative than the heterosexual individuals studied, the clinical diagnosis of all the persons in the sample was checked. Here, again, clear-cut differences were found.

Whereas 78 per cent of the highly heterosexual patients were found to be neurotic and 22 per cent borderline psychotic or outrightly psychotic, the proportion of borderline and psychotic patients rose to 37 per cent in the bisexual, 41 per cent in the predominantly homosexual, and 57 per cent in the inverted group. When tested for statistical significance, it was found that the homosexual and inverted patients had significantly more borderline and psychotic patients among them than did the highly heterosexual patients.

The hypothesis was then considered that the relative lack of creativity among the homosexual and inverted patients might well be related to the seriousness of their emotional disturbance. To check on this hypothesis, a comparison was made between the heterosexual neurotics and the homosexual and inverted neurotics. It was found that whereas 39 per cent of the former group showed little or no creativity, 50 per cent of the homosexual group showed equally little creativity. In other words, even when clinical diagnosis was held constant, the highly heterosexual group still proved to be more creative than the highly homosexual group. This difference, however, did not prove to be statistically significant.

Investigation of the degree of improvement in the highly heterosexual and the highly homosexual groups of patients was also made. It was found that while 97 per cent of the individuals in the heterosexual group made distinct or considerable improvement, 16 per cent of the bisexuals, 32 per cent of the predominantly homosexuals, and 64 per cent of the inverts made little or no clinical improvement. It was further found that in regard to overcoming their specific homosexual problem, 100 per cent of the bisexuals, 54 per cent of the homosexuals, and 28 per cent of the inverts made distinct or considerable improvement.

It would appear reasonable, from the foregoing findings, to make the following (highly tentative) conclusions:

1. Homosexual patients, in general, and inverts in particular are significantly less creative than highly heterosexual patients and, as far as their creativity is concerned, seem to benefit less from psychotherapy.

2. Homosexual patients, in general, and inverts in particular

are significantly more emotionally disturbed than are highly heterosexual patients.

3. Homosexual patients, in general, and inverts in particular show significantly less clinical gain in the course of intensive psychotherapy than do clearly heterosexual individuals.

4. One of the main reasons for the significantly greater creativeness of heterosexual over homosexual patients would seem to be the significant relationship which exists between severe emotional disturbance and lack of creativity.

5. Psychotherapy is of distinct value in helping homosexuals become less emotionally disturbed, less homosexual, and more creative; but, on all three counts, it is less effective with predominant homosexuals than with bisexuals and much less effective with homosexuals who maintain sex role inversion than it is with those who are not inverted.

These conclusions concerning homosexuality and creativity are not, of course, to be taken as gospel, since they are based on a single study by one psychotherapist; and other studies of similar or different heterosexual and homosexual populations might well produce other results. As has often been said of psychological experiments in the field of learning theory, the rats in one laboratory simply do not seem to run the same way as the rats in a rival group's laboratory; and it is possible that the human guinea pigs used in my clinical study or my personal assessments of their performance have been unconsciously manipulated by me to obtain the kind of results and conclusions just delineated.

It is also possible, however, that this pioneer study of human homosexual behavior—which I believe is the first recorded investigation to make use of a logically justifiable control group of emotionally disturbed and highly heterosexually oriented individuals—*has* been productive of valid findings and conclusions. If so, it presents an interesting supplemental question: namely, granted that homosexuals may be generally less creative than heterosexuals, how can we account for the preponderance, today, of so many outstandingly creative homosexuals in such fields as music, the theatre, designing, and the dance? I think we can account for this seeming paradox in several ways:

Firstly, it may be noted that the seeming preponderance of homosexuals in certain fields of artistic endeavor is perhaps not as great as, at first blush, it seems to be. It is very easy for most of us, no doubt, to recall several outstanding playwrights of this generation who are homosexual. But how many of us can actively bring to mind even a small proportion of the outstanding playwrights who are heterosexual? Frequently, outstanding creators who are homosexual turn out to be, precisely because of their homosexuality and allied disturbances, unusual characters, and therefore are easily remembered in any discussion; while outstanding creators who are heterosexual, and who may well be living a quiet home-life in a non-sensational way, are less quickly called to mind.

Secondly, a reasonably high proportion of homosexuals who are generally acknowledged to be creative are not actually so in the sense used in the present discussion. This, particularly, is true of many performers, such as dancers, actors, and singers, who may have decided talent and do well in their artistic fields of endeavor, but who really have little or no inventiveness or originality. It is my feeling that many homosexuals devote themselves to the performing arts, and eventually become proficient at these arts, largely because they are interested in achieving fame and approval rather than because they are truly creative (though this is true, of course, of many heterosexuals as well). Moreover, homosexuals in our society often have considerable experience at acting in their real-life roles, since to be thoroughly honest about their homosexuality might well be disastrous at times. Their unusual interest in the performing arts may possibly be related to this real-life role playing and may not necessarily stem from basic creativity.

Thirdly, it is particularly to be noted that the creative fields of endeavor in which homosexuals seem to excel are almost exclusively the artistic and esthetic rather than the scientific, professional, managerial, or other fields. In contemporary America, however, there are probably a great many more highly creative individuals working steadily in nonartistic than in artistic areas; and, when we remember the high proportion of homosexuals in esthetic fields, we tend to forget the low proportion who may be outstandingly creative in nonesthetic modes of endeavor. We also forget the fact that whereas creative artists, writers, composers, and choreographers tend to be in the public eye and to acquire a high degree of renown, tens of thousands of contemporary physicists, biochemists, medical researchers, psychologists, political scientists, economists, etc. lead highly creative existences and make notable contributions to our culture without ever achieving public renown.

On several counts, then, it may be doubted whether the seemingly high proportion of creative homosexuals in certain fields of endeavor is really as high as appears, or whether it actually proves that homosexuals are generally more inventive than heterosexuals. More artistic or esthetic they may perhaps be; but not necessarily, on the whole, more creative.

Assuming that, in spite of the number of outstanding creators in our society who are overt homosexuals, the average homosexual may not be nearly so creative as he could potentially be nor even so creative as the highly heterosexual person is, the important question would arise: Why is this so? Is there anything about the condition of being homosexual which interferes with and often seriously sabotages creativity?

My answer to this question would be: Yes, there very often, though not always, is something about the condition of being predominantly homosexual or inverted which blocks an individual's potential creativeness. How so? In the following ways:

1. As indicated previously in this chapter, and as I have shown in other writings (Ellis, 1955c, 1960, 1962b), exclusive and inverted homosexuals are not only more disturbed than heterosexuals but there are good reasons to believe that they are *necessarily* neurotic or psychotic. This is not because they practice homosexual acts (which in themselves are normal enough) but because they rigidly stick to these activities while living in a society which (unfortunately and unfairly) severely

punishes them for doing so. Fixed homosexuality is not inborn but arises when an individual is exceptionally *fearful* of having heterosexual relations, or is *fetichistically fixated* or *obsessively-compulsively attached to* members of his or her own sex. The fears, fixations, or obsessive-compulsive attachments which drive human beings not merely to homosexual activity but to exclusive or inverted homosexuality are almost invariably caused by and intimately related to the fixed homosexual's deep-seated feelings of guilt, inadequacy, and worthlessness—that is, caused by his irrational and groundless negative self-evaluations.

Because fixed and inverted homosexuals are so intrinsically self-hating and so thoroughly absorbed in a futile attempt to raise their estimations of themselves by inducing *others* to accept and approve them, they spend inordinate amounts of time and energy, as do most seriously disturbed persons, in focusing on *how they are doing* at a problem instead of on the problem *itself*. Consequently, they are often unable to devise new solutions to artistic and scientific problems and, by the definition employed in this chapter, to be highly creative.

2. Fixed homosexuals and inverts, as Donald Webster Cory (1956, 1960) has shown, are torn between the desire to rebel against their society, on the one hand, and to conform to it and to their homosexual subsociety, on the other hand. Most of the time, as far as I can make out from my clinical studies of homosexuals, they spend much more time conforming to and being highly imitative of their homosexual groups than they do in outward rebellion. In fact, it is my impression that homosexuals, on the whole, are among the most imitative, most conventional, and most acceptance-demanding people in our ultra-conforming culture. And their basic conformity and lack of ideological risk-taking, I would say, often prevents them from looking for the truly novel and original aspects of life and art and from being half as creative in practice as they potentially and theoretically are.

3. Fixed homosexuals who adopt a sexually inverted role are even more disturbed than are homosexuals who maintain their own sex role. Dr. Daniel Brown, an outstanding clinical psy-

chologist who has spent more time studying sex role inversion than probably any living scientist (Brown, 1961), tells me (personal communication) that he has not been able to find in all of recorded human history a single example of a thoroughgoing invert who was a well-known highly creative individual.

I am sure that such persons will eventually turn up—especially, perhaps, among lesbians who have adopted a thoroughly masculine role of living—but I would wager that they will always be exceptionally rare. For anyone who is *so* disturbed as to completely forego his or her own sex role and to behave as if he or she actually were a member of the other sex is almost certain to be too disorganized and unobjective to focus adequately on devising inventive and original solutions to difficult artistic or scientific problems.

4. Fixed homosexuals and inverts, in our country, are usually so blamed, persecuted, and partially excommunicated from normal social life that, in addition to their original fears, hostilities, and self-hatred which induced them to adopt exclusively homosexual patterns of life, they frequently also acquire a secondary disturbance as a result of society's disapproval. Both their primary and secondary disturbances then combine to keep them absorbed in their own problems and to divert considerable amounts of time and energy which they might otherwise devote to creative problem-solving.

5. Homosexuality, as I have pointed out in my book, *Sex Without Guilt* (1958b), is frequently adopted as a mode of life because, perversely enough, it is conceived as an easier way out than an individual's tackling the difficulties which our society puts in the way of his achieving satisfactory heterosexual relations. Young homosexuals can often obtain easier and quicker sex satisfaction than the heterosexual who must usually spend considerable time and money getting a girl to bed or to the altar and who, if he marries, must then accept even greater social, economic, child-rearing, and other responsibilities.

But individuals who do adopt homosexuality largely because it is an easier and less responsible mode of life also tend to look for the easy way out in other aspects of existence; and when it comes to the study, self-discipline, practice, and hard work that is usually necessary for creative achievement, they goof on that just as they goof on their sex and personal problems. Many of them, therefore, who have considerable potential creativeness never actually realize their own potentialities, but end by being desperately dillettantish, pseudointellectual, and bored with themselves.

For purposes of public show these people give the appearance of being artists, litterateurs, and esthetes; but they are not really vitally absorbed in any pursuit—except the autistic and narcissistic contemplation of their own navels and the dire fear that someone will figuratively or literally cut off their testicles. This fear, alas, applies as much to the imagined testes of the butch-type lesbian as to the real ones of the fixed male homosexual.

What, then, is to be done about this sorry state of affairs? How may bisexual, homosexual, and inverted individuals be helped to overcome their emotionally crippled state and to achieve their greater creative potential? The best answer to this question, I am afraid, is to have them reared in such a manner that they do not become homosexual deviants in the first place. For, as I have stressed in previous writings (Ellis, 1956c, 1960, 1962b) and as many other recent writers have also emphasized (Allen, 1949; Bergler, 1956; Cory, 1961; Fink, 1954; Henry, 1955; London and Caprio, 1950; Robertiello, 1959; Stekel, 1934; Westwood,1953), fixed homosexuality is a learned reaction and, as such, can definitely be unlearned.

Even sex role inversion, including attempts of individuals to get rid of their own sex organs and acquire those of the other sex, is not inherited; but as Daniel Brown (1961) and John Money (1961) have recently indicated, is usually a result of very early imprinting and is theoretically treatable. As almost all authorities agree, today, it is certainly possible to bring up a child so that he will not become a fixed homosexual or an invert; and that, in regard to homosexuality, should probably be our main goal.

Assuming—as it is, alas, very safe to assume—that many individuals have been and will continue to be reared so that they are bisexual, homosexual, or inverted, the solution to their problem is not sex hormone injections, tranquilizing drugs, shock treatment, nor any other physical procedure that has yet been devised. A saner societal attitude, including more liberal acceptance of heterosexual relations, would probably help prevent much fixed homosexuality and encourage homosexuals to live more healthfully with themselves while they are still deviated. Intensive psychotherapy is and will probably continue to be the only effective method of cure.

This is not to say that, up to the present time, therapists have been remarkably effective in treating homosexuals. They haven't. This is largely because most fixed homosexuals have no great desire to change themselves and even when they come for therapeutic help will frequently not make the effort required for change. Moreover, many psychotherapists, partly led astray by early misconceptions of Sigmund Freud himself (1960) have taken a defeatist attitude toward the treatment of homosexuality and have mainly tried to adjust homosexuals to their problem rather than to make a serious attempt to help them rid themselves of this problem.

When, however, the therapist himself is strongly heterosexual; when he is not heavily burdened by orthodox psychoanalytic preconceptions; when he sees homosexuality as a general personality problem rather than a specific sex issue; when he does not moralize or blame his homosexual patients; and when, in particular, he ruthlessly and actively uncovers and attacks the irrational and self-defeating philosophies of life which invariably lie behind fixed homosexual behavior, he may well have considerable success in helping homosexuals to be unafraid of and to thoroughly enjoy heterosexual participation and to become considerably less self-hating, other-directed, and hostile and more self-directed and truly creative.

As noted previously in this chapter, the great majority of bisexuals, the majority of fixed homosexuals, and about a fourth of the inverts I have seen for intensive psychotherapy have been considerably or distinctly improved, both sexually and generally, by treatment. As an illustrative case, let me summarize the rational-emotive therapeutic approach employed with a patient who came for therapy primarily because he had been exclusively homosexual all his life and thought that it was about time he settled down and married. He had read about my work with homosexuals in a magazine and was self-referred. In addition to this homosexual problem, he suffered from heart palpitations which had been consistently diagnosed as being of purely psychogenic origin, and he wondered whether something could be done about them. He vaguely thought that he might have other problems, but was not certain what they were.

The patient, 35 years of age, was living in Brooklyn with his parents and operating his disabled father's toy factory. He had been brought up as a Catholic, but no longer considered himself a believer. He was the only son of what he described as a "very religious and very neurotic" mother and "an exceptionally weak, dominated father," who had been disabled by a serious stroke two years before the patient came for treatment. He had always been quite close to his mother, and usually did her bidding even though he bitterly resented her persistent attempts to control him and his father. He liked but did not respect his father.

The patient, whom we shall call Caleb Frosche, was born and reared in Brooklyn; had a shy, uneventful childhood; spent three unhappy years in the Navy; always did well in school; did some college teaching for a short time after obtaining his doctorate in zoology; and reluctantly took over his father's business, after the father had had a serious stroke, and was carrying it on successfully. Caleb had a few dates with girls when he went to high school, but was afraid to make any sexual overtures, for fear of being rejected, and consequently had not ever kissed a girl. While in the Navy he was plied with liquor by two other sailors and induced to have his first homosexual experience at the age of 19. Since that time he had engaged in homosexual acts every two or three weeks, always making his contacts at public urinals and never having any deep relationships with his partners. He occasionally dated girls, mainly to convince others that he was heterosexual, but he was not par-

ticularly attracted to any of them and never made any advances
or got seriously involved.

Shortly after his father began to have difficulties with his
heart—when Caleb was 25—the patient began to experience
sudden attacks of heart palpitation and chest pain. These would
spontaneously subside a few minutes after they began, but he
would be left in a shaken condition for several hours or days
afterward. Continual medical examinations had revealed no
heart pathology, and he referred to himself as a "cardiac neurotic."

Caleb was one of the early patients treated with rational-
emotive psychotherapy. His first major symptom which was
attacked in the course of therapy was his pattern of exclusive
homosexuality, as this was the aspect of his behavior with which
he was most concerned. In tackling Caleb's homosexual pattern,
I first carefully explained why this mode of behavior is neurotic.
I showed him that although homosexual activity is not in itself
a product of emotional disturbance, its fixed or exclusive form
is invariably a neurotic manifestation because it rigidly, prejudicedly, and fetichistically eliminates *other* modes of sexual fulfillment, notably heterosexuality. Thus, the homosexual in our
society, out of some illogical fear or hostility, arbitrarily forfeits
sexual desire and satisfaction with half the population of the
world; and, to make his behavior still more illogical in our
society, confines himself to sex acts with those partners with
whom he is most likely to get into serious legal and social
difficulties, including arrest and blackmail.

Caleb was shown, at the start of therapy, that there would
be no attempt on the therapist's part to induce him to surrender
his homosexual desires or activities in their own right—since
there was no logical reason why he should not, at least, maintain deviated *desires*—but that the goal of therapy would be to
help him overcome his irrational blocks against heterosexuality.
Once he overcame those, and actively desired and enjoyed sex
relations with females, it would be relatively unimportant, from
a mental health standpoint, whether he still had homosexual

leanings as well, or whether he occasionally (and non-self-defeatingly) engaged in homosexual acts.

The basic assumptions behind Caleb's homosexual pattern of behavior were then quickly brought to light. From questioning him about his specific homosexual participation, it was revealed that he invariably would enter a public urinal or a gay bar, would wait around until some male approached him, and then, whether this male appealed to him or not, would go off to have sex relations. On never a single occasion, in 16 years of homosexual activity, had he ever actively approached a male himself.

On the basis of this and allied information, it was made clear to Caleb that his outstanding motive for remaining homosexual was his strong fear of rejection by (*a*) all women and (*b*) most males. He was so convinced that he might be rejected if he made sexual approaches to either women or men, that he had arranged his entire sex life so that no active approach, and consequently no possibility of rejection, was necessary. He had obviously acquired his fear of rejection, as further questioning soon brought out, at an early age, and it was probably related to the fact that he had been a rather chubby and unattractive boy, and that even his own mother had kept remarking that he would have trouble finding and winning an attractive girl.

Rather than spend much time belaboring the point that Caleb's fear of rejection probably stemmed from his childhood, the therapist convinced him, on purely logical grounds, that this was so since he had apparently feared being rejected by girls when he was in his early teens, and his fear must have originated sometime prior to that time. The therapist, instead of harping on Caleb's childhood days, tried to get, as quickly as possible, to the source of his fear of rejection: namely his illogical *belief* that being disapproved by a girl (or a fellow) was a terrible thing. Said the therapist:

T. Suppose, for the sake of discussion, you had, back in your high school days, tried, really tried, to make some sexual passes at a girl, and suppose you had been unequivocally rejected by her. Why would that be terrible?

P: Well—uh—it just would be.

T: But *why* would it be?

P: Because—uh—I—I just thought the world would come to an end if that happened.

T: But *why*? Would the world *really* have come to an end?

P: No, of course not.

T: Would the girl have slapped your face, or called a cop, or induced all the other girls to ostracize you?

P: No, I guess she wouldn't.

T: Then what *would* she have done? How would you—*really* —have been hurt?

P: Well, I guess, in the way you mean, I wouldn't.

T: Then why did you think that you would?

P: That's a good question. Why did I?

T: The answer, alas, is so obvious that you probably won't believe it.

P: What is it?

T: Simply that you thought you would be terribly hurt by a girl's rejecting you merely because you were *taught* that you would be. You were raised, literally raised, to believe that if anyone, especially a girl, rejects you, tells you she doesn't like you, that this is terrible, awful, frightful. It isn't, of course; it isn't in any manner, shape or form awful if someone rejects you, refuses to accede to your wishes. But you *think* it is, because you were *told* it is.

P: Told?

T: Yes—literally and figuratively told. Told literally by your parents—who warned you, time and again, did they not?—that if you did wrong, made the wrong approaches to people, they wouldn't love you, wouldn't accept you—*and that would be awful, that would be terrible.*

P: Yes, you're right about that. That's just what they told me.

T: Yes—and not only they. Indirectly, figuratively, symbolically, in the books you read, the plays you saw, the films you went to—weren't you told the same thing there, time and again, over and over—that if anyone, the hero of the book, you, or anyone else, got rejected, got rebuffed, got turned down, they *should* think it terrible, should be hurt?

P: I guess I was. Yes, that's what the books and films really say, isn't it?

T: It sure is. All right, then, so you *were* taught that being rejected is awful, frightful. Now let's go back to my original question. Suppose you actually did ask a girl for a kiss, or something else; and suppose she did reject you. What would you *really* lose thereby, by being so rejected?

P: Really lose? Actually, I guess, very little.

T: Right: damned little. In fact, you'd actually gain a great deal.

P: How so?

T: Very simply: you'd gain experience. For if you tried and were rejected, you'd know not to try it with that girl, or in that way, again. Then you could go on to try again with some other girl, or with the same girl in a different way, and so on.

P: Maybe you've got something there.

T: Maybe I have. Whenever you get rejected—as you do, incidentally, every time you put a coin in a slot machine and no gum or candy comes out—you are merely learning that this girl or that technique or this gum machine doesn't work; but a trial with some other girl, technique, or machine may well lead to success. Indeed, in the long run, it's almost certain to.

P: You're probably right.

T: O.K., then. So it isn't the rejection by girls that *really* hurts, is it? It's your *idea*, your *belief*, your assumption that rejection is hurtful, is awful. *That's* what's really doing you in; and that's what we're going to have to change to get you over this silly homosexual neurosis.

Thus, the therapist kept pointing out, in session after session, the illogical fears behind the patient's fixed homosexual pattern of behavior—and *why* these fears were illogical, *how* they were merely learned and absorbed from Caleb's early associates, and especially how *he* now kept re-indoctrinating himself with the fears by parroting them unthinkingly, telling himself over and over that they were based on proven evidence, when obviously they were completely arbitrary and ungrounded in fact.

The patient's fear of rejection, of losing approval, or having others laugh at him or criticize him, was examined in scores of its aspects, and revealed to him again and again. It was not only revealed but forcefully *attacked* by the therapist, who kept showing Caleb that it is necessarily silly and self-defeating for anyone to care too much about what *others* think, since then one is regulating one's life by and for these others, rather than for oneself. Moreover, one is then setting up a set of conditions for one's own happiness which make it virtually impossible that one will ever be happy.

Caleb's homosexual pattern of behavior, then, was consistently, forthrightly assailed not on the grounds of its being immoral or wrong, but solely on the grounds of its being self-defeating and self-limiting—and of its stemming from basic, largely non-sexual assumptions which had ramifications in all the rest of his life, and which kept him from enjoying himself in many other ways as well.

At the same time that the philosophic assumptions underlying Caleb's fear of rejection and his consequent homosexual behavior were being directly questioned and attacked, he was encouraged by the therapist to date girls, so that he could, in actual practice, overcome his fears concerning them. He was warned that his first attempts at dating might well result in embarrassment, awkwardness, and failure; but was told that only by working through such situations and feelings was he likely to overcome his irrational fears of females.

On his first date, which he made the week following his first therapy session, Caleb saw a girl who was very nice and refined, but who was quite cold and who obviously had severe problems of her own. On his second attempt, he met a librarian, a year younger than he, who was warm and accepting, and with whom he immediately began to pet heavily, but who also turned out to be severely disturbed. While still going with her, he went to a party with a girl whom he had known in a friendly way for some time, but whom he had never actually dated; and he wound up by having intercourse with her, which he thoroughly enjoyed. The girl, however, moved to another town shortly thereafter, and he did not see her again.

While Caleb was seeing these girls, the therapist went over with him in detail his behavior with and his reactions to them. He was given specific information and instruction as to how to make dates; what to expect from the girls; how to understand them and their problems; how to avoid being discouraged when he was rebuffed; what kinds of sexual overtures to make and when to make them; etc. His mistakes and blunders were gone over in an objective, constructive manner; and he was shown how, instead of blaming himself for these mistakes, he could put them to good self-teaching uses.

After he had seen the therapist seven times, on a once a week basis, Caleb met a girl whom he thought most desirable, and was sure, at first, that he would not be able to get anywhere with her. The therapist consistently encouraged him to keep seeing her, even when things looked rather black in their relationship. Largely because of the therapist's encouragement, Caleb did persist, and soon began to make headway with this girl. He not only managed to win her emotional allegiance; but in spite of the fact that she had a history of sexual indifference, he gradually awakened her desires and, through heavy petting, was able to give her, much to her own surprise, tremendous orgasmic release. She was the one who finally insisted that they have coitus, and this, too, proved to be supremely enjoyable for her and Caleb.

The thing that most impressed Caleb, however, was not his sexual prowess with the girl but his ability to win her emotional responsiveness against initially great odds, after he had first convinced himself that he could never succeed. His basic philosophy of his own worthlessness, or the necessity of his failing at anything he really wanted very badly, was rudely shaken by this practical lesson in the value of continuing to fight against odds.

Although Caleb's homosexual proclivities were barely mentioned after the first two sessions, and no direct attempt was made to get him to forego them, he completely and voluntarily renounced homosexuality as soon as he began to be sexually and emotionally successful with females. By the time the twelfth week of therapy had arrived, he had changed from a hundred per cent fixed homosexual to virtually a hundred per cent heterosexual. All his waking and sleeping fantasies became heterosexually oriented, and he was almost never interested in homosexual contacts.

As soon as I had made the point that Caleb's homosexual problems stemmed mainly from his feelings of inadequacy and fear of failure, and as soon as depropagandizing and activity forces were set in motion against his fixed homosexuality, I began to make a frontal attack on Caleb's heart palpitations. Here, a little psychoanalytically-oriented interpretation was first done, in order to show Caleb the connection between his psychosomatic symptoms and his father's stroke, and also to relate his symptoms to his mother's tendency to baby him when he was physically ill and to his intense dislike for having to take over his father's factory instead of pursuing his own chosen career.

Largely, however, a rational analytic attack was made on the *secondary* rather than the *primary* cause of Caleb's psychosomatic symptoms. That is to say, he was shown that although symptoms of this sort commonly arise because an individual is afraid of having a stroke like his father had, or wants his mother to baby him, or strives for the neurotic gain of being able to quit a disliked activity, such symptoms are secondarily *maintained* because they themselves become a focal point for fear and self-blame.

As I noted to Caleb at one point:

"Granted that you *originally* acquired your heart palpitations because of the two feelings, irrational fear and hostility, which cause virtually all neurotic symptoms. The more important question is: Why do you maintain these symptoms?"

"Yes, why do I? Especially when they're so bothersome!"

"A large part of the answer is that *you fear and hate the symptoms themselves.* Out of a feeling of panic, let us say, your heart starts beating wildly. But then, because you are a human being who can observe and talk to himself about his observations, you *feel* that it is beating wildly."

"I certainly do! And then I push the panic button."

"Yes. You push the panic button by immediately saying to yourself: 'Oh, my God! Look at my heart beating like that. I could easily die!' You also say, when you discover that your symptom is psychogenic rather than just physical, 'Oh, my heavens! What an idiot I am for letting myself go like this. I'd better stop this nonsense!' Then, finally, you say to yourself, after awhile: 'How terrible! I am *not* stopping this symptom. In fact, I *can't* stop it. This proves that I am a *hopeless* idiot, a hopeless weakling!'"

"That really fixes it for me, doesn't it?"

"It sure does. As if your heart palpitations were not bad enough, you make them infinitely worse by continually telling yourself how terrible, how fearful they are—telling yourself that you're an idiot, an incompetent for having them—and telling yourself that you're hopeless because you can't get rid of them. Of course, under *these* conditions, the original fears which caused you to have these palpitations in the first place will instead of gradually fading away, become more and more pronounced—because you are literally *making* them become more and more pronounced—in the second place."

"I'm literally digging my own grave, then, aren't I?"

"Not exactly. Very few people die of neurosis. Maybe it would be better if they did. But they live miserably on."

Over and over again, I proved to Caleb that every time he was experiencing his heart palpitations he was (*a*) telling himself some fear- or hostility-creating nonsense to bring them on, and (*b*) then telling himself some even greater tommyrot to aggrandize and perpetuate them. I insisted that Caleb was thereby constantly reinforcing two of his basic irrational philosophies of living: first, the idea that he must be perfectly competent, achieving, and successful in everything he did; and second, the idea that when he did anything badly, or made a mistake while doing it, he should blame himself and consider himself an idiot and a blackguard. These philosophies, of arrant perfectionism and self-blame, *must* necessarily lead him to acquire some kind of symptoms, such as his heart palpitations, and then to aggravate and perpetuate these symptoms.

Considerable time was spent, then, unmasking and interpreting Caleb's fundamental assumptions regarding perfectionism and self-blame, and showing him that these could and must be replaced by other assumptions: especially the beliefs that a human being should do, rather than do well; should try to be reasonably adequate rather than perfect. Particularly in relation to his secondary neurosis of blaming himself for being neurotic and for having psychosomatic symptoms, Caleb was shown that he should not concentrate on what a hopeless idiot he was for having his palpitations, but on how to accept himself even though, for the present, he was neurotically afflicted.

When Caleb finally began to see that his having his symptoms was unfortunate and unpleasant, but that it was not a crime or a catastrophe, these symptoms began to abate. As he remarked during the ninth session: "The less I blame myself for the things I experience, the less I begin to experience them. It's really remarkable!"

Although I had intended to get around to attacking Caleb's vocational problems in a forthright rational-emotive manner, there actually was no specific need to resort to this kind of attack, as he managed to make it himself as a by-product of some of the new ideas he was learning in the course of his therapeutic sessions. What I did was to give him the general idea that an individual becomes emotionally healthy when he is able to ask himself what *he* would most like to do in life, when he digs deeply behind his early acquired and unthinkingly retained prejudices to see whether this is what he *really* wants to do, and when he then goes ahead to try to do exactly that.

Caleb was at first blocked in this respect because, although he had deep resentments against both his father and his mother, he felt strongly obligated to carry on his father's business merely because his parents wanted him to do so. He felt that they would be terribly hurt if he did not stick to this business and believed that it was wrong for him to hurt them in this manner. I, as his therapist, insisted that he also consider another viewpoint: namely, that it was wrong for him not to think of himself as well as his parents, because morality consists of self-interest as well as interest in others.

If Caleb, I pointed out, was indifferent to his own career, and his parents strongly wanted him to operate their factory, then he might as well help or appease them in this regard. But if he distinctly wanted a career of his own, then he had a perfectly good moral right to choose this career over the preferences of his parents; and if they insisted on hurting themselves by his choice, then that was largely their problem and perhaps he could help them do something about solving that kind of a problem.

Only once during the therapeutic sessions with Caleb was the matter of morality and his .own vocational goals discussed. But a good many other times we did talk about the general problem of a healthy individual's standing on his own two feet and deciding what *he* wants to do in life and then, without *unduly* hurting others, striving to fulfill his own wants. Suddenly, to my surprise, Caleb himself brought up the issue of his career in the eighteenth session. He brought it up, moreover, as a *fait accompli*—an issue which he had resolved himself. Said Caleb at this time:

"I've decided one thing definitely, Doctor Ellis. Whether my father lives for a long time or not, and no matter how my mother feels about the matter, I am getting out of the business during the next year. I've already begun sending out letters looking for a teaching job in my own field next Fall, and that's going to be it. I thought very carefully about what we've been saying, and you're absolutely right. I only have one life to live, and goddam it, I'm going to live it from now on mainly for me. The only thing I ever wanted to do career-wise was to teach zoology and one day, perhaps, write a definitive text in the field. Come what may, I'm going to do it!"

Unexpectedly, at the nineteenth session of therapy, Caleb said that he thought he would discontinue the sessions for the present because he thought he would like to do it on his own.

He said he knew that he wasn't by any means completely cured but he felt that he was well on his way to getting over the main problems with which he had come to therapy, and that he would like to see how he could handle them from here on in himself.

I felt at the time that this was a somewhat premature close to the sessions in spite of the great progress Caleb had made in a relatively short period of time. I felt that, as happens in many such instances, Caleb would have considerable difficulty going on by himself and that he would probably return for more help in a few weeks or months. I kept my doubts to myself, however, and mainly encouraged Caleb to try going it alone as long as he felt free to come back at any time if he did get into serious difficulties. Caleb said with sincerity that he certainly would return before he let things get truly bad again; but he repeated that he wanted to try things for himself for awhile.

As it happened, Caleb never did return. A three-year-later checkup, however, showed that he had married the fourth girl he dated, and that they are the proud parents of a son. He is teaching zoology in a Midwestern university and is getting along well, if not perfectly, in most respects. He is completely disinterested in homosexual relations and is free from the psycho-somatic heart symptoms with which he came to therapy.

One of the most interesting aspects of this case is that some basic issues in Caleb's life were virtually never discussed during the entire therapeutic procedure—partly because I thought that some of them would be analyzed in more detail later and partly because I believed that some of them were largely irrelevant to Caleb's main problems. Thus, I felt that his homosexual pattern of behavior was, at least in part, caused by his over-attachment to his mother, which included some elements of an incest tabu and the feeling that no other girl would be good enough for him.

In the entire course of therapy, however, relatively little refer-ence was made to Caleb's relations with his mother, and no detailed analysis was done in this connection. Nonetheless, his deviated sex pattern radically changed in the course of therapy —because, in all probability, the *main* cause of his homosexuality was not his Oedipal attachment to his mother but his severe feelings of inadequacy and fear of rejection, which *were* thoroughly analyzed and attacked during therapy.

By the same token, although Caleb's hostility to his father was never thoroughly interpreted to him, largely because the therapy ended before this aspect of his behavior was minutely investigated, he wound up by being, on the one hand, much less hostile toward and, on the other hand, more able to break with his father. This was because his basic philosophy of blaming both himself and others was steadily and powerfully attacked in the course of therapy. Once this philosophy started to change, he had no need of being jealous and hostile toward his father.

In any event, a swift frontal attack was made by the therapist on the basic assumptions or irrational philosophies underlying Caleb's symptoms; and after less than six months of therapy, radical reorganizations in his life goals and his overt sexual and nonsexual behavior occurred. An individual who would have been considered too difficult and rigid a case for therapy by Freud and his early followers was helped to overcome his longstanding homosexual neurosis and to make several other notable changes in his patterns of living.

Similarly, rational-emotive psychotherapy has been effectively employed (by myself and an increasing number of other practitioners) in many other instances of fixed homosexuality and other types of serious sexual deviation. Although deviants continue to be most difficult patients (partly because they are getting clear-cut sexual advantages from their deeply ingrained perverted behavior), they are not intrinsically more difficult to deal with than many other severely disturbed persons; and the results of forthrightly and quite actively attacking their unconscious philosophic premises is often highly rewarding.

15

The Treatment of Schizophrenia*

One of the most frequent questions that I am asked in regard to rational-emotive psychotherapy, particularly when I discuss my work at professional gatherings, is: "Granted that your technique has excellent advantages when it is used with ordinary neurotics, or with people who have serious problems but are not really too disturbed, can it work with out and out psychotics, especially with paranoid schizophrenics or severe obsessives?"

My usual answer to this question is: "Let us face it: psychotic individuals are the most difficult kind of patients for any type of psychotherapy; and results in this connection are usually quite discouraging. Even when they are temporarily helped, they frequently slip back, without any warning, into severe psychotic states. Personally, I believe that most of them were *not* merely raised to be the way they are, but in a very important sense they were born with distinct psychotic tendencies, and then usually had these tendencies significantly exacerbated by their early upbringing." (Dilger, 1962; Keeley, 1962; Martí-Ibáñez, 1960; Masor, 1959; Wolpe, 1961a).

Nonetheless, I believe that psychotics in general and schizophrenics in particular can usually be significantly helped (if rarely truly cured) by intensive psychotherapy. And of all the methods of psychotherapy that I have seen used with psychotic patients, rational-emotive therapy is one of the most efficient techniques ever invented.

One of the first attempts I made at using RT with a psychotic patient was back in 1955, when I was seeing a paranoid schizo-

---

* This chapter is an expanded version of "Hypnotherapy with Borderline Psychotics," *J. General Psychol.*, 1958, 59, 245-253.

phrenic man of 38 who was insanely jealous of his wife and who kept insisting that whenever he called home during the day and she was out, she must have been having sex relations with a neighbor, a tradesman, one of his partners, or any other male with whom she might possibly come in contact. I showed him how his stories about her doings were quite contradictory, and how she couldn't possibly be doing half the things he was convinced she was doing; but at first I made little headway.

I then switched to his own paranoid ideas, and attempted to show him how they stemmed not from any external events that were occurring, but from his own belief that it would be a horrifying, ego-destroying thing if his wife *were* as unfaithful as he thought she was. "You keep saying," I told him, "that *she* would be such a double-crossing bitch if she were unfaithful to you; and that *that* is the problem. But this is nonsense: since even if she were as adulterous as you think she is, that would only be *her* problem and it would not necessarily be *yours*. All you would have to do, under the circumstances, would be to accept fully the fact that she had this problem, and then calmly decide either to stay with her and help her get over it, or else to leave her and let her take her problem to some other marriage."

"But how could I calmly decide to do such a thing," he asked, "when, well, she's doing such a terrible thing? How can you expect me to be *calm* about that?"

"You're proving my very point," I replied. "Just because you *can't* be calm about her presumably having a problem, you obviously have one yourself. And your problem is not her being unfaithful, but your depreciating yourself *if* she were."

"How do you mean? I would give myself a hard time if *she* were caught in the act?"

"Well, *wouldn't* you? If you actually did catch her in the act, would you calmly say to her, 'Look, dear, if you can't be faithful to me, then let's just break up this marriage, and be done with it,' or wouldn't you, instead, brood, think how terrible it would be if someone, anyone *found out* about your being cuckolded, and generally worry your head off about it?"

"I—I think maybe you're right. I guess—yes, I would give myself a hard time. I'd be worrying about what the others were thinking about *me*."

"Exactly. And *that's* where your paranoid thinking stems from. You're so afraid that *you* would be made to look bad if she were unfaithful, and dwell so catastrophically all the time on that 'horrible' prospect, that you can't do anything but think all day about whether she *is* out with some other fellow. Then, one short step from there, you look for the evidence that she is unfaithful, and sooner or later you find something suspicious; then you keep looking; then you find something still more suspicious; then you finally start concluding that she simply *must* be adulterous. Actually, your 'evidence' consists only of your suspicions. But your real suspicion is not that *she* would be a bitch if you caught her in the act, but that *you* would be a weakling who had an adulterous wife. Your *own* feeling is the real issue here; and her behavior is important only insofar as it gives you an excuse, as it were, to have this feeling."

"An excuse to have it?"

"Yes, because actually you have the feeling to begin with. You are certain right at the start, before she does anything, that you *would* be worthless if she did cuckold you. So her cuckolding you, if such an event actually occurs, is an overt excuse for your giving vent to your own underlying feeling, that was always there before she did or thought of doing her act. In fact, it seems to me that you might well be *disappointed* if you did not find her cuckolding you—for then your basic negative view of yourself would not be justified. And it looks to me like you almost *want* to prove that you are a no-good slob, and are exactly the kind of a person whom a wife would cuckold."

"I don't know. Maybe you're right, but I don't quite see it. Why would I *want* to think I am a slob? I can see that you *may* be right. But I can't quite see that you are."

"See! Now you're looking for exact evidence of *my* rightness, just as you keep looking for exact evidence of your wife's wrongness. Like most paranoid individuals, what you're really interested in is certainty, in controlling your entire environment, and seeing all possible answers, right and wrong, to the questions in this environment, so that there is no possibility of doubt or indecision on your part. You *insist* on perfect answers—even perfect wrong answers. And the world, of course, consists of approximations and probabilities, not of perfect answers. But, being unwilling to tolerate such approximations, you keep looking for the exact answers. And when they are not for the moment existent, you *create* them—as you are now creating this so-called adulterous behavior on the part of your wife."

"But how do you know that I'm creating it? It could exist."

"Certainly it *could*. But what are the probabilities? Actually, your accusations against your wife are very funny."

"I don't find anything funny about them!"

"No, you wouldn't. But to accuse a poor, namby-pamby, terribly frightened woman like her of running around all over town looking for any man to approach and to jump into bed with is highly ridiculous. Why, she's almost as frightened as you are of what other people think of her. And even if she *wanted* to have affairs with other men, the chances are ninety-nine out of a hundred that she would refuse, or would at least put each one of them off for a year or two before she gave herself to him. From what you tell me, she's even afraid to have sex relations with you on many occasions, because she thinks it's so terrible if she doesn't have a full orgasm, and hates herself if she doesn't. And you have *this* poor, scared woman taking the great risks of running all over town, from one man's bed to another! It's really very funny!"

At this point, I couldn't help bursting out laughing at the very idea of this patient's timid, inhibited wife being aggressively promiscuous, as he kept accusing her of being. And my laughing at the very thought of this idea seemed to have more effect on the patient than any of my other words or actions. Noting this, I continued in the same vein as before, interpreting to him both his own fear of what people think, and how this related to his paranoid delusions, and also his wife's similar fears, and how they were connected with the infinitesimally small possibility of her engaging in adulterous relations.

"So you really think my wife would never do it?" the patient asked.

"I certainly think she never would. In fact, there is just as little chance of her doing what you're accusing her of as there is of your taking it well if you actually found her in an adulterous situation. Both of you are so similarly afraid of doing *anything* that others might consider wrong or indecorous that, on your side, you would never condone her adultery even if you had no sex desire for her yourself, and she would never condone her own adultery, even if she were dying for sexual fulfillment and you refused to give her any. Two minds, peculiarly enough, with a single ego-destroying thought!"

"But you said before that we both, my wife and I, were only trying to protect our egos. How, then are we ego-destroying?"

"No, you're both trying to protect your *weak* egos, your *false* pride. An individual who has a good ego or true pride does not have to keep protecting himself about the views of others, except when real practical issues are involved. Generally, he likes himself so much that he can be comfortable *even* when others disapprove his behavior. But people like you and your wife, with weak egos, or with the notion that it is terribly important what others think of you (which is the same thing as having a weak ego), constantly have to protect their false pride. And by this kind of protection they actually destroy their true egos—destroy what *they* really would want to do in life."

"Oh."

"Yes, you can say that again!"

My paranoid patient was momentarily thoughtful. And after I had continued, for a good many more sessions, to show him how utterly ridiculous it was to think a scaredy-cat wife like his would seek out affairs with other men, he gradually, to my surprise, gave up the idea and began to have a much better relationship with her. He did not stop being schizophrenic; and he continued to do typically self-sabotaging acts and to engage in paranoid ruminations from time to time. But he did show considerable improvement and he was able to keep working steadily and to maintain better relations with others.

Whereas, before I saw this patient, he had been institutionalized twice and had had several series of shock treatments on an outpatient basis, he has had no recurring crises for the last six years and seems to have settled down to a stabilized mode of living. He gets fleeting ideas, every once in a while, that his wife is being unfaithful; but at these times he is able to recall our talks on the subject, including my genuine amusement at the idea that his wife would be aggressively adulterous, and he quickly convinces himself that his ideas are groundless, and settles down to a good period of adjustment again.

In many other instances, I have been able to talk schizophrenics out of the notion that they absolutely must be loved and adored by all the significant people in their lives; and I have helped them to accept the reality that they often will not be approved by others.

With hostile schizophrenics—and to some degree I believe that almost all of them are underlying quite hostile—I have had perhaps even a harder time in talking them out of their hostility. Although they can often be helped to understand that there is no good reason why people *should* act the way they want these people to act, they still seem to *want* to argue, and blame, and hate; and sometimes no technique that I can think of, including that of giving them considerable therapeutic support and approval, will induce them to do otherwise.

At the same time, unusual progress in this regard can sometimes be made. A 40-year old exceptionally hostile schizophrenic woman hated her husband, her daughter's boyfriend, and all her neighbors. For many months I could make no headway whatever in getting her to see that, however many mistakes and wrongdoings these various individuals may have committed, hating them was not going to rectify their behavior and was only going to keep her as miserable as she had been almost all the days of her life. "But they *are* no good!" she would keep screaming at me, when I kept trying to show her that her enemies were fallible humans and should therefore be forgiven for their "sins."

I nonetheless persisted. All our sessions sounded like duplications of the first one: with her gripes being endlessly repeated, and with my counter-arguments being steadfastly and unblamefully presented against them. Finally, when she complained one day that one of her neighbors had unfairly beaten her (the patient's) daughter when the girl had been arguing with the neighbor's child, I vigorously insisted that the beating the daughter received from the neighbor was much less harmful than the verbal beating which the patient was giving this daughter almost every day in the week, and that the verbal sallies she kept making against her husband and other people were also cruel to these people as well as harmful to the patient herself.

Again to my surprise, this schizophrenic woman accepted my vigorous interpretations and began, thereafter, to discuss blaming and its consequences with me in a much more temperate and at times compassionate manner. Although this patient, too, was never entirely cured, and still gives herself and others a difficult time on many occasions, she is much less a blamer and arguer than she was before I started seeing her, and she is able to calm herself down on many occasions when previously she upset herself tremendously, and often remained upset for hours or for days afterward.

Borderline (or ambulatory) schizophrenics are much easier to help psychotherapeutically than are full-fledged schizophrenics; and RT is one of the best methods of helping them. Here, again, it must be admitted that goals of therapy must often be realistically limited, since there is some evidence that even borderline psychotics may have organic as well as psychological causes for their severe disturbances, and the clearing up of the psychological aspects of their sickness may not fully eliminate the organic element. What this organic element in psychosis may be, and exactly what can be done about it, is not at present clear; but there is good reason to think that eventually our knowledge in this respect will be bettered.

According to the theory of rational-emotive therapy, psychotics as well as neurotics are telling themselves some kind of nonsense, at point B, after something occurs to them at point

A, in order to produce their negative reactions (especially extreme anxiety and hostility) at point C. But where neurotics *can* but do not make adequate cognitive discriminations at point B, to produce sensible results at point C, there is a possibility that psychotics actually *cannot* make such discriminations adequately, or else that they have unusual difficulty in making them. Consequently, neurotics (though difficult enough to reorient) are much more teachable than are psychotics; and only with considerable effort can an effective therapist show a psychotic patient how to discriminate between his true and his false generalizations and to undermine his own irrational thinking.

Thus, whereas both neurotics and psychotics usually believe that they are worthless individuals, the latter do so in a far more conclusive way. Why? Because, I believe, it is easier for people with real thinking deficiencies to make this than the opposite conclusion. Thus, the psychotic is probably saying to himself something like this: "I am handicapped by my own inability to think clearly and deal correctly with other people; therefore I have difficulties with these other people; and therefore I am worthless." The first part of this sentence may well be true—because he well *may* be organically handicapped in his thinking; and the second part may also be true. But his conclusion is still a false one.

It is easier, however, for him to make this false conclusion than to say to himself: "I am handicapped by my own inability to think clearly; therefore I have difficulties with other people; so I'll just have to make the best of my life, anyway, in spite of these difficulties; and, even though others may devalue me as a person, I can be quite valuable to myself and not think that I am worthless." But evaluating oneself highly, in this manner, even when others give one a low evaluation, is intrinsically more difficult (even for a so-called normal individual) than evaluating oneself less highly. It requires *extra* steps in thinking, *extra* discriminations.

Neurotics are probably those who, for one reason or another, refuse to use their able thinking powers, and therefore fail to make these extra discriminations, and end by falsely thinking that they are worthless when they make mistakes or displease others. But when helped by a therapist to make such extra discriminations, they can and often do make them, and get over their difficulties. Psychotics, I hypothesize, cannot *as easily* make these extra discriminations; and some serious psychotics probably cannot really make them at all. They therefore hang on to their poor generalizations (which I again contend are easier to make and require relatively little hard thinking) and refuse to budge from these.

Psychotics, moreover, may feel more comfortable with these old and tired (though self-defeating) false generalizations, because they *can* successfully make them; and they may derive a certain "ego" satisfaction from their paranoid and false thinking. It "fits" together well, this false thinking; or at least seems to do so. And though the jigsaw puzzle they are working on is "completed" largely because they fill in only the easy parts and let the difficult parts go, they manage to feel quite "satisfied" with the parts they have filled in. Moreover, the society in which they reside actually helps them believe that they *are* worthless to themselves if they are relatively valueless to others; so they have little incentive to work to complete the puzzle of a good or happy life and to figure out that they can be valueless to others and *still* be worthwhile to themselves.

Nonetheless, full-fledged and borderline psychotics can be helped, especially if the therapist realistically views them as possessing a thinking deficiency, and works to help them at least partly overcome this deficiency. All the rational-emotive techniques employed with neurotics can also be employed with psychotic patients; but usually they have to be given more structuring, more encouragement, and more emphasizing of their potential assets than neurotics have to be given.

Even hypnotherapy may at times be effectively used with borderline psychotic patients, although it is not by any means necessarily the treatment of choice, and is only rarely used in my own practice. This is not only because borderline patients are not the best hypnotic subjects; but more because even when they are hypnotizable there is considerable danger of their becoming more disorganized and disoriented than they normally are.

Suggestion is a two-edged sword when employed with all kinds of patients, and it can especially lead to somewhat bizarre results when used with borderline schizophrenics. Thus, I once noted that one of my borderline patients had several checks in his checkbook all filled out, ready to pay his telephone bill, his grocer, his department store account, etc. When I asked him why he didn't make out these checks at the time he actually paid them, instead of in advance, he replied that he had thought that I had advised him to do things in this precise manner. What I actually had said was that if he wanted to get the full benefit of the time spent with me, it would be well if he had *my* check made out when he entered the session, instead of spending some of his time making it out at the end of the session. He had generalized this suggestion into a rigid pattern of making out *all* his checks.

Even more important is the fact that borderline psychotics are usually autistic, disorganized, highly unrealistic individuals who have great difficulty in buckling down to accepting the harsh and inexorable facts of everyday living. Under hypnosis, they frequently tend to go off into even greater flights of fancy; and the task of then getting them to accept an integrated, positive, fairly well organized pattern of living often becomes more difficult than it is in the course of non-hypnotic therapy.

Nonetheless, there are occasions on which I deliberately employ hypnosis with borderline patients—particularly when they show interest in being hypnotized and when they appear to be reasonably good subjects. On these occasions when hypnosis is employed, I usually find a somewhat dichotomous distribution in regard to ease of hypnosis. That is to say, I find that some of the patients, especially the younger ones, are quite suggestible, dependency-oriented, and easily hypnotizable; while others, even when they themselves ask to be hypnotized, fight desperately against it and are almost impossible to put in a trance. Even those who do enter a hypnotic state tend to go into a light rather than a deep trance, and often spontaneously awake when disturbing material is discussed or when there are loud street noises.

The main technique I employ with borderline psychotics whom I hypnotize is the same that I use with my nonpsychotic hypnotherapeutic subjects—that is, a combination of hypnosis and rational-emotive psychotherapy. When used in conjunction with hypnosis, RT becomes a training in a special kind of auto-suggestion which might be termed *autosuggestive insight*. All hypnotic suggestion that is therapeutically successful probably works largely through autosuggestion—since unless the patient *himself* takes over the suggestion of the hypnotherapist, and consciously or unconsciously keeps thinking about them when the therapist is no longer present, only the most short-lived kind of results are likely to follow. But when the patient does keep repeating and repeating to himself what the hypnothera-pist has originally repeated to him, long-lasting therapeutic effects may occur.

Therapeutic autosuggestion may be divided into three major categories. The first of these may be called *autosuggestion with-out insight*, and is typified by the work of Bernheim, Coué, and many others who have taught their patients to parrot to them-selves sentences such as: "I can get better," "The pain is going away," "I am not afraid," etc. Without any knowledge whatever of how their disturbances arose in the first place, or why their autosuggestions work in the second place, many such patients apparently overcome neurotic symptomatology, and some of them are probably even "cured."

The second type of autosuggestion that is used for therapeutic purposes may be called *autosuggestion with direct insight*. This technique is well illustrated in a case of Bowers, Brecher, and Polatin (1958). Dr. Bowers, working with a severely schizo-phrenic patient, got him to separate himself into two parts, Walter Positive and Walter Negative, and then, under hypnosis, systematically set about pushing Walter Negative out of the patient's body. Gradually, after months of letting Walter Posi-tive fight his own battles in hypnosis, which seems to have been accompanied by his continually suggesting to himself that the good Walter could conquer the bad Walter, the patient made a remarkable recovery.

In the course of being treated, Dr. Bowers' patient not only made an excellent social recovery, but also developed considerable insight into some of his previous illogical thinking. He was able to see that by rebelling against his father he was only cutting off his nose to spite his face; that by performing poorly in the sexual area he was trying to avoid his father's sadism; and that his father was really like a raging, angry little terrier whose bark was far worse than his bite. Concomitant with therapeutic suggestion and autosuggestion, Walter was able to surrender several false *ideas* or *beliefs* about his father—and thus *really* to rid himself of the influence that had produced the bad Walter, or Walter Negative.

When *autosuggestion with direct insight* takes place a similar phenomenon occurs, but with a salient addition: namely, insight into the autosuggestive process itself. Such insight arises from a thoroughgoing understanding of *why* suggestion and autosuggestion work. Bernheim (1887) was one of the first to realize that suggestion, with or without hypnosis, is often a most effective therapeutic tool. But neither he nor any of his followers seem to have grasped very clearly *why* this is so—probably, ironically enough, because the answer to the problem is so simple.

The answer to this riddle, in the light of the theory of rational-emotive psychotherapy, is simply that suggestion and autosuggestion are effective in removing neurotic and psychotic symptoms because *they are the very instruments which caused or helped produce these symptoms in the first place*. Virtually all complex and sustained adult human emotions are caused by ideas or attitudes; and these ideas or attitudes are, first, *suggested* by persons and things outside the individual (especially by his parents, teachers, books, etc.); and they are, second, continually *autosuggested* by himself.

Thus, Dr. Bowers' patient, Walter, was brought up in a social milieu which first *suggested to* (or taught) him that his father was fearsome, that he must at all costs avoid his father's sex patterns of behavior, that he must rebel against his father even if he had to cut off his nose to spite his face, etc. And then, after internalizing the irrational ideas, Walter *autosuggested* them to himself, over and over, until he thoroughly believed them, and automatically or unconsciously acted on the (false) assumption that they were true.

Just because Walter's disordered emotions resulted from illogical ideas, and just because these ideas were originally ingrained by repetitive suggestion and autosuggestion, it is not difficult to see why Dr. Bowers' positive counter-suggestion, as well as Walter's positive counter-autosuggestion, finally were instrumental in helping him overcome the originally ingrained negative thoughts and consequent feelings. And just as Walter first was induced by suggestion and autosuggestion to "understand" or get "insight" into how fearsome his father was, so with the counter-suggestion and autosuggestion of a positive nature could he understand and get insight into this same father's innocuousness.

The one thing that Walter apparently did not understand at the close of therapy was why and how the original suggestion and autosuggestion led to his illogical beliefs, and how and why the later suggestion and autosuggestion led to his more logical, and hence less schizophrenic, beliefs. This additional measure of insight into how and why irrational ideas and feelings arise, and how patients can go about attacking and invariably defeating such senseless beliefs, is what rational therapy tries to give. Thus, in Walter's case, a rational hypnoanalytic approach would have attempted to show him that, *in general,* human beings in our society are reared to believe (by suggestion and autosuggestion) many irrational notions; that once they believe these notions they *must* become more or less emotionally disturbed; and that the only thoroughgoing way for them to overcome their disturbance is to admit that their notions are irrational, to attack them with counter-suggestion and autosuggestion, and to replace them with more rational ideas.

To illustrate, consider the case of a borderline schizophrenic whom I saw awhile ago. This 31 year old male had had 10 years of therapy previously, but had always managed to avoid being hospitalized. He was exceptionally fearful, dependent, and compulsive; and, although he had no outright delusions or hallucinations, was quite hostile toward virtually everybody, and felt that the whole world was against him and that he kept failing in school and business because of the obstacles which people deliberately kept putting in his way. He would continually ask what was the "right" way to do things and he would become utterly confused and disorganized when there was any possibility that he might make a mistake.

This ambulatory schizophrenic was seen privately for about a year before any hypnotherapy was attempted. In the course of this time, he was shown that he had several basic irrational ideas—especially that it was a dire necessity that he be loved by everyone for everything he did, and that he be perfectly competent in all the tasks he performed.

The origin of these ideas, in the patient's relationships with his parents and his indoctrinations by his culture, was discussed; but more time was spent in showing him why his beliefs were irrational than in demonstrating how he originally came to believe them. He was also shown how and why such illogical ideas generally arise, and how human beings normally autosuggestively keep indoctrinating themselves with these senseless notions. He was taught that if he stopped this kind of indoctrination, and instead kept contradicting his irrational views and consistently brought their inanity to his own conscious attention, they would soon start disappearing, and the fearful, dependent, and compulsive behavior to which they led would concomitantly tend to disappear.

Some distinct progress was made with this borderline schizophrenic patient. He began to see for himself that he really didn't *have* to be loved by everyone; that no great catastrophe occurred—unless *he* made it occur—when someone did not accept him; that his incompetencies were not great crimes, but merely challenging hurdles he could actually enjoy tackling. He still, however, kept lapsing into irrational thinking and wanted to know if he could not obtain some additional help in overcoming it.

Partly at his own suggestion and partly at mine, hypnosis was discussed and he was more than willing to try it. In spite of this willingness, he was not a good subject at first, since he had conscious fears of what might happen if he surrendered himself completely to someone else, and his attention kept wandering while I was trying to hypnotize him. On two occasions, just as he seemed to go under hypnosis he suddenly opened his eyes and sat up on the sofa.

Finally, in the course of the fourth attempt at hypnosis, the patient went into a light to medium trance, but still appeared to be restless and always on the verge of waking. No attempt was made to explore early memories or derive additional insight into psychodynamics—partly because the patient did not seem receptive to this kind of probing, and partly because it is not normally emphasized in the course of rational-emotive psychotherapy.

Instead, direct suggestion was given. But, while including some directives for the patient to do certain acts of which he was normally afraid, the suggestion mainly took the form of having him *think* differently about these acts rather than merely *do* them. Thus, on one occasion the therapist said:

"You now have trouble, we know, in attending dances and meeting new girls, but you are not going to have much difficulty doing so in the future. This is because you are now beginning to realize that *you* are causing your own difficulties; that you become embarrassed and ashamed to meet girls because *you* think it is terrible and horrible to be rejected by them.

"But you are no longer going to think that, no longer going to indoctrinate yourself with that nonsense. You are going, instead, to realize that there *is* nothing terrible in being rejected by someone whom you would like to meet; that the terror is completely in your head, and has no objective existence; that it exists only because you keep *telling* yourself that it exists; and that, in this sense, you keep *making* it exist.

"You are beginning to see, now, that you don't *have* to create this nonsense, this false terror, that you don't *have* to be afraid. You are beginning to see that you can go onto the dance floor, ask a perfectly strange girl to dance, and not give a damn whether she accepts or rejects you. You are beginning to see that, on the law of averages, you *must* be rejected many times if you are also to be accepted many times, and that it really *doesn't matter* if you are rejected. You are beginning to see, to show yourself over and over, that the worst that can happen, if a girl rejects you, is that she will think badly of you, think you are an idiot, or are clumsy, or are ugly, or something like that; and that *it doesn't matter* what she thinks, it doesn't really affect you at all. It is what *you* think that matters—what you really feel you are. And if *you* know that you are not an idiot, are not clumsy, are not ugly, what she thinks has no importance whatever.

"You are beginning to see, moreover, that it doesn't even matter greatly if you *are* stupid or incompetent or ignorant or imperfect in some respects. For none of us, you are seeing more and more clearly, can be perfectly adequate and fine in *all* respects; all of us have our distinct imperfections and failings; and as long as we are reasonably able in *some* ways, it is not necessary that we be A Number One in *all* ways.

"You are going to try, therefore, and keep trying to ask girls to dance at the next affair you attend. And you are going to realize that, in this as in all other human affairs, it is only practice that makes perfect, that you cannot expect to be very good at the start, that you will make lots of errors before you get used to what you are doing and develop a good technique of doing it. And you are going to realize, especially, that it is not the achievement, the success of doing the thing that is important so much as the honest trial, the giving yourself a chance, the trying to do what you want to do, whether or not you succeed at doing it.

"You are going to keep trying, therefore. And whenever you fail, which at times you are bound to do, and you start getting frightened or ashamed of failing, of having others dislike you or think you are incompetent, you are going to question, question, *question* your own feeling of fear or shame. You are going to ask yourself: 'Why am I fearful or ashamed? What is so frightful or shameful about failing or being thought badly about? What difference does it make? What's the catastrophe? What's the crime?' You are going to keep questioning, questioning, questioning your fear and your shame: observing carefully when they arise, asking yourself why they arise, showing yourself, in each and every single instance, that *you* make them arise.

"You are going to watch yourself, in other words, create and cause your shame and your fear by telling yourself sentences, such as 'Oh, my God, what a fool she thinks I am for asking her to dance! How awful it is that she thinks I'm such an idiot!' And, observing yourself tell yourself such silly sentences, such fear- and shame-creating sentences, you are going, instead, to start telling yourself other, more sensible, realistic sentences, such as: 'So she thinks I'm a fool for asking her to dance. So what? What difference does it make?' Or: 'So she didn't accept me this time. So I'll keep trying until someone does accept me. What difference does it make how often I get rejected, as long as I eventually get accepted?'

"You are going to see, as you are already beginning to see, that all your shame and fear are creations of your own: consist of silly, illogical sentences that you keep telling yourself; and that you can change these sentences, tell yourself more sensible things, and thus eliminate the shame and the fear. You are beginning to see that all sustained negative emotions that people feel stem from their *own* internalized sentences, rather than from outside events, and that if they only changed these sentences, substituted more sensible ones, and really came to believe the substance of the more sensible sentences, all their irrational shame and fear, all their emotional disturbances, would vanish.

"You are going out, then, to this dance on Saturday night, and to dance after dance, dance after dance, and you are going to keep asking girls to dance, keep dancing with them, getting to know them, making dates with them. And while you are doing this, you are going to keep telling yourself there is nothing to be afraid of, nothing to be ashamed of, that your shame and your fear are your own creations, as everybody's illogical shame and fear are their own creations, and that you can uncreate them just as you created them, that you can tell yourself sensible and sane instead of unsensible and silly sentences, and with these sensible and sane sentences rid yourself of all needless shame and fear.

"You are going to do this: to think, to think; to question, to question; to stop catastrophizing; to say, 'So what!' instead of, 'Oh, how awful!'; to show yourself that things and reactions outside you are not as important as you have been thinking they are. And, thinking this way, telling yourself the right kind of sentences, you are going to keep dancing and dating, dancing and dating, until you find little difficulty and much enjoyment in doing so."

After the very first hypnotherapeutic session using this rational approach, the patient said that he received a real lift, greater than he had ever previously experienced as a result of a therapy session. Although only a few more sessions thereafter were devoted to hypnosis, he continued to improve considerably, and to believe that much of his improvement stemmed from the boost given him by hypnotherapeutic procedures. After another year of rational psychotherapy without the use of hypnosis he was discharged as significantly recovered. An informal checkup two years later showed that he appeared to be maintaining his recovery.

Several other patients, including borderline schizophrenics and neurotics, have also been treated with a similar combination of rational psychotherapy and hypnotherapy, and the results have been almost uniformly good. Whether, however, the hypnotic adjunct to the method of rational analysis is itself very effective is difficult to say, since the use of the method without hypnosis has been quite efficacious in its own right. My own feeling is that it is usually preferable to use rational-emotive therapy *without* hypnosis, in almost all cases, since the individual who improves his thinking processes and his state of mental health without any gimmicks or crutches is more likely to have increased self-confidence and to sustain his initial improvement than is the patient with whom hypnosis or other specialized techniques of this sort have been employed. I am therefore making no plea for the use of hypnotic measures; and use these measures very sparingly in my own practice.

When used without giving the subject insight into the autosuggestive process, hypnosis verges too closely on blind suggestion—which, even when it is therapeutically efficacious, has distinct disadvantages and limitations. As Platonov (1959) has noted:

> It is necessary to delimit phenomena connected with the conscious perception of the word and its suggestive influence. Dubois was, apparently, the first to point out the necessity for clearly delimiting the conceptions of suggestion and persuasion which before him had usually been confused. In addition, according to Verworn "suggestion is an artifically produced idea arising without the control of criticism and accepted by force of it almost blindly." A. Forel emphasizes that *"we must not regard the influence of one man on another by reasoning as a suggestion."* . . . Y. Katkov correctly observes in one of his studies that there is a dialectical relationship between the conscious perception of speech and its suggestive influence. Verbal influence perceived critically *cannot be suggested*, because it is perceived passively without criticism, may easily become *suggested*, even though it may contradict past experience and be severed from present reality.

These earlier investigators have correctly seen that suggestion and persuasion are not only different, but in some significant ways quite antagonistic. When an individual, on blind faith, accepts a suggestion, even a suggestion that he rid himself of some neurotic symptom, he is doing the right thing for the wrong reason: becoming "better" by surrendering his ability to think for himself. Although he may thereby lose his symptom, he is not only making no real inroads against his basic disturbance, but may actually be aggravating it: since this disturbance, at bottom, *is* his tendency unthinkingly to accept and be dependent upon outside authority (Ciardi, 1962; Maltz, 1960).

Similarly, individuals who surrender their symptoms and become "better" as a result of reassurance, abreaction and catharsis, transference bonds, reciprocal inhibition, operant conditioning, positive thinking, or various other kinds of non-insightful or semi-insightful techniques, may truly be "cured" in the sense that they do not reacquire their disturbed symptoms again, but it is dubious that they are "cured," in the sense that they are not likely to acquire *other* symptoms. It is true, as Bruner, Goodnow, and Austin (1956) point out, that some of the most creative problem-solvers are individuals whose actual performance runs well ahead of their ability to state verbal justifications for it. But unless such verbal justification is eventually forthcoming, such persons will have to keep solving their basic life problems over and over again, instead of finding a general solution that can be reapplied whenever a problem arises that is similar to the ones they have just solved.

"Cures" by hypnotic or nonhypnotic suggestion, in other words, have relatively little prophylactic value, because the "cured" individual does not realize precisely *how* he got better, and he has to keep running back to the suggester when he gets into trouble again. He therefore does not truly become stronger in his own right, or become less liable to get himself into further emotional difficulties (Jackson and Kelly, 1962).

Because of this serious limitation of suggestion, rational-emotive psychotherapy mainly attempts to work through persuasive rather than suggestive techniques. For in the course of persuading someone to change his views, the therapist has to induce the patient to *think* differently—to *challenge* his own unthinking assumptions. But in the course of suggestion, the therapist largely induces the patient to *accept* new ideas on faith, rather than truly to think them through. Ideas that are at first accepted on a suggestive basis may *later* be experimentally tried and reaccepted on the basis of factual evidence. But they also may never be rethought through and may remain imbedded in a foundation of faith unfounded on fact—which is irrational and neurotic.

When properly employed, however, hypnotic and nonhypnotic suggestion may help. For it has been found that neurotic and borderline psychotic patients can be in some instances appreciably helped with suggestion and autosuggestion that is accompanied by direct insight into the suggestive process.

If these patients are taught to understand that their disturbances largely originated in parental and societal suggestion, and were then and are now being unconsciously carried on by autosuggestive reindoctrination; if they are subjected to forceful and repetitive counter-suggestion by the therapist; and if, above all, they are shown how they can counter-autosuggestively keep depropagandizing themselves, with conscious verbalizations as well as actions, so that they no longer believe in the illogical and irrational beliefs that underlie and cause their emotional disturbances, they can then be led to face and accept reality and to think clearly about themselves and their relations to others. This kind of rational therapy, with or without hypnotic reinforcement, seems to provide an excellent mode of attack on some of the most longstanding and deep-seated states of psychopathology.

It must again be emphasized, however: psychotics are most difficult to treat successfully with any of the presently known forms of psychotherapy. They may well have a thinking disorder that is organically as well as psychologically based; and their difficulties in focusing and discriminating in a rational and not self-defeating manner are quite probably at least partly endogenous.

Precisely because of the severity of their disturbances, RT is one of the very best methods of choice in treating psychotics. It presents a view of life and a cognitive-emotive approach to reality that is unusually clear, understandable, and teachable. It avoids unstructured fantasy-chasing, free association, symbol production, and other vague and amorphous approaches to therapy that frequently help psychotics become even more confused than they are when they first come to therapy. It makes considerable use of persuasion, reëducation, information-giving, and other structured techniques which help psychotics to focus in a more integrated manner on the reality-testing aspects of life (Brady *et al.*, 1962).

RT is an unusually permissive and nonblaming method of

therapy that gives maximum aid to psychotics who are almost invariably excessively self- and other-blaming. It allows the therapist specifically to help psychotic patients manage their lives, and temporarily lean on his saner judgment and better wisdom, until they are truly able to attempt to manage their own disorganized existences.

Where the essence of psychosis, then, is disorientation, confusion, nonintegration, and poor focusing and discriminating (which are sometimes taken to the defensive extremes of paranoid super-rigidity), the essence of rational-emotive therapy is a high degree of logical structuring, clear-cut focusing, and analytic discrimination. Consequently, RT often gets good results with psychotics in fairly short order, while other forms of therapy (especially classical psychoanalytic and nondirective modes of treatment) permit and abet interminable floundering and concomitant maintenance or worsening of the psychotic process.

Rational-emotive psychotherapy certainly is not effective with all psychotics; and it helps many of them in a relatively ameliorative rather than truly curative kind of way. But few if any other forms of therapy have a better all-around record with borderline and severely psychotic patients than has the consistently rational approach to treatment.

16

The Treatment of a Psychopath with Rational-Emotive Psychotherapy*

So-called psychopaths, or individuals suffering severe character disorder whose behavior is distinctly antisocial, are exceptionally difficult to treat with any form of psychotherapy. They only rarely come for treatment on a voluntary basis; and when they are involuntarily forced into treatment they tend to be resistant, surly, and in search of a "cure" that will involve no real effort on their part. Even when they come for private treatment, they are usually looking for magical, effortless "cures," and they tend to stay in treatment only for a short period of time and to make relatively little improvement.

Psychoanalytic techniques of approaching psychopaths are particularly ineffective for several reasons. These individuals are frequently nonintrospective and nonverbal; they tend to be not overly bright or well educated; they are impatient of long-winded procedures; and they are highly skeptical or afraid of involved psychological analysis or interpretation. It is therefore only the exceptional psychopath who can be helped with analytic methods such as those employed by Lindner in his *Rebel Without a Cause* (1944). Considerably modified techniques of interpretation, such as advocated by Cleckley (1950) and Schmideberg (1959), are usually recommended, instead of the classical psychoanalytic methods.

Before attempting to treat any young delinquents or older criminals in my present private practice of psychotherapy, I had

---

* This chapter is expanded from "The Treatment of a Psychopath with Rational Psychotherapy," *J. Psychology*, 1961, 51, 141-150. Also published in Italian, *Quaderni di Criminologia Clinica*, 1959, 1, 173-184.

considerable experience in examining and treating them when I was Chief Psychologist at the New Jersey State Diagnostic Center and later Chief Psychologist of the New Jersey Department of Institutions and Agencies. At that time I became impressed with the fact that whether the offender was a thief, a sex deviate, a dope addict, or a murderer, about the very worst way to try to help him rehabilitate himself was to give him a moral lecture, appeal to his conscience or superego, or in any way blame him for his misdeeds.

I began to see that, in their own peculiar ways, virtually all these offenders really were anxious and guilty underneath their facade of psychopathic bravado; and that, in fact, their criminal acts were frequently committed as a defensive attempt to protect them against their own feelings of low self-esteem. I saw that many of them were already being compulsively driven to psychopathic behavior by underlying guilt and anxiety; and that to endeavor to make them more guilty and anxious, as is often at first attempted in some forms of counseling and psychotherapy, would hardly help them lose their need for their compulsive defenses.

Instead, I found that if I temporarily showed the offender that I was *not* critical of his behavior, and if I at first allied myself with him (if necessary) against the authorities of the institution in which he was incarcerated (and whom he almost invariably saw as being persecutory), a notable degree of rapport could be established between us. Then, once the prisoner felt that I was really on his side, it was often possible to show him that his pattern of criminal behavior was not merely immoral and antisocial (which he of course knew without my telling him so) but that, more importantly, it was *self-defeating*. If I could convince him, which I often could, that however much society might be (from his standpoint, justifiably and revengefully) harmed by his crimes, he *himself* was inevitably even more self-sabotaged by these acts and their usual consequences, then I had a fairly good chance of getting him to change his behavior in the future.

My many investigatory and therapeutic relationships with

criminals taught me, then, that so-called hardened psychopaths, like other disturbed human beings, act in an irrational and self-defeating manner because they believe, quite falsely, that they are helping themselves thereby. And when they are calmly, unblamefully, and yet vigorously disabused of this belief, they are often capable of radically changing their philosophic orientation and their antisocial behavior which springs from that orientation. Because many or most of the classic psychopaths are, as Cleckley points out, basically psychotic, they are often most difficult to treat; and one must usually be content with reasonably limited gains in therapy with them. Nonetheless, remarkable improvements in their general living patterns, and particularly in the reduction of their antisocial behavior, may result from proper treatment.

Partly as a result of my experiences in treating youthful and older offenders, as well as considerable experience in working with run-of-the-mill neurotics and psychotics, I have in recent years developed the technique of rational-emotive psychotherapy expounded in this volume. A case involving the rational therapeutic treatment of a psychopath will now be described.

The patient was a 25 year old son of a well-to-do family and had been engaging in antisocial behavior, including lying, stealing, sexual irresponsibility, and physical assaults on others since the age of 14. He had been in trouble with the law on five different occasions, but had only been convicted once and spent one year in the reformatory. He displayed no guilt about his offenses and seemed not at all concerned about the fact that he had once helped cripple an old man whose candy store he and his youthful comrades had held up. He had had two illegitimate children by different girls, but made no effort to see them or contribute to their financial support. He came for psychotherapy only at the insistence of his lawyer, who told him that his one chance of being put on probation, instead of being sent to prison, for his latest offense (rifling several vending machines) was to plead emotional disturbance and convince the court that he was really trying to do something to help himself get better. He was first seen by a psychiatrist, who diagnosed him as a hopeless psychopath and thought that treatment would be futile. But I agreed to see him because I thought he presented a challenging problem for psychotherapy.

For the first few sessions the patient was only moderately cooperative, kept postponing appointments without good cause, and came 10 or 15 minutes late to almost every interview. He would listen fairly attentively and take an active part in the session; but as soon as he left the therapist's office he would, in his own words, "forget almost everything we said," and come in for the next session without giving any thought to his problems or their possible alleviation. It was not that he was resentfully resisting therapy; but he quite frankly was doing little or nothing to "get with it."

During the first several sessions, I made little attempt to get the full details of the patient's history. I merely determined that he was the only son of a doting mother, who had always given him his way, and of a merchant father who had ostensibly been friendly and permissive, but who actually had held up to him almost impossibly high standards of achievement and who was severely disappointed whenever he fell below these standards. The patient—whom we shall call Jim—had behaved as a spoiled brat with other children, over whom he was always trying to lord it; had never lived up to his potentialities in school; had started to gain attention from his peers and his teachers at an early age by nasty, show-off behavior; and had been able to get along only reasonably well with girls, one or more of whom he usually managed to have serve him while he sadistically exploited her masochistic tendencies.

Although the patient was quite intelligent and could easily understand psychodynamic explanations of his behavior—such as the possible connection between his failing to satisfy his father's high standards of excellence and his trying to prove to others, by quite opposite antisocial actions, how "great" he was —no attempt to interpret or clarify such connections was made. For one thing, he stoutly opposed such "psychoanalytic crap" whenever the psychodynamics of his situation were even hinted at; for another thing, the rational-emotive therapist frequently makes relatively little use of this kind of historical clarification, since he deems it highly interesting but not necessarily conducive to basic personality change.

Instead, the patient's current circumstances were first focused upon, and he was quickly and intensively shown that he kept defeating himself in the present—as well as in the past. Thus, he kept discussing with me the possibility of his violating the terms of his bail and "skipping out of town." Without being in the least moralistic about his idea or taking any offense at the implied notion that therapy was not going to help him and therefore he might as well go on living the kind of life he had always lived, I calmly and ruthlessly showed Jim that (*a*) he had very little likelihood of being able to skip town without being caught in short order; (*b*) he would only lead a life of desperate evasion during the time he would remain free; and (*c*) he would most certainly know no mercy from the court if and when he was recaptured. Although, at first, he was most loath to accept these grim facts, I patiently persisted in forcing him to do so.

At the same time, I kept showing Jim the silly and totally unrealistic philosophies behind his self-defeating notions of trying to skip bail. He was shown that he was grandiosely and idiotically telling himself that he *should* be able to do what he wanted just because he wanted to do so; that it was totally unfair and unethical for others, including the law, to stand in his way; and that it was utterly catastrophic when he was frustrated in his one-sided demands. And these assumptions, I kept insisting, were thoroughly groundless and irrational.

"But why," asked Jim at one point in the fourth session, "shouldn't I want things to go my way? Why *shouldn't* I try to get what I want?"

Therapist: No reason at all. To want what you want when you want it is perfectly legitimate. But you, unfortunately, are doing one additional thing—and that's perfectly illegitimate.

Patient: What's that? What's the illegitimate thing?

T: You're not only *wanting* what you want, but *demanding*

it. You're taking a perfectly sane desire—to be able to avoid standing trial for your crimes, in this instance—and asininely turning it into an absolute *necessity.*

P: Why is that so crazy?

T: For the simple reason that, first of all, *any* demand or necessity is crazy. Wanting a thing, wanting any damn thing you happen to crave, is fine—as long as you admit the possibility of your not being able to get it. But as soon as you demand something, turn it into a necessity, you simply won't be able to *stand* your not getting it. In that event, either you'll do something desperate to get it—as you usually have done in your long history of antisocial behavior—or else you'll keep making yourself angry, exceptionally frustrated, or anxious about not getting it. Either way, *you* lose.

P: But suppose I *can* get what I want?

T: Fine—as long as you don't subsequently defeat your own ends by getting it. As in this case. Even assuming that you could skip bail successfully—which is very doubtful, except for a short while—would you *eventually* gain by having to live in terror of arrest for the remainder of your life or by having to give up everything and everyone you love here to run, let us say, to South America?

P: Perhaps not.

T: Perhaps? Besides, let's assume, for a moment, that you really could get away with it—that you really could skip bail and wouldn't get caught and wouldn't live in perpetual fear. Even then, would you be doing yourself such a great favor?

P: It seems to me I would! What more could I ask?

T: A lot more. And it is just your *not* asking for a lot more that proves, to me at least, that you are a pretty sick guy.

P: In what way? What kind of crap are you giving me? Bullshit!

T: Well, I could get highly "ethical" and say that if you get away with things like that, with rifling vending machines, jumping bail, and such things, that you are then helping to create the kind of a world that you yourself would not want to live in, or

certainly wouldn't want your friends or relatives to live in. For
if you can get away with such acts, of course, others can, too;
and in such a pilfering, bail-jumping world, who would want
to live?

P: But suppose I said that I didn't mind living in that kind
of world—kind of liked it, in fact?

T: Right. You might very well say that. And even mean it
—though I wonder whether, if you really gave the matter careful thought, you would. But let us suppose you would. So I
won't use that "ethical" argument with a presumably "unethical" and guiltless person like you. But there is still another
and better argument, and one that you and people like you
generally overlook.

P: And that is?

T: That is—your own skin.

P: My own skin?

T: Yes, your own thick and impenetrable skin. Your guiltless,
ever so guiltless skin.

P: I don't get it. What the hell are you talking about?

T: Simply this. Suppose, as we have been saying, you are
truly guiltless. Suppose you, like Lucky Luciano and a few
other guys who really seem to have got away scot-free with a
life of crime, really do have a thick skin, and don't give a good
goddam what happens to others who may suffer from your
deeds, don't care what kind of a world you are helping to
create. How, may I ask, can you—you personally, that is—manu-
facture and maintain that lovely, rugged, impenetrable skin?

P: What difference does it make how I got it, as long as it's
there?

T: Ah, but it does!—it does make a difference.

P: How the hell does it?

T: Simply like this. The only practical way that you can be
guiltless, can maintain an impenetrable skin under conditions
such as we are describing, where you keep getting away with
doing in others and reaping criminal rewards, is by hostility—
by resenting, hating, loathing the world against which you are
criminally behaving.

P: Can't I get away with these things without hating others? Why can't I?

T: Not very likely. For why would a person do in others without hating them in some manner? And how could he not be at least *somewhat* concerned about the kind of dog-eat-dog social order he was creating unless he downed his potential concern with defensive resentment against others?

P: I don't know—. Why couldn't he?

T: Have *you*?

P: Have I, you mean, managed not to—?

T: Exactly! With your long history of lying to others. Leading them on to do all kinds of things they didn't want to do, really, by your misleading them as to your feelings about them. The girls you got pregnant and deserted, for instance. The partners in crime you double-crossed. The parents whose help you've always run back for after breaking promise after promise to them? Would you call that *love* you felt for these people? Affection? Kindliness?

P: Well—uh—no, not exactly.

T: And the hostility, the resentment, the bitterness you felt for these people—and must keep perpetually feeling, mind you, as you keep "getting away" with crime after crime—did these emotions make you feel good, feel happy?

P: Well—at times, I must admit, they did.

T: Yes, at times. But really, deep down, in your inmost heart, *does* it make you feel good, happy, buoyant, joyous to do people in, to hate them, to think that they are no damn good, to plot and scheme against them?

P: No, I guess not. Not always.

T: Even most of the time?

P: No—uh—no. Very rarely, I must admit.

T: Well, there's your answer.

P: You mean to the thick skin business? You mean that I thicken my skin by hating others—and only really hurt myself in the process.

T: Isn't that the way it is? Really is? Isn't your thick skin—like the lamps made of human skin by the Nazis, incidentally

—built of, nourished on little but your own corrosive hatred for others? And doesn't that hatred mainly, in the long run, corrode you?

P: Hm. I—. You've given me something to think about there.

T: By all means, think about it. Give it some real, hard thought.

In a similar manner, in session after session with this intelligent psychopath, I kept directly bringing up, ruthlessly examining, and forthrightly attacking some of his basic philosophies of living, and showing him that these philosophies underlay his antisocial thoughts and behavior. I made no negative criticism or attack on the patient *himself*: but merely on his ideas, his thoughts, his assumptions which (consciously and unconsciously) served as the foundation stones for his disordered feelings and actions.

It was quite a battle, the therapeutic process with Jim. Intelligent he was, and he had little difficulty in ostensibly seeing the things I pointed out, and even quickly agreeing with them. But his behavior, which mirrored his *real* beliefs, changed little at first, and he only (as do so many patients) gave lip-service to the new ideas that we were discussing. Finally, after a year of rational-emotive therapy, Jim was able to admit that for a long time he had vaguely sensed the self-defeatism and wrongness of his criminal behavior, but that he had been unable to make any concerted attack on it largely because he was afraid that he *couldn't* change. That is, he believed that (*a*) he had no ability to control his antisocial tendencies; and that (*b*) he would not be able to get along satisfactorily in life if he attempted to live more honestly.

I then started to make a frontal assault on the philosophies behind Jim's defeatist feelings. I showed him that an individual's inability to control his behavior mainly stems from the *idea* that he cannot do so, the *notion* that longstanding feelings are innate and unmanageable, and that he simply *has to* be ruled by them. Instead, I insisted, human feelings *are* invariably controllable—if one seeks out the self-propagandizing sentences (e.g., "I must do this," "I have no power to stop myself from doing that," etc.) which one unconsciously uses to create and maintain these "feelings."

Jim's severe feelings of inadequacy—his original feelings that he never could gain the attention of others unless he was a problem child and his later feelings that he could not compete in a civilized economy unless he resorted to lying or thieving behavior—were also traced to the self-propagated beliefs behind them—that is, to the sentences: "I am utterly worthless unless I am always the center of attention, even though I gain this attention by unsocial behavior." "If I competed with others in an honest manner, I would fall on my face, and that would be utterly disgraceful and unforgivable." Et cetera.

These self-sabotaging beliefs, and the internalized sentences continually maintaining them, were then not merely traced to their source (in Jim's early relations with his parents, teachers, and peers) but were logically analyzed, questioned, challenged, and counterattacked by the therapist, until Jim learned to do a similar kind of self-analyzing, questioning, and challenging for himself. Finally, after considerable progress, retrogression, and then resumption of progress, Jim (who by that time had been placed on probation) voluntarily gave up the fairly easy, well-paid and unchallenging job which his family, because of their financial standing, had been able to secure for him, and decided to return to college to study to be an accountant.

"All my life," he said during one of the closing sessions of therapy, "I have tried to avoid doing things the hard way—for fear, of course, of failing and thereby 'proving' to myself and others that I was no damn good. No more of that crap any more! I'm going to make a darned good try at the hard way, from now on; and if I fail, I fail. Better I fail that way than 'succeed' the stupid way I was 'succeeding' before. Not that I think I *will* fail now. But in case I do—so what?"

A two-year follow-up report on this patient showed that he was finishing college and doing quite well at his school work. There is every reason to believe that he will continue to work and succeed at his chosen field of endeavor. If so, a self-defeating psychopath has finally turned into a forward-looking citizen.

In this case, the patient's high intelligence and good family background unquestionably contributed to making him a more suitable prospect for psychotherapy than the average psychopath would usually be. The same technique of rational-emotive psychotherapy, however, has also been recently used with several other individuals with severe character disorders and symptoms of acute antisocial behavior, and it appears to work far better than the classical psychoanalytic and psychoanalytically-oriented methods which I formerly employed with these same kinds of patients.

This is not to say or imply that RT works wonders with all psychopaths. It (or any other known type of psychotherapy) doesn't. Even mildly neurotic patients can and usually are difficult to reorient in their thinking: since, as pointed out in the early part of this book, almost all human beings find it *easy* to behave idiotically about themselves and others. Psychopaths and psychotics (who, to my way of thinking, seriously overlap) find it still more difficult to change their own self-defeating ways. Even when they are not organically predisposed to be aberrant (which they probably usually are), their disordered and delusive thinking is so deeply ingrained that only with the greatest effort on their and their therapists' part can effective inroads against their slippery thinking be made.

Not only, therefore, must the therapist who treats psychopaths himself be unusually sane and nonblaming, but he must be able to vigorously maintain a challenging, circuit-breaking attitude: so that by his very persistence in tackling the slipshod cognitions of his antisocial patients, he at first makes up for their tendency to goof in this very respect. Left to their own devices, psychopathic individuals brilliantly avoid facing basic issues and evade accepting a long-range view of life. If the therapist utterly refuses to let them get away with this kind of cognitive shoddiness, but at the same time refrains from scorning them for presently having it, he has some chance—not, to be honest, a very good but still a fair chance—to interrupt and help break up the rigidly set rationalizing patterns which the psychopath keeps inventing and sustaining.

Directness, forcefulness, and freedom from moralizing are among the most effective methods in the armamentarium of the therapist who would assail the citadels of psychopathy. These therapeutic attributes are all heavily emphasized in rational-emotive psychotherapy; and it is therefore hypothesized that this technique is one of the most effective means of treating individuals with severe character disorders.

17

Rational Group Therapy

Although I employed group psychotherapy a decade ago and found it to be an effective means of treating institutionalized young delinquents, and although I have been a member of the American Group Psychotherapy Association for a good many years, I resisted doing group therapy with adults in my private practice until fairly recently. One of the main reasons for my resistance was an awareness, through my patients and my professional contacts, of what often was transpiring in the type of psychoanalytically-oriented group therapy which is most prevalent in New York City.

The more rational I became as a therapist, the more irrational most psychoanalytic group therapy seemed to be; and I wanted no part in adding to the New York scene some additional "therapeutic" groups in which patients were encouraged to view each other as members of the same family, to ventilate without ever really eradicating their hostility, to regress to so-called pregenital stages of development, and generally to become sicker (though perhaps more *gratifyingly* sicker) than they had been before entering therapy.

As the theory and practice of rational-emotive psychotherapy developed, however, I began to see how it could be logically applied to group therapy, and I sometimes used it in small groups consisting of members of the same family. Thus, I would fairly frequently see husbands and wives during the same session; and sometimes I saw their children or parents or other relatives along with them. I also occasionally saw a patient and his or her friend simultaneously.

One thing that I particularly noted in the course of seeing these small groups was that considerable therapeutic time was often saved, in that whatever I had to teach one patient was sometimes just as effective with the spouse or other attending patient. Moreover, if I saw, say, a husband and wife together, and convinced even one of them that he was acting irrationally, and that if he looked at his own internalized sentences and challenged and changed them he could behave much more rationally and less neurotically, then this one convinced patient frequently was able to do a better job with the other, less convinced patient than I was able to do myself. The convinced patient became a kind of auxiliary therapist; and his playing this kind of a role frequently was of enormous help, both to the other patient and to himself (Bach, 1954; Hunt, 1962).

Noting this kind of effect from very small therapeutic groups, I decided to experiment with larger groups, and formed my first regular rational therapy group, consisting of seven members, in 1958. From the start, the group was a great success. The members not only enjoyed the sessions but seemed to be appreciably benefited by them. And some members, who had had several years of prior individual therapy and made relatively minor gains, were able to make much greater progress after they had been steady members of a group for awhile. Soon the original group began to expand in size, as more members wanted to join; and at present, I have five fairly sizable groups going on a once-a-week basis.

Rational group therapy is significantly different from many other kinds of group therapy in several respects. In the first place, the groups tend to be larger than are psychoanalytic or other types of groups. Although I naively thought, when I began my first group, that seven or eight members were quite enough to crowd into a single group, I soon began to see that larger groups were not only quite practical but actually had distinct advantages. With the larger groups, for example, sessions tend to be more lively; more new material, and less stewing around in the same old neurotic juices, tends to arise; more challenging points of view are presented to any individual who brings up his problem during a given session; and, from the standpoint of educational economy, when productive sessions are held more "pupils" are present to learn and benefit from the professional resources (the trained therapist) present.

In consequence of its being able to deal adequately with fairly large groups of patients, rational-emotive group therapy is also financially economical, since each patient may be charged a quite reasonable fee for the hour-and-a-half session in which he participates once a week.

As a result of practical experience, therefore, I soon found it feasible to expand my groups to 10, 12, and sometimes even as many as 14 regular members. At first, I permitted the group members to socialize with each other fairly easily outside the group sessions; but when such socialization soon resulted in lying and evasion on the part of some of the group members who were becoming too friendly with other members, the rules were stiffened, and socialization was confined to the members going, as a group, for coffee after the session (without the presence of the therapist).

Other than this, alternate group sessions, when the therapist is not present, were not allowed, since my observations have led me to believe that group patients who have alternate sessions and who socialize with each other outside the group frequently adopt therapy as a way of life, isolate themselves from other outside contacts, and lead a kind of sheltered, and often very sick, existence which enables them to *avoid* facing and working out some of their main relationship problems and life difficulties.

From the start, rational group therapy has taken a highly didactic and well-integrated course, in that the session normally begins with someone's presenting a troubling problem (or continuing a problem presented at the previous session). Then the other members of the group, acting as auxiliary therapists of a sort, question, challenge, and analytically parse the thinking of the presenting patient, pretty much along the same lines as a rational therapist would handle his patient in an individual interview. If the presenter, for example, says that his boss yelled at him that day and he got very upset, they want to know exactly what he told himself to make himself upset, why he believes this nonsense that he told himself, how he is going to contradict it, what he is going to do the next time the boss yells at him, what the general philosophic principle of his upsetting himself is, etc., etc.

After one patient has been therapeutically interviewed by the other members of the group in this rational-emotive manner, a second or third patient is usually also handled in a similar manner during a given session; though on some occasions the entire session may be devoted to the problems of a single patient, especially one who has not previously presented any of his disturbances in the group. Meanwhile, considerable interaction and rational analysis of this interaction also takes place.

Thus, if one group member is too insistent that another member has a certain problem or should do this or that about his problem, he may be interrupted and challenged by any member of the group as to why he is upsetting himself so much about the first person's problem, or why he is projecting or distorting so much in relation to this problem; and soon the second person rather than the first one may be the center of the group's therapeutic attention. Similarly, if individuals in the group remain too silent, talk too much, keep talking about but never working on their problems, or otherwise acting inappropriately, they may be spontaneously challenged by other group members (or by the therapist) and objectively questioned about their group behavior.

No holds are barred in the group; and no subject of any kind is tabu. If individuals are reluctant to discuss certain aspects of their lives, they may be permitted to remain silent for awhile. But ultimately they will almost certainly be questioned; and their stubborn silences or evasions will be rationally analyzed, until they are convinced that there *is* nothing for them to be ashamed of, that there *is* no horror in revealing themselves to other group members.

Actually, with a few exceptions, the content and the language of the members' statements is unusually free at most times; and sex deviants, thieves, participants in incest, impotent and frigid individuals, paranoid patients, and other committers of socially disapproved acts are continually talking up and discussing their deeds quite openly. So honest is the general tenor of discussion in most instances that the dishonest or avoidant individual soon begins to feel uncomfortable and often feels compelled to bring up whatever fantasies or overt acts he has been hiding.

At the same time, there is no deliberate emphasis on the "true confession" type of session, or on abreaction or catharsis for their own sake. Individuals in the group are often encouraged, by the therapist or by other group members, to speak out and to discuss problems that are bothering them, but that they feel ashamed of discussing. However, they are encouraged to do so not for the cathartic release that they will get thereby, but to show them, on a philosophical level, that there really *is* nothing frightful about their revealing themselves to others, and that the world will *not* come to an end if they do so.

Thus, when anyone is afraid to speak up (as is common, especially among new members of the group), he is not forced to do so against his will. Rather, he is normally asked: *"Why* don't you want to tell us your problem? What are you afraid will happen if you do speak up? Do you think that we won't like you if you tell us the 'terrible' things you have done? Suppose we *don't* like you—what horrible event will *then* occur?" With this kind of questioning, which actually consists of an attack on the philosophic assumptions of the shy or hesitant group member, he is not only induced to ventilate his thoughts and feelings, but to challenge his own premises and to see that there is no good *reason* for his remaining silent.

Similarly, when a group member obviously dislikes what some other member is doing or saying, but will not admit his feelings of dislike or anger, he is frequently encouraged by other group members to express his feelings more openly and honestly. But, again, the purpose of his being urged to express himself is not to help him ventilate or gain emotional release. Rather, it is to show him that (*a*) there is no good reason why he should not behave as he feels, and (*b*) there is often even less good reason for his feeling the way he does and for cherishing this self-defeating feeling.

Thus, a member of one of my groups said nothing for the first several sessions he attended, but sat frowning and pouting at many things that the other group members were saying. He was finally challenged: "Well, let's have it, Joe. What's eating you?" At first he insisted that he wasn't upset in any way about what was going on in the group, but had merely been thinking of things outside the group when he frowned and pouted. But then several group members pointed out that when Jack had said this, or Marion had said that, Joe always stewed or sulked or otherwise showed evident negative feeling. How come?

"All right," Joe finally said, "I guess I have been angry. Damn angry, in fact! And why shouldn't I be? Jack keeps talking about himself all the time as if he were the only person in the room, and all the rest of us are just here to hear him and to help him with his problems; and he obviously doesn't give a damn about helping anyone else but himself. And Marion, well, she goes over the same thing, time and again, and asks us to tell her what to do, but she's really not interested in doing anything for herself and makes absolutely no effort to change. I think that she just wants our attention and has no intention of changing at all. So why should I waste my time telling her anything, when she's not even really listening?"

A couple of the group members immediately began to defend Jack and Marion, and to say that they weren't exactly doing what Joe was accusing them of; and that Joe was grossly exaggerating their poor group behavior. But one girl interrupted these two defenders and said:

"Look, this is not the point. Let's suppose that Marion and Jack are acting just as you, Joe, say they are, and that in a sense they're wasting the time of the rest of the group. So? What do you expect disturbed people to do—behave like little angels in a situation like this? Sure they're doing the wrong thing. That's what they're here for! If they were acting the way you seem to want them to act, they wouldn't need therapy at all. Now the real question is: Why the hell can't you *take* their kind of behavior, and try to help them—and help yourself through trying to help them—change it? Sitting in the corner and pouting

like you have been doing for the last several sessions isn't going
to help you, them, or anyone!"

"Yes," another member of the group chimed in: "Let's assume
that Jack and especially Marion—whom I think you're quite
right about, incidentally, because I find her, very often, an awful
pain in the ass myself, and heartily agree with you that she's
not trying very hard to use the group, except to *avoid* doing
anything about her problem—let's suppose that they're both just
wasting our time acting the way they do, and not really trying
to solve their problems. So what? What do you expect neurotics
like any of us to do, anyway—act like perfectly sane and healthy
people? But, as Grace said, that's not the point. The real point
is that *you* are upsetting yourself because Jack and Marion are
behaving in their typical upset way. Now what are *you* telling
yourself in order to make yourself angry at them?"

Several of the other group members also chimed in, not to
induce the angry member to admit he was angry or to get
him to give "healthy" vent to his anger; but, rather, to get him
to look behind his anger, and discover what *he* was doing to
create it. At first, he was startled with this approach, for he felt
that he had a perfect *right* to be angry at Jack and Marion. But
a short while later, he began to see that other issues were involved, and said:

"Yeah, I'm beginning to get it now. You're not just trying to
get me to say what I feel, though that's important, too, I guess,
as long as I actually feel it, and I'm not doing myself any good
pouting like this and hiding my feelings. But you're really trying
to get me to look behind my feelings, and to ask myself what I
am doing to create them. I never thought about it that way
before, but just as I'm sitting here, I can see you're right. For
I was telling myself, while Marion was talking, that she has no
intention whatever of changing her ways, and that she's therefore
imposing on the rest of us, and especially on myself, whom I
think, yes, I think I do want to change, although maybe I'm just
rationalizing pretty much the same way she does. Anyway, I kept
telling myself that she shouldn't be acting in this anti-group and,
yes, I guess anti-me way. And I see now that I'm wrong: there's

no reason why she shouldn't be acting this way, though it would be much better for her if she weren't."

"And besides," said one of the other group members, "you're not helping her in any way by getting angry at her, as you have been doing, isn't that so?"

"Yes, you're absolutely right. If I really want to help Marion, then I shouldn't be angry at her, but should tell her that I don't think that she's really trying to get better, and should try to help her see why she's not trying, and then I might be, uh, really helpful instead of, uh—"

"Stewing in your own juices!"

"Yes, stewing in my own juices. I'm beginning to see that it's my problem for not expressing myself helpfully to her, but for becoming angry and, well, you know, I just thought of something this very minute! It could be, yes, it could well be that I was becoming angry at her because I wanted to help her, and didn't know how to, and thought it was terrible that I didn't know how to, and was afraid to take a chance and speak up, and perhaps put my foot in it before her and before the rest of the group. And I—I, yes, I guess I've been sitting here and stewing because I really hated myself for not knowing how to help her, or at least trying to speak up to try to help her, and then I was blaming her for putting me in this position, when I, of course, really put myself in it, by being afraid to speak up, and I was seeing her as the cause of my keeping my mouth shut when she wasn't, really, at all."

"In other words," said the therapist, "you blamed yourself for not being able to help Marion. Then you blamed her for putting you on this self-blaming spot, as it were. Then you said to yourself—blaming again, mind you!—'She just is unhelpable and really doesn't want any of us to help her, so why doesn't she stop this stuff she is talking about when she is pretending she is trying to get help from us and—'"

"—Yes, and then I kind of almost saw what I was doing, even before the group started pointing it out to me, and I blamed myself, once again, for doing it, and for not talking up myself about it, for not bringing out *my* problem, and letting someone like Marion, instead, go on blathering about her problems when she really doesn't intend to do—. See! I can see it right now. I'm already beginning to blame her again and I can feel the blood and the temper rising in me."

"Pretty firmly and strongly set, this blaming habit, isn't it?" asked the therapist. "But don't get discouraged, now, and start blaming yourself for having the blaming habit. That would be the final ironical straw! As long as you can objectively see what you're doing, how you're blaming, as I think you are now beginning to see, the vicious circle, or set of concentric interlocking circles, of blame can be broken. In time! And with effort!"

"Yes, hell knows it's taking *me* a long enough time," interjected one of the other group members. "But it's slowly coming along. And I really do think that I blame myself just a little bit less every other day. Now if I can only apply it to others, and stop blaming people like Marion—who still, I am also forced to confess, gives me a pain in the ass, too, with her talky-talky circumlocutions—"

"You mean," interrupted another group member, "whom *you* give *yourself* a pain in the ass about."

"Yes. Thank you. Whom I give *myself* a pain in the ass about. Well, when I stop *that* kind of blaming, maybe I'll get somewhere myself and be able to live more comfortably in this unholy world."

"You can say that again!" said the group member who had first been pounced upon for his silent pouting.

Although, then, in rational group therapy there is considerable emotional ventilation and expression of cross-feelings by and among the group members, the philosophic purpose of this ventilation is continually brought to light and examined. The final aim, as in all rational-emotive therapy, is to *change* the negative thoughts and feelings of the participants, rather than merely to offer them "healthy" and gratifying expression.

Some of the main advantages of group forms of RT are as follows:

1. Since RT is mainly a mode of attitudinal de-indoctrination,

the individual who has an entire group of individuals, including many who are at least as disturbed as he is, attacking and challenging his irrational self-indoctrinations may be more effectively encouraged and persuaded to challenge his own nonsense than may the individual who merely has a single therapist showing him how self-defeating he is. No matter how sane, intelligent, or effective a therapist may be, he is still only one person; and all his work with a patient may often fairly easily be edited out, by the patient's telling himself that the therapist is wrong, stupid, crazy, misguided, etc. It is often harder for a resistant patient to ignore the therapeutic influence of 10 or 12 people than it is for him to by-pass a single therapist.

2. In rational-emotive group therapy, each member of the group who actively participates serves as a kind of therapist in his own right, and tries his best to talk the other members of the group out of their self-sabotaging. In so doing, he usually cannot help seeing that he has just as silly and groundless prejudices himself as have the other people he is trying to help; and that just as they must give up their nonsense, so must he give up a great deal of his. The more stubbornly the other group members hold on to their irrational premises, the more he may be able to note his own stubbornness in holding on to his own. Moreover, the better arguments he may devise, sometimes on the spur of a moment, to assail another group member's illogical views, the better he is sometimes able to use similar arguments to defeat his own defeatism. In group RT, the patients all tend at various times to take the role of a therapist; and this kind of role-playing, as Corsini, Shaw, and Blake (1961) and Moreno and Borgatta (1951) have shown, is an effective method of self-teaching.

3. In rational-emotive group therapy, as in most forms of group treatment, the mere fact that a patient hears the problems of the other group members is sometimes quite therapeutic. Believing, when he first enters therapy, that he is uniquely disturbed or worthless, he soon finds that his problems are no different from other people's; and that he has plenty of company in the world of emotional disturbance. He may therefore

see that he is *not* necessarily hopeless, and that he (like the others) can get over his troubles. Particularly, when a disturbed group member sees equally neurotic individuals slowly but surely improve in the course of group therapy, he is likely to tell himself that at least it is *possible* for him to improve, too —whereas, previously, he may have thought this to be virtually impossible.

4. Disturbed individuals who think about their upsets seriously often come up with individual answers which can be effectively applied by others. Sometimes the specific terminology that they employ to attack their difficulties may be taken over and usefully applied by other group members. Sometimes their philosophic content is helpful. Sometimes the practical homework activity assignments that they give themselves may be successfully applied by others. Thus, one of my patients set herself the task of making an actual written account of what she was telling herself just prior to her becoming upset about something. Then, when she became upset about something similar again, she would pull out her previously made list and go over it, to see what she probably was telling herself *this* time. And she would find it easier to work with and challenge her own negative thinking in this manner. Two other members of her group, on hearing her technique of tackling her own internal verbalizations, used the method themselves and found it quite helpful.

5. Frequently a group member, especially one who has been defensively preventing himself from observing his own behavior clearly (because, with his self-blaming philosophy of life, he would then be compelled to give himself a difficult time), is able to observe, in the course of group treatment, the neurotic behavior of others; and after seeing *their* behavior, is able to recognize this same kind of activity or inactivity in himself. Thus, a good many patients who have little to talk about in individual therapy, because they are glossing over some of their major difficulties, at first listen to the disclosures of others in their group, and *then* they find that they have much to talk about—both in the group itself and in their individual therapy sessions. These people need a sort of spark from without to

enable them to see what they are doing; and the group work provides them with this kind of spark in many instances.

Moreover, the mere fact that Jim, who is himself quite hostile, is safely removed from Joe's behavior, frequently enables him to see how hostile Joe is without at first recognizing his own hostility. But after he has seen Joe's (and perhaps Jack's, and Judy's, and Jill's) hostility, he is able to edge up, as it were, on his own anger, and admit that it exists.

6. Group homework assignments are often more effective than those given by an individual therapist. If the individual therapist tells a shy patient that he simply has to go out and meet other people, in order to overcome his fear of them, the patient may resist following the therapist's suggestion for quite a period of time. But if an entire group says to him, "Look, fellow, let's have no nonsense about this. We want you to speak to the people in your class at school even though you think it's going to kill you to do so," then the patient may more easily give in to group pressure, may begin to push himself into social activity, and may quickly see that it really *doesn't* blight his entire existence if he fails to be accepted by everyone to whom he talks.

The mere fact that other group members are doing healthier things, after coming to therapy, than they ever did before, may persuade one member to try these same kinds of things; and the fact that he is going to have difficulty explaining to the group that he has *not* carried out its homework assignment may give him the extra drive needed to get him to carry it out. When a group member does healthy acts because of group pressure, he may be doing the right thing for the wrong reasons—that is, getting "better" out of his dire need for group approval. So this kind of "progress" is by no means always genuine movement, but it may at times be of considerable temporary help.

7. Whereas, in individual therapy, the patient can often give a seemingly honest but yet very false account of his interactions with other people, in a group situation his own account is not even needed in many instances, since he *does* socially interact right within the group itself. Therefore, the therapist may liter-

ally see how he is interacting, without relying on his reports. In one instance, for example, one of my patients kept coming to me for weeks, telling me how he was refusing to become hostile any more, no matter how his wife or boss provoked him. But after he had been in a group for only a few sessions, it was obvious that he *still* was much more hostile to others than he realized that he was; and this fact could be forcefully brought to his attention and worked at.

8. A group offers a disturbed individual more hypotheses about the causes of some of his behavior than almost any individual therapist might be able to offer him. In one case, one of my patients had been upset about his relations with his girlfriend for many weeks, and both the therapist and his group, in individual and group sessions, had given him many hypotheses as to why he was upset, such as: he was afraid he couldn't get another girlfriend if she left him; he thought it unfair that she was difficult to cope with; he identified her with his dominating mother; etc. The patient carefully considered all these hypotheses, but felt that none of them really rang a bell in his head.

Finally, however, one of the quietest members of his group, who rarely had anything constructive to offer, at this point, wondered whether, just as in his own case, the patient was worried about his failure to make any significant progress in his relationship with this girl, and was blaming himself for failing to effectively apply his therapy-learned insights to the relationship with her. This hypothesis rang a real bell; and the patient saw more clearly what he was telling himself and began to work on one of his basic problems—fear of failing at the therapy process itself.

9. In some instances, group therapy offers patients, especially those who may be slow to warm up to considering their own problems at any given time, a chance to get more intensively at the bottom of some of their disturbances than does the usual form of individual therapy. Thus, a group therapy session generally lasts for an hour and a half (against an individual session of 45 minutes). If, during this time, a given patient is discussing

his problems with the group; and if he then, immediately after, continues to discuss himself for an hour or two more, over coffee with some members of the group, he may finally begin to see things about himself that it would have been much more difficult or even impossible for him to see if he merely had the usual 45 minute single session.

By the same token, his two-, three-, or four-hour total therapeutic participation on a given day, even if he himself is relatively silent during this time, may make such a total impact on the patient that he may continue to think constructively and objectively about himself for hours or days afterward; while, after a single session of individual therapy, he may time and again tend to return to his usual evasions of thinking concertedly about himself.

In many respects, therefore, rational group therapy (like many other forms of group therapy) has concrete advantages over individual psychotherapy. But it has disadvantages, too. An individual in a group naturally cannot receive as much specialized attention from the therapist as he can when he has individualized sessions. When he sees the therapist alone, he is much more likely to get a degree of concentration on his problem, of consistent focusing on his main tasks, and of steady persuasion, challenging, and encouragement that will almost certainly be significantly diluted when he is but one individual in a group of 10 or 12.

Moreover, group therapy is not suited to all patients. Some are too afraid of group contacts even to try it; some are too sick to stick with it when they do try it; some are so suggestible that they take all therapeutic suggestions, both good and bad, with equal seriousness, and therefore may be more harmed than helped by group treatment. Most general psychotherapy patients, I have found, are sufficiently ready for group therapy even when they have first started therapy, and can appreciably benefit from it. Many of them have a hard time in the group for the first several weeks; but if they stick at it, they find it easier and easier, and benefit enormously.

Just as group therapy is unsuitable for some patients, so is

it practically mandatory for others. I have seen quite a few
patients who have severe socializing problems, and who seem to
be almost impossible to help when they are only in individual
therapy, for the simple reason that they can be significantly
improved only if and when they have more contact with others,
and through this contact (and the therapeutic supervision that
continues while they are having it) work through their relationship problems. But they refuse, these patients, to do anything
at all about making the required social contacts; and they can
go on for years of regular therapy, indefinitely refusing. Finally,
they quit therapy in disgust, feeling that they have not been
greatly benefited—which, in their cases, is true.

These same individuals, if they can somehow be forced or
cajoled into joining a therapeutic group, usually still prove to
be difficult patients, in that they say very little, do not interact
with other group members, and continue to lead their lonely
lives in the midst of the group process. Quite commonly, however, they can be pressured by the therapist and the group to
participate more and more in the group activity; and after a
time, and sometimes not too long a time, they are socializing
much better and are beginning to work through their relationship difficulties.

I have no hesitation, after considerable experience with this
kind of patient, in forcing some of them into group therapy by
merely telling them that I will not see them any longer on a
purely individual basis. Most of the time, this kind of force is
not necessary; since individual patients can be persuaded by
normal means to join a group. But in the several cases in which
I have forced someone to join one of my groups, the worst that
has happened is that they have left the group after a few sessions; and in more than half the cases they have stayed with
the group and begun to benefit significantly from their association with it.

My experience with rational-emotive group psychotherapy
during the past several years has shown that group work, when
effectively done, is not merely an adjunct to individual therapy
but actually an important part of it. For individual sessions tend

to be more interesting and helpful as the member participates in a group. Behavior which the patient exhibited in the course of group sessions may be discussed in detail during the individual sessions; and, similarly, material gone over during individual therapy may be helpfully employed in the course of group sessions.

Ideally, I find that if I see my patients for regular individual sessions (usually about once a week) at the start of therapy, and after a few introductory sessions get them into a once-a-week group session, maximum benefit results. After from one to three months of this individual and group therapy combination, most patients can thereafter be seen once a week in group and once every other week (or even less often) in individual therapy. After a year or two (and sometimes less) has gone by on this kind of basis, most patients can be seen regularly mainly in the group, with individual sessions being infrequent or entirely absent.

All told, the total length of therapeutic contact in most completed cases is from two to four years. But during this period the patient has perhaps been seen for about 75 to 100 times for individual sessions and about 150 times for group sessions. In terms of time and money expended by the patient, this is a considerable saving over classical psychoanalysis or most kinds of psychoanalytically-oriented psychotherapy. And the results, from almost the beginning weeks of therapy until the end, are far better in most instances than the results that seem to be obtained by other therapeutic methods.

Rational group psychotherapy, then, is an integral part of rational-emotive analysis. Group participation is almost ideally adaptable to the rational approach; and many of the severe limitations and the anti-therapeutic results of psychoanalytic group therapy are eliminated or significantly decreased by the use of this kind of group method.

18

Rational Therapy and Other Therapeutic Approaches *

A major critique of most of the existing schools of psychotherapy is well in order; and someday I hope to be able to find the time to do a voluminous and well-documented book along these lines. Because of space limitations, however, this kind of critique will not be attempted, even in a summary way, in the present volume. Rather, a brief attempt will now be made to indicate some of the main differences between the rational-emotive approach to psychotherapy and that taken by some of the other prominent schools of therapeutic practice.

RT and Freudian Psychoanalysis. Much has previously been said in this volume regarding the differences between RT and Freudian psychoanalytic practice, so these differences will be only summarily reviewed here. Classical psychoanalysis mainly consists of the application of the techniques of free association, dream analysis, the analysis of the transference relationship between the analyst and analysand, and the direct psychoanalytic interpretations of the analyst to the patient. In rational-emotive psychotherapy free association and dream analysis are infrequently employed, not because they do not produce salient or interesting material about the patient, but because most of this material is irrelevant to curing him and is inefficiently produced in terms of the time, effort, and money that are expended

---

* This chapter is an expanded version of "Rational Psychotherapy and Individual Psychology," *J. Individ. Psychol.*, 1957, 13, 38-44 and some of the material appearing in Paul Krassner and Robert Anton Wilson, "An Impolite Interview with Albert Ellis," *The Realist*, March and May, 1960, reprinted in Paul Krassner, *Impolite Interviews.* New York: Lyle Stuart, 1961.

in order to obtain it (Loevinger, 1962; Starer and Tanner, 1962).

A specific transference neurosis between the therapist and patient is virtually never deliberately created in the course of RT; but when normal transference and counter-transference relations do come up in the course of therapy, they are either directly interpreted and dealt with; or, on occasion, they are simply noted and employed by the therapist but not specifically interpreted to the patient. It is considered more important in RT to interpret and work through the patient's emotional transferences from his parents (and other important figures in his early life) to his associates and intimates *outside* therapy (such as his mate, his friends, and business associates) than to interpret every detail of his emotional transferences to the therapist.

Rather than over-emphasizing the importance of the transference relationship itself, the rational-emotive therapist often spends considerable time analyzing and observing the *philosophic basis* of all transference phenomena: that is, the patient's illogical *beliefs* that he *must* be loved by the therapist (and others); or that he *must* hate a frustrating or unloving therapist (or other significant person in his life); or that he *must* behave in the present pretty much the same way as he behaved in his early life and relationships.

Instead, therefore, of merely revealing important transference phenomena to the patient, the rational therapist philosophically and ideologically *attacks* the foundations on which these phenomena continue to exist; and he thereby helps uproot both positive and negative transferences that are defeatingly binding the patient and forcing him to behave in a compulsive, inefficient manner. Where, therefore, many therapists feel that they effectively handle and interpret transference processes to their patients, the rational therapist feels that most of these therapists actually give only lip-service to the cause of uprooting transference phenomena; and, in fact, by their artificially creating transference neuroses, or encouraging positive transferences to the therapist, they often actually abet rather than undermine disturbance-creating transference.

In regard to the analysis of the Oedipus and Electra complexes, the rational therapist again feels that the Freudians largely describe these processes rather than remove their deepest roots. For he believes that the real philosophic source of an Oedipus complex (if and when it actually exists to a serious degree) is not the patient's infantile association with his mother and father, but his acquiring a false set of *beliefs* about these relations: namely, his beliefs that *it would indubitably be terrible* if he were caught masturbating, if he lusted after his mother, if his father jealously hated him, etc. The rational therapist, when he finds a real Oedipus complex, vigorously attacks the beliefs which support it, and thus more thoroughly does away with it (and most of its pernicious side effects) than does classical psychoanalytic therapy.

The rational therapist is much closer in his technique to psychoanalytically-oriented psychotherapists, especially those of the Horney, Fromm, and Alexander schools, than he is to the classical analyst. As do these neo-Freudian (or neo-Adlerian) analysts, he uses considerable direct interpretation to show his patients how their past behavior is connected with their present malfunctioning, and how they have been unduly indoctrinated with ideas and attitudes which are now defeating their own ends.

The rational therapist, however, spends less time on past events in the patient's life than do most psychoanalytically-oriented therapists; and, more especially, he goes far beyond their interpretation by forcefully *attacking* the patient's early-acquired philosophies of living, once he has analytically revealed them and convinced the patient that they still strongly persist.

The rational therapist also uses considerably more suggestion, persuasion, activity homework assignments, and other directive methods of therapy than the usual psychoanalytically-oriented therapist does; and when he uses them, he does so on theoretical rather than purely empirical grounds.

RT and Jungianism. Although Jung's theories differ radically in many respects from those of Freud and Adler, Jungian therapy seems to be largely derived from the practical views of these two pioneers; and Jung has noted (1954) that "the severer neuroses usually require a reductive analysis of their symptoms and states. And here one should not apply this or that method indiscriminately but, according to the nature of the case, should conduct the analysis more along the lines of Freud or more along those of Adler." However, Jung continues, "when the thing becomes monotonous and you begin to get repetitions, and your unbiased judgment tells us that a standstill has been reached, or when mythological or 'archetypal' contents appear, then is the time to give up the analytical-reductive method and to treat the symbols analogically or synthetically, which is equivalent to the dialectical procedure and the way of individuation."

RT overlaps Jungian therapy in that it views the patient holistically rather than only analytically; holds that the goal of therapy should as much be the individual's growth and development as his cure from mental disturbance; firmly encourages the patient to take certain constructive steps; and particularly emphasizes his individuality and his achieving what *he* really wants to do in life. Philosophically, therefore, rational-emotive therapy is in many ways closer to Jungian analysis than it is to Freudian technique.

At the same time, the rational therapist rarely spends much time observing or analyzing his patients' dreams, fantasies, or symbol productions, as they are employed in Jungian practice; and he is not particularly interested in the mythological or "archetypal" contents of the patients' thinking. He considers this material to be informative and often fascinating, but not particularly relevant to the patient's basic philosophic assumptions, which he contends are normally present in simple declarative and exclamatory internalized sentences, and do not have to be sought for in symbolic form.

The rational therapist also feels that most patients are already so preoccupied with their vague, fantasy-like, mythological thinking that encouraging them to do more of this kind of ideation during therapy frequently hinders their clearly seeing what they are telling themselves to create their own upsets. Particularly in the case of schizophrenic and borderline psychotic individuals, he would not employ this kind of confusing technique; and even with run-of-the-mill neurotics, he would prefer to help them see what they are nonsensically reiterating to themselves in the present rather than to dig up any archetypal material which may or may not have relevance to their current disturbances.

RT and Adlerian Therapy. When the first public paper on rational-emotive therapy was given in 1956, it was pointed out by Dr. Rudolf Dreikurs and other Adlerians that there seemed to be a close connection between many RT views and some of the basic thinking of Alfred Adler. At the time I gave this paper, I was not myself aware of some of the basic similarities between the Adlerian and RT therapeutic systems, although I had previously been acquainted with the writings of Adler (1927, 1929, 1931) and had been favorably impressed by them. It was not until I reread these writings and also read the more contemporary presentations of Ansbacher and Ansbacher (1956), Dreikurs (1950, 1956), and other Adlerians that I realized the significant degree of overlap of the Adlerian and RT viewpoints.

Rational-emotive therapy, for example, holds that it is people's irrational *beliefs* or *attitudes* which usually determine their significant emotional reactions and lead to their disturbances. Adler continually emphasized the importance of the individual's style of life and insisted that "the psychic life of man is determined by his goal." The common factor is that both—beliefs and attitudes on the one hand and life goals on the other—are a form of thought.

Adler noted that when an individual is neurotic, "we must decrease his feeling of inferiority by showing him that he really undervalues himself." Rational therapists teach their patients that their feelings of inadequacy arise from the irrational beliefs that they should be thoroughly competent in everything they do, and that they should consequently blame themselves when they make any mistakes or when someone disapproves of them.

The rational-emotive therapist makes relatively little use of the Freudian notion of a highly dramatic "unconscious" in which sleeping motivations lie ever ready to rise up and smite the individual with neurotic symptoms (Ellis, 1950, 1956b); but he does keep showing his patients that they are unconsciously, or unawarely, telling themselves statements, naively believing these unconsciously-perpetuated statements, and significantly affecting their own conduct thereby. Adler says much the same thing in these words: "The unconscious is nothing other than that which we have been unable to formulate in clear concepts. It is not a matter of concepts hiding away in some unconscious or subconcious recesses of minds, but of parts of our consciousness, the significance of which we have not fully understood."

Adler points out that the therapist "must be so convinced of the uniqueness and exclusiveness of the neurotic direction line, that he is able to foretell the patient's disturbing devices and constructions, always to find and explain them, until the patient, completely upset, gives them up—only to put new and better hidden ones in their place." This, in his own terms, is exactly what the rational therapist does; because he knows, even before he talks to the patient, that this patient *must* believe some silly, irrational ideas—otherwise he could not possibly be disturbed. And, knowing this, the rational-emotive therapist deliberately looks for these irrationalities, often predicts them, and soon discovers and explains them, or mercilessly reveals their flaws, so that the patient is eventually forced to give them up and replace them with more rational philosophies of living.

The rational therapist, as emphasized in this book, insists on *action* as well as *depropagandization,* and often virtually or literally forces the patient to do something to counteract his poor thinking. Adler wrote in this connection: "The actual change in the nature of the patient can only be his own doing."

Speaking of individuals with severe inadequacy feelings, Adler noted that "the proper treatment for such persons is to encourage them—never to discourage them." The rational therapist, more than almost any other kind of psychotherapist, particularly gets at long-ingrained negative beliefs and philosophies by persuading, cajoling, and consistently encouraging the patients to be more constructive, more positive, more goal-oriented.

The practitioner of RT believes that human beings are not

notably affected by external people and things, but by the views they take of these people and things, and that they therefore have an almost unlimited power, through changing their sentences and their beliefs, to change themselves and to make themselves into almost anything they want. Said Alfred Adler in this connection: "We must make our own lives. It is our own task and we are masters of our own actions. If something new must be done or something old replaced, no one need do it but ourselves."

In many important respects, then, RT and Alfred Adler's Individual Psychology obviously overlap and support each other's tenets. There are, however, some significant differences. Although it has been reported (Munroe, 1955) that Adler's therapeutic technique was often quite persuasive and even commanding, as the rational therapist's technique candidly is in many instances, Adler himself espoused a more passive view: "Special caution is called for in persuading the patient to any kind of venture. If this should come up, the consultant should say nothing for or against it, but, ruling out as a matter of course all generally dangerous undertakings, should only state that, while convinced of the success, he could not quite judge whether the patient was really ready for the venture" (Ansbacher and Ansbacher, 1956, p. 339).

It is mainly, however, in the realm of his views on social interest that Adler would probably take serious issue with the rational therapist. For the latter believes that efficient human behavior must be primarily based on *self*-interest; and that, if it is so based, it will by logical necessity also have to be rooted in *social* interest. Adler seemed to believe the reverse: that only through a primary social interest could an individual achieve maximum self-love and happiness.

Ansbacher and Ansbacher report in this connection: "To the most general formulation of the question, 'Why should I love my neighbor?' Adler is reported to have replied: 'If anyone asks me why he should love his neighbor, I would not know how to answer him, and I could only ask in turn why he should pose such a question.'" The rational therapist would tend to take a different stand and to say that there is a very good answer to the question of why one should love one's neighbor, or at least why one should take care not to harm him: namely, that only in so doing is one likely to help build the kind of society in which one would best live *oneself*.

The rational therapist believes, in other words, that self-interest *demands* social interest; and that the rational individual who strives for his own happiness will, *for that very reason*, also be interested in others. Moreover, the rational therapist tends to believe, with Maslow (1954) and other recent personality theorists, that the human animal *normally* and *naturally* is helpful and loving to other humans, provided that he is not enmeshed in illogical thinking that leads to self-destructive, self-hating behavior.

Where Adler writes, therefore, "All my efforts are devoted toward increasing the social interest of the patient," the rational therapist would prefer to say, "Most of my efforts are devoted toward increasing the self-interest of the patient." He assumes that if the individual possesses rational self-interest, he will, on both biological and logical grounds, almost invariably tend to have a high degree of social interest as well.

In some theoretical ways, then, and in several specific elements of technique, RT and Individual Psychology significantly differ. Thus, rational-emotive therapy particularly stresses disclosing, analyzing, and attacking the concrete internalized sentences which the patient is telling himself in order to perpetuate his disturbance; and it is much closer in this respect to general semantic theory and philosophical analysis than it is to Adlerianism. It also tends to make less use of dream material and of childhood memories than Adlerian therapy does.

It is interesting and important to note, however, that in many ways RT and Individual Psychology amazingly agree. That Alfred Adler should have had a half century start in stating some of the main elements of a theory of personality and psychotherapy which was independently derived from a rather different framework and perspective is indeed a remarkable tribute to his perspicacity and clinical judgment.

RT and Nondirective or Client-Centered Therapy. Rational-emotive psychotherapy largely originated as an empirical revolt against the passive methods of classical Freudian psychoanalysis and Rogerian nondirective therapy. In my early days as a counselor and therapist, I experimentally employed considerable degrees of passivity and nondirectiveness in my work with patients. I discovered that although this method was enormously gratifying to many individuals (though often not to the most intelligent ones, who soon "got on" to it and saw that they were getting back from the therapist little more than they were giving him), it was abysmally unhelpful in any deep-seated sense. The patients often received significant insights into themselves through nondirective therapy; but they only rarely used their insights to change their fundamental philosophies and patterns of behavior. Rational-emotive therapy, therefore, developed as a means of seeking some more effective way of getting patients not only to *see* but to *change* their irrational life premises.

The aims of Rogerian client-centered therapy and those of RT have much in common and are similar to the aims of most schools of therapy. Thus, Rogers (1951) notes that the altered human personality, after effective therapy takes place, generally includes (*a*) less potential tension or anxiety, less vulnerability; (*b*) a lessened possibility of threat, less likelihood of defensiveness; (*c*) improved adaptation to life; (*d*) greater self-control; (*e*) greater acceptance of self and less self-blaming; and (*f*) greater acceptance of and less hostility to others. These are all definite goals of rational-emotive psychotherapy.

The Rogerian method, moreover, is somewhat akin to the rational method, in that the client-centered or nondirective therapist appears to help his patients primarily by fully accepting them in spite of their incompetencies, misdeeds, and disturbances; remaining unanxious and unperturbed himself; serving as a good integrated model for his patients; and forcefully communicating to them his unconditional regard and empathic understanding of their internal frames of reference. In a manner different from the nondirective reflection of their feelings, the rational therapist communicates to his patients that he unconditionally accepts and forgives them, in spite of their immoral or inefficient acts, and that he can remain unhostile and unanxious no matter what material they bring up during his sessions with them.

Indeed, just because the rational-emotive practitioner believes, in fact and in theory, that no one is ever to blame for anything he does, and that blame and anger are dysfunctional and irrational feelings, he is beautifully able to communicate to his patients that he *really* does not hate them or think them worthless when they act in "bad" and ineffective ways. In this respect, he is most accepting and permissive—probably much more so than many psychoanalytic, nondirective, or other therapists.

At the same time, the rational therapist goes far beyond the Rogerian therapist in that, in *addition* to accepting his patients fully and non-blamefully, he actively *teaches* them to accept themselves and others without blaming. He not only sets them an excellent example by his own non-blaming behavior; but he also didactically demonstrates why they should accept themselves. In terms of his active persuasion, teaching, debating, and information-giving, he deviates widely from the nondirectiveness and more passive acceptance of the followers of Carl Rogers. Although the rational therapist has *some* belief in the innate capacity of human beings to help themselves when they are non-judgmentally accepted by others, he also accepts the limitations of extremely disturbed persons to be thereby benefited; and he consequently does something *more* than unconditionally accepting them in order to help them truly to accept themselves and others.

RT and Existentialist Therapy. As in the case of its overlapping of Rogerian aims, rational-emotive therapy also overlaps significantly the aims of Existentialist therapy. As previously noted in this volume, the main aims of the Existentialist therapists are to help their patients define their own freedom, cultivate their own individuality, live in dialogue with their fellow men, accept their own experiencing as the highest authority, be fully present in the immediacy of the moment, find truth through their own actions, and learn to accept certain limits in life (Braaten, 1961;

May, 1961; Royce, 1962; Thorne, 1961). RT practitioners largely accept these views, though they may use somewhat different terminology and emphasis.

Like the Rogerians, however, the primary (and often sole) technique of the Existentialist therapists, in their endeavors to help their patients achieve these individualistic aims, is to have open, honest, unrestricted Existentialist encounters with these patients. In the course of these encounters, presumably, the patients see that the therapists truly follow their own codes, and are individuals in their own rights, relatively free from the dictates of other-directedness; and consequently they begin to emulate the therapists in these regards and to free themselves from their neurotic, convention-bound behavior.

The practitioner of RT, on the other hand, feels that while the Existentialists' goals are fine and their experiential encounters with patients are quite possibly helpful in many instances, they (like the Rogerians) fail to accept the grim reality that most emotionally disturbed individuals, and especially serious neurotics and psychotics, are so strongly indoctrinated and self-propagandized by the time they come for therapy that the best of Existential encounters with their therapists are frequently going to be of relatively little help to them. In fact, because such encounters are immediately gratifying, they may actually divert patients from working for long-range therapeutic goals. Because Existentialist therapy techniques are somewhat vague and unstructured, they may help seriously disturbed persons to become even more disorganized and confused. Because the therapist serves as such a good model to his patients, unguided self-hating patients may tell themselves that they could not possibly be as good as he is, and may blame themselves ever more severely.

For a variety of reasons such as these, the rational therapist feels that most Existentialist therapists are better theoreticians than practitioners; and that, in addition to whatever healthful encounters they may personally have with their patients, more direct teaching, persuasion, and discussion is often needed to jolt them out of their deeply intrenched circularly negative thinking. Moreover, just because serious neurotics and psychotics are frequently directionless and disoriented, they often require a most direct and highly focused form of therapy that is anathema to most Existentialist thinking. Free encounters with other human beings are marvelous for relatively healthy persons. It is doubltful whether many seriously aberrated individuals can successfully take or withstand this kind of relationship before they are more authoritatively helped to discipline their thinking.

RT and Conditioning-Learning Therapy. There is considerable agreement between rational-emotive theory and practice and the work of the conditioning-learning therapists, such as Dollard and Miller (1950), Eysenck (1961), Ferster (1958), Mowrer (1953, 1960a), Rotter (1954), Salter (1949), Shaw (1961), Wolpe (1958, 1961a), and some Soviet psychotherapists (Myasischev, Bassin and Yakovleva, 1961; Sakano, 1961).

On theoretical grounds, the rational therapist accepts the main premises of the learning theorists, and believes that human beings are largely conditioned or taught to respond inefficiently to certain stimuli or ideas, and that they can consequently be reconditioned, either ideationally or motorially, in the course of a therapeutic process. He is skeptical, however, about the scope of the deconditioning treatment of therapists, such as Salter and Wolpe, who largely concentrate on symptom-removal and who do not aim for any basic philosophic restructuring of the patient's personality. He also feels that when deconditioning therapists do succeed with their patients, they have usually unwittingly induced these patients to change their internalized sentences, and have not merely got them to respond differently to the stimuli that are presented to them.

Rational-emotive therapy, in other words, attempts to put deconditioning techniques within a verbal or ideational framework rather than to use them in their simpler forms. It tries to recondition not merely the individual's neurotic response (such as his fear of animals or his anger at poor automobile drivers) but to change the philosophic basis of this response, so that neither the current fear or hostility nor similar responses will tend to rise again in the future.

RT is therefore quite compatible with deconditioning techniques, and itself includes some amount of verbal deconditioning. But it deals with the patient in a broader and more ideational frame of reference and attempts to give him a concept and a technique of resolving *any* of his illogically-based activities rather than merely providing him with a means of overcoming his *current* irrational fear or hostility.

RT and Other Schools of Therapy. Rational-emotive psychotherapy has something in common with several other psychotherapeutic schools; but at the same time, it has significant differences from them. Thus, it parallels much of the thinking of the General Semanticists. But it also provides a detailed technique of psychotherapy which is so far absent among the followers of Korzybski (1933); and its personality theory and its system of therapy are much broader in scope and application than the theory and practice of the semanticists.

RT has little quarrel with some of the views of Wilhelm Reich (1949) and his followers, especially their notion that emotional disturbances tend to be mirrored in the individual's posture, gestures, and motor habits, and that helping a disturbed person to release his muscular and other physiological tensions may help him to face and work through some of his psychological problems. By the same token, RT sometimes makes use of techniques of physical relaxation, especially those espoused by Jacobson (1942), as an adjunct to psychotherapy. The rational therapist believes, however, that manipulative and relaxational approaches to therapy are largely palliative and diversional and that they rarely, by themselves, get to the main sources of emotional difficulties.

What the Reichians and other physiopsychotherapeutic practitioners do not seem to see is that if one physically manipulates a patient, especially in a sexual way, one may often be unwittingly depropagandizing him and may consequently do him more good by this unwitting depropagandization than by the physical strokings or pokings.

Thus, if John Jones irrationally thinks that sexual participation is a wicked business, and his Reichian therapist (particularly if she is a female therapist) keeps manipulating parts of his body often enough, Jones is quite likely to say to himself: "Well, what do you know! Sex can't be so wicked after all." And he may actually lose some of his inhibitions and unhinge some of his character armoring.

The question is, however: Is it really the Reichian manipulations that are helping the patient, or is it the new *ideas* that he is indirectly deriving from such physical manipulations of his body? The rational therapist, while having no serious objection to physical aspects of psychotherapy, almost invariably sticks mainly within the ideological rather than the physiological realm and helps change bodily armorings mainly through changing ideation, rather than vice versa.

Because of his activity-directive leanings, the rational-emotive therapist has no prejudice against various other modes of therapy in which patients are physically handled, manipulated, or coaxed into some kind of action (Hamilton, 1961). Thus, if he wishes to do so, there is nothing in his theoretical orientation which prevents him from using some of the techniques employed in the course of Gestalt therapy, hypnotherapy, experiential therapy, conditioned reflex therapy, or psychotherapy by reciprocal inhibition [all of which schools are ably outlined in Robert A. Harper's *Psychoanalysis and Psychotherapy: 36 Systems* (1959)].

Again, however, RT goes considerably beyond the main practices of these various therapeutic schools and, in addition at times to using some of their methods, invariably includes a forthright didactic approach to and attack on the basic philosophic orientation of the patient (Wolf, 1962).

RT is much closer, in its eclectic respects, to Adolf Meyer's psychobiologic therapy (Meyer, 1948; Muncie, 1939) than it is to most active-directive therapies, since RT stresses highly verbal and spoken *as well as* so-called nonverbal or nonvocalized therapeutic methods. It is not, however, a thoroughly eclectic approach, since it does have and rests upon a centralized *theory* of human disturbance and of psychotherapy. And in keeping with its theory, it is distinctly more assertive and frankly counter-propagandistic than are the therapies which it most significantly seems to overlap, such as Adler's Individual Psychology, Thorne's directive therapy, Johnson's General Semantics, most of the learning theory therapies, and Phillips' assertion-structured therapy (Stark, 1961).

All told, RT is, at one and the same time, highly rational-persuasive-interpretive-philosophical *and* distinctly emotive-directive-active-work-centered. Peculiarly enough, this seems to be a rare combination, except among today's frankly eclectic therapists. But rational-emotive therapy is based on a structured theoretical framework that gives a clear-cut rationale for the variety of specific techniques it employs. In the last analysis, this is one of its most distinguishing characteristics: that it presents a firm theoretical outlook and plausible rationale for the many therapeutic methods which it does (and also does not) employ.

19

A Consideration of Some of the Objections to Rational-Emotive Psychotherapy *

Whenever I or my colleagues who believe in and practice rational-emotive psychotherapy present our views to a professional or a lay audience, and particularly to the former kind of groups, the air tends to become blue with vigorous objections, protests, and counter-perorations. The psychoanalytically-inclined individuals in our audience become quite disturbed because, they vigorously contend, we are not sufficiently depth-centered; and the Rogerians and their nondirective cohorts object because we are presumably too cold-blooded and do not have enough unconditional positive regard for our patients.

In considering the highly emotionalized objections that are often raised against RT principles and procedures by sundry adherents of different schools, it would be easy to say "That's *their* problem!" and let it go at that. And perhaps it *is* the problem of those who so strongly object to RT that they get terribly disturbed at our views. It is also, however, very much *our* problem if some of the objections raised to rational-emotive procedures are valid. And unless we frankly and clearly answer these objections, the validity of our *own* assumptions and techniques will remain very much in doubt. Let me, therefore, consider some of the most cogent and relevant protests that have been raised against RT and try to answer them with a minimum of irrational evasiveness or hostility.

* This chapter is an expanded version of papers presented at graduate psychology department colloquia at the University of Minnesota. the State University of Iowa, the Veterans Administration Centers at St. Paul, Minnesota and Knoxville, Iowa, the Michigan Society of School Psychologists, and the University of Kansas Medical Center in 1961 and 1962.

Is RT too unemotional, intellectualized, and over-verbal? It is often objected that any rational approach to therapy tends to be too intellectualized, unemotive, and over-verbal. Some answers to this charge are as follows:

1. There may well be forms of rational or didactic psychotherapy that do not adequately consider the emotional aspects of human nature; but it is doubtful that RT is one of these techniques. It begins with the assumption that disturbed people have anxious or hostile *feelings;* and, more than most other schools of therapy, it entertains the hypotheses that some of these feelings are biologically rooted—that there is a normal *tendency* of humans *easily* to become excessively fearful and angry, and that it is most difficult (though not impossible) for them to understand, control, and to some degree eradicate this tendency. It is the job of effective therapy, the rational-emotive therapist contends, to show the disturbed individual how he can challenge and change his biologically based (as well as his environmentally inculcated) tendencies toward irrational, over-emotionalized behavior and to help him become *more,* though probably never *completely,* rational.

2. In the actual process of therapy, most rational-emotive sessions start with the patient's current *feelings:* with his describing exactly how badly or well he felt when this event or that relationship occurred in his life. The patient is not asked to talk about his thoughts or deeds, but largely about how he *feels* about these ideas and actions. Then, when his feelings prove to be negative and self-defeating, he is shown their cognitive and ideational sources. That is to say, he is shown how he concretely and literally *creates* most of his self-destructive emotions by consciously or (more usually) unconsciously telling himself certain exclamatory and evaluative sentences. Thus, when he feels hurt by being rejected, he is shown that his feeling is created by (*a*) the fairly sane internalized sentence, "I don't like being rejected," and by (*b*) the decidedly insane sentence, "It is *terrible* being rejected; and because I don't like it, I can't *stand* to be rejected in this fashion."

3. The critic who accuses the rational-emotive therapist of

ignoring or intellectualizing feeling and emotion is making a false dichotomy between so-called emotion and so-called thought. Actually, the two are closely interrelated; and sustained emotion, particularly in an adult, largely consists of self-evaluative thoughts or attitudes (Arnold, 1960). Human adults mainly feel good because (*a*) they receive pleasant physical sensations (such as good odors, tastes, sounds, sights, and caresses) and (*b*) they *think* or *believe* that some person or thing is delightful or charming. And they *feel* bad because they encounter unpleasant physical stimuli and they *think* or *believe* that some person or thing is horrible, frightful, or terrible.

Rudolf Arnheim (1958) has recently published a most astute paper showing that emotion cannot be divorced from perceiving or thinking. And V. J. McGill, in his book, *Emotions and Reason* (1954), has noted that "it is as difficult to separate emotions and knowing, as it would be to separate motivation and learning. . . .Emotions . . . include a cognitive component and an expectation or readiness to act; their rationality and adaptive value depends on the adequacy of these two components in a given situation."

Rational-emotive therapy not only encourages human beings to guiltlessly seek and accept all kinds of harmless physical sensations (such as sex and gustatory pleasures), but it also invites a long-range hedonistic approach to satisfaction that emphasizes the pleasures and lack of pain of *tomorrow* as well as the satisfactions of today. Nor is RT anti-emotional: since it is highly in favor of the individual's having a wide range of experiences and emotions, including many of the moderately "unpleasant" ones. It is merely opposed to, and devises highly effective counter-measures against, frequent, prolonged, or intense negative or self-defeating emotional states, such as dysfunctional anxiety (as opposed to justified and self-preserving fear) and senseless hostility (as opposed to feelings of irritation and annoyance which encourage world-changing behavior).

4. Wolpe (1956) has noted that "it is not to be expected that emotional responses whose conditioning involves automatic subcortical centers will be much affected by changes in the patient's

intellectual content." Wolpe seems to assume, however, that emotional responses in human beings *first* result from conditioning that involves automatic subcortical centers and *later* continue to occur in an automatic manner. This is a dubious assumption. The chances are that in most instances an individual (such as a young child) first tells himself something like: "Oh, my heavens, it would be terrible if my mother did not love me!" and that he *then* becomes conditioned, perhaps on subcortical levels, so that whenever his mother frowns, criticizes, or otherwise indicates that she may not love him, he starts being horribly anxious. If this is true, then much of his so-called automatic subcortical emoting is really based on his holding, unconsciously, distinctly cortical philosophies of life. For if he did not continually believe that it *is* terrible for his mother or for some other beloved person to reject him, it is doubtful whether his subcortical neurotic reactions would still be maintained. And philosophies of life, as far as I can see, are normally (though perhaps not always) held on cortical rather than subcortical levels, and can be changed by modifications of the individual's thinking.

Moreover, assuming that there are some emotional responses whose conditioning involves automatic subcortical centers which cannot fully be affected by changes in the person's intellectual content, rational-emotive therapy is one of the relatively few techniques which include large amounts of action, work, and "homework" assignments of a so-called nonverbal (though actually of a nonspoken) nature.

Thus, in the course of individual RT sessions, the therapist who is seeing, say, a patient who has a fear of riding in airplanes, will do his best to persuade, cajole, induce, or even command his patient to take airplane rides. And in rational-emotive group therapy sessions, an individual who is afraid to participate in the group discussion or to tell the group about some of his presumably shameful behavior will often be urged and practically forced by the therapist and other group members to work out his fears in action as well as in theory.

Although most rational therapists do not practice Wolpe's specific techniques of deconditioning fearful patients by using hypnotic desensitization or special apparatus, or by presenting the patient with specific objects which he fears, there is nothing in RT theory that prevents us from using these kinds of techniques. On the contrary, the theory states that human beings propagandize themselves into behaving irrationally by consciously and unconsciously, verbally and actively convincing themselves of nonsense; and that the *two* main counter-propagandizing forces that will help them change their underlying beliefs and their disturbed behavior are thinking *and* acting: challenging and contradicting their internalized sentences, on the one hand, and forcing themselves to *do* the things of which they are irrationally afraid, on the other.

5. Appel (1957) has stated that "psychotherapy is essentially the psychological, social, and emotional influence of one individual on another. It cannot remain entirely within the intellectual realm, as the patient is more than just his ideas." This is, of course, a true statement; but it does not negate the principles of RT.

As shown in the early chapters of this book, rational-emotive therapy sees the human being as possessing *four* basic processes —perception, movement, thinking, and emotion—all of which are integrally interrelated. But it also contends that a large part of what we call emotion is little more or less than a certain kind —a biased, prejudiced, or strongly evaluative kind—of thinking.

Although, then, the patient is more than just his ideas, for all practical purposes the fact remains that, especially as regards his emotional disturbance, he is *mainly* his ideas; and that therefore the most important method of helping him overcome his disturbance is through helping him change his conscious or unconscious ideas. Practically all forms of psychotherapy, including Wolpe's reciprocal inhibition therapy and Wilhelm Reich's character unarmoring by physical manipulation of the patient, explicitly or implicitly include some important emphasis on changing the patient's ideas. Almost by definition, in fact, the term *psycho*therapy means some form of verbal communication between the patient and therapist; otherwise, the term *physio*therapy would be used instead.

Rational-emotive therapy, as noted above, emphasizes overt activity and homework assignments by the patient. It also (as will be discussed in more detail below) includes some kind of relationship between the patient and the therapist. More than most other kinds of therapies, however, it explicitly stresses the direct, logical-persuasive intervention of the therapist to help change the patient's ideas, since it holds that man is a uniquely symbolizing and thinking animal and that his neuroses and psychoses are largely, though not entirely, a result of his irrational thinking.

6. Alan Watts (1960) holds that "there is much to suggest that when human beings acquired the powers of conscious attention and rational thought they became so fascinated with these new tools that they forgot all else, like chickens hypnotized with their beaks to a chalk line. . . . Intellect is not a separate ordering faculty of the mind, but a characteristic of the whole organism-environment relationship, the field of forces wherein lies the reality of a human being." The implication here is that highly intellectualized modes of psychotherapy cannot get at the basic problem of the total human organism and therefore have a limited scope.

To some extent, Watts' criticism of rationalism is valid, since ultra-rationalistic thinking (which is a kind of religious dogma) may well ignore the sensing and experiencing of areas of human existence. One of the basic philosophic aspects of rational-emotive therapy, however, is an emphasis on hedonism, pleasure, and happiness rather than (in the Platonic or Schopenhauerian sense) on the so-called joys of pure intellect and idea.

Perhaps the main goal the patient of RT is helped to attain is that of commitment, risk-taking, joy of being; and sensory experiencing, as long as it does not merely consist of short-range, self-defeating hedonism of a childish variety, is encouraged rather than spurned. Even some of the Zen Buddhist strivings after extreme sensation, or *satori*, would not be thoroughly incompatible with some of the goals a devotee of rational-emotive living might seek for himself—as long as he did not seek this mode of sensing as an escape from facing some of his fundamental anxieties or hostilities (Hora, 1961).

7. Rollo May (May, Angel, and Ellenberger, 1958) has pointed out that preoccupation with technique does not get to the source of a patient's problems; and that therefore all rational systems of psychotherapy may be limited in their curative effects. It is true that rational therapists *may* become preoccupied with technique—but so, of course, may any other kinds of therapists, including Freudian, nondirective, and Existentialist practitioners. Although the term "rational" has tended to become synonymous with "highly technical" in industrial and economic fields of discourse, this synonymity does not necessarily exist in the field of rational therapy.

This is not to say that in rational-emotive analysis a definite, teachable technique of therapy does not exist; for it does. Much of what any rational therapist does, especially his method of quickly determining what is really and fundamentally bothering the patient, and his procedure of incisively getting this patient to challenge and question his basic irrational assumptions, can clearly be specified and effectively be taught to any open-minded therapist who wants to learn this method. In this sense, a good deal of the *modus operandi* of RT is more clear-cut and specifiable than the methods of most other schools of therapy.

To a large extent, however, the rational-emotive therapist teaches his patients by example: by, in his relationships with these patients, serving as a relatively nondisturbed model. Unless he has taught himself how to be unanxious and unhostile in his relations with his patients (and others), the therapist is not likely to be able, convincingly, to show them how to eliminate (rather than merely express or cover up) their own basic anxieties and hostilities.

The rational-emotive therapist's so-called techniques of therapy, therefore, largely consists of the use of himself, of his own person, and of what could well be called his experiential encounters with his patients. In Freudian terms, this would be called his transference relations with the patients; but it is doubtful whether this would be an accurate use of the term transference, since Freud meant by the word the analyst's serving as both a good and a bad parental figure to the patient.

In RT, however, the therapist serves largely as a good or sane model and does not encourage the patient's undergoing a classical transference neurosis. If transference and counter-transference phenomena arise, they are faced and interpreted; but no special fetichistic emphasis is placed on them, as is done in Freudian and Sullivanian treatment.

In any event, RT uses the patient's experience with the therapist in addition to its conscious and direct employment of didactic methods whereby the therapist, as a kind of wise authoritative figure, literally teaches the patient how to think more clearly and more scientifically about himself and his close associates. And because the well rationally-analyzed therapist really *doesn't* care too much about what others think of him and really *isn't* grandiosely hostile with those who do not agree with him, he is unusually free to be *himself* in the therapeutic relationship and to enjoy thoroughly natural expressions of his own thoughts and feelings in the course of this relationship. By thus being himself he is uniquely free of artificially acquired technique for technique's sake and is far removed from being the rational*ist* straw-man that he is sometimes accused of being by those who do not truly understand what he is doing and being.

8. In psychotherapy, Rollo May (May, Angel, and Ellenberger, 1958) has also stated, "We have tended to commit the error of placing too much weight on verbalization. . . . Verbalization, like formulation in the psychotherapeutic session, is useful only so long as it is an integral part of experiencing." The charge that rational therapists over-emphasize verbalization is one of the most common objections to their activity. This charge is largely invalid because those who make it do not seem to be clear about what verbalization is, and almost always confuse it with speaking.

The word "verbal," as English and English point out in their *Comprehensive Dictionary of Psychological and Psychoanalytical*

Terms (1958), means "pertaining to, taking the form of, consisting of, words in any form: spoken, heard, seen, written, or thought." If this is so, it would clearly appear that the vast majority of human thinking, and particularly the type of thinking which leads to disturbed behavior, is verbal—or, more specifically, consists of internal verbalization of ideas, attitudes, and evaluations that the individual has usually learned fairly early in his life and that he keeps endlessly repeating or auto-suggesting to himself for the rest of his days.

Almost every time a person performs a neurotic act—for example, irrationally fears meeting strangers—he is most verbally saying something to himself, such as: "Oh, how terrible it would be if I met these strangers and they did not like me!" And it is his internal verbalization which largely constitutes or causes his disturbance.

Since much of what human beings internally verbalize is done on an unaware or unconscious basis, and much of what they even consciously verbalize is never expressly spoken, their emotional disturbances are often not closely correlated with their *spoken* verbalizations; and it will consequently help them relatively little if a therapist merely gets at their spoken words, phrases, and sentences. But if this therapist accurately and incisively keeps revealing to disturbed people what their entire range of internal *and* external verbalizations is, and if he effectively shows them how to see for themselves, and then to vigorously keep challenging and attacking, their own irrational (spoken and unspoken) verbalizations, it will be quite difficult for them to remain disturbed.

The rational therapist, then, is intensively and extensively occupied with his patient's conscious and unconscious verbalizations. And so, whether they are aware of the fact or not, are virtually all other kinds of psychotherapists. Thus, although the Rogerian therapist may be overtly saying little to the patient, he is by his manner and attitude covertly saying—or verbalizing—a host of important things. And, by his overt and his covert verbalizations, he is finally helping the patient to say to *himself* something along these lines: "Even though I hate myself for doing the things I have been doing, my therapist obviously accepts me and is on my side. Therefore, maybe I am *not* the awful person I have been thinking I am; and maybe I *can* accept myself less blamefully."

Similarly, the Reichian therapist, by very dint of his physically manipulating his patient, is (overtly and covertly) signaling, saying, or verbalizing a significant therapeutic message. And he is finally inducing his patient to say to *himself* something of this nature: "I can see by the physical manipulations of my therapist that I really *am* terribly inhibited, physically and emotionally. And since *he* obviously is not inhibited in these respects, and *he* is able to evoke unarmored responses in me, there seems to be no reason why *I* cannot release myself in a similar manner."

Without some such internal verbalizations as these, it is doubtful if any psychotherapy would be effective. And even if, by some miracle, it were originally efficacious on a purely non-verbal level (if it is truly imaginable for human beings to communicate in totally nonverbal ways), it is almost impossible to conceive this therapy's having truly lasting effects. For unless a patient finally communicates clearly with himself and does so in *some* kind of internal language, how can he keep himself from falling back into his old neurotic or psychotic behavior? Unless, in *some* kind of words, phrases, or sentences, he thoroughly convinces himself that it is *not* terrible when he fails at some task or when people don't love him, and that it is *not* necessary that the world and its people refrain from frustrating him, how can he prevent himself from becoming, once again, just as disturbed as he was before he started any mode of psychotherapy?

Although, therefore, both patients and therapists may *talk* too much, and may thereby restrict and constrict a healthy flow of sensations and emotions, if they are efficiently *verbal* (or *thinking*) they will normally tend to become less inhibited and much better able to feel deeply and to release their feelings. *Amount* of verbalization is not the issue here; but *efficiency* or *quality* of internal verbalization is.

The rational therapist, especially at the beginning of therapy, tends to be more consciously verbal and more talkative than most other therapists. But he particularly strives to be, and to teach his patients to be, effectively, insightfully, and organizedly verbal. Later, as the patient becomes more adequately and integratedly verbal, the therapist tends to become less talkative. The initiate in scientific thinking is now learning from his teacher and is showing how well he can apply the scientific method to his own behavior.

9. It is often objected that since much of human disturbance is learned on the early-childhood, preverbal level, it is impossible to remove this disturbance with highly verbal forms of analysis (Schactel, 1947; McClelland, 1951). The first answer to this objection is that the hypothesis that human disturbance is largely learned on a preverbal level has never been convincingly validated, and there is much reason to believe that most serious neurotic manifestations which *are* clearly the result of learning are learned after a child is nine months of age— that is, after he begins to verbalize.

Assuming that prior nonverbal learning does contribute significantly to the individual's emotional disturbances, it would appear that once the child acquires the power to verbalize to himself and others, he retranslates his preverbal behavior into verbal terms, and is thenceforth bothered by (or, actually, bothers himself by) these translated verbal signals of his disorder.

Thus, assuming that the child becomes terrorized by the absence of his parents when he is too young to verbalize, we may well surmise that once he does begin to verbalize he translates this terror into external or internal phrases or sentences and tells himself something like: "Isn't it horrible that my parents have left me! Maybe they'll never come back. They probably don't love me. And this proves that I am worthless." With such internalized sentences as these does the child, it would appear, take over and (what may be more important) significantly add to his preverbally acquired disturbances.

If this is so, then by the time the individual (whether he is a young child or an adult) comes for psychotherapy the best (and, in fact, almost only) way to reach him and to help him undermine his early-acquired disturbances is to be therapeutically verbal with him. That is, as mentioned above, he must be shown exactly what he is irrationally verbalizing (though not necessarily overtly speaking) to himself and how he can specifically challenge and undermine his own self-defeating verbalizations. This means that even if many individuals learn to become severely neurotic on a preverbal level (which is as yet unproven), it would appear that their disturbances are actually *maintained* in highly verbal ways and can be undermined mainly by their seeing and changing their own verbalizations.

As Dollard and Miller (1950) aptly note, effective psychotherapy largely consists of the verbal labelling and resorting of preverbal categories, so that these become accessible to the methods of symbolic or linguistic manipulation characteristic of adult problem-solving.

10. It is often objected that rational procedures become an end in themselves, lose sight of human feeling and happiness and lead to more evils than they alleviate. Thus, Daniel Bell (1956) has noted that "utilitarian rationality knows little of time as *durée*. For it, and for modern industrial life, time and effort are hitched only to the clocklike, regular 'metric' beat. The modern factory is fundamentally a place of order in which stimulus and response, the rhythms of work, derive from a mechanically imposed sense of time and pace. No wonder then that Aldous Huxley can assert: 'Today, every efficient office, every up-to-date factory is a panoptical prison in which the workers suffer . . . from the consciousness of being inside a machine.'" Jack Jones (1958) has also stoutly upheld the view that rationalism must logically lead to statism, authoritarianism, and communism and must thereby help stifle men's freedom and spontaneity.

This notion that extreme rationalism can be emotion-destroying and freedom-usurping indeed contains a germ of truth—if one admits the dubious proposition that an extreme rationalist is truly rational. For, as Dr. Robert A. Harper and I indicate in our book, *A Guide to Rational Living* (Ellis and Harper,

1961a), a rational approach to life hardly means a one-sided, monolithic kind of rationality. A definition of the word *rational*, as it is used by modern exponents of rationality and by a rational-emotive therapist, is: showing reason; not foolish or silly; sensible; leading to efficient results for human happiness; producing desired effects with a minimum of expense, waste, unnecessary effort, or unpleasant side effects.

Replying to critics of rationality, such as Bell and Jones, Starobin (1959) has asked: "Is Reason at fault in our troubles, or has it been the driving of Reason beyond its limits which it should inherently have, by its own definitions? Is it Reason *per se* which must be abandoned, or is it the dehumanization of the rationalist tradition, that split of rationalism from its own purpose which was to serve and to save man?" And as Hilgard (1958) has noted: "The very knowledge of our own irrationality is a triumph for rationality. This sounds paradoxical, but it is not really so. Only a clear-thinking man is capable of discovering his own mechanisms of self-deception; only rational processes can reveal the areas of irrationality."

11. It is often objected that RT leads to intellectualizing and rationalizing, or to some form of psychological defensiveness which is hardly the real goal of effective therapy. Here again there seems to be a needless semantic confusion. Although rationalizing, in a philosophic sense, means to make rational or to make conform to reason, in a psychological sense it means to devise superficially rational or seemingly plausible explanations or excuses for one's acts, beliefs, or desires, and usually to make these excuses without being aware that they are masking one's real motives. Psychologically, therefore, rationalizing or excusing one's behavior is the opposite of being rational or reasonable about it.

Similarly, although to intellectualize, in a philosophic sense, means to reason or to think, in a psychological sense it means to *over*emphasize intellectual pursuits (such as mathematics or abstract art) and to consider them superior to other pursuits (such as popular drama or music). To intellectualize also, psychologically, has come to mean to think about one's emotional problems in such a detailed and compulsive manner as to deny their true existence and to avoid rather than attempt to solve them.

Although, therefore, the principles of rational-emotive therapy strongly favor a highly reasonable approach to human life, they do not favor a rationalizing or intellectualistic approach in the sense that these terms are often used in modern psychology. To reason one's way out of one's emotional difficulties is to be highly sane and sensible. But to rationalize or intellectualize about one's self-defeating behavior is to help perpetuate it endlessly. Those who accuse the rational-emotive therapist of encouraging rationalizing and intellectualizing do not understand his theory and practice, but are tying them up with old-time absolutistic rationalist views to which he does not subscribe.

Is the use of reason essentially limited in human affairs and psychotherapy? A serious set of objections that is often raised against rational-emotive therapy concerns itself with the essential limitations of reason. Included in this set of objections are the following points:

1. It is held by some critics that rationalism, in the philosophic use of this term, is an outdated and unrealistic philosophy, since it consists of (*a*) the principle or practice of accepting reason as the only authority in determining one's opinions or course of action, and (*b*) the philosophic theory that the reason, or intellect, is the true source of knowledge, rather than the senses. These two elements of rationalism, it is contended, are unvalidated and unscientific.

I, for one, quite agree with the critics of absolutistic or eighteenth century rationalism and am more than willing to admit that it *is* an untenable position today. The modern devotee of reason, as I have pointed out in a paper on "Rationalism and its Therapeutic Applications" (Ellis, 1959), does not believe absolutely or perfectionistically in the power of reason but does believe that, although man cannot live by reason alone, he can considerably aid his existence and lessen his disturbances by thinking clearly, logically, consistently, and realistically.

A rational therapist, moreover, is not anti-empirical but accepts the idea that scientific knowledge must, at least in principle, be confirmable by some form of human experience. He is distinctly an empiricist and a realist; but he also takes a semi-idealistic or phenomenalist view, in that he believes that human reactions are not usually caused by external stimuli or events, but by the individual's own perceptions and interpretations of these external occurrences. Rational-emotive therapy is not closely allied with or dependent on the philosophic doctrine of rationalism, except insofar as it is opposed to all forms of supernaturalism, spiritualism, mysticism, revelation, dogmatism, authoritarianism, and antiscientism (see Chapter 6).

2. Reason itself, as many modern critics have pointed out, has its inherent limitations. As Jack Jones (1959) indicates, "It is reason which introduces an artificial mode of consciousness. This is the suspension of the *au naturel* projection of desire in order to regard the thing 'objectively'—i.e., as a 'fact.' . . . The idea of human goal or purpose is derived increasingly from theory and not from desire. That is, the *rational consciousness becomes its own end,* and is projected as such backward and forward through the historical record."

William Barrett (Suzuki, 1956) similarly notes that "in science itself, modern developments have combined to make our inherited rationalism more shaky . . . Heisenberg in physics, and Gödel in mathematics, have shown ineluctable limits to human reason." Again, Gombrich (McCurdy, 1960) insists that "the meaning of human expression will always elude scientific explanation. . . . The rational approach can help to eliminate such mistakes [as thinking that intuition must always be superior to reason] by showing what a work of art cannot have meant within the framework of its style and situation. Having thus narrowed down the area of misunderstanding it must retire. . . . Created as a tool to help us find our way through the world of things, our language is notoriously poor when we try to analyze and categorize the inner world."

Most recently, George Boas (1961) has published a book, *The Limits of Reason,* in which he points out that "eternal" statements, whether in the form of scientific laws or ethical norms, violate, disfigure, and over-simplify nature as we experience it in time. Logic, Dr. Boas contends, has nothing to do with history, because logic, or reason, must by its very nature reject change; and reason cannot encompass variety, ambiguity, or the particularity of love and pain. It also cannot come to terms with memory, duration, or hope, since the very essence of hope is to be unreasonable (Greene, 1961).

Although critics like Jones, Barrett, Gombrich, and Boas may be somewhat too enthusiastic in demonstrating its bounds and limitations, there is little doubt that they are in some respect correct. Reason is no more infallible or perfect than is man himself; it *has* distinct disadvantages and limits. But as Finch (1959) has noted in defense of rationality: "To be aware of the limits of reason is to be 'reasonable,' and this was the 'liberal' attitude suggested by Socrates, who recommended, as Plato quoted him, only 'a *hesitating* confidence in human reason.' Not to see any 'horizontal' limits to human reason at all is to be 'rationalistic' and in modern times that means totalitarian."

Robert Anton Wilson (1959) also hauls Jack Jones over the coals for his attack on reason and points out that although rationality certainly has its limitations—a rationalist—or, better, a reasonable—society may well provide for deeper and more intense feelings of human emotion than may an irrational culture. Frankel (1958) similarly remonstrates with William Barrett and some of his irrationalist and Existentialist cohorts by pointing out that "no contemporary advocate of the scientific and rationalistic philosophies condemned by the Existentialists would deny that reason is the instrument of a limited and finite creature entangled in sect, sex, and historical circumstances. But it is surely remarkable to conclude from this fact that when we try to understand the irrational we should do so in an irrational way. We do not have to be mad to understand madness, and the geologist who understands stones need not be a clod himself. If even orderly thought is fallible, as it surely is, it is doubtful that our passionate impulses are going to provide surer avenues to the truth."

Granted, then, that reason is fallible and that it has intrinsic limitations, this does not gainsay the fact that it is one of the very best tools available to investigate the sources of human disturbance and to help humans overcome their own irrational assumptions and deductions. Other psychotherapeutic tools— such as the therapist's relating to the patient, having an experiential encounter with him, serving as a good model of behavior, giving him supportive help, etc.—may also be valuable procedures. But just as reason *alone* may not help many patients to overcome their emotional upsets, it is equally unlikely that a therapist's refusal to employ *any* kind of persuasive logic will enable him intensively or permanently to help his patients. A purely rational approach to therapy has its clear-cut limitations; but a thoroughgoing irrational approach is usually disastrous (Schwartz and Wolf, 1958).

3. It is often held that human beings are *naturally* irrational and illogical; and that therefore any kind of rational psychotherapy cannot possibly be of much help to them. Curiously enough, the theory of rational-emotive therapy fully accepts the fact that human beings are naturally—yes, biologically—disposed to be irrational and that only with the greatest of difficulty can they induce themselves to be fairly consistently logical in their behavior.

I have personally believed for some years that man inherits a predisposition to think unclearly during his childhood and that it is very easy, and entirely statistically normal, for him to continue unthinkingly to accept and act upon, during his adulthood, the most ridiculous, unsensible, and often insane assumptions and conceptions. I also happen to believe, in the light of much recent experimental and clinical evidence, that tendencies toward severe mental disturbances, especially chronic schizophrenia, are often congenital or inherited and that mental illness is as much biological as a sociopsychological problem.

Nonetheless, I am most optimistic about the possibilities of psychotherapy, if it is based on adequate theory and practice. For just because human beings normally *do* tend to be irrational, I believe that they have to be *un*biologically (or even to some extent *anti*-biologically) reared so that they can gradually be taught to overcome their innate thinking handicaps. Particularly by the didactic, persuasive, active, and relationship techniques of rational-emotive therapy even individuals with some of the worst kinds of cognitive handicaps (whether of an inborn or early-acquired origin) can, I hold, be taught to check their own assumptions, to generalize more accurately, to deduce more logically, to think more calmly, and otherwise to use their innate mental capacities up to their own best limits.

No matter how much rational therapy (or any other kind of psychotherapy) individuals with limited reasoning capacities receive, I am sure that they will always to some degree remain irrational and self-defeating. None of us is a perfect, consistently logical thinker; and none of us, in consequence, will ever live a completely undisturbed existence. So be it. But just because human beings *are* basically irrational and because they *do* time and again easily defeat their own best interests, they particularly need the help of a trained therapist to help them minimize, if never entirely surmount, their innate reasoning limitations. The more irrational they are, in fact, the better a case can be made for their going for rational-emotive psychotherapy or some similar kind of treatment.

Is RT a superficial, suggestive form of psychotherapy? A major set of objections to RT is that it is a superficial form of therapy, largely based on suggestion and "positive" thinking, failing to get at patients' deeply buried unconscious thoughts and feelings, leading to symptom removal rather than real cure, and encouraging relapses on the part of presumably cured individuals. Some answers to this set of objections are as follows:

1. Those who accuse rational therapists of being superficial in their treatment do not understand that the main aim of RT is to help the patient to clearly see what his own basic philosophic assumptions or values are and to significantly change these life premises. This kind of attempt to change the individual's fundamental philosophy of living, and *not* any special aspect of psychotherapeutic technique, is what truly seems to distinguish depth-centered from superficial therapy.

Take, for example, a therapist who employs hypnosis, and

who induces his overly fearful patient to undergo the deepest possible kind of hypnotic trance state. Then, while his patient is in a state of deep, deep trance, this therapist suggests to him that he will no longer be afraid of—say—automobiles, he will no longer be afraid of automobiles, etc. Assuming that this form of therapy would actually work (which at least sometimes it would), has any truly deep form of therapy occurred?

The answer is: No. The patient, in all probability, still has the basic set of irrational values with which he came to therapy, and even though he becomes no longer afraid of automobiles, the chances are that his underlying anxiety and lack of self-confidence will not be greatly ameliorated.

Suppose, instead, this same patient is not hypnotized but is induced by a therapist to relive his earliest traumatic experiences with automobiles; and suppose that, in the course of doing so, he gets over his fears of cars and is able to enjoy riding in them for the rest of his life. Even though his abreactive sessions with the therapist, in this case, may have been very intense or "deep," it is questionable whether he has significantly changed his basic philosophy. At most, he will probably have changed the internalized sentence, "I can't stand automobiles, they are terribly frightful," to "What's so frightful about automobiles—they may actually be enjoyable." But the rest of his life and his basic philosophy that *something*, such as an automobile, can be made fearful when it really isn't that fearful, will not have been changed.

Finally, suppose that a patient who is afraid to compete in business learns, in the course of classical psychoanalysis, that he has a severe Oedipus complex, that he really fears his father will castrate him because he has lusted after his mother, and that therefore he is afraid to compete in business with other men, whom he envisions as father-surrogates or as rivals for his mother's bed. Even here, if this individual overcomes his fear of competition by seeing that it stems from his early fear of competing with his father for his mother's love, he will only have partly changed his basic philosophy of life—which, in its more generalized form, probably holds that *all* failure and lack of approval is terrible, horrible, and awful, and that therefore if his father (or any other man) hates him it is catastrophic.

Even in this presumably deepest of the deep psychoanalytic form of therapy, therefore, the patient we are discussing, while distinctly helped to overcome one of his serious life problems through acquiring some insight into the origin of his behavior, may not extensively or intensively change his basic value system. While he is *less* neurotic at the close than at the beginning of therapy, he still may be distinctly over-fearful and hostile in many significant aspects of his life.

All these examples merely go to show that the depth of the therapeutic technique may have little correlation with the depth of the basic cure. No matter how close to the patient's unconscious thoughts or feelings a therapist may at times get, nor how intensely he may induce the patient to abreact, nor how far back in the individual's history he may incisively cut, only symptomatic or partial cure may still be effected. And it is quite likely that in the vast majority of cases of so-called depth therapy, only such symptomatic and partial changes in the patient's underlying philosophies of life do occur (Wolpe, 1961b).

In rational-emotive psychotherapy, on the other hand, a concerted effort is made to uncover, analyze, attack, and significantly change the individual's fundamental philosophic assumptions—or to uproot what Alfred Adler (1927) called his basic goals or his style of life. In this sense, the rational therapist often goes far deeper than the abreactive therapist, the relationship therapist, and even the classical psychoanalyst, even though their techniques may sometimes *appear* to be exceptionally deep.

For many therapists, alas, do not adequately seem to tackle the most *generalized* forms of irrational thinking that make and keep patients seriously disturbed, even when they do tackle *some* of the aspects of this disordered thinking. The rational-emotive therapist, on the contrary, usually tries to get at *all* the main illogical assumptions of his patients—including their false beliefs that they *need* to be accepted and approved, that they *must* be perfectly successful, that they *shouldn't* have to accept harsh reality, that they *can't* control their own destinies, etc.

And he does not consider his job as a therapist finished unless and until he somehow induces his patients to see clearly and to forcefully keep uprooting their fundamental self-defeating premises and deductions.

For this reason it is difficult to imagine how any therapist can attempt to be more depth-centered than the rational therapist tries to be. At times, of course, the practitioner of RT may not succeed in his work. And occasionally, with patients who are too old, quite unintelligent, or impossibly rigid, he may try (as do almost all therapists at times) for limited goals. But his general principles lead him to attempt the most complete re-structurings of human personality that are possible for disturbed people to make. And although his techniques may sometimes seem to be deceptively simple and superficial, they are actually, especially with regard to their far-reaching results, unusually penetrating and deep.

2. The charge that rational-emotive therapy fails to get at patients' deeply buried unconscious thoughts and feelings is as groundless as the charge that it is not a depth-centered form of treatment. While Sigmund Freud (1924-1950; 1938), with real strokes of genius, revealed and examined some of man's unconscious processes far better than any other person before his time, he was unfortunately mistaken in his notion that the royal roads to "the unconscious" are primarily those of free association, dream interpretation, and analysis of the transference relationship between the analyst and his patient. These Freudian techniques of getting at unconscious thoughts and feelings are certainly at times effective; but they are limited and cir-cumscribed in their own right and rarely get at the exact and concrete unconscious phrases and sentences that the individual is telling himself to create his disturbances.

Thus, a patient may be totally unaware that he hates his mother; and he may be shown, after hours of associating, re-lating his dreams, and having his transference reactions to his analyst interpreted, that much evidence points to the fact that he really does hate her. He may then admit his hostile feelings and, because of his admission, work through them—or, at the very least, feel better about admitting them. In other words, he may, through these psychonalytic techniques, be helped to hate his mother consciously rather than unconsciously. And perhaps —though this is a big perhaps—he may be induced not to hate her any longer.

This patient, however, in the great majority of instances will never understand through undergoing classical psychoanalysis (a) what his unconscious hatred of his mother concretely and specifically consists of or what truly causes it; nor (b) how, precisely, he can go about giving up hating his mother and, for that matter, his hating other human beings. In rational-emotive therapy, however, he will be shown exactly of what his hatred consists and how he can concretely uproot it.

That is to say, he will be shown that his hatred consists of and is *not* caused by his mother's nasty behavior but his own internalized sentences *about* that behavior—by, for example, his own self-statements: "My mother *shouldn't* be acting the nasty way that she is acting!" and "I can't *stand* her acting the way she does, because I am such a worthless person that I can't live with her disapproval and nastiness."

In the course of RT, moreover, the patient will be shown that he is saying the same kind of sentences about many other people as well; and that he can objectively examine, parse the logic of, and intelligently question and challenge these silly self-sentences, until he no longer believes them. He will thereby not only be able to see or understand—and I mean *truly* understand—his hostility toward his mother, but will be able to effectively eliminate it and the disturbances stemming from it.

But how, it may be asked, will this patient be able to see that he unconsciously hates his mother, if his therapist does not use free associations, dreams, transference analysis, and other psychoanalytic techniques? Very simply. The rational-emotive therapist *knows,* on theoretical grounds, that the patient must be saying some kind of nonsense to himself or else he wouldn't be disturbed and come for therapy in the first place. And the therapist also knows that much of what the patient is telling himself must be unknown to him, or be unconsciously believed and self-promulgated. Knowing this, the therapist can use many different techniques—including even the relatively inefficient ones of free association and dream analysis—to make the patient aware of his important unconsciously held beliefs.

Thus, the therapist can show the patient that there is a significant gap between what he *thinks* he believes (e.g., that he loves his mother) and what his behavior (e.g., his rarely visiting his mother or his continually fighting with her when he does see her) proves that he really believes. Or the therapist can show the patient that he behaves toward motherlike figures in a consistently hostile manner, and that consequently there is a good chance that he feels angry toward his own mother as well. Or the therapist can teach the patient, by the therapist's own behavior and by didactic methods, that it is self-defeating for the patient to hate anyone; and, after seeing that he need not hate others, even when they act badly toward him, the patient may *then* realize that he has hated his mother all his life and that he no longer need do so. Or the therapist can in many ways help the patient to remove his *own* self-blaming tendencies. Once these are ameliorated or eradicated, the patient may easily be able to admit many things, such as hostility toward his mother, that he would have been most ashamed to admit, to himself or others, previously.

There are, then, perhaps a score of means, in addition to those employed in conventional psychoanalysis, which the therapist can employ to show the patient (a) that he does unconsciously hate his mother, and (b) that he need not hate her nor anyone else who is nasty to him. And all other unconscious thoughts and feelings can similarly be unpsychoanalytically (as well as psychoanalytically) revealed (Whyte, 1960). RT, in that it invariably tries to disclose—*and* to truly understand and eradicate—the negative, self-sabotaging unconscious ideation, motivation, and emotional responses of the patient, is in some ways much more concerned with unconscious processes than is even classical psychoanalysis. It is *also* distinctly concerned with the indi-

vidual's *conscious* self-destructive thoughts and feelings; but it
in no way minimizes or neglects his important unconscious
thinking and emoting.

It should perhaps be emphasized again that, as briefly noted
two paragraphs back, RT has, in addition to the usual methods
of getting at people's unconscious processes, a rather unique
method—and that is the easy and almost automatic disclosure of
their deeply buried thoughts and feelings *after* the rational
therapist has induced them to change some of their basic assumptions and values. Let it be remembered in this respect that,
according to Freudian theory, people largely repress their conscious aims and wishes, and force these back into their unconscious minds, because their Superegos cannot stand the urgings
of their Ids and Egos, and consequently make them feel thoroughly ashamed of some of their own aims and wishes.

In rational-emotive theory, we do not believe that there is *an*
Unconscious or that anyone's thoughts and feelings can be
scientifically reified into entitities entitled the Superego, Id, or
Ego. We do, however, believe that people frequently have
conflicting philosophies about their urges—that they believe, for
example, that sex satisfactions are good and also believe that
sex desires are heinous. When their values conflict, and when
they feel the urge to do something they consider, at one and
the same time, to be good and bad, they tend to feel terribly
ashamed of their urge or their active expression of it. And,
being ashamed, they sometimes do repress or actively look
away from (in Harry Stack Sullivan's words, "selectively in-
attend") their "shameful" urges.

If this is so, and if one of the main principles of RT is that
the individual is to be taught that there is *nothing* that he is to
be ashamed of, *nothing* that he should legitimately blame himself for (even though there are many of his thoughts and acts
which he may objectively disapprove and should make concerted efforts to change), it can be seen that to the degree that
the rational-emotive therapist succeeds with his patients and
actually induces them to stop blaming themselves for their
mistakes and fallibilities, he effectively and often dramatically

removes the necessity of their repressing or hiding their immoral or uncommendable thoughts and feelings. Under these circumstances, ideas and emotions that they have deeply buried in their so-called unconscious minds may easily be brought to light again, and frequently are.

Consequently, after only a few sessions of rational psychotherapy, patients may unrepress and confront themselves with deep-seated hostilities, sex feelings, and anxieties that they unconsciously held for many years. Although this phenomenon happens in other types of therapy as well, it often occurs because therapists *un*wittingly help their patients to stop blaming themselves and others. In RT, the process of the therapist's helping the patient to overcome his self- and other-directed blame and hostility is most conscious, is done on theoretical as well as practical grounds, and is often unusually effective.

3. It is frequently contended by those who have a superficial knowledge of rational psychotherapy that it is the same kind of process advocated by Emile Coué, Norman Vincent Peale, and other advocates of "positive thinking." The patient, according to these critics, simply parrots to himself that day by day in every way he is getting better and better, or that God or his therapist loves him and that he is therefore a worthwhile creature; and he thereby, they claim, temporarily surrenders some of his neurotic symptoms. That some RT patients (as well as many patients of other forms of therapy) do this kind of thing cannot be denied; but that these patients are following the rational-emotive psychotherapeutic technique is untrue.

If anything, RT largely consists of showing the individual how he is continually reindoctrinating himself with negative, silly philosophies of life, and how he must see, examine, understand, challenge, and question these negative philosophies. It is thus a truly analytic school of therapy; and it heartily advocates contradicting the negative rather than "accentuating the positive." One of the main reasons for this is that it has been empirically found that when disturbed people accentuate the positive, and tell themselves that they are really worthwhile, need not be afraid of anything, feel kindly toward others, and are getting better and better every day, they are still beautifully and almost miraculously able *at the very same time* to keep asserting and believing highly negative things about themselves.

In particular, the person who keeps telling himself sane sentences, such as: "There is really nothing to be afraid of in my relations with others; I would like them to accept me, but I can get along without their love and approval," can very easily keep telling himself, with much more force and conviction, "But it *is* terrible if others do not like me; and it *would* be catastrophic if they strongly disapproved of me." Indeed, the mere fact that the individual is consciously telling himself that he does *not* care too much if others disapprove of him can prevent him from realizing that he much more strongly believes that he *does* unduly care about their disapproval.

Couéism or "positive thinking," therefore, is usually a glossing over and a covering up of the underlying and still very-much-alive-and-kicking neurotic process. It is akin to the "sour grapes" mechanism from *Aesop's Fables,* where the fox, not being able to reach the grapes, and afraid that the other animals would look down on him for not being able to succeed, pretended that he really didn't want the grapes in the first place. The fact is, of course, that he really *did* want them. And, instead of healthfully saying to himself, "Well, I do want these grapes, but I cannot reach them. Tough! And if others scorn me for not being able to get the grapes, that's their problem," he falsely told himself (and the others): "Who needs grapes? I don't really want them." The fox thereby *felt* good, at least temporarily; but his underlying problem was of course not solved, since he *did* still want the grapes and *did* demand the approval of his witnesses.

Similarly, no matter how often you autosuggestively tell yourself that things are going to be all right, or God is with you, or it isn't necessary that everyone love you, there is a good chance, if you have for many years rigidly held on to the opposite, negative point of view, that you still basically believe that things are going to be catastrophic, that the Devil is after you, and that it *is* necessary that everyone adore you. Facing this human tendency and trying to cope with it squarely, the rational-emotive therapist tries to show his patient that "positive thinking" will not help and that he must fully—and I mean *fully*—keep admitting to himself that his old negative thinking is still there, must continually—and I mean *continually*—question and challenge and uproot this negative thinking until it really —and I mean *really*—is killed off.

This does not gainsay the fact that RT, like virtually all other forms of psychotherapy, makes considerable use of suggestion. Actually it has to: since, according to its basic theory, humans become emotionally disturbed because, to a large degree, irrational assumptions and modes of deduction are first *suggested* to them by their parents, teachers, and other forces in their society; and then, and often more importantly, they keep resuggesting these same false assumptions to themselves day after day, week after week, year after year. If this is so, then obviously some form of counter-suggestion is necessary to do away with the early-imposed and later-reiterated suggestion.

Many individuals, such as Bernheim (1887), Coué (1923), and Platonov (1959), have seen the importance of suggestion in psychotherapy. Even Freud realized that what he called the gold of psychoanalysis was often mixed with the dross of suggestion to effect therapeutic progress. What virtually none of these therapists have fully realized, as is pointed out in Chapter 15 of this book, is that the main reason why suggestive therapy works so well in many instances is because the patient's disturbances largely originate in the suggestions of those around him and his autosuggestions which carry on the original propaganda to which he subscribes.

The best kind of solution to this problem, therefore, is not his or a therapist's vigorous counter-suggestion, but the patient's attaining clear *insight* into his autosuggestive process and his using this insight so that he can effectively keep contradicting and challenging his negative, self-destroying autosuggestions.

This is what happens in rational-emotive psychotherapy. The patient is concretely shown how he keeps autosuggesting the same kind of nonsense that was originally suggested to him by his parents and other propagandizing sources in his society; and he is taught how to analyze logically, to parse semantically, and to counterattack philosophically his own internalized values. Only *after* he has thereby learned to attack and keep vigorously uprooting his own forceful negative autosuggestion will he be able to suggest to himself truer and more workable philosophies of life.

Thus, only *after* he has truly convinced himself that it is *not* terrible if others do not approve of him, or if he fails to achieve certain things in life, or if he has to keep disciplining himself to attain certain future pleasures, only *then* will the patient honestly and convincingly be able to tell himself: "I *can* live without So-and-So's approval. I *am* intrinsically worthwhile, whether or not I succeed at my work. It *is* more rewarding to discipline myself for future gains than to strive only for the short-range pleasures of today."

Rational-emotive therapy, in other words, is largely an insightful counter-suggestive rather than a Pollyanna-ish autosuggestive form of treatment. It fully acknowledges the enormous power of suggestive and counter-suggestive forces in human beings, teaches the patient how to understand and use these forces for his own benefit, and thereby helps give him a measure of control over his own behavior that is unfortunately rare among modern men and women. It is also a form of therapy, as noted above, that stresses counter-suggestive *action* as well as verbal depropagandization. It consequently uses what might be called depth suggestion rather than superficial, parrotted suggestive techniques.

4. It is sometimes objected that RT can only effect symptom-removal rather than actual cure of underlying emotional disturbances, partly because patients glibly follow some of its basic tenets and do not actually go about rooting out their deep-set irrationalities. Just because rational-emotive therapy often works very well after patients have experienced it for a short time, these patients (as Harper [1960c] has pointed out) may not keep undermining their own irrational thinking as in-

tensely and as prolongedly as they actually should if they want to become truly cured.

These allegations are, of course, true of many patients—and of patients of all kinds of therapies, not merely RT. As soon as some individuals begin to feel better after relatively few sessions of psychotherapy, they think they are completely well, or believe that further treatment is unnecessary, too expensive, or otherwise too inconvenient; and they consequently leave therapy. This may be particularly true of individuals participating in efficient psychotherapies, such as RT, since in inefficient therapies some patients may get less benefit at the beginning and may consequently stay with the therapist longer. On the other hand, there seem to be a great many patients who if they are not quickly and appreciably helped by their therapist leave after one or a few sessions and do not return to him or perhaps to any therapist.

The main point is that rational-emotive therapists do not view the patient as being cured when he has, in a short period of time, made significant improvements. Their main aim is to effect a thoroughgoing change in the value systems of most of their patients; and they are not satisfied with superficial "cures." They tend to see patients less frequently than do many other therapists; but may see them for a fairly long period of time, since they realize that the process of basic personality change is almost necessarily a time-consuming affair, and in many respects lasts the patient's lifetime.

The patient of RT is never considered "cured" or minimally disturbed until he has learned to truly and consistently challenge his underlying irrational assumptions, to think in a fairly straight manner about himself and his intimate associates as well as about external things and events, and to stand on his own two feet without any dire need for support from the therapist or anyone else. These kinds of therapeutic goals are obviously anything but superficial.

5. It is sometimes contended that although individuals may well overcome some of their worst emotional disturbances with

the help of RT, they will tend to do so in a temporary manner and will eventually suffer serious relapses. Abelson (1959) indicates that "in time the effects of a persuasive communication tend to wear off." This, some critics hold, is what occurs with the persuasion that takes place in RT.

The first answer to this objection is that there is no evidence that the good effects of rational-emotive psychotherapy wear off more quickly or to a greater extent than the effects of any other kind of therapy. It is most probable that a large percentage of individuals who have had successful experiences with all kinds of therapists later relapse to some extent; and it is also probable that some of them become just as emotionally disturbed again as they were prior to therapy. But there is no evidence that this is truer of RT than of non-RT patients.

Although no systematic follow-up studies have yet been done with patients treated with RT, I have had unofficial checkups on many of my own patients, and I find that those who complete therapy to my as well as their own satisfaction rarely suffer major relapses, and that when they do retrogress they tend to do so in a minor manner that can be overcome by the patient himself or with a few additional sessions of therapy. I find consistently better results in this respect than I did when I practiced, first, classical psychoanalysis and, later, psychoanalytically-oriented psychotherapy.

This is not to say that relapses do not occur with successfully treated RT patients. They do. But my present hypothesis is that these relapses occur less frequently and less drastically than they occur in individuals treated with other forms of therapy, including classical psychoanalysis.

One of the reasons why relapses are not too likely to occur when a patient has been successfully treated with RT is that the essence of the technique is not merely to persuade the patient that he is thinking illogically and that he must henceforth think more rationally about himself and others. Rather, its essence is the teaching of the patient to change his own basic self-persuasive or autosuggestive methods.

That is to say, the disturbed individual not only thinks inefficiently when he comes to therapy, but he almost always does not know *how* to think logically about himself. The very *concept* of questioning and challenging his own assumptions, and of truly applying scientific methods of perception, analysis, and generalization to his relations with himself and others, is foreign to him; and in the course of RT he is helped to learn and accept this concept.

While undergoing successful RT treatment, moreover, the patient, by using his newly acquired concepts of questioning and challenging his own thinking processes, is usually led to acquire a radically new way of life. His philosophy of being, his personal code of morality and moralizing, his degree of dependency on many of his fellows, his courage to be himself: these important aspects of his life are likely to change significantly. Consequently, a quick or total relapse to his old disturbed ways of thinking, feeling, and behaving is most unlikely. Even if his presenting painful symptoms temporarily return, his way of looking at himself and the world will tend to be much different from his previous self- and world-view; and he will not completely relapse.

6. It is sometimes objected that RT is superficial in that it adjusts the patient all too well to his poor life situation and stoically induces him to tolerate what may well be intolerable conditions. This objection is a misinterpretation of the philosophy of Stoicism; and it assumes that rational-emotive psychotherapy strictly follows Stoic teachings, which it does not.

Epictetus, one of the main proponents of Stoicism, did not say or imply that one should calmly accept *all* worldly evils and should stoically adjust oneself to them. His view was that a person should first try to change the evils of the world; but when he could not successfully change them, *then* he should uncomplainingly accept them. Thus, he wrote: "Is there smoke in my house? If it be moderate, I will stay; if very great, I will go out. For you must always remember, and hold to this, that the door is open."

Some Stoics, such as Marcus Aurelius, took the doctrine of accepting the inevitable to extremes and were irrationally over-fatalistic. Thus, Marcus Aurelius advised: "Accept everything which happens, even if it seem disagreeable, because it leads to this, to the health of the universe and to the prosperity and felicity of Zeus. For he would not have brought on any man what he has brought, if it were not useful for the whole." To this kind of fatalistic philosophy, rational-emotive therapists of course do *not* subscribe.

Nor does RT attempt to adjust the individual to his society, even though it helps him remain undisturbed when he is forced, by outside influences, to do so. On the contrary, because it helps the individual to stand firmly on his own ground and not to *need* the complete acceptance of his fellows, it enables him to adjust minimally to his culture as far as giving up his own individualism is concerned.

Patients who undertake rational-emotive analysis normally acquire the philosophy that it is wise to accept unpleasant people and circumstances when (*a*) it is of practical advantage to do so, or (*b*) there really is no other choice. Thus, they learn unanxiously and unhostilely to accept an unfair supervisor or boss when (*a*) their job has unusual advantages aside from their contact with this overseer, or (*b*) it is presently impossible for them to get a better position with a less unfair boss.

At the same time, however, the rational individual will strive to accept unpleasant conditions only *temporarily* and will do everything in his power (in spite of what others may think of him *personally*) to change these conditions. Being relatively unanxious and unhostile, he will normally be able to modify undesirable situations more quickly and effectively than if he wasted considerable time and energy fearing and fuming against the people or conditions around him.

When faced with a correctable and not too risky situation, the rational individual will tend to rebel against it in a definite but discreet way. Thus, if he knows that some people will disapprove and actively interfere with him if he practices nudism, he will publicly refrain from doing so but will quietly and discreetly arrange to be a nudist in his own home or in special protected circumstances.

The truly rational person, then, will always be something of a rebel—since only by rebelling against stultifying conformity to some degree can a human being in our society maintain a good measure of his own individuality (Lindner, 1953). But he will not childishly rebel for the sake of rebelling. He will fight against unnecessary restrictions and impositions; temporarily accept what is truly inevitable; and remain undisturbed whether he is fighting or accepting.

7. It is sometimes alleged that RT is too crassly hedonistic and that it teaches people to enjoy themselves at the expense of their deeper or more rewarding commitment. This is a false charge, since one of the main tenets of rational-emotive psychotherapy is the Stoic principle of long-range rather than of short-range hedonism.

Just about all existing schools of psychotherapy are, at bottom, hedonistic, in that they hold that pleasure or freedom from pain is a principal good and should be the aim of thought and action. This is probably inevitable, since people who did not believe in a hedonistic view would continue to suffer intense anxiety and discomfort and would not come for therapy. And therapists who did not try in some manner to alleviate the discomfort of those who did come to them for help would hardly remain in business very long. The rational-emotive therapist, therefore, is far from unique when he accepts some kind of a hedonistic world-view and tries to help his patients adopt a workable hedonistic way of life.

It has been empirically found through the ages that the short-range hedonistic philosophy of "Drink, eat, and be merry, for tomorrow you may die," is unrealistic: since most of the time you *don't* die tomorrow, but are much more likely to live and rue the consequences of too much drinking, eating, and merrymaking today. Consequently (as Freud, for one, kept stressing) the reality principle of putting off present pleasures for future gains is often a much saner course to follow than the pleasure principle of striving only for present gains. This reality principle, or the philosophy of long-range hedonism, is consistently stressed in RT.

Instead of being encouraged to do things the "easy way," the patient is helped to do them the more *rewarding* way—which, in the short run, is often more difficult. RT, while embracing neither the extreme views of the Epicureans nor those of the Stoics, strives for a more moderate synthesis of both these ways of life. In the course of the therapy process itself, a fundamental principle of RT is that the patient must work, work, work at changing his own basic assumptions and his self-defeating behavior if he is truly to overcome his emotional disturbances.

Ineffective patterns of behavior are conceived as originating in unthinking or child-centered views and of being *maintained* by the individual's verbal reindoctrinations and motor habits. It is therefore deemed that practice makes *im*perfect; and that only considerable counter-practice will undo the existing inefficiencies.

RT, then, is a highly active, *working* form of treatment—on the part of both the therapist and his patient. Less than almost any other kind of psychotherapy does it give the patient immediate gratification, personal warmth from the therapist, or encouragement for him indefinitely to cherish his childish, short-range hedonistic impulses. In this sense, once again, it eschews symptom-removal and false therapeutic gains to get, as quickly as possible, to the very heart of the patient's basic irrational philosophies of life and to induce him, verbally and actively, to work, work, work against his own self-sabotaging beliefs.

Is RT too directive, authoritarian, and brain-washing? Another major set of objections to rational-emotive psychotherapy is set forth by those who insist that it is too directive, authoritarian, and brain-washing. Some of the specific charges raised in this connection will now be answered.

1. Those who allege that RT is too authoritarian and controlling do not seem to face the fact that virtually *all* psychotherapies, including the nondirective, passive, client-centered, and existentialist techniques, are actually distinctly authoritative and controlling. The therapist, because of his training and experience, is invariably some kind of an authority in his

field; and by virtue of the fact that he is presumably less disturbed than his patient, and is often older and/or wiser, he is something of an authority- or parental-figure. Even if *he* does not look upon himself in this manner, the members of his clientele almost invariably do. And, whether he likes it or not, a considerable portion of his effectiveness with his patients results from his being or appearing to be something of an authority figure to them (Lederer, 1959; London, 1961; Schoen, 1962).

Even the most nondirective and passive kind of therapist, moreover, *is* nondirective or passive because he believes that he *should* take this kind of role with his patients; and he more or less deliberately takes it. Similarly, the most existentialist or spontaneous therapist believes that he *should* be existentialist or spontaneous when he is in session with his patients. Otherwise, of course, if he believed anything else, the nondirective therapist would be more directive and the spontaneous therapist less spontaneous.

In accordance with their belief-systems, therefore, therapists deliberately assume *some* kind of role with their patients; and to the extent that they do so they are distinctly authoritative, technique-centered, controlling, and calculating. The real question is not *whether* the therapist is authoritative and controlling but *in what manner* he exerts his authority and his control.

Not only are all psychotherapies more or less authoritative but they are also to some degree authoritarian. Even though their ultimate goal is the attainment of individual freedom of judgment and action by the patient, directly or indirectly these therapies show the patient that he must do or think *this* instead of *that* if he is to stop his own self-defeating tendencies. Although nondirective and passive therapists maintain the illusion that they are entirely democratic in their means as well as their ends, this is nonsense: since they very precisely, albeit cleverly and subtly, attempt to get the individual to channel his thoughts and feelings in one direction rather than in another.

A straightforward, directive therapist, for example, will tell his patient: "I think that if you keep feeling and acting in a hostile manner to others you will only defeat your own ends. Therefore, I would advise you to look into your own heart, see that your hostility is self-defeating, see what you are doing needlessly to create this hostility, and teach yourself how not to create it in the future." A so-called democratic, nondirective therapist will say to the same patient: "I feel rather uncomfortable while talking to you about your hostility. I feel that perhaps you are getting hostile to me, too. And I feel that perhaps I would not want to feel as hostile as you are now feeling. Do you feel that my feeling about you and your hostility may be right?"

In this indirect, and presumably more democratic and less authoritarian manner, the nondirective therapist is really saying to the patient: "Look, brother: let's not fool ourselves. I know and you know that your hostility only serves to make me and other people uncomfortable and doesn't get you the kind of reactions you want from other people and from yourself. Wouldn't it therefore be much better if you explored your hostile feelings and learned how to give them up?"

Similarly, other kinds of therapists who try to help the patient see that he is unnecessarily hostile, no matter how passive or indirect their approach may be, are actually (though perhaps more subtly) as directive and authoritarian as is the rational-emotive therapist. But while the latter employs his authority, his direct teaching, and his advice-giving honestly and openly, the former appears to be more devious.

Carl Rogers (Krout, 1956) has stated that insofar as therapists set for themselves any such goals as helping their patients work out better relationships with their wives, "we enter the realm of values and to a certain extent set ourselves up as arbiters of what is right." True; but is this bad?

Emotional disturbance, I must keep insisting, largely consists of the individual's acquiring and reindoctrinating himself with illogical, inconsistent, and unworkable values; and effective therapy must partly consist of helping him deindoctrinate himself so that he acquires a saner and more constructive set of values (Callahan, 1960). There is always the danger, of course, that the therapist will be authoritarian in a pernicious way, or that he may use his authority to induce his patient to acquire *his*, the therapist's, particular brand of beliefs. But this is a danger in all kinds of therapy, including so-called nondirective psychotherapy; and as long as the therapist is aware of this danger, and faces the possibility of what the Freudians call his counter-transferences, he can take steps to minimize the likelihood of his being too authoritarian. Thus, he can keep reminding himself that the main goal of therapy is to help the patient stand on his *own* feet and to become independent of the therapist as well as of others. Nonetheless: in any effective kind of therapy, the danger of authoritarianism on the part of the therapist is not likely to be removed entirely.

Let it be remembered, in this connection, that the therapist has every right to let his own values be known in the course of the therapeutic sessions. First of all, being a human being, he must have values; and it is pointless to pretend that he doesn't (Hudson, 1961). Secondly, being well trained and presumably little disturbed himself, there is a good chance that he will tend to have saner, more workable values than his patients, and that he will be able to present these in a reasonably objective, unpunitive, understanding manner. Thirdly, since he will consciously or unconciously tend to communicate his values to his patients, it is better that he do so overtly rather than covertly, with full consciousness of what he is doing. Fourthly, the more open he is about presenting his own values, the more spontaneous and unartificial, the more courageous and committed to his own views, he is likely to be.

2. The assumption of those who are powerfully set against open display of authority on the part of the therapist is that it results in brain-washing and the undemocratic imposition of the therapist's views upon the patient. This is a highly questionable assumption.

For one thing, the anti-authority school of thought seems to forget that patients are usually exceptionally disturbed individuals whose irrational thoughts and feelings are most deeply and rigidly set by the time they come for treatment. Although it is quite true that these patients, as Fromm (1955), Horney (1950), Maslow (1954), Rogers (1951), Sullivan (1953), and others have recently emphasized, have enormous self-actualizing and self-reconstructive potentials, the fact remains that they also have powerful self-destructive drives and that much encouragement, nondirective listening, warmth, and spontaneous encounters by and with their friends and associates have not helped them to achieve their potentials for healthy living. At the time they come for therapy, therefore, stronger and even more constructive measures are needed in order that they may be helped to help themselves.

As has been empirically discovered by primitive medicine men, by members of the clergy, by general medical practitioners, by pre-Freudian psychologists and psychiatrists, and by other kinds of mental healers during the past centuries, a strong show of authority by a therapist, even when his particular theory is wrong or his techniques largely consist of mumbo-jumbo, is frequently curative. Lederer (1959), reviewing some of the magical, religious, and mystical modes of therapy of the past and present, hypothesizes that the best technique may well be the therapist's highly authoritative belief in himself and his powers and his firm conveying of this belief to his patients. "Any movement in therapy," he states, "is not correlated with what the therapist analyzes, but springs nonspecifically from his relative lack of anxiety"—which is tied up, Lederer believes, with the therapist's authoritative manner.

This hypothesis is quite extreme and does not, in all likelihood, explain many of the factors of effective treatment. But Lederer's point does seem to have *some* validity; and it is probably correct to state that the therapist's authoritativeness is *one* of the most helpful tools he can use to encourage people to reconsider and reconstruct their own self-defeating philosophies of life. It is also probably true that nondirective or passive techniques of therapy will achieve poor results with many, and perhaps the great majority, of patients, even though they may have *some* usefulness with other patients.

It likewise seems clear that when individuals come for therapy they are already distinctly brain-washed—by their parents, their intimate associates, their teachers, and by many of the mass media of our society; and that they consequently believe all kinds of ultra-conforming, anti-individualistic ideas. What psychotherapy does is effectually to *un*brain-wash or counter-brain-wash them, so that they can really begin to think for themselves. Because a mode of therapy like rational-emotive analysis accomplishes this *anti*-brain-washing in a highly efficient and often reasonably quick-acting way is certainly no reason to accuse the practitioners of this kind of therapy of being fascistic or communistic brain-washers.

As Skinner (1956) has pointed out, "Education grown too powerful is rejected as propaganda or 'brain-washing' while really effective persuasion is decried as 'undue influence,' 'demagoguery,' 'seduction,' and so on." This, to some extent, is what seems to be happening in the field of psychotherapy: where the less efficient groups accuse the more efficient practitioners of engaging in brain-washing.

It should not be forgotten that in didactic methods of psychotherapy, such as those which are vigorously employed in RT, it is not the *patient* but his irrational *ideas* which are forcefully attacked by the therapist. In political-economic brain-washing, the individual is *himself* attacked. Either he is physically threatened or abused; or else he is taught that he is a worthless *person* unless he changes his thinking to suit that of his captors or rulers (Sargant, 1957). In rational-emotive therapy, however, the patient is virtually never blamed, criticized, or attacked, since blaming and devaluating individuals are deemed, in RT theory, to be the root of practically all evils.

The therapist, again, is not interested in inducing the patient to change his basic irrational thinking for the therapist's sake, but only for his *own* greater well-being. This therapeutic motivation is exactly the opposite of that of the political-economic brain-washer, who obviously does not care for the rights or well-being of the individual but only for those of the state or system he, the brain-washer, upholds.

3. Another criticism of RT is somewhat akin to the Rogerian

view expressed above that it is unethical for therapists to inject their own values into their work with patients. This other view, as expressed by Spotniz (1958), is that it is unscientific for the therapist to provide the patient with the benefits of his own wisdom. This view seems to be most peculiar. If it was scientific of Copernicus, Galileo, Einstein, and other great thinkers to provide us with what proved to be their highly wise hypotheses and experiments—which in the early stages of their work were nothing but inspired guesses—it is difficult to see why it is unscientific for trained therapists to hypothesize and to experiment with their patients, even though their hypotheses may sometimes turn out to be unsubstantial or invalid.

With each of his patients, in fact, the therapist, no matter to which active or passive school he belongs, is essentially hypothesizing that the patient's disturbances stem from certain causes and that if he, the therapist, somehow induces the patient experimentally to think and act in ways different from those in which he has previously been thinking and acting the patient's disturbances will be significantly ameliorated. This, it seems to me, is essentially a scientific procedure—even though the therapist's chief hypotheses (or theoretical framework) may be invalid or the patient may not carry out the experiment the therapist is trying to induce him to undertake to prove or disprove these hypotheses.

Moreover, if (as Spotnitz claims) it is unscientific to provide the patient with the benefits of the therapist's own wisdom, is it more scientific to provide him with the benefits of the therapist's stupidity? Wisdom, in the last analysis, is scientifically arrived at, in that the wise individual starts with many assumptions (or hypotheses), checks them against his and others' experiences, and winds up with fewer but wiser—meaning, more empirically validated—theories. Is it not more scientific for the therapist to use his well-validated, wise assumptions than to try to work with his patients with some less valid, unwiser assumptions?

4. It is often objected that the methods of RT are much too directive and that they discourage the patient from thinking

for himself and becoming truly self-sufficient and self-actualizing. This criticism has some validity, since it is certainly possible for a highly directive, active therapist to run his patient's life and thereby unconsciously if not consciously encourage the patient to continue to be dependent.

The fact remains, however, that patients are not running their lives well when they come for therapy; and many are hardly living at all. They consequently require more than a little push; and a comprehensive review of the literature that I did several years ago (Ellis, 1955a) indicated that if they get this push by a highly active-directive therapist they frequently are, after awhile, able to become more adequately self-directive. In recent years, therefore, active-directive methods of psychotherapy, particularly in the case of exceptionally disturbed patients, have been used more frequently than ever.

In rational-emotive therapy it has been found that it is not too difficult, if the therapist is consciously aware of the basic goals of therapy and of his own limitations as a human being, to push, persuade, cajole, and occasionally force patients into anxiety-destroying thought and action, thereby to help them build confidence in themselves, and then to let them take over the direction of their own lives. This is particularly true since RT is rarely done on a three to six times a week basis, but is usually done once a week, or even once every other week; so that there is relatively little danger of the patient becoming overly dependent on the therapist.

It again should be remembered that when a patient is distinctly disturbed there is little chance of his being truly independent and of his thereby taking concrete advantage of his theoretical ability to make his own democratic decisions. Once, however, a therapist has vigorously attacked this patient's self-destructive ideas, the patient *then,* for the first time in his life in many instances, becomes truly capable of being independent and free.

Just as a student of physics or language is not really free to use physical laws or employ a foreign tongue to his own advantage and in accordance with his own wishes until he has been helped (preferably by a quite active-directive teacher) to master the rudiments of these subjects, so a disturbed individual is not free to make his own marital, vocational, recreational and other decisions until, often, he has been helped by an active-directive therapist to master the rudiments of his self-verbalizations. Freedom and self-mastery, as has been noted for centuries by wise philosophers, require self-knowledge. And in the last analysis, it is significant knowledge about himself that the rational-emotive therapist actively and forcefully helps his patient acquire.

Does RT work with extremely disturbed or mentally limited patients? A set of objections that is sometimes raised against RT revolves around the allegation that it may work very well with a limited number of patients but that it could not possibly be used effectively in treating patients who are not too intelligent or educated, or who are psychopathic, obsessive-compulsive, or psychotic. Let us now consider these objections.

1. The notion that RT works well only with highly intelligent and educated individuals is not supported by any existing evidence. On the contrary, because of its simplicity and its clarity, rational-emotive psychotherapy seems to work better with less intelligent, poorly educated, economically deprived patients than most of the usual psychoanalytic, nondirective, existential, or other therapies.

Highly intelligent patients, it must be admitted, seem to improve more quickly and more significantly with almost any kind of psychotherapy, including RT, than do moderately intelligent or relatively stupid patients. With RT, they often make phenomenal gains after just a few therapeutic sessions. However, the rational-emotive therapist can accept patients of relatively low I. Q. and minimal educational background who could not possibly be helped by classical analysis and most other complex schools of psychotherapy; and he can appreciably help these individuals to face many of their most fundamental problems and to a considerable degree stop blaming themselves and others. As long as he is content with limited goals with such patients, he can teach them some of the basic theories and practices of RT and can help them to become significantly less irrational than when they first came for therapy.

2. RT, as I have shown in Chapter 16 of this book, is definitely applicable to the so-called psychopaths or individuals with severe character disorders. With the use of rational-emotive psychotherapy, such severely disturbed individuals can often be shown how they are defeating their own best interests and how they must change their ways if they are to keep out of serious future trouble. These patients with severe behavior disorders are difficult patients for any kind of therapist; and they certainly give the rational therapist a rough time as well. But again, with the persistent use of RT they can be benefited in more cases and to a greater extent than they probably can be with almost any other mode of psychotherapy.

3. As with the treatment of psychopaths, the treatment of obsessive-compulsives is exceptionally difficult with any form of psychotherapy, including RT. In my own clinical experience, I have found that serious obsessive-compulsives are rarely neurotic but are almost always psychotic. And psychotics, especially severe and chronic ones, are treatable by any kind of psychotherapy only if the therapist is realistically able to accept limited goals and face the fact that he is probably not going to have any complete "cures."

It is my own view, after much study of the subject, that most severe states of psychosis are basically biological in origin and that they do *not* merely originate in the early experience of the afflicted person. I also believe that borderline psychotics usually, though not necessarily always, inherit or congenitally acquire a predisposition to think in a slippery manner and consequently to relate poorly to others, to be exceptionally fearful, to have unusually low ego-strength, and to be quite hostile.

This is not to say that I take a pessimistic view toward the treatment of psychosis and borderline psychotic states. On the contrary, I take the somewhat optimistic view that psychotics can be significantly helped, with an effective mode of psychotherapy, to overcome much, though rarely all, of their biological handicaps. I doubt whether most psychotics are, in our present state of knowledge, likely to be truly cured. But I do feel that they can be appreciably aided and that many of them can be so improved that, for all practical purposes, they eventually behave in only moderately "neurotic" or even so-called "normal" ways.

Whereas several forms of psychotherapy, especially classical psychoanalysis, are clearly contraindicated in the treatment of psychosis, rational-emotive therapy can be appropriately employed with almost any kind of psychotic, and it will tend to have more effectiveness than most other standard forms of psychotherapy. This is because RT, very directly and simply, and in terms that most psychotics can well understand, attacks the central issues of psychosis: namely, the huge catastrophizing, self-blaming, and hostile tendencies that almost all psychotics have. It also is a highly active-directive mode of treatment that often produces good results with apathetic and inert individuals.

Sometimes, with psychotic patients, a preliminary period of unusual acceptance, reassurance, and ego-bolstering has to be undertaken, before the rational therapist can gain sufficient contact and rapport with the withdrawn or over-agitated individual to be able to employ some of his other logical-persuasive methods. But it is surprising how often the rational-didactic approach can be used almost from the start with chronic psychotics (Shapiro and Ravenette, 1959). Usually, these patients will need much firmer and longer periods of logical persuasion than will serious neurotics. But if the therapist is willing to keep pounding away, against odds, and ceaselessly to show these individuals that they *are* irrationally blaming themselves and others; that they *must* keep terribly upsetting themselves if they continue to be ultra-moralistic; and that they *can* observe, understand, and counterattack their specific, endlessly repeated blaming sentences; and if the therapist, at the same time, is able to be a consistent, non-blaming model, he may finally, after a considerable expenditure of time and effort, be able to break into the rigidly held irrationalities of some of the most severely psychotic patients and induce them to think and behave more (though rarely completely) sanely.

20

The Limitations of Psychotherapy

The impression may somehow be gained from what has previously been said in this book that psychotherapy, when done
in a rational-emotive manner, is a simple process that merely
involves showing patients that their "emotional" problems stem
from their own illogical internalized sentences, demonstrating
how they can parse and challenge their self-verbalizations, and
then (after a few weeks) sending them on their merry, live-
happily-ever-after way. But this view of the near-miraculous,
easily-derived benefits of RT (or any other brand of psychotherapy) is sadly mistaken. In fact, it is downright misleading.

The difficulty with the presentation of any technique or method is that the presenter is almost exclusively interested in showing how this method *is* done—and, of course, how it is *successfully* done. He knows perfectly well, in most instances, that his
particular system of teaching music, playing tennis, practicing
psychotherapy, or what you will, does not work equally well
for all persons under all circumstances; and he even knows that
for some individuals it will not work at all. But he also knows
that the rival methods in his field are just as limited as is his;
and he (competitively) prefers to show those instances in which
his technique *does* work and others' rules don't. He especially,
therefore, emphasizes his successes and minimizes his failures;
and the readers of his tracts may well gain the impression that
failures are virtually nonexistent.

So it is in the field of psychotherapy. Freudians, Adlerians,
Jungians, Sullivanians, Horneyites, Rankians, Rogerians, Ellisians,
etc. all present many accounts of the successful employment of
their particular therapeutic methods; and rarely do they give

clear-cut instances of failure. The successful cases they present, moreover, often tend to be unusually *good* successes: that is, those which were obtained with a minimum degree of difficulty and a maximum devotion to these therapists' own theory and practice. The poor, partial, or later-relapsing "successful" cases are much less often published.

So it is with the cases in this book. Almost all of them were originally selected to illustrate articles in professional journals and were chosen for the express purpose of showing how rational-emotive therapy works. They were not naturally chosen to show how it does *not* work; and, consequently, particularly when taken as a whole, they give a somewhat false impression that RT is not only invariably successful, but that its successes are mostly obtained in a dramatic manner, after the patient has had only relatively few sessions of psychotherapy.

This, of course, is bound to be misleading. Even the most successful and efficient forms of psychotherapy, as Astin (1961), de Grazia (1952), Eysenck (1953), The Joint Commission on Mental Illness and Health (1961), and others have pointed out, do not have notable records of cures. And especially when therapy is done in a private practice setting, where patients have to weigh the hard-earned dollars they are paying for treatment against the possibility of gaining from it, many individuals leave therapy after a short length of time after they have made only minimal or no gains. Although several recent exponents of new ways in psychotherapy, including Berne (1957), Phillips (1956), Rosen (1953), Thorne (1957), Wolpe (1958), and Ellis (1957b), have reported that they obtain up to 90 per cent improvement in their psychotherapy cases, there is little indication that by "improvement" they mean a complete and irreversible removal of their patients' underlying disturbances. Symptomatically, these patients have significantly changed as a result of treatment; but changes in their basic philosophies of living seem to be less far-reaching (Seeman, 1962).

It is particularly often noted, by laymen as well as professional observers, that most psychotherapy practitioners are themselves hardly the very best models of healthy behavior. Instead of being minimally anxious and hostile, as on theoretical grounds one might expect them to be if their own theories work well, they are frequently seriously emotionally disturbed, even after they have undergone lengthy psychoanalytic or other treatment.

It has also often been observed that individuals who are immensely benefited by psychotherapy, and who temporarily lose all or most of their presenting neurotic or psychotic symptoms, frequently relapse; and within a few years after they have completed therapy, they are almost as seriously disturbed as they were. It has likewise been noted that patients who are significantly improved when they are treated in an institution or when their living conditions are bettered, frequently slip back into the old disturbed ways of thinking and behaving when they go back to their homes or when their environment again worsens.

From all this and much similar evidence, it would appear that the results of even the most effective forms of psychotherapy are, as yet, distinctly limited. In probably the majority of instances, the able psychotherapist has to work for a considerable period of time, and under highly discouraging conditions, with the majority of his patients. And even when he helps them significantly to improve, they stubbornly continue to cling to a considerable number of the irrationalities with which they first came to therapy, and often to behave self-defeatingly all over again once they have led themselves and their therapist to believe that they had considerable insight into the causes of their disturbances and that they were already making good use of this insight.

The phenomenon of the individual's recalcitrance in getting and staying better in the course of his working with a psychotherapist has long been noted in professional literature and has usually, especially by the psychoanalysts, been given the name "resistance." Unfortunately, however, the concept of resistance has long been endowed with a psychodynamic quality that seems only very partially to explain what it is and why it so consistently arises. That is to say, it has been all too easily assumed that that patient, either consciously or unconciously, *deliberaately* and *wilfully* resists cure. More specifically, it has been alleged that the patient, for his own neurotic or psychotic reasons, really does not *want* to get better; or that he *fears* giving up his disturbance and the neurotic gains resulting from it; or that he is waging some kind of personal, transference-relationship battle between himself and the therapist, and that because of this battle he is not really *trying* to get better.

Doubtless, these psychodynamic reasons for resistance to therapy are sometimes cogent; but it is most unlikely that they give the full answer to the problem of resistance. I frequently explain to my own patients that they are refusing to work hard against their own disturbances for the same two basic reasons why they became disturbed in the first place: namely, needless anxiety and childish rebelliousness. That is to say, they are afraid (because of their own irrational definition of failure being equivalent to worthlessness) that they are not good enough or competent enough to overcome their disturbance; so, rather than try and risk failure, they don't really try. And they are so convinced that they *shouldn't* have to work to get better (because, again, they irrationally define the world as a place where they *should* be helped over their difficulties and *should* have a protecting fairy godmother) that, again, they don't try to work very hard at helping themselves.

Although I feel that I am probably quite correct in making these interpretations to my patients, and although many of them fully agree with me that they are resisting therapy out of illogical anxiety and/or grandiosity, I still feel that these psychodynamic explanations of resistance do not quite cover the facts. Something very important seems to be omitted here; and that something, I am fairly well (though not dogmatically) convinced is bound up with the inherent biological limitations of a human organism to think straight, and especially to think clearly and logically about his own behavior, for any consistent length of time. Resistance to new ideas is such an important and statistically normal part of human living that even great scientists, as Barber (1961) recently has shown, frequently resist acceptance of valid scientific discovery.

Before I go into further detail about the biology of human

thinking and behaving, let me face the possibility that what I am going to say could also be explained on environmental grounds. If, as I am going to hypothesize, human beings have clear-cut tendencies *easily* and *naturally* to become seriously emotionally disturbed, and then to offer determined resistance to overcoming their disturbances, it may well be that both these tendencies follow from their early upbringing, and are therefore the result of environmental conditioning.

I think that this argument is rather specious even if and when some supporting experimental data can be presented in its favor, since it largely ignores the biological substratum on which the environmental conditions work. Take, for example, two notable experiments relating to the creation and removal of experimental neurosis in animals. In the first of these experiments, Liddell (Hoch and Zubin, 1950; Hunt, 1944), found that, by forcing sheep to be protractedly vigilant, he could easily induce them to behave neurotically; but once he got them to be neurotic, it was almost impossible to get them to be non-neurotic again.

Solomon and Wynne (1954), reviewing their own and others' experiments with rats and dogs, conclude that a principle of the partial irreversibility of traumatic anxiety reactions exists and that, according to this principle "there will be certain definite limitations on the 'curing' of behavior arising from early, 'primitive' traumatic experiences. This will also hold true for psychosomatic symptoms which may be a more direct manifestation of early conditioning. Complete freedom from a *tendency* to manifest such symptoms could not be expected, even with the most advantageous course of therapy."

According to these findings, it would seem clear that environmentally or experimentally induced anxiety in several different kinds of animals can produce neurotic states that are thereafter highly resistant to change; and the conclusion may consequently be drawn that resistance to therapy may well be, in human as well as lower animals, a product of the intensity of the early-acquired, environmentally caused disturbance.

This would be a rash conclusion, however, since it begs the important question: *why* do sheep, rats, dogs, or humans, once they are driven neurotic by external situations in which they are placed, thereafter stubbornly resist all kinds of therapy? And one fairly obvious answer to this question might well be: Because they are inherently the kind of animals who, once they become emotionally disturbed, find it most difficult to change.

If men and women, for example, were *not* the kind of beings they are—if, say, they were Martians, Venusians, or what you will—it is quite possible that they could then become seriously emotionally disturbed and *not* be too resistant to therapeutic change. But, of course, they are *not* Martians or Venusians; they are human. And there is probably something about their humanity, and particularly about the kind of nervous system which goes with their humanness, which makes it *easy* or *natural* for them to resist therapy, even when it is indisputably shown (as under experimental conditions, it may be shown) that their emotional disturbances directly result from the environmental conditions to which they are subjected.

The main point I am making, then, is this: that however much external stimuli and events may contribute to an individual's becoming emotionally disturbed, it would seem safe to assume that he becomes disturbed in the first place and resists treatment in the second place partly or largely because he is human—and because, as a human, he was born with a specific kind of neuromuscular constitution. At bottom, then, his becoming and remaining disturbed is partly a biological as well as a psychosociological phenomenon; and rather than our merely looking for the psychodynamic roots of his disturbance and his resistance, we might well further the science of human behavior by looking for the biological roots as well (Breland and Breland, 1961; Eysenck 1960; Martí Ibáñez, 1960; Masor, 1959; Razran, 1962; Simeons, 1960).

For many years, as I have investigated the origins of the neurotic and psychotic processes of hundreds of patients, and as I have watched these patients react well or poorly to my psychotherapeutic efforts, I have speculated about the biological (as well as the psychodynamic) roots of their becoming and remaining disturbed. I have thus far come up with several hypotheses in this connection, which I shall now briefly attempt to outline. What, I have asked myself, are some of the main biological common denominators that make it relatively easy for virtually *all* men and women to act self-defeatingly on many occasions even when they are not intrinsically stupid or uneducated as far as impersonal modes of problem-solving are concerned? My tentative list of these biological determiners of human neurosis and resistance to therapy follows.

Prolonged period of childhood. Every normal human being undergoes a prolonged period—at least 10 or 12 years—of childhood. During this time, his mental age is necessarily fairly low, even though his intelligence quotient may be unusually high. A child, compared to what he himself will be when he reaches late adolescence or adulthood, *is* unintelligent, incompetent, and over-emotional. Moreover, if he lives (as he almost always does) in some kind of adult world, he *is* vulnerable, weak, and in constant danger of starvation, pain, injury, death, etc.

In consequence, the child's thoughts, emotions, and behavior, however appropriate they may be be when he is still young, *are* almost always a poor training ground and preparation for the kind of thinking, emoting, and acting that he will have to do if he is to live sanely as an adult. Depending on his early upbringing, his childhood experiences may be more or less helpful for the kinds of roles he is likely to be called upon to play later in life; but we can be reasonably certain that these experiences will never be *too* helpful and that they will often be exceptionally misleading, dysfunctional, and unhelpful for his future existence.

Moreover, the child's early experiences are, by necessity, primal ones. They occur before his adolescent or adult experiences; take place when he is quite impressionable; transpire when he has few or no prior impressions to unlearn; and are often literally forced on him by external people and events. On both neurological and sociological grounds, therefore, it is only to be expected that these early impressions will usually be firmly fixed in his psyche and influential on his behavior long before his adolescent and adult experiences begin to affect him. Under these conditions, he can hardly be expected to be free of *some* kind of prejudice in favor of his early-acquired behavior patterns, however inappropriate these may be for his later adult adjustment.

Difficulty of unlearning. Once he has learned, and particularly when he has over-learned, to do something, the human being is the kind of organism that has difficulty unlearning. Even when he learns new things, he frequently learns them on top of the old; and he still retains many of the elements of the old teachings. Consequently, if he gets in the habit of doing something that is fairly appropriate in his younger days (such as crying when he is frustrated) and discovers that this same kind of behavior is inappropriate in later years, he will still have difficulty in giving up the old habit patterns, however much he realizes that they are no longer functional. Unlearning requires considerable work and practice; it does not automatically follow the acquiring of insight into the dysfunctionality of the habit that is to be unlearned. And human beings, as we shall note below, find great difficulty engaging in *consistent* work and practice.

Inertia principles. Just as inanimate objects are subject to the principles of inertia, so do humans seem to be similarly limited. To get a car started, one has to give it extra gasoline and put special effort into aligning its gears. Once it is well started, less gas and less effort will be required, and it will tend to run smoothly (according to a corollary of the principle of inertia, which states that a moving object will keep moving until some special force is exerted to stop it).

Similarly, once a human being gets into action, of a physical or mental nature, he tends to sail smoothly along in this activity. But to push himself originally into this action, he frequently needs extra determination. But it is often quite difficult and onerous for him to exert this extra energy—even though, once it is exerted, he may reap tremendous rewards. So he will frequently balk or rebel against this initial energy expenditure, and will inappropriately remain where he is—which may well be right in the midst of his own self-defeatism. Thus, after learning that if he is to overcome his neurotic fear of, say, bicycle riding, he must force himself to ride and ride and ride bicycles, an individual will find it easier *not* to push himself into the bicycle riding than to push himself (especially while his fear is still extant) to do it. Consequently, he will make little effort to overcome his neurosis.

Short-sightedness. It is a normal propensity of most humans to be short-sighted about many things, and even to fall back on short-sightedness after they have temporarily been longer-sighted. Thus, the child wants the pleasure of spending his pennies on candy *right now* rather than the pleasure to be derived by saving the pennies and *later* buying a more substantial toy with them. And the adult wants the rewards of a higher-paying job *right now* even though he (reluctantly) recognizes that this job is a dead end and that another position, that now pays substantially less, will eventually lead to a higher maximum wage.

Even when the adult is *for the moment* future-oriented rather than short-sighted, he often finds it very difficult to remain consistently so since he *is* being presently frustrated by his longer-range planning, and he rarely can be *absolutely certain* that he is making the wisest choice by accepting this present frustration. At best, there is a higher *probability* that this longer-range hedonism will lead to better results than a shorter-range hedonism; and humans seem to be the kind of animals who do not like to live by probability, even when they have no other real choice.

Prepotency of desire. Virtually all animals seem to survive largely because of the prepotency of their desires. The lion *desires* meat; and the rabbit *likes* vegetation; and both consequently live instead of starving to death. Even the flower that seeks the sun may be said to "desire," to "like," or "want" sunshine. Normal human babies certainly seem to desire the mother's breast, or the nipple of a bottle, or the removal of a pin in their side; consequently, they survive. Many things which are not needed for survival, such as the approval of others or the mastery of a difficult task, are also strongly desired by human children and adults; and, for the most part, the desire for these things is sensible enough, since the human being is such that he receives greater pleasure and is able to behave more efficiently when he has these desires gratified.

Many other things, however, are momentarily desirable but in the long run undesirable or harmful. The consumption of alcohol, drugs, and too much food, for example, may be in this class. Other things are desirable, but cause immediate pernicious effects—such as some foods which have allergic reactions in certain individuals. Still other things are unpleasant or undesirable (such as vile-tasting medicines) but have quick or delayed good effects. Some activities (such as playing tennis) are highly desirable in one set of circumstances (e.g., when the weather is moderate) and equally undesirable in other circumstances (e.g., when the day is very hot).

The point is that the human organism seems to be so constructed that there is little relationship between what it desires (either because of inborn tendencies or because it has been favorably conditioned in a certain direction) and what it wisely should do or refrain from doing for its own best benefit or survival. And desire, especially for the moment, often strongly tends to outweigh wisdom. There is usually no reason why a human being *has* to get what he desires; but when his wants and preferances are powerful (as they often are), he tends to feel such physical or psychological discomfort when his desires are unsatisfied that it is very easy for him to *believe* that they *must* be satisfied; hence he normally or "naturally" *tends* to favor his current strong desires over either his present or his future *general* well-being.

It is even possible that many individuals are so equipped biologically (or by early conditioning on top of their original biological tendencies) that some of their desires are considerably stronger than those of other individuals; and that therefore it is much harder for these persons to resist unwise or self-destroying desires than it is for other persons to resist exactly the same desires. It is also possible that, when they are in a desirous state, some people have much more difficulty than others in thinking clearly and dispassionately about whether it is wise for them to gratify their desires.

Thus, young children may well be virtually unable to think straight when they have a strong desire to eat, play, or urinate; and many older individuals may be congenitally afficted in a similar manner. Such individuals, however intelligent and educated they might otherwise be, might well tend to behave in a much less wise and hence "neurotic" manner than other less generally bright and sophisticated persons.

In any event, it is postulated that strong desire normally prejudices the desiring individual in such a way as to interfere with his wise, self-preserving choices of action; and that there is often a tendency for highly desirous individuals to be less able to think straight while they are in a state of want or deprivation than while they are undesiring. This common prejudice and interference with straight-thinking is probably significantly related to neurotic behavior.

Over-suggestibility. A normal human being is an unusually suggestive animal, particularly during his early childhood. On even slight provocation, he tends to go along with, imitate, and often slavishly follow the views and behavior of others (Tabori, 1959, 1961). His unusual suggestibility is probably in some way related to the large size of his cerebral cortex; and it has distinct advantages, since without it much useful and self-preserving social learning, cooperativeness, division of labor, etc. would not take place. But, as is the case in relation to so many of his useful capacities and abilities, the human person seems to have an over-abundance of suggestibility and imitativeness, and he often finds it most difficult to arrive at a discriminating cutoff point where it would be wiser for him to be less suggestible and more independent-thinking, less conforming and more original (Bowser, 1962).

As usual, the calculation of a perfect cutoff point for the balancing of his suggestibility-independence tendencies is made difficult for the average individual by the peculiar exigencies of his life space and life span. Thus, when he is very young and weak, imitating and conforming to others is probably most helpful to him; when he is older and stronger, it can easily become stultifying. When he works for a dictatorial boss, he might well be (or at least seem to be) quite accepting and docile; but when he goes into business for himself, he needs more initiative and risk-taking. With his relatives and family members, it is often wiser for him to adjust himself to difficult existing circumstances; but in the choice of his personal friends, he might just as well be considerably more independent, and choose people who readily accept and conform to his ways of thinking and behaving.

Since, then, there cannot easily be a general, invariant rule for a given individual's employing his propensities for both conformity and independent thinking, the average person finds it quite difficult to keep adjusting in a flexible, wise manner to the various circumstances and people he is likely to keep encountering during his life; and he frequently tends—that is, finds it *easy*— to behave in either an over-suggestible or over-stubborn, and hence neurotic, manner.

Over-vigilance and over-caution. Without some kind of fear reactions, a human being would not long survive; since there are distinctly hazardous conditions in his world and he must somehow learn to prevent, avoid, and meet them. But sensible degrees of vigilance and caution very closely overlap insane degrees of the same traits. It is relatively easy for a vigilant person who appropriately watches the cars as he walks across the street inappropriately to start worrying about being hit by a car when he is on the sidewalk, or even when he is safely ensconced at home. Where human beings, unlike lower animals, are sanely prophylactic on many occasions, they also tend to become idiotically over-prophylactic on many other occasions, and neurotically give themselves enormous difficulties by scrubbing their teeth ten times a day, locking the doors of their car several times before they feel safe, avoiding riding in airplanes because a few hundred people out of the millions who use them are killed each year, etc.

It is terribly easy, moreover, for a person who is appropriately afraid of real dangers to become equally afraid of wholly or almost-wholly imaginary ones. Thus, the individual who is sensibly wary of losing his job, often tends to become illegitimately afraid of what every single person in the office is thinking of him at all times—when, actually, what these people think of most of the things he believes, says, or does will have little or no effect on his continuing to hold his job. The human condition, as the existentialists point out, includes *some* degree of existential fear or anxiety; and it also seems to include a *tendency* toward too much, too intense, and too frequent—that is, neurotic —anxiety. This biological tendency toward over-anxiety can, I would strongly hypothesize, definitely be overcome as a result of rational upbringing or reëducation. But it does, normally, exist; and it must, in order to be overcome, be fully faced and continually tackled.

Grandiosity and over-rebellion. It is obviously dysfunctional when an individual grandiosely feels that the universe should revolve around him, that others should do his bidding, and that he should cut off his nose to spite his face by violently rebelling against all the necessary difficulties and restrictions of life. But what is rarely recognized in the psychological (and particularly the psychoanalytic) literature is the *normal human* components of grandiosity and over-rebelliousness.

A child, to a certain degree, is *healthfully* grandiose, rebellious, and hostile. By egotistically thinking that the world *should* be the way he would like it to be, he often helps himself overcome the expectable difficulties of his childhood existence; and frequently, thereby, he becomes stronger and more self-confident. It is therefore *natural* for him to be something of a monster, unfairly to try to get his way against well-nigh impossible odds, and ungracefully and surlily to usurp the rights of others.

It is also easy, unless he is specifically and calmly trained not to do so, for this same child to continue to be overly-rebellious and grandiose as he grows into adolescence and manhood. He will, as noted previously in this chapter, have other, counteracting tendencies as well: particularly those favoring conformity and suggestibility. But on many occasions, because he *is* human, and because it *would* be lovely if he could induce the whole world to do his bidding, a human being who is chronologically adult will find it exceptionally easy to refuse to accept grim reality and will pigheadedly continue to fight City Hall when he almost certainly will defeat his own ends in the process. His biological urges for self-expression, however partially civilized they may become, perpetually tend to remain somewhat primitive and childlike, and consequently to prejudice him in favor of reasonably frequent self-defeating or neurotic behavior patterns.

Extremism. There is something about the nature of human beings—and particularly about the nature of some humans more than others—which makes it horribly difficult for them to take the middle ground, or the position of the Aristotelian mean, on many or most important questions. Instead of having moderating corrective tendencies when they engage in some form of extreme behavior, humans often tend to jump from one extreme to another—and thereby defeat their own best ends.

Thus, when an individual has been ultra-conservative or conforming and discovers that he is not getting sufficient satisfaction with this position, you would think that he would merely go ahead somewhat to a less conservative position. Very frequently, however, he will do nothing of the sort: he will jump to an exceptionally radical or unconforming position—which he may then soon find to be equally as unsatisfying as he found his previous stand to be. The middle ground, perhaps because it tends to be relatively undramatic, ordinary, and boring, tends to be eschewed by millions of humans; and, instead, they cling doggedly and precariously to one or another jagged peak, and thereby keep themselves continually unbalanced and upset.

It is possible that some of the basic elements of the human nervous system, which frequently work on all-or-none rather than on middle-ground principles of excitation and response, prejudice the human person to respond in extreme rather than moderate manners in his thinking and acting. Whatever the cause may be, it seems to be clinically observable that most "normal" people, and particularly most emotionally disturbed ones, tend to react in self-defeating extremist ways on many occasions; and that there is good reason to believe that this kind of response pattern is a normal biological component of being human.

Oscillation and erraticness. Human personality, as Murphy

(1947), Maslow (1954), and many other observers have pointed out, is generally replete with tendencies toward change, oscillation, erraticness, and imbalance. Although homeostasis, or the *restoral* of states of equilibrium and balance, is also a basic attribute of human (and other) animals, in between their states of homeostatic balance they have distinct periods of being off-balance. Most people, moreover, do not seem to be able to maintain states of equilibrium and stability for any considerable period of time. They become bored, listless, and irritable if they have to continue the same kind of work or same kind of life for month after month, year after year; and, to break the monotony, they usually require vacations, periods of goofing, bouts of drinking, or some other form of radical change.

Life, unfortunately, often does not allow the periods of break and leeway that men and women commonly seem to demand in the course of their living routines. A mother just cannot leave her young children every few weeks or so and go off on a binge; and a husband or even a young unmarried male cannot afford to stay home from his job and take some time at the race-track or lolling around neighborhood bars. The breaking of bad habits, moreover, usually requires a steady, almost invariant, pattern of reëducation. Anyone who diets for three weeks and then stops dieting for the next week will probably (*a*) gain back all the weight he has lost, and (*b*) fail to get to the point where he almost automatically finds it *easy* to continue dieting. The laws of inertia, which we referred to earlier in this chapter, require that interruptions of a given mode of behavior be sufficiently *steady* and *consistent* before they begin to become highly effective and semi-automatic.

A sort of biological vicious circle tends to exist, in other words, before a maladaptive pattern of behavior can be overcome. First, the malfunctioning habit pattern becomes easy to maintain and hard to break, so that it requires *persistent* counter-behavior to interrupt; and then, to make things worse, the persistent counter-behavior itself becomes difficult to maintain because, after a relatively short time, it seems to be boring and unexciting, while

(in consonance with fact of biological oscillation) the temporary reëstablishment of the old, maladaptive behavior pattern
seems exciting and pleasurable.

. On two main counts, then, the old habits become hard to
break and the new ones (at first) hard to substitute for them.
After a while, when the new habits persist for a long enough
time, the vicious circle unwinds, and it may actually become
difficult to reëstablish the old ways again. But until that time
arrives, the individual has the very devil of a time giving up his
self-defeating ways and replacing them with less neurotic behavior patterns.

Automaticity and unthinkingness. One of the distinct advantages of the human organism is that it takes over certain learned
patterns of behavior and soon begins to perform them automatically, habitually, unthinkingly. Thus, the child first laboriously
learns to tie his shoelace; but after a time, he is tying it unthinkingly, with very little conscious effort. If this process of
automaticity and habituation did not exist, humans would be
woefully inefficient and would spend huge amounts of time and
energy performing many tasks that they now do quickly.

Automaticity, however, has its distinct disadvantages. Because,
for example, a person learns to tie his shoelaces quite efficiently,
he may unthinkingly keep purchasing shoes with laces, when
(with a little extra thought) he could purchase them or fix them
up with elastic partitions or some other device that would enable him to dispense with shoelace tying. Similarly, because an
individual successfully adapts or adjusts himself to living with
an inefficient car, or in a noisy neighborhood, or with a quarrel-
some spouse, he may not think about making a basic change in
his situation, since he no longer finds it *too* intolerable. But
it is quite possible that it would be much wiser if he did think
about change rather than continued toleration.

Once an individual becomes used to a neurotic way of behaving, he may unthinkingly perpetuate that behavior pattern and
may find it exceptionally difficult to force himself to think in
such a manner that he finally breaks it. Thus, if he becomes terribly anxious and begins to use alcohol, drugs, or sleep as a

method of evading (rather than facing and working through) his anxiety, he may soon find himself unthinkingly reaching for a drink, a pill, or a bed when his anxieties rise. Almost before he can even give himself a chance to say to himself, "Now, look: you don't have to be anxious. Let's see what's bothering you, and do something about it," he may find himself on his way to a state of drunkenness or relaxation that *then* precludes his doing any further thinking about his basic problems. Consequently, it remains very easy for him to perpetuate his neurosis and unusually difficult for him to attack it.

Forgetfulness. Freud and his followers, in stressing the repressive aspects of forgetfulness, have failed mightily to consider the importance of its nonrepressive or normal aspects. It would appear to be one of the most normal things in the world for an individual to keep forgetting that something is noxious or nonbeneficial to him, even when he has plenty of evidence of its potential harmfulness (Mark, 1962).

Thus, the person who suffered miserably from his own allergic reactions to strawberries last summer will sometimes forget his misery when he sees how delicious they look today, and will rashly consume them again. The woman whose husband criticized her mercilessly for several years, and who finally divorced him because of his nastiness, will only very vaguely remember his behavior a few months later (especially after she has been lonely or sexually deprived because of their separation) and will remarry him—only to be startled, within a week or two, into remembering what a horribly critical person he really *is*. The man who carefully diets for a period of time, and is overjoyed at losing 30 or 40 pounds, will gradually forget, after awhile, that he simply *cannot* afford to eat potatoes or drink beer; and, before he knows it, he will have gained back almost all the lost weight again.

Probably in most of these instances, as the Freudians have emphasized, there is a distinct wish-fulfilling or Pollyannaish element in neurotic forgetting. The individual *wants* to forget that he cannot touch strawberries, or remarry his or her mate, or go back to drinking beer; and he consequently finds it *easy* to do this kind of forgetting. But over and above this wishfully-induced form of forgetfulness, there is every reason to believe that memory traces *naturally* fade, and that the mere passage of time itself interferes with clear-cut remembrance of desirable aspects of behavior.

Take, again, the person who is allergic to strawberries. He soon discovers, when he keeps eating this fruit, that he has unusually distressing reactions; and, remembering these reactions, he wisely decides to forego eating strawberries again. But after he has not had any berries for a long enough period of time and has consequently had no distressing allergic reactions, it would indeed be remarkable if he remembered his distress as clearly as when he had been fairly regularly experiencing it. Consequently, it is quite expectable and normal for him to forget some of the most painful details of his allergic reaction, and only to remember them again *after* he has rashly tried strawberries again. To say, therefore, that he *only* forgets about the disadvantages of his eating strawberries because he *wants* to do so or because he has *repressed* his painful memory of previously eating them is to ignore some of the obvious nonpsychodynamic aspects involved in his case.

Because, it is hypothesized, human beings have highly expectable and normal tendencies to forget the painful results of their behavior, it is woefully easy for them to act self-defeatingly in the first place and to return to self-sabotaging modes of behavior even when they have once temporarily conquered these dysfunctional behavior patterns.

Wishful thinking. As noted in the last section, many instances arise when a person wishfully-willfully forgets that he'd better do this or refrain from that pattern of living. It is to Freud's great credit that he first saw the mechanism of wishful thinking in its fullest flower and described its enormous influence on life. Implicit in much Freudian literature, however, are the assumptions that (*a*) wishful thinking is an unusual or abnormal manifestation; and that (*b*) it largely arises as a result of early childhood experiences.

On the contrary, there is much reason for believing that human animals have an inborn tendency to expect a thing to exist because they strongly want it to; and that this tendency is one of the most usual and at least statistically normal aspects of being human. In all times and climes, people have dreamed up supportive gods, fairies, leprechauns, etc. who would (for a few prayers or sacrifices, to be sure) bring them rain, food, fertility, or other things they craved; and there is reason to suspect that almost any self-respecting cerebral cortex that has the power to imagine future events will in large part tend to use its power to fantasize the fulfillment of its owner's heartfelt desires. If—as we hypothesized previously in this chapter—men and women have a prepotency of desire, it is only to be expected that they will use their imaginative powers to convince themselves that their wants *will* be satisfied.

The very normality of wishful thinking, however, frequently leads to neurotic results. For, whether we like it or not, the world is not a place where most of our strongest desires are gratified; and it *is* an area where many of our gratifiable desires must be appreciably postponed before they are fulfilled. Consequently, although it is perfectly sane to *want* our desires to be satisfied, it is not equally sane for us to *expect* them to be.

Our strong tendencies to think in a wishful manner, therefore, continually run headlong into the grim realities of our own and our world's limitations. Unless we somehow learn to challenge, check, and realistically keep re-assessing our wishful thinking (which it is possible but quite difficult for most of us to do), we tend to behave neurotically. Moreover, when once we are neurotic, our wishful-thinking tendencies apply to psychotherapy as well as to everything else; and we often cavalierly *expect* therapeutic miracles that are not likely to occur. When, in consequence, disillusion sets in, our own concerted *efforts* to help ourselves get better are minimized, and resistance to therapy results.

Ineffective focusing and organizing. In order to keep thinking straight about his own behavior and to plan his life well, man has to keep focusing adequately on the problems at hand and to organize many diverse elements of his existence into integrated wholes. Thus, if he is to do a simple task, such as catching a plane at 3:00 P.M., he has to arrange for tickets, pack, notify people that he will be away, arrange for transportation to the airport, dress properly for his flight, let his friends or business associates on the other end of the trip know when he will arrive, etc. This simple task therefore requires considerable planning, clock-watching, and organizing. And if he does not force himself to focus and to keep focusing on various aspects of the task at hand, he will almost certainly miss his plane, take along the wrong things, fail to have accommodations when he arrives, or otherwise importantly miss out on some important aspects of his trip.

Although it is not too difficult for most people to focus, from time to time, on one aspect or another of their lives, it seems to be quite difficult for them to *sustain* their focusing in an effective manner. For one thing, too many stimuli other than the ones they immediately want to focus upon keep coming to their attention. Thus, while thinking about and planning his airplane trip, the average man will also want to or have to keep in mind, to some extent, his relations with his family and his associates, his various hobbies and interests, his general goals in life, his hunger and sex desires, etc. He rarely can *just* focus on his trip and forget everything else. But if he tries to keep his *general* life satisfactions in mind, he may very well neglect some salient aspects of the trip. Either way, it would seem, there is no perfect answer to his problem of being generally *and* specifically satisfied; and he must keep changing his focus, almost from minute to minute, and then refocusing again on this or that aspect of his immediate or long-range requirements.

For even the most stable and "normal" individuals, it is hypothesized, proper and consistent focusing on present and future goals is distinctly difficult. As we have just noted, there seem to be too many things in life on which, at one and the same time, we have to focus. Then, even if we do have the opportunity to focus adequately on some significant phase of our existence, and are doing well with this phase, we tend to become satiated or bored with it; and, against our own best interests, we frequently *want* to think of something else. Again: although at one moment we think that we *should* focus on on this person or thing, our interests tend to wander and become divided; so that at another moment we think that, no, maybe we'd better focus, instead, on *that* individual or situation.

As usual, there seems to be no real surcease from the toil and turmoil of planned living; our abilities both to continue sustained focusing until a given task is well done and to be able flexibly to shift our focus to an equally or more important task appear to be strictly limited, even when we are generally bright and informed. It is relatively easy, therefore, for us to become under- or over-focused on a given situation, and thereby to defeat our own best (and especially our best long-range) aims. Again, moreover, once we are in a neurotic stew, and are desperately seeking a way out, we often find it difficult to focus adequately and sustainedly on *that* situation; and we may resist getting better not because we really do not *want to improve* (as psychoanalysts commonly interpret) but largely because we cannot adequately focus, especially in a short period of time, on such improvement. Not taking these focusing difficulties into account, we frequently conclude that we can't improve, and we give up the battle for mental health.

Unsustained effort. Somewhat related to inefficient focusing is the tendency of human beings to fail to continue sustained efforts, to give up easily, to be "lazy" as regards prolonged exertions. Many persons (unlike those we mentioned in our section on inertia) have no difficulty in getting themselves under way; but once they are sailing along, they soon tire, become bored, and give up continuing any concerted effort. This tendency toward unsustained effort is in part the result of poor motivation and fear of failure; the individual gives up because success does not come as quickly as he thinks it should, or he is afraid that he will not be guaranteed success, so he sees no motive in continuing his efforts.

As usual, however, there is reason to believe that not *all* unsustained effort is related to anxiety or rebellion; and it is even possible that some people's fear of failure and rebelliousness against continuing certain projects largely stem from their biological difficulties in sustaining their efforts.

Most young children, for example, are easily distractible, have poor attention span, and will not continue to do a difficult task for any length of time. This is not because they are emotionally disturbed; but because they are normal children. It is quite likely, therefore, that many or most adults have these same inborn childish tendencies; and that although they definitely *can* continue to work at a difficult or long-range task for a considerable period of time, they find it *hard* to do so and have to be unusually well motivated to sustain their efforts.

If this hypothesis is correct, then it would explain much of the resistance encountered in psychotherapy. For, as noted several times in this book, once an individual is behaving self-defeatingly and has done so for a period of time, his habits of malfunctioning can be permanently broken only if, for another period of time, he works and works and works *against* his neurotic tendencies. But, obviously, if he has an inborn tendency *not* to work at difficult tasks for any length of time, he will (in addition to whatever other psychodynamic reasons for resisting therapy he may have) find it most difficult to keep exerting therapeutic effort and quite easy to give up long before he has significantly improved and maintained his improvement.

Over-emphasizing injustice. It is probable that man is not born with a clear-cut sense of unfairness or injustice, but that he learns what is right and what is wrong and is taught how to hate others who are "wrong." Nonetheless, the history of human civilization shows that man *very easily* becomes a moralistic animal; and there is some reason to believe that the ease with which he becomes moralizing, blaming, and injustice-collecting is biologically rooted. Given any kind of social upbringing whatever, and learning to discriminate between his own acts and possessions and those of others, it is reasonably certain that any normal or average human being will tend to covet others' possessions, feel unjustly deprived when he cannot perform as adequately as they can, blame them for being significantly different from himself, and feel that fate or the world is unkind to him for not giving him whatever he strongly wants.

I am positing, in other words, that human feelings of envy, jealousy, and hatred are biologically rooted as well as environmentally fostered. There is little doubt, as many anthropological studies have shown, that some peoples are more cooperative and less hostile than are other peoples, and that their lack of hostility seems to be largely related to their upbringing. But this does not gainsay the fact that it is very *easy* for an individual to have deep-seated feelings of unfairness and to hate others who he thinks are taking advantage of him. With enough training, especially in rational thinking, we can take an average child and rear him to be nonhostile, or even take a negative and nasty child and convert him to more cooperative and less moralizing ways. It seems to be a lot easier to rear than not to rear a child to be an injustice-collector; and it is even conceivable that if human beings did not have very *normal* tendencies to be angry and aggressive against other animals who seemed to be depriving them of their wants (or endangering their existence), the human race would never have survived.

If the hypothesis that man has a biological tendency to be blaming and hostile is warranted, then it easily can be seen how this tendency would frequently (especially in a fairly well-ordered and cooperative society such as our own) prejudice him against others and would induce him to behave on many occasions in a self-defeating way. For the world (as yet) *is* full of injustices, inequities, discriminating rules, etc.; and anyone who tends to become unduly riled by these social, political, and other differences, and to demand that *he* invariably get the best of what life has to offer, will surely encounter stiff opposition and will probably not get everything he wants. What he will get, of course, is a rise in his own blood pressure or tension level.

Again: injustice-collectors will tend to be poor psychotherapy choices, since they will be inclined to believe that (*a*) they *shouldn't* be emotionally upset (when some others are relatively unsettable), and (*b*) they *shouldn't* have to work hard at getting over their disturbances (when some others can get over their difficulties much easier). Anyone, therefore, who has a pronounced biological tendency to collect injustices and to be moralistic will tend to become and to stay neurotic.

Over-emphasizing guilt. Like the tendency to blame others, the propensity to blame oneself (or to be guilty) may also in part be biologically based. This is not to deny that much or most of the intense guilt of men and women is acquired in the course of their early upbringing; for it would certainly seem to be. But here again we must suspect that if virtually all humans in all parts of the civilized and uncivilized world are intensely guilty or ashamed of many things they do, man must somehow be the kind of animal who, *par excellence,* is guilt-inducible.

Child-rearing practices are particularly instructive in this connection. It is theoretically possible to bring up a youngster so that when he does wrong acts he is calmly penalized and so that when he does right acts he is calmly rewarded. But nearly all the peoples of the world seem to rear their children so that when they do the wrong things they are angrily cursed, upbraided, and punished—that is, severely blamed. This is probably because it has been empirically discovered, over the centuries of human history, that blaming a child is one of the quickest and presumably most effective methods of influencing his behavior. He is *normally* a blame-accepting animal; and his parents, teachers, bosses, and other supervisors have discovered that they can therefore control him by making him guilty about something he has done or not done.

To be more specific, it can be hypothesized that because of man's limited powers to make fine discriminations (to be discussed below) as well as his tendency to be overly-swayed by his immediate desires (discussed previously in this chapter), he usually finds it immensely difficult to see the difference between saying: (a) "My *performance* is poor, because I just behaved wrongly or badly," and (b) "*I* am worthless, because my performance is poor." Although it is *possible* for him to see that his performance does not equal himself, it is hard for him to make this fine discrimination, even when he is generally bright and informed. Consequently, he tends to blame himself (rather than objectively give a low rating to his performance) when he fails in any way or is proven to be "wrong" instead of "right."

If this is true, and if it is also true (as we have been insisting throughout this book) that self-blame is the very essence of feelings of anxiety and worthlessness, then it would appear that man *easily* tends to make himself anxious and neurotic. He doesn't *have* to do so, of course; but the biological cards are heavily stacked in favor of his becoming emotionally disturbed. Only by concerted focusing on and thinking about the problem of wrongdoing and blame could man *not* come to self-defeating conclusions in this connection. And, as we have also seen in this chapter, concerted and consistent focusing on *any* life problem is itself difficult for the average human being. So, again, the chances of his *not* confusing objective acceptance of wrongdoing with pernicious imposing of blame are rather slight.

If we are still on the right track, and it is true that man illegitimately but quite easily blames himself for his actual or potential performances and thus becomes anxious and self-hating, then it should also be obvious that once an individual becomes thus disturbed, he will also have relatively little chance of calmly and sensibly helping himself to overcome his disturbance. For he will first blame himself for becoming disturbed; and then, unless he very quickly gets better, will tend to blame himself severely for remaining disturbed. The usual terribly vicious circle of neurosis and resistance to therapy is thereby established.

Excitement-seeking. Although man has a distinct love for security, stability, and steadiness, he also is the kind of animal that finds great satisfaction in variety, adventure, and excitement-seeking. Moreover, the more secure and stable his life is, the more he may tend to find it monotonous and boring and to want to do something startlingly different. His excitement-seeking tendencies might well be advantageous if only his mode of living were sanely organized, so that he could mix a fair degree of adventure with a reasonable amount of security. But this, alas, is not often true.

On the contrary, modern competitive life tends to be highly unadventurous. And the conformity that exists in our society is

even more unexciting. Adult responsibilities, as we normally define them, leave little leeway for big-game hunting in Africa, for
exchanges of sexual partners, for exciting job opportunities. The
individual's innate adventure-seeking tendencies consequently
have to be squelched; and tension results. In many instances,
the excitement-seeking is entirely surrendered; but loss of *joie
de vivre* and a monotonous existence loom in its place. In other
instances, the individual brashly breaks out of his over-confine-
ment and goes to opposite extremes: becomes a drug addict, a
derelict, an irresponsible gambler, a criminal, or some other kind
of person who almost totally surrenders security and stability.

Moreover, even when the individual is generally stable, his
excitement-seeking trends may rise up to smite him. Thus, a
single week spent at the race-track may bankrupt an otherwise
responsible person for several years; or a night of drunken riot-
ousness in a whore house may lead to the breakup of a man's
fairly good marriage of 20 years' standing.

Much of this kind of thrill-seeking is of typical neurotic origin,
and stems from an individual's childish rebelliousness or his anxiety about being a weak nonentity. But excitement-seeking of
a more normal nature is probably built into the biological foundations of most average people; and at times it prejudices them
in favor of engaging in self-defeating behavior. It is also quite
possible that some individuals (such as juvenile delinquents)
have more of this in-built kind of excitement-seeking than
have others; and that some of their life activities are significantly
influenced (though not entirely determined) by their inborn
physiological trends.

As usual, if an individual is in trouble partly as a result of
his excitement-seeking tendencies, he will find his psychotherapeutic efforts appreciably handicapped by these same trends.
For psychotherapy, as we must keep insisting, requires hard
and steady work by the patient; and excitement-trended individuals are rarely receptive to the prospects of such kind of
work. They goof on therapy as well as on some other responsible
aspects of their lives; and they consequently resist getting better.

Stress-proneness. According to the findings of Selye (1956) and his associates during the past two decades, the normal human being is unusually prone to negative reactions to prolonged stress. Following either extreme physical or unusual psychological stress, the human body seems to react with (*a*) an alarm reaction followed by (*b*) a period of adaptation to the stressor agent which continues until the body's vital energy is expended and psychophysical exhaustion sets in (Richter, 1960).

If this is true—and there seems to be considerable experimental and clinical evidenc? that it is—then we are fairly safe in saying that when the human individual is placed in poor physical or psychological circumstances, as of course he frequently is as he goes through the average kind of life that is common today, he tends to become physically and mentally exhausted. Under these conditions, neurotic, maladaptive behavior on his part is only to be expected in many instances.

What is worse, once the individual does become psychologically upset following prior conditions of stress, he then will experience this upset as *another* form of stress; and he will consequently tend to become more upset and unable to function. Obviously, too, when this individual is already terribly disturbed, and he wants to do something to help himself get better, his psychophysical organism will frequently tend to be in such a state of near-total collapse by the time he comes for help, that he will simply be in no condition to be able to help himself or to benefit very much from the outside help he receives. This may well be why some exceptionally seriously disturbed individuals cannot be treated at all with psychotherapy when they are first seen, but first must go through a period of physical rest and rehabilitation before they can be successfully approached with psychotherapy.

In any event, physiological mechanisms of stress *normally* predispose many individuals to states of emotional disturbance. This is not to say that physical stress *alone* often leads to emotional breakdown; for it is probable that it does not. But many or most people are so constructed that whenever they allow themselves, because of some poor philosophy of living, to become upset, their physiological stress mechanism then takes over and causes them much more psychophysical discomfort than would otherwise occur.

Similarly, individuals with underlying allergic reactions will often, as a result of upsetting themselves psychologically, experience profound physical sequelae which, if they did not become upset in the first place, would probably rarely or never occur. Although ideational factors are most important in these connections, it would be folly if we lost sight of the basic genetic and congenital factors which also importantly exist in these cases.

Lack of self-perspective. It would appear that it is perfectly normal and expectable for the average individual (as well as the above-average individual, too) to be considerably less able to view himself and his own behavior objectively than he is able to view others and their actions. Just as one's own voice invariably sounds different to oneself than it does to others, so in the great majority of instances do one's other attributes tend to be viewed distortedly or myopically by oneself.

Part of the individual's own lack of objectivity may simply result from focusing difficulties. When he is viewing another, he can easily focus concertedly on what this other person is saying and doing—whether, for example, the other is nervous or calm, loving or hating. But he does not have sufficient leisure, in most instances, to observe himself while he is actively saying or doing something: for the good reason that he must focus, at this particular time, on the saying or the doing rather than on the observing. He can sit back *after* he has said or done something and watch himself and the effect he has had on others; but he finds it almost impossible fully to watch himself *while* he is actually performing. In fact, if he watches himself very closely while he is performing, he tends to perform very badly, since he is then not really paying too much attention to *what* he is doing, but to *how* he is doing it.

It is quite difficult, moreover, for a person to assess his own performances *objectively*, since he is usually too involved in their outcome. If Jones sings either badly or well, he doesn't particularly care too much one way or the other; and he can therefore objectively observe just how badly or well Jones is singing. But if he himself sings badly, he often thinks it is *dreadful* that he should sing that way. Therefore, he has a stake in either (*a*) refusing to observe how badly he has actually sung, or (*b*) over-emphasizing the poor quality of his singing because it is so far removed from the ideal that he thinks he *should* obtain.

Human self-evaluations, in other words, tend to be moralistic rather than objective; and the emotions intrinsically tied in with a man's moralizings frequently obscure his observations of his own performances. Moreover, once he becomes moralistic and unobjective, he frequently tends to upset himself severely; and then his condition of upsetness further hinders accurate self-observation.

On several counts, then, human beings normally find it very difficult to objectively assess their own doings. In consequence, they frequently tend to become either overly or underly critical of their performances, and to behave self-defeatingly. Then, as ever, once they recognize their neurotic behavior and try to do something about it, they *still* tend to lack perspective about their psychotherapeutic efforts; and they frequently unwittingly sabotage such efforts. Thus, a patient may falsely believe that he is entirely cured of his emotional disturbance when he has really made only slight improvement; or he may believe that he isn't getting better at all when, in fact, he is making significant improvements in his thought and behavior. In either eventuality, his lack of self-perspecive may sabotage his psychotherapeutic endeavors.

Discrimination difficulties. Even the most intelligent human beings may have inherent discrimination difficulties in some or many respects. Thus, a man may be a talented art critic, medical diagnostician, or logician; and in his own particular field may earn a well-justified reputation for discriminating between what is valuable or trashy, diseased or well, true or false. But in his private life he may have enormous difficulty telling when to be easy-going and when to be firm with his wife and children. Or he may have the devil of a time distinguishing between the legitimacy of showing himself how wrong he is about something and the illegitimacy of blaming himself for being wrong about this thing. And because of his discrimination difficulties regarding certain aspects of his personal life, he may get into serious trouble with himself and others (Mark, 1962).

What is being hypothesized here (as is true of virtually all the major headings we are discussing in this chapter) is that it is intrinsically *hard* for an average human being, no matter how intelligent he may be, to make many important ethical, personal, and social discriminations which it is necessary that he make successfully if he is to avoid defeating his own best interests. And, conversely, it is *easy* for this same average person to be slipshod, careless, and lackadaisical about making these kinds of discriminations. This is not to say that none of us *can* properly discriminate between efficient and inefficient ways of handling our affairs, nor to say that we cannot *learn* to do so in a more effective manner. We *do* apparently have discriminating capacities; and we *can* learn to use them more adequately. But it is still hard, awfully hard, to actualize our potentials in this respect, and it is so terribly easy to fail to do so.

Our discrimination difficulties—assuming that they do exist and have biological as well as socially learned roots—tend to interfere with our therapy as well as our lives. For successful psychotherapy essentially consists of convincing a disturbed person that he *can* be more discriminating about his life choices than he has hitherto been, and showing him precisely how he can increase and sharpen his discriminating abilities. And, because of the natural difficulties of the human individual in becoming and remaining interpersonally discriminant, psychotherapy is usually accomplished against the grain, and only after considerable time and effort on the part of both therapist and patient.

Thus, if there is a normal tendency for a disturbed person to fail to discriminate properly between the wrongness of his *acts* and the evilness of *himself,* and a therapist tries to help his patient overcome this tendency, it is only to be expected that he will have to be most forceful and convincing in his teachings and that, no matter how effective he may generally be, many or most of his patients are going to resist seeing what he is driving at, or see it and then fail to retain their new insights, or see how to make finer and saner life discriminations and then refrain from practicing their improved discriminating powers for a sufficient period of time until they become almost automatic or "second nature." Both patient and therapist have uphill battles to wage; and it is hardly surprising that before any final victory is won, there will be much sallying back and forth over the initial battle lines.

Over-generalization tendencies. A special kind of discrimination difficulty (and also a special mode of extremism) is that form of ineffective thinking which is called over-generalization. Some learning theorists practically define neurosis as over-generalization; and they are probably not too wide of the mark. For anxiety largely consists of the notion that it will be *catastrophic* (rather than merely annoying or inconvenient) if a certain event occurs; a phobia means that an individual *can't stand* something (rather than that he strongly dislikes it); an obsessive-compulsive act implies that a person *must* do something (rather than his merely wanting to do it very much); and hostility connotes an individual's convincing himself that someone *should not* be the way he is (rather than his believing that it would be lovely if this person wasn't the way he is). All these neurotic beliefs, as close examination will show, are based on rash and groundless over-generalization rather than on wisely discriminated constructs.

It is hypothesized (once again!) that the human being is that kind of animal that not only is biologically equipped (doubtless because of the complexity of his cerebral cortex) with the highly advantageous ability to organize his perceptions into wide-ranging conceptions or generalizations, but that he also is innately equipped with the decidedly disadvantageous ability to over-generalize. With very little difficulty, he can truly conclude that blemished apples are usually worse to eat than are unblemished ones. And with almost equally little difficulty he can falsely conclude that *all* blemished apples are bad to eat and that *all* unblemished ones are delectable. More to the point, he can *easily* conclude that because something is annoying, it is

terrible, and that because it would be undesirable if people
didn't approve him, it would also be horrendous.

Similarly, a disturbed individual who is trying to become less
disturbed can easily over-generalize in regard to therapeutic
principles Thus, as he learns in therapy about some of his unconscious negative feelings, he can easily conclude: "Well, seeing that I am *so* hostile, this proves that I really *am* worthless!"
Or, as he learns in rational-emotive psychotherapy to question
his self-defeating assumptions, he can easily over-generalize and
obsessive-compulsively begin to question *all* his assumptions. In
many ways, in the course of therapy, he can use his over-generalizing tendencies to sabotage the curing process (Warshaw and
Bailey, 1962)

Slow learning tendencies. Many or most human beings normally seem to learn many things quite slowly. Sometimes, there
are psychodynamic reasons for their slow learning. Thus, they
may, out of fear of failure, not be focusing properly on what
they are learning; or they may be trying to impress others instead of trying to learn; or be so preoccupied with grasping various subjects *immediately* that they have difficulty in grasping
them at all. But in many instances there would appear to be
physiological reasons for slow learning, with the learner naturally requiring a great many repetitions or experiences before
he finally sees that you simply *cannot* have your cake and eat
it, or that you *can* survive quite well if some significant person
rejects you.

If some individuals are slow learners, they will inevitably tend
to defeat many of their own best interests. *Eventually,* they will
learn that they just cannot act in a certain way and get the most
out of life; but before that eventuality arrives, they will behave
neurotically. Slow learning, moreover, is not necessarily related
to faulty intelligence, since some of the greatest geniuses the
world has known seem to have been *profound* but not necessarily
fast thinkers.

Slow learners, almost by definition, will also tend to resist
reasonably rapid therapeutic change. If their therapist keeps

working with them persistently and forcefully enough, they will finally get and use his sane messages. But they may have to go the long way round, do things the super-hard way, and give themselves an enormously hard time before they decide that there *is* no sensible way to behave other than that which he is trying to teach them and that, for their own sakes, they simply *must* question and challenge their own self-sabotaging philosophic assumptions.

Rashness and over-impulsivity. A certain degree of rashness and impulsivity is a healthy component of human personality. If a child were not a rather impulsive, risk-taking kind of animal who rushes in where angels fear to tread, he would never gain much of the experience and self-confidence that he needs to develop adequately. But just as impulsivity has its most normal and advantageous qualities, so does it appear to be equally normal and *dis*advantageous for an individual to be quite rash and over-impulsive. For where, exactly, is one to draw the line between healthy assertiveness and unhealthy foolhardiness? And how is the average young child, let alone the average adult, to know how and where to draw this line?

Rashness, in other words, would seem to have its clear-cut biological (as well as its socially encouraged and learned) components. And its biological aspects are almost certain to make it easy for the average individual, at many times in his life, to leap before he looks and to take all kinds of unwise chances. Many of the brightest people who ever lived were obviously neurotically over-impulsive; and there is no convincing evidence that they were all specifically reared to be rash in their early environmental surroundings. Indeed, the chances are that many of the world's outstanding generals, explorers, statesmen, inventors, and artists were born with far more than the average share of impulsivity, and that their biological heritage in this respect constituted at least one of the main reasons for their becoming outstanding.

Just as rashness often drives an individual to neurotic behavior, it may also help slow down his therapeutic progress. Over-impulsive people usually do not *like* the steady grind of learning and practicing that is necessary for effective therapy to take place. They frequently tend to gravitate toward half-baked, crackpot notions of therapy (such as the Reichian orgone boxes or primitive voodoo ceremonies) that are most unlikely to bring about any real cure. When getting along reasonably well in some sane form of psychotherapeutic treatment, they sometimes enthusiastically see themselves as cured, and stop treatment, when they have just scratched the surface of their basic disturbances. On several grounds the very impulsivity which actually may have helped to propel them into some kind of treatment in the first place may finally block their steadily and slowly going ahead to a thoroughgoing alleviation of their neuroses.

Perceptual time lag. Humans and other animals have in most aspects of their lives a perceptual immediacy that enables them to survive. As soon as a dangerous situation occurs, they generally *see* or *sense* its existence, and they take counter-measures against it. Thus, the deer instantly sees or smells the approach of the lion, and quickly takes flight; and the human being sees that his auto is about to collide with another car, and immediately turns the steering wheel, puts on the brakes, or takes some other kind of protective action.

In many aspects of one's emotional life, however, there is a distinct time lag between one's perceptions and one's responses. Thus, a man imbibes heavily of alcohol today, and all that he immediately perceives is a feeling of release or euphoria. He does *not* at the moment see that he will have a feeling of drowsiness in a little while and a hangover tomorrow. Or a woman gets terribly angry at her mother or husband and perceives, almost instantly, that she feels good at telling her "persecutor" off. But she does *not* perceive that her gastric juices are flowing wildly and that eventually she may help herself acquire an ulcer.

If the heavy drinker and the angry woman did, at the precise moment they are imbibing or becoming irate, perceive all the major physical and emotional consequences of their acts, they might well learn to resist drinking or becoming angry. But their quite normal and natural time lag in these respects makes it most difficult for them to exert the kind of self-control today that will help them to be happier tomorrow.

To make matters worse, there seems to be a continual lag, or perhaps we should call it a comprehension lag, between the average person's thinking and emoting. Not only does the individual fail to see, at the moment he is getting angry, that his anger will probably have serious negative consequences for himself, but he especially fails to see that his anger almost always follows after and is caused by his thinking. He observes someone behaving wrongly or badly and he quickly becomes angry; and then he erroneously relates his anger to the behavior of this other person and believes that *it* causes his upset.

The angry individual fails to see, however, that he invariably has a pronounced thought just prior to his anger—to wit, "That dirty So-and-So *should* not have done what he did; I can't *stand* his behaving in that wrong manner!"—and that it is *his* thought and not the other *person's* action which really causes his own anger. Moreover, he often becomes so involved and absorbed in his angry feelings, that he finds it almost impossible to believe that they are related to any kind of thinking. For he *feels* his emotions deeply; and the thoughts that caused them are not really felt (even though they are experienced) or viscerally perceived.

Even in those instances in which the individual is quite capable of seeing that his feelings are integrally related to his thoughts, he is usually (and, again, normally) incapable of seeing this very sharply *while* his intense feelings are in progress. Thus, the woman who gets terribly angry at her mother may *later*, after her anger has run its course and been dissipated or diverted mainly by the passing of time, perceive that she really *didn't* have to make herself angry, and it *was* her own illogical thinking that produced her strong emotion. But while her anger itself lasts, she may be almost totally incapable of perceiving the connection between it and her own thinking. Her time lag between becoming angry and recognizing that she actually thought up her own anger is usually so long, that by the time she gets around to observing and working at her anger-creating thoughts it is much too late to prevent her from venting her spleen on her mother and from defeating some of her own best interests in the process.

Moreover, if this woman generally recognizes the connection between her anger and her illogical thinking considerably after the anger has passed, she is almost necessarily going to be fairly ineffective about teaching herself not to become angry again the next time a similar situation with her mother occurs. If a tennis player sees, while he is engaged in playing a match, that he is hitting the ball too hard and therefore lobbing it over his opponent's back line, he will usually, *right then and there*, force himself to take gentler swings at the ball; and in a short period of time, he will often be able to correct his game. But if the angry woman, while arguing with her mother, right then and there does *not* try to correct herself (that is, to challenge her own irrational thinking and induce herself to become less angry) she will be in much the same position as the tennis player who thinks about and tries to correct his game only when he is lying in bed at night and is nowhere near a tennis court. Obviously, she is going to have a most difficult time practicing not becoming angry.

Because, then, of the perceptual and comprehension time lags involved in much of our emotional behavior, and especially in our perceiving that our emotions almost always are integrally connected with our thinking, it should be obvious that we will *easily* tend to behave self-defeatingly on many occasions and that we will have great *difficulty* in undoing our own neurotic self-sabotaging.

Ease of survival with disturbance. Individuals who are seriously handicapped physically have difficulty surviving in a competitive world; and when they do survive, they often cannot mate easily or have offspring. Consequently, any genetic tendency toward handicap which they may have tends to be eliminated. Serious emotional disturbance, however, can be indulged in for many years and rarely seems to shorten the individual's life or to prevent him from having many offspring. Biological tendencies toward such disturbance can therefore easily be passed on to one's descendants, and may continue to thrive unabatedly for generation after generation.

What is more important, perhaps, in any particular instance of neurosis is that the afflicted person soon discovers that, however handicapping his disturbance is, he rarely will die of it, nor even appreciably shorten his life by continuing to be afflicted by it. He therefore will rarely have a *dire need* of ridding himself of his neurosis; and, considering the onerousness of the efforts which he will usually have to make to eradicate it, he may well find it seemingly easier to go on living with it than to work hard against it.

To make matters still worse, many neurotic symptoms (as the psychoanalysts have pointed out for many years now) carry with them distinct gains. No matter how debilitating a person's disturbance is, he usually finds that, with practice, he can *easily* adjust to it. There is a familiarity and a predictableness about it that makes it seem almost like an old friend; and he soon comes to know the *limits* of its handicaps. Thus, an individual who is afraid to speak up in public can, after years of practiced maneuvers, fairly easily manage to avoid being called on, to have suitable excuses handy in case he is called upon, to stay home from gatherings where he may be asked to speak, etc. Eventually, he will become so practiced at avoiding public speaking that he will hardly be anxious about doing so, except on rare occasions. And so it becomes hardly worth his effort, he believes, to try to overcome his fear.

Neurotic gains may be even much more specific. By neurotically adopting and maintaining a homosexual way of life, for example, a male in our society can derive distinct substitute sex satisfactions, can find it easier to pick up male than female companions, can save money that he would have to spend courting girls, and can avoid the responsibilities of marriage, child-rearing, and home-making.

Because it is often so easy for an individual to survive with neurotic handicaps, and even to derive clear-cut gains from his symptoms, it is fairly obvious why many persons acquire neurotic symptomatology in the first place and why they will make practically no concerted effort to rid themselves of their symptoms in the second place. They learn to live with their neurosis and—almost—like it! And the biologically based *ease* of their being able to do so is one of the most important factors in their becoming and remaining emotionally disturbed.

Physical malaise. Many individuals, particularly females, are normally afflicted with all kinds of physical malaise which makes it exceptionally easy for them to become depressed, panicked, hostile, or otherwise emotionally disturbed. Women, for example, very easily tend to become depressed a few days before the start of their menstrual cycles; and most men and women tend to feel disturbed when they have severe colds, infections, illnesses, or states of fatigue.

It may well be that, during these periods of physiological debility, the individual is not as well able to muster his thinking resources as he is at other periods of his life, and that consequently he then is prone to think irrationally and to bring on negative emotional states. Or it may be that pathways of physical pain and malease tend to overlap with avenues of psychological responsiveness, and that the former negatively affect the latter (just as, on many occasions, the latter negatively affect the former).

In any event, few people *feel* good when they are in the throes of an intense headache, toothache, spell of respiratory wheezing, or other physical irritation. And since man is normally prey to many short and prolonged ailments and diseases, he can often easily become emotionally upset partially as a result of bodily discomfort. Moreover, when people are acutely or chronically ill, they frequently do not feel sufficiently energetic to tackle their psychological problems; and any psychotherapeutic attempts they may make at this time may easily be sabotaged.

Difficulty of sustained discipline. Although man at times enjoys a certain amount of sustained discipline, he also finds it onerous, in that it tends to become boring and monotonous and to interfere with spontaneity and freedom. Especially when he is young, but also when he is well on in years, he normally finds it terribly difficult to keep dieting, studying, planning, saving, or loving *forever*. And yet, alas, this is exactly what he has to do in many, many instances if he is to refrain from woefully defeating some of his most cherished aims. To gain one kind of freedom—especially freedom from anxiety—he frequently has to surrender various other kinds of freedom—especially the freedom to do exactly what he wants when he wants to do it.

In this respect, as in so many similar ones, man is continually torn between two opposing kinds of behavior, both of which have their distinct advantages and neither of which can entirely be foregone if he is to live a maximally happy kind of existence. Thus, to achieve a non-neurotic pathway he must (at various times and sometimes even at exactly the same time) be reasonably spontaneous *and* disciplined, flexible *and* firm, active *and* relaxed, cautious *and* risk-taking, hedonistic *and* altruistic, childlike *and* adult. This is awfully difficult! And, in a sense, he can never entirely win.

As we have previously noted, the moderate, sensible line of behavior between the two extreme and self-defeating ways of acting on both sides of this line, is often exceptionally narrow and winding; and it is easy, all too easy, to deviate from it. It is therefore statistically normal for human beings to keep straying from the ideal path; and neurotic or self-defeating behavior must be looked upon as something of a usual rather than a rare occurrence.

As ever, just as it is difficult for the average (or above-average) person to be sustainedly self-disciplined and thereby to remain unneurotic, it is just as (or even more) difficult for him to maintain steady discipline when he is trying to uproot his neurosis. For it is easier and more spontaneous for neurotics to let themselves act according to their disordered feelings rather than to keep observing, analyzing, and challenging the basic ideologies that lie behind these feelings (as they have to do in any effective form of psychotherapy). Peculiarly enough, even when disturbed individuals are over-disciplined—as, for example, when they are engaging in obsessive-compulsive behavior—it is still easier, at least in the short run, for them to cling to this dysfunctional and rigid kind of discipline than it is for them to force themselves to become more flexible and more sensibly disciplined. Almost *any* pathway that a human being is traveling along at a given moment seems to him to be more spontaneous and enjoyable than would be his forcibly turning to a new, less chartered path. And, as previously noted in this book, even though his long-range goals and happiness might well be benefited by his changing his route, the tenacity of his short-range hedonistic goals may well win out for the present—and, alas, for many presents to come.

Therapeutic handling of biological tendencies toward irrational behavior. If what we have been pointing out in this chapter is even half true, it would appear that there are a great many inborn human tendencies toward irrational thinking and behaving; and that therefore it is hardly surprising that virtually all human beings, whatever the culture in which they are reared, easily become and remain neurotic or psychotic. If so, what are some of the basic solutions that can be suggested for this problem?

One solution, obviously, would be to change human nature. If man is easily a victim of emotional disturbance because he is "human," then the less human he might be enabled to become the less disturbed he might be. Changing his basic biological structure by drugs, operations, genetic breeding, etc. might be a possible answer in this connection.

Unfortunately, this answer is not, at the moment, either very clear or possible. Even if man's biological essence could be radically altered by some breeding or postbreeding procedure, it is not even reasonably obvious what specific alterations would be desirable. Shall we, for example, try to change people's structure so that they become naturally and easily more cautious, stable, and work-oriented? Or shall we, on the contrary, try to make them more adventurous, spontaneous, and carefree? Shall we endeavor to increase their suggestibility and docility (so that they will be easier to get along with)—or to strengthen their independence and grandiosity (so that they would be more individually expressive)?

Until a great deal more experimentation has been done in

respect to what it would truly be best for humans, for the sake of themselves and others, to be, it would be awfully rash for us to try fooling around with their biological make-up. Almost every basic trait has its distinct advantages as well as its disadvantages; and, as yet, there is no telling exactly what will happen if one of the present outstandingly human traits (such as suggestibility or excitement-seeking) is either biologically over-emphasized or de-emphasized.

Moreover, there exists a kind of balanced ecological relationship between the appearance of certain human traits and other (desirable and undesirable) traits; and if one outstanding trait were somehow eliminated or pronouncedly emphasized, the effects that would ensue are almost impossible to imagine or predict. Considerable experimental investigation would have to be done in this respect before reasonably valid answers could be given.

There may be various other disadvantages, moreover, to changing the basic biological structure of human beings, even if this becomes (as it is increasingly becoming) quite possible to do. If the biological basis of neurosis were completely overcome, it is possible that men and women would be too alike and undifferentiated to enjoy each other very much; that they would eventually lose much of their motivation for living and striving (including the challenge of working with and trying to surmount their own biological limitations); that they might become too over-specialized (as did some prehistoric animals) and therefore less capable of ultimate survival; etc. Quite probably, it will be to the advantage of the human race if we breed out or otherwise biologically eliminate some of the clearly "bad" characteristics, such as extreme mental deficiency, psychosis, and physical handicaps. But there is no evidence that we would become or remain essentially better off if we tried to eliminate *all* the neuroticizing tendencies which we have outlined in this chapter.

The other solution to the problem of our biological predispositions to emotional disturbance is for human beings to try to acquire an unusually good philosophy of life which will enable them, albeit with much continual effort, to live successfully and happily *in spite of* their intrinsic handicaps. Or, stated differently, assuming that people are not (at least in the immediate future) going to become appreciably less neurotic by biochemical means, they'd better try to change their internal and external environments so that they can best live with their existing handicaps.

This means, as is often forgotten by psychologists and psychiatrists, *two* things instead of one. The first of these things, as the Freudians and others have pointed out for years, is that the individual should understand the environmental influences on his life, and do his best to alleviate, or stop fomenting, their pernicious influences. Thus, he should understand that his parents blamed him severely when he was very young, and that he does not *have* to keep blaming himself in a similar manner now.

The second thing, which is sadly neglected by many psychologists, is that a person should understand the *biological* influences on his life, and do his best to alleviate or stop aiding *them*. Thus, in addition to ceasing to give himself an *unnecessary* hard time by carrying on the blaming that his parents (and others) showed him how to do during his youth, he must teach himself to combat and surmount his "necessary" difficulties—that is, his innate tendencies to blame and punish himself for normal mistakes and errors.

Similarly with other aspects of an individual's disturbances. Where it is sometimes relatively easy to see that he learned various anxieties and hostilities and that he can, with effort, unlearn these negative feelings, it is often harder for him to accept the fact that he was born with certain tendencies toward making himself anxious and hostile, and that he can also counter *these* tendencies. Perhaps the main issue here is that of effort versus near-magic. For if a man learned to hate his father and now neurotically hates all men who resemble him, there is a kind of magic about getting insight into his early hatred and, through this insight, being able now to undo the hatred of men who are similar to his father. This magical and almost effortless quality of insight into learned behavior is what makes the psychoanalytic kinds of therapy so attractive to so many patients who actually derive very little benefit from prolonged analyses.

If, on the other hand, a person fully accepts the facts that his tendency to hate those who do not immediately gratify his wishes, and that his hatred of his father as well as his later hating other men who resemble him actually originated in a biologically-based tendency to hate anyone who does not go along with his grandiose conception of himself, a much more difficult therapeutic task is now at hand. For insight into his inherited tendencies to hate others will *not* magically eliminate these tendencies, even though it will pinpoint the precise area at which they may be attacked. *After* he gains this kind of insight, the individual will have to *keep* working and working, with its help, to contradict and challenge his own innate (as well as early acquired) grandiose trends.

If, in other words, a man were purely associationally conditioned to hate his father and men who resemble him, he could simply understand this form of conditioning, and could say to himself: "Well, this is ridiculous! So my father was a hostile and persecutory person who blamed me severely when I was young. But these other men are *not* my father; so why should I hate them as well as him?" And, with this degree of insight, his hatred of his father might well remain; but the hatred of the other men could quickly vanish.

This, however, is not a true description of the situation. Actually, if the biological underpinnings of emotional disturbance described in this chapter exist, this situation involves a complexity of elements, such as these: (*a*) A person has a fundamental, innate tendency to want or demand his own way and to abhor frustration. (*b*) His father, for various reasons of his own (including the reason that *he* wants *his* way and does not want to be frustrated), behaves badly toward the son by being non-accepting and thwarting. (*c*) For "natural" reasons (his discomfort at being thwarted) as well as artificially and unnecessarily acquired reasons (such as the fairy-tale acquired unrealistic philosophy that he *should* not be thwarted), the son becomes terribly hostile toward his father. (*d*) When he later meets other men who resemble his father, he hates them too because (*1*) he associates them to the father and the prior discomfort of being thwarted and (2) he is still (because of his biologically-based tendencies toward grandiosity) terribly resentful of the possibility of being disapproved and thwarted and there *is* a chance (however slight) that these new men will balk him just as his father previously did.

If these conditions better describe the origin of a person's hostility than does the simpler hypothesis of associational conditioning, it can be seen that insight into the process will not of itself undo his hostility. For he still has to face the fact that he *does* naturally tend to be grandiose (today as well as in the past), and that the only full solution to the problem is for him to tackle and bring his feelings of grandiosity down to reasonable proportions. For if—and only if—this kind of attack on his own basic tendencies occurs, will he be able (*a*) really to understand and accept his father's original thwarting, and hence be able to stop blaming and being hostile toward him; and (*b*) truly to see and eliminate his own undue feelings toward others *whether or not* they resemble his father.

More concretely, a full solution of the problem will require a man's own saying to himself, as soon as he begins to feel hostile: (*a*) *I* am creating my own hostility; it is *not* being created by external people or things (such as my father or men who resemble him). (*b*) I am creating this hostility because, first, I have natural grandiose tendencies which make me think that I should always be catered to by others and, second, I have picked up, somewhere along the line, unrealistic philosophies of life which help me bolster these natural tendencies. (*c*) My natural grandiose tendencies that lead to my hostility are going to be quite difficult for me to combat, just because they are part and parcel of my being human; but nonetheless I can work against them, when they arise, by saying to myself: "I *don't* have to get what I want, even though I want it very badly; and it is *not* horrible and awful if my father or other men do not satisfy my wants." In this manner, I can work philosophically *against* my own self-defeating tendencies to think unclearly about my being frustrated by others. (*d*) Similarly, my acquired unrealistic philosophies which help me bolster my natural tendencies toward grandiosity and low frustration tolerance can also be fought and changed, so that I no longer am victimized by believing them.

If, whenever an individual feels hostile either toward his father or toward other men who resemble him, he questions and challenges his negative emotions in this philosophic manner, then not only will the associationally conditioned aspects of his neurotic behavior tend to become extinguished, but all the other important aspects of his unnecessary (albeit partially "normal") hostility to others will tend to be both specifically and generally ameliorated. This, exactly, is the aim in rational-emotive therapy: not merely to challenge and question the individual's "abnormal," psychodynamically created, or personally induced irrational thinking and behaving; but, just as importantly, also clearly and unblamefully to accept the existence of his "normal," innate tendencies toward irrationality, and clearheadedly to fight those as well.

This is not to say that RT tries to turn the individual into a nonhuman or a superhuman being. It doesn't. And, in that it realistically assesses and at least temporarily *accepts* the full measure of his humanity, it is more in consonance with his humanity, than are many other forms of psychotherapy which unwittingly look upon man as a kind of superhuman animal. But after objectively accepting man for what he is, RT does frankly attempt to help him become a more rational, more efficient person in many ways. *Perfectly* sensible and effective it does not think he is ever likely to be; but *more* logical and *less* self-defeating than is his normal and abnormal wont, it does have some confidence in his becoming.

References

Abelson, Herbert I. *Persuasion.* New York: Springer, 1959.

Adkins, L. J. The creative factor in man. *Christian Century,* Jan. 14, 1959.

Adler, Alfred. *Understanding human nature.* New York: Greenberg, 1927.

Adler, Alfred. *The science of living.* New York: Greenberg, 1929.

Adler, Alfred. *What life should mean to you.* New York: Blue Ribbon Books, 1931.

Alexander, Franz, and French, Thomas M. *Psychoanalytic therapy.* New York: Ronald, 1946.

Allen, Clifford. *The sexual perversions and abnormalities.* London: Oxford, 1949.

Ansbacher, H. L., and Ansbacher, Rowena R. (Eds.). *The individual psychology of Alfred Adler.* New York: Basic Books, 1956.

Appel, Kenneth E. Psychotherapy: general principles. *J. So. Carolina Med. Assn.,* 1957, 53, 371-378.

Arnheim, Rudolf. Emotion and feeling in psychology and art. *Confin. Psychiat.,* 1958, 1, 69-88.

Arnold, Magda. *Emotion and personality.* 2 vols. New York: Columbia University Press, 1960.

Astin, Alexander W. The functional autonomy of psychotherapy. *Amer. Psychologist,* 1961, 16, 75-78.

Ausubel, David P. Personality disorder is disease. *Amer. Psychologist,* 1961, 16, 69-74.

Ayer, A. J. *Language, truth and logic.* New York: Dover Publications, 1947.

Bach, George R. *Intensive group psychotherapy.* New York: Ronald, 1954.

Bain, Read. Review of Lipset and Lowenthal's *Culture and social character. Science,* 1962, 135, 32.

Bakan, D. Clinical psychology and logic. *Amer. Psychologist,* 1956, 11, 655-662.

Baker, Blanche M. Toward understanding. *One,* 1959, 7, No. 1, 25-26.

Barber, B. Resistance by scientists to scientific discovery. *Science*, 1961, 134, 596-601.

Barrett, William. *Irrational man*. New York: Doubleday, 1958.

Bartlett, Frederick. *Thinking*. London: Allen & Unwin, 1958.

Behr, Zalman. Consciousness and practice in rational psychotherapy. *Science & Soc.*, 1950, 17, 193-210.

Bell, Daniel. *Work and its discontents*. Boston: Beacon, 1956.

Bell, David. Science and Dr. Ellis. *Mattachine Rev.*, 1959, 5, No. 7, 5-7.

Bergler, Edmund. *Homosexuality*. New York: Hill & Wang, 1956.

Berlyne, D. E. *Conflict, arousal and curiosity*. New York: McGraw-Hill, 1960.

Berne, Eric. Ego states in psychotherapy. *Amer. J. Psychother.*, 1957, 11, 293-309.

Bernheim, H. *Suggestive therapeutics*. New York: London Book Co., 1887, 1947.

Boas, George. *The limits of reason*. New York: Harper, 1961.

Bousfield, W. A., and Orbison, W. D. Ontogenesis of emotional behavior. *Psychol. Rev.*, 1952, 59, 1-7.

Bowers, M. K., Brecher, S., and Polatin, A. Hypnosis in the study and treatment of schizophrenia. Manuscript, 1958.

Bowser, Hollowell. The long, shrill city. *Sat. Review*, Jan. 27, 1962, 24.

Braaten, Leif J. The main theories of "existentialism" from the viewpoint of a psychotherapist. *Ment. Hyg.*, 1961, 45, 10-17.

Brady, John Paul, and others. MMPI correlates of operant behavior. *J. Clin. Psychol.*, 1962, 18, 67-70.

Branden, Nathaniel. The emotional side of human nature. *Objectivist Newsletter*. January 1962, 3.

Breland, Keller, and Breland, Marian. The misbehavior of organisms. *Amer. Psychologist*, 1961, 16, 681-684.

Bronowski, J. Science and human values. *Nation*, 1956, 183, 549-556.

Brown, Daniel G. Transvestism and sex-role inversion. In Ellis, Albert, and Abarbanel, Albert (Eds.). *Encyclopedia of sexual behavior*. New York: Hawthorn Books, 1961.

Brown, Roger W. *Words and things*. New York: Basic Books, 1960.

Bruner, Jerome S., Goodnow, Jacqueline J. and Austin, George. *A study of thinking*. New York: Wiley, 1956.

Brunswik, E. *The conceptual framework of psychology*. Chicago: Chicago University Press, 1952.

Buber, Martin. *Between man and man*. Boston: Beacon, 1955.

Bull, Nina. An introduction to attitude psychology. *J. Clin. Exper. Psychopathol.*, 1960, 27, 147-156.

Burke, Kenneth. *A rhetoric of motives.* New York: Prentice-Hall, 1950.

Burke, Kenneth. *A grammar of motives.* New York: Prentice-Hall, 1954.

Burrow, Trigant. *Science and man's behavior.* New York: Phillosophical Library, 1953.

Callahan, Roger. Value orientation and psychotherapy. *Amer. Psychologist*, 1960, 15, 269-270.

Cameron, D. E. *General psychotherapy.* New York: Grune & Stratton, 1950.

Cassirer, Ernst, *Essay on man.* New York: Doubleday Anchor Books, 1953.

Chambers, Jay L., and Lieberman, Lewis R. Variability of normal and maladjusted groups in attributing needs to best-liked and least-liked people. *J. Clin. Psychol.*, 1962, 18, 98-101.

Church, Joseph. *Language and the discovery of reality.* New York: Random House, 1961.

Ciardi, John. The Armenian heresy. *Sat. Rev.*, January 27, 1962, 27.

Clausen, John A. Review of Yehudi Cohen's *Structure and Personality. Science*, 1961, 134, 662.

Cleckley, H. *The mask of sanity.* St. Louis: Mosby. 1950.

Cobb, Stanley. *Emotions and clinical medicine.* New York: Norton, 1950.

Cohen, Arthur R., Stotland, Ezra, and Wolfe, Donald M. An experimental investigation of need for cognition. *J. Abnorm. Soc. Psychol.*, 1955, 51, 291-294.

Combs, A. W., and Snygg, D. *Individual behavior.* New York: Harper, 1960.

Corsini, Raymond J., Shaw, Malcolm E., and Blake, Robert R. *Role playing in business and industry.* New York: Free Press, 1961. 1961.

Cory, Donald Webster (Ed.). *Homosexuality: a cross cultural approach.* New York: Julian, 1956.

Cory, Donald Webster. *The homosexual in America.* New York: Castle Books, 1960.

Cory, Donald Webster. Homosexuality. In Ellis, Albert, and Abarbanel, Albert (Eds.). *The encyclopedia of sexual behavior.* New York: Hawthorn Books, 1961.

Coué, Emile. *My method.* New York: Doubleday, Page, 1923.

Cuber, John F., Harper, Robert A., and Kenkel, William F. *Problems of American society.* New York: Holt, 1956.

de Grazia, Sebastian. *Errors of psychotherapy.* New York: Doubleday, 1952.

Dejerine, J., and Gaukler, E. *Psychoneurosis and psychotherapy.* Philadelphia: Lippincott, 1913.

de Laguna, Grace. Culture and personality. *Amer. Anthropol.,* 1949, 51, 379-391.

Deutsch, F., and Murphy, W. F. *The clinical interview.* New York: International Universities Press, 1955.

Diaz-Guerrera, Rogelio. Socratic therapy. In Standal, Stanley W., and Corsini, Raymond J. (Eds.). *Critical incidents in psychotherapy.* Englewood Cliffs, N. J.: Prentice-Hall, 1959.

Diggory, James C. Sex-differences in judging the acceptability of actions. *J. Soc. Psychol.,* 1962, 56, 107-114.

Dilger, William C. The behavior of lovebirds. *Sci. American.* January 1962, 89-99.

Dollard, John, and Miller, Neal. *Personality and psychotherapy.* New York: McGraw-Hill, 1950.

Dreikurs, Rudolf. *Fundamentals of Adlerian psychology.* New York: Greenberg, 1950.

Dreikurs, Rudolf. *The Adlerian approach on the changing scope of psychiatry.* Chicago: Author, 1955.

Dubois, Paul. *The psychic treatment of nervous disorders.* New York: Funk & Wagnalls, 1907.

Eichenlaub, John E. *The marriage art.* New York: Lyle Stuart, 1962.

Eisenstein, V. W. (Ed.). *Neurotic interaction in marriage.* New York: Basic Books, 1956.

Ellis, Albert. *An introduction to the scientific principles of psychoanalysis.* Provincetown, Mass.: Journal Press, 1950.

Ellis, Albert. Application of clinical psychology to sexual disorders. In Brower, Daniel, and Abt, Lawrence A. (Eds.). *Progress in clinical psychology.* New York: Grune & Stratton, 1952.

Ellis, Albert. *New approaches to psychotherapy techniques.* Brandon, Vermont: Journal of Clinical Psychology, 1955a.

Ellis, Albert. Psychotherapy techniques for use with psychotics. *Amer. J. Psychother.,* 1955b, 9, 452-476.

Ellis, Albert. Are homosexuals necessarily neurotic? *One,* April, 1955c, 3, No. 4, 8-12.

Ellis, Albert. An operational reformulation of some of the basic principles of psychoanalysis. *Psychoanal. Rev.*, 1956a, 43, 163-180. Also published in Feigl, Herbert, and Scriven, Michael (Eds.). *Minnesota studies in the philosophy of science. Vol. I.* Minneapolis: University of Minnesota Press, 1956a.

Ellis, Albert. A critical evaluation of marriage counseling. *Marr. Fam. Living*, 1956b, 18, 65-71.

Ellis, Albert. The effectiveness of psychotherapy with individuals who have severe homosexual problems. *J. Consult. Psychol.*, 1956c, 20, 191-195.

Ellis, Albert. *How to live with a neurotic.* New York: Crown, 1957a.

Ellis, Albert. Outcome of employing three techniques of psychotherapy. *J. Clin. Psychol.*, 1957b, 13, 334-350.

Ellis, Albert. Neurotic interaction between marital partners. *J. Counseling. Psychol.*, 1958a, 5, 24-28.

Ellis, Albert. *Sex without guilt.* New York: Lyle Stuart, 1958b.

Ellis, Albert. Rationalism and its therapeutic applications. In Ellis, Albert (Ed.). *The place of value in the practice of psychotherapy.* New York: American Academy of Psychotherapists, 1959.

Ellis, Albert. *The art and science of love.* New York: Lyle Stuart, 1960.

Ellis, Albert. *The folklore of sex.* New York: Grove Press, 1961a.

Ellis, Albert. Frigidity. In Ellis, Albert, and Abarbanel, Albert (Eds.). *The encyclopedia of sexual behavior.* New York: Hawthorn Books, 1961b.

Ellis, Albert. What is "normal" sex behavior? *Sexology.* 1962a, 28, 364-369.

Ellis Albert. *The American sexual tragedy.* New York: Lyle Stuart, 1962b.

Ellis, Albert, and Harper, Robert A. *A guide to rational living.* Englewood Cliffs, N. J.: Prentice-Hall, 1961a.

Ellis, Albert, and Harper, Robert A. *Creative marriage.* New York: Lyle Stuart, 1961b.

English, H. B., and English, Ava C. *A comprehensive dictionary of psychological and psychoanalytical terms.* New York: Longmans, Green, 1958.

Eysenck, H. J. *Uses and abuses of psychology.* London: Penguin, 1953.

Eysenck, H. J. Levels of personality, constitutional factors, and social influences: an experimental approach. *Int. J. Soc. Psychiat.*, 1960, 6, 12-24.

Eysenck, H. J. (Ed.). *Handbook of abnormal psychology.* New York: Basic Books, 1961.

Feigl, Herbert, and Scriven, Michael (Eds.). *Minnesota studies in the philosophy of science. Vol. I.* Minneapolis: University of Minnesota Press, 1956.

Feigl, Herbert, and Sellers, Wilfred (Eds.). *Readings in philosophical analysis.* New York: Appleton-Century-Crofts, 1949.

Fenichel, O. *Psychoanalytic theory of neurosis.* New York: Norton, 1945.

Ferenczi, Sandor. *Further contributions to the theory and technique of psychoanalysis.* New York: Basic Books, 1952.

Ferster, C. B. Reinforcement and punishment in the control of human behavior by social agencies. In Social aspects of psychiatry. *Psychiat. Res. Rep.*, 1958, No. 10, 101-118.

Festinger, Leon. *A theory of cognitive dissonance.* Evanston, Ill.: Row, Peterson, 1957.

Finch, Roy. The totalitarian mind. *Liberation.* Summer, 1959, 6-11.

Fink, Harold K. *Long journey.* New York: Julian Press, 1954.

Fink, Harold K. Why do husbands and wives cheat? II. *Real Life Guide*, February 1962, 26-39.

Frank, Jerome. *Persuasion and healing.* Baltimore: Williams and Wilkins, 1961.

Frankel, Charles. Review of William Barrett's *Irrational man. New York Times Book Rev.*, Sept. 7, 1958, p. 8.

Frazer, J. G. *The new golden bough.* New York: Criterion, 1959.

French, Thomas M. *The integration of behavior.* 4 vols. Chicago: Chicago University Press, 1952-1960.

Freud, Anna. *The ego and the mechanisms of defense.* London: Hogarth, 1937.

Freud, Sigmund. *The future of an illusion.* London: Hogarth, 1927.

Freud, Sigmund. *Collected papers.* London: Imago Publishers, 1924-1950.

Freud, Sigmund. *Basic writings.* New York: Modern Library, 1938.

Freud, Sigmund. *Outline of psychoanalysis.* New York: Norton, 1949.

Freud, Sigmund. *Letters.* New York: Basic Books, 1960.

Freud, Sigmund, and Breuer, Josef. *Studies in hysteria.* New York: Basic Books, 1895, 1957.

Friedman, Ira. Phenomenal, ideal and projected conceptions of self. *J. Abnorm. Soc. Psychol.*, 1955, 51, 611-615.

Fromm, Erich. *Escape from freedom.* New York: Farrar & Rinehart, 1941.

Fromm, Erich. *Man for himself.* New York: Rinehart, 1947.

Fromm, Erich. *Psychoanalysis and religion.* New Haven: Yale University Press, 1950.

Fromm, Erich. *The sane society.* New York: Rinehart, 1955.

Glover, Edward. *An investigation of the techniques of psychoanalysis.* Baltimore: Williams & Wilkins, 1940.

Goldstein, Kurt. The concept of health, disease, and therapy. *Amer. J. Psychother.*, 1954, 8, 745-764.

Greene, Maxine. Review of George Boas' *The limits of reason. Sat. Rev.*, Jan. 18, 1961.

Grimes, Pierre. Alcibiades. A dialogue utilizing the dialectic as a mode of psychotherapy for alcoholics. *Quart. J. Studies Alc.*, 1961, 22, 277-297.

Guze, Henry. Mechanism and psychotherapy. In Ellis, Albert (Ed.). *The place of value in the practice of psychotherapy.* New York: American Academy of Psychotherapists, 1959.

Hamilton, Eleanor. *Partners in love.* New York: Ziff-Davis, 1961.

Hamilton, G. V. *An introduction to objective psychopathology.* St. Louis: Mosby, 1925.

Hamilton, Prudence. *The greatest role in the world.* New York: Vantage, 1962.

Harper, Robert A. *Psychoanalysis and psychotherapy: 36 systems.* Englewood Cliffs, N. J.: Prentice-Hall, 1959.

Harper, Robert A. A rational process-oriented approach to marriage. *J. Family Welfare*, 1960a, 6, 1-10.

Harper, Robert A. Marriage counseling as rational process-oriented psychotherapy. *J. Individ. Psychol.*, 1960b, 16, 192-207.

Harper, Robert A. Talk at the Advanced Training Seminar of the Institute for Rational Living, Inc., Nov. 5, 1960c.

Hartman, Robert S. *The measurement of value.* Crotonville, N. Y.: General Electric Co., 1959.

Hartmann, Heinz, Kris, Ernst, and Loewenstein, Rudolph M. Comments on the formation of psychic structure. *Psychoanal. Stud. Child.*, 1947, 2, 5-30.

Hartmann, Heinz, Kris, Ernst, and Loewenstein, Rudolph M. Notes on the theory of aggression. *Psychoanal. Stud. Child.*, 1949, 3, 9-36.

Hartmann, Walter. The free will controversy. *Amer. Psychologist,* 1961, 16, 37-38.

Henry, George W. *All the sexes.* New York: Rinehart, 1955.

Herzberg, Alexander. *Active psychotherapy.* New York: Grune & Stratton, 1945.

Hilgard, Ernest R. *Theories of learning.* New York: Appleton-Century-Crofts, 1956.

Hilgard, Ernest R. *Unconscious processes and man's rationality.* Urbana: University of Illinois Press, 1958.

Hirsch, Edwin W. *Modern sex life.* New York: New American Library, 1957.

Hitschmann, E., and Bergler, E. Frigidity in women. *Psychoanal. Rev.*, 1949, 36, 45-53.

Hoch, P. H., and Zubin, J. (Eds.). *Anxiety.* New York: Grune & Stratton, 1950.

Hoffer, Eric. *The true believer.* New York: Harper, 1951.

Hoffer, Eric. *The passionate state of mind.* New York: Harper, 1955.

Hooker, Evelyn. The adjustment of the male overt homosexual. *J. Proj. Tech.*, 1957, 21, 18-31.

Hora, Thomas. On meeting a Zen master socially. *Psychologia,* 1961, 4, 73-75.

Horney, Karen. *Neurotic personality of our time.* New York: Norton, 1937.

Horney, Karen. *New ways in psychoanalysis.* New York: Norton, 1939.

Horney, Karen. *Neurosis and human growth.* New York: Norton, 1950.

Hovland, Carl I., and Janis, Irving L. *Personality and persuasibility.* New Haven: Yale, 1959.

Hudson, John W. *Values and psychotherapy.* In manuscript, 1961.

Hunt, J. McV. (Ed.). *Personality and the behavior disorders.* New York: Ronald, 1944.

Hunt, Wilson L. Psychotherapy as a group process. *J. General Psychol.*, 1962, 66, 61-69.

Israeli, Nathan. Creative art: a self-observation study. *J. General Psychol.*, 1962, 66, 33-45.

Jackson, C. W. Jr., and Kelly, E. Lowell. Influence of suggestion on subjects' prior knowledge in research on sensory deprivation. *Science*, 1962, 135, 211-212.

Jacobson, Edmund. *You must relax.* New York: McGraw-Hill, 1942.

Johnson, D. M. *The psychology of thought and judgment.* New York: Harper, 1955.

Johnson, Wendell. *People in quandaries.* New York: Harper, 1946.

Joint Commission on Mental Illness and Health. *Action for mental health.* New York: Basic Books, 1961.

Jones, Jack. To the end of thought. *Newspaper,* 1958, No. 6, 1-35.

Jones, Jack. Ideology in the fourth dimension. *Liberation,* Summer, 1959, 12-17.

Jung, C. G. *The practice of psychotherapy.* New York: Pantheon, 1954.

Keeley, Kim. Prenatal influence on behavior of offspring of crowded mice. *Science,* 1962, 135, 44-45.

Kelly, George. *The psychology of personal constructs.* New York: Norton, 1955.

Kinsey, Alfred C., Pomeroy, Wardell B., and Martin, Clyde E. *Sexual behavior in the human male.* Philadelphia: Saunders, 1948.

Kinsey, Alfred C., Pomeroy, Wardell B., Martin, Clyde E., and Gebhard, Paul H. *Sexual behavior in the human female.* Philadelphia: Saunders, 1953.

Kleegman, Sophia J. Frigidity. *Quart. Rev. Surg. Obstet. & Gynecol.,* 1959, 16, 243-248.

Kline, Milton V. *Hypnodynamic psychology.* New York: Julian Press, 1955.

Korzybski, Alfred. *Science and sanity.* Lancaster, Pa.: Lancaster Press, 1933.

Korzybski, Alfred. The role of language in the perceptual process. In Blake, R. R., and Ramsey, G. V. (Eds.). *Perception.* New York: Ronald, 1951.

Krout, Maurice H. (Ed.). *Psychology, psychiatry and the public interest.* Minneapolis: University of Minnesota Press, 1956.

Kupperman, Herbert S. Frigidity: endocrinological aspects. *Quart. Rev. Surg. Obstet. & Gynecol.,* 1959, 16, 254-257.

LaBarre, Weston. *The human animal.* Chicago: University of Chicago Press, 1955.

Lederer, Wolfgang. Primitive psychotherapy. *Psychiatry,* 1959, 22, 255-265.

Levine, Maurice. *Psychotherapy in medical practice.* New York: Macmillan, 1942.

Lewis, C. L. The nature of ethical disagreement. In Feigl, Herbert, and Sellars, Wilfrid (Eds.). *Readings in philosophical analysis.* New York: Appleton-Century-Crofts, 1949.

Lichtenberg, Philip. Comparative value and ideational action. *J. Soc. Psychol.,* 1962, 56, 97-105.

Lindner, Robert. *Rebel without a cause.* New York: Grune & Stratton, 1944.

Lindner, Robert. *Prescription for rebellion.* London: Gollancz, 1953.

Lipset, Seymour, and Lowenthal, Leo (Eds.). *Culture and social character.* New York: Free Press, 1961.

Liswood, Rebecca. *A marriage doctor speaks her mind about sex.* New York: Dutton, 1961.

Loevinger, Jane. Measuring personality patterns of women. *Genet. Psychol. Monogr.,* 1962, 65, 53-136.

London, Louis S., and Caprio, Frank S. *Sexual deviations.* Washington: Linacre, 1950.

London, Perry. The morals of psychotherapy. *Columbia Univ. Forum,* Fall, 1961.

Low, Abraham A. *Mental health through will-training.* Boston: Christopher Publishing Co., 1952.

Lynn, David. The organism as a manufacturer of theories. *Psychol. Rep.,* 1957, 3, 353-359.

Maltz, Maxwell. *Psychocybernetics.* Englewood Cliffs, N.J.: Prentice-Hall, 1960.

Mark, Henry J. Elementary thinking and the classification of behavior. *Science,* 1962, 135, 75-88.

Marschak, J. Rational behavior, uncertain prospects and measurable utility. *Econometrica,* 1950, 18, 111-141.

Martí-Ibáñez, Felix. *Centaur.* New York: MD Publications, 1960.

Maslow, A. H. *Motivation and personality.* New York: Harper, 1954.

Masor, Nathan. *The new psychiatry.* New York: Philosophical Library, 1959.

May, Rollo. *Man's search for himself.* New York: Norton, 1953.

May, Rollo. *Existential psychology.* New York: Random House, 1961.

May, Rollo, Angel, Ernest, and Ellenberger, Henri F. (Eds.). *Existence: a new dimension in psychiatry and psychology.* New York: Basic Books, 1958.

McClelland, D. C. *Personality.* New York: Sloane, 1951.

McCurdy, H. G. Review of E. H. Gombrich's *Art and illusion. Contemp. Psychol.,* 1960, 5, 241-243.

McGill, V. J. *Emotions and reason.* Springfield, Ill.: Charles C Thomas, 1954.

Mead, G. H. *Mind, self and society.* Chicago: University of Chicago Press, 1936.

Melzack, Ronald. The perception of pain. *Scientific Amer.,* Feb. 1961, 41-49.

Menninger, Karl. *Theory of psychoanalytic technique.* New York: Basic Books, 1958.

Mercer, J. D. *They walk in shadow.* New York: Comet, 1959.

Meyer, Adolf. *The commonsense psychiatry of Dr. Adolf Meyer.* Edited by Dr. Alfred Lief. New York: McGraw-Hill, 1948.

Miller, J. G. Review of Joint Commission on Mental Health's *Action for mental health. Contemp. Psychol.,* 1961, 6, 293-296.

Money, John. Hermaphroditism. In Ellis, Albert, and Abarbanel, Albert (Eds.). *The encyclopedia of sexual behavior.* New York: Hawthorn Books, 1961.

Moreno, J. L., and Borgatta, E. F. An experiment with sociodrama and sociometry in industry. *Sociometry,* 1951, 14, 71-104.

Morris, C. W. *Signs, language, and behavior.* New York: Prentice-Hall, 1946.

Moustakas, Clark. Self-exploration of teachers in a seminar in interpersonal relations. *J. Individ. Psychol.,* 1957, 13, 72-93.

Mowrer, O. H. (Ed.). *Psychotherapy: theory and research.* New York: Ronald, 1953.

Mowrer, O. H. *Learning theory and behavior.* New York: Wiley, 1960a.

Mowrer, O. H. Some constructive features of the concept of sin. *J. Counseling Psychol.,* 1960b, 7, 185-188.

Mowrer, O. H. "Sin," the lesser of two evils. *Amer. Psychologist,* 1960c, 15, 301-304.

Muncie, Wendell. *Psychobiology and psychiatry.* St. Louis: Mosby, 1939.

Munroe, Ruth. *Schools of psychoanalytic thought.* New York. Dryden, 1955.

Murphy, G. *Personality.* New York: Harper, 1947.

Myasischev, V., Bassin, F. V., and Yakovleva, Y. K. (Eds.). *The first psychiatric congress in Czechoslovakia. Psychiatry in the USSR and Czechoslovakia.* Washington: U.S. Joint Publications Research Service, 1961.

Pastore, Nicholas. A neglected factor in the frustration-aggression hypothesis. *J. Psychol.,* 1950, 29, 271-279.

Pastore, Nicholas. The role of arbitrariness in the frustration-aggression hypothesis. *J. Abnorm. Soc. Psychol.,* 1952, 47, 728-731.

Peller, Lili E. The child's approach to reality. *Amer. J. Orthopsychiat.,* 1939, 9, 503-513.

Perls, Frederick, Hefferline, Ralph, and Goodman, Paul. *Gestalt therapy.* New York: Julian Press, 1951.

Permyak, Yevgeny. The work principle in education. *Soviet Rev.,* 1962, 3, No. 1, 17-22.

Phillips, E. Lakin. *Psychotherapy.* Engelwood Cliffs, N. J.: Prentice-Hall, 1956.

Piaget, Jean. *The language and thought of the child.* New York: Humanities Press, 1952.

Piaget, Jean. *The moral judgment of the child.* Glencoe, Ill.: Free Press, 1954.

Piers, G., and Singer, M. G. *Shame and guilt.* Springfield, Ill.: Charles C Thomas, 1953.

Platonov, K. E. *The word as a physiological and therapeutic factor.* Moscow: Foreign Languages Publishing House, 1959.

Rand, Ayn. *For the new intellectual.* New York: Random House, 1961.

Rank, Otto. *Will therapy and truth and reality.* New York: Knopf, 1945.

Rapoport, Anatol. Scientific approach to ethics. *Science,* 1957, 125, 796-799.

Razran, Gregory. Inheritance in Soviet medicine, psychology, and education. *Science,* 1962, 135, 248-253.

Reich, Wilhelm. *Character analysis.* New York: Orgone Institute Press, 1949.

Reichenbach, Hans. *The rise of scientific philosophy.* Berkeley: University of California, 1953.

Reid, Mark. Nudism, Freud and preventive psychiatry. *Nude Living,* February 1962, 18-27.

Reik, Theodor. *Listening with the third ear.* New York: Rinehart, 1948.

Richter, C. P. Biological clocks. *Proc. Nat. Acad. Sci.,* 1960, 46, 1506-1530.

Riesman, David, Glazer, Nathan, and Denney, Reuel. *The lonely crowd.* New York: Doubleday Anchor Books, 1953.

Robbins, Bernard S. The myth of latent emotion. *Psychotherapy,* 1955, 1, 3-29.

Robbins, Bernard S. Consciousness: the central problem in psychiatry. *Psychotherapy,* 1956, 1, 150-153.

Robertiello, C. *Voyage from Lesbos.* New York: Citadel, 1959.

Rogers, Carl R. *Client-centered therapy.* Boston: Houghton Mifflin, 1951.

Rogers, Carl R. The necessary and sufficient conditions of therapeutic personality change. *J. Consult. Psychol.,* 1957, 21, 459-461.

Rokeach, Milton. *The open and closed mind.* New York: Basic Books, 1960.

Rosen, John N. *Direct analysis.* New York: Grune & Stratton, 1953.

Rosenfeld, Albert. The spell of that old quack magic. *Life.* January 12, 1962, 20-22.

Rotter, Julian B. *Social learning and clinical psychology.* New York: Prentice-Hall, 1954.

Royce, Joseph R. Psychology, existentialism, and religion. *J. General Psychol.,* 1962, 66, 3-16.

Russell, Bertrand. *The conquest of happiness.* New York: Pocket Books, 1950.

Ryle, G. The work of an influential but little-known philosopher of science: Ludwig Wittgenstein. *Scientific Amer.,* 1957, 197, No. 3, 251-259.

Sakano, N. Interaction of two signal systems. *Psychologia,* 1961, 4, 92-112.

Salter, Andrew. *Conditioned reflex therapy.* New York: Creative Age, 1949.

Salzinger, K. Experimental manipulation of verbal behavior. *J. Gen. Psychol.,* 1959, 61, 65-94.

Sargant, William. *Battle for the mind.* New York: Doubleday, 1957.

Sarnoff, Irving, and Katz, Daniel. The motivational bases of attitude change. *J. Abnorm. Soc. Psychol.,* 1954, 49, 115-124.

Sartre, Jean Paul. *Existentialism and human emotion.* New York: Philosophical Library, 1957.

Schactel, E. G. On memory and childhood amnesia. *Psychiatry,* 1947, 10, 1-26.

Schmideberg, Melitta. Some practical problems in the treatment of delinquents. *Psychiatric Quart. Suppl.,* 1959, 23, 235-246.

Schoen, Stephen M. The psychotherapeutic command. *Amer. J. Psychother.,* 1962, 16, 108-115.

Schwartz, Emanuel K., and Wolf, Alexander. Irrational trends in contemporary psychotherapy: cultural correlates. *Psychoanalysis and Psychoanal. Rev.,* 1958, 45, 65-74.

Seeman, Julius. Psychotherapy and perceptual behavior. *J. Clin. Psychol.,* 1962, 18, 34-37.

Selye, Hans. *The stress of life.* New York: McGraw-Hill, 1956.

Shand, Harley C. *Thinking and psychotherapy. New Haven: Yale,* 1961.

Shannon, C. E. *The mathematical theory of communication.* Urbana: University of Illinois Press, 1949.

Shapiro, M. B., and Ravenette, A. T. A preliminary experiment on paranoid delusions. *J. Mental Sci.,* 1959, 105, 77-83.

Shapiro, Stewart B. A theory of ego pathology and ego therapy. *J. Psychol.,* 1962, 53, 81-90.

Shaw, Franklin J. (Ed.). *Behavioristic approaches to counseling and psychotherapy.* Univ. Alabama Stud., 1961, No. 13.

Simeons, A. T. W. *Man's presumptuous brain.* New York: Dutton, 1960.

Skinner, B. F. *Science and human behavior.* New York: Macmillan, 1953.

Skinner, B. F. Critique of psychoanalytical concepts. *Sci. Monthly,* 1954, 79, 300-385.

Skinner, B. F. Freedom and the control of men. *Amer. Scholar,* 1956, 25, 47-65.

Snyder, William U., and others. *Group report of research in psychotherapy.* State College, Pa.: Pennsylvania State College, 1953.

Solomon, Richard L., and Wynne, Lyman C. Traumatic avoidance learning. *Psychol. Rev.,* 1954, 61, 353-385.

Spotnitz, Hyman. Comment on Schwartz and Wolf's *Irrational trends in psychotherapy. Psychoanal. & Psychoanalytic Rev.*, 1958, 45, 74-78.

Staats, A. W., and others. Operant conditioning of factor analytic personality traits. *J. General Psychol.*, 1962, 66, 101-114.

Standal, Stanley W., and Corsini, Raymond J. (Eds.). *Critical incidents in psychotherapy.* Englewood Cliffs, N. J.: Prentice-Hall, 1959.

Starer, Emanuel, and Tanner, Henry. An analysis of responses of male schizophrenic patients to Freudian-type stimuli. *J. Clin. Psychol.*, 1962, 18, 58-61.

Stark, Paul. Success in psychotherapy—a common factor. *Amer. J. Psychother.*, 1961, 15, 431-435.

Starobin, Joseph R. How much reason? *Liberation*, Summer, 1959, 18-19.

Stekel, Wilhelm. *The homosexual neurosis.* New York: Physician's and Surgeon's Book Co., 1934.

Stekel, Wilhelm. *Technique of analytical psychotherapy.* New York: Liveright, 1950.

Stewart, Louis H. Social and emotional adjustment during adolescence as related to the development of psychosomatic illness in adulthood. *Genet. Psychol. Monogr.*, 1962, 65, 175.

Stokvis, B. Results of psychotherapy. In Stokvis, B. (Ed.). *Topical problems of psychotherapy.* Vol. I. New York: S. Karger, 1960.

Sullivan, Harry Stack. *Conceptions of modern psychiatry.* Washington: William Alanson White Foundation, 1947.

Sullivan, Harry Stack. *The interpersonal theory of psychiatry.* New York: Norton, 1953.

Suttie, Ian D. *The origins of love and hate.* London: Kegan, Paul, 1948.

Suzuki, D. T. *Zen Buddhism.* New York: Doubleday Anchor Books, 1956.

Symonds, Percival M. *Dynamics of psychotherapy.* New York: Grune & Stratton, 1956-1959.

Szasz, Thomas S. The myth of mental illness. *Amer. Psychologist*, 1960, 15, 113-118.

Szasz, Thomas S. The uses of naming and the origin of the myth of mental illness. *Amer. Psychologist*, 1961, 16, 59-65.

Tabori, Paul. *The natural science of stupidity.* Philadelphia: Chilton Co., 1959.

Tabori, Paul. *The art of folly.* Philadelphia: Chilton Co., 1961.

Thorne, Frederick C. *Principles of personality counseling.* Brandon, Vermont: Journal of Clinical Psychology, 1950.

Thorne, Frederick C. An evaluation of eclectically-oriented psychotherapy. *J. Consult. Psychol.,* 1957, 21, 459-464.

Thorne, Frederick C. *Personality: a clinical eclectic view.* Brandon, Vermont: Journal of Clinical Psychology, 1961.

Tillich, Paul. *The courage to be.* New York: Oxford University Press, 1953.

Voget, Fred W. Man and culture. *Amer. Anthropol.,* 1960, 62, 943-965.

von Neumann, J., and Morgenstern, O. *Theory of games and economic behavior.* Princeton: Princeton University Press, 1944.

Walker, Kenneth, and Strauss, E. B. *Sexual disorders in the male.* Baltimore: Williams and Wilkins, 1952.

Walker, Kenneth. A rare case when a doctor's lie was justified. *Sexology.* 1962, 28, 446-448.

Warshaw, Leon, and Bailey, Mattox. A study of Q-sort generalizations in the form of constellations within personalities. *J. Clin. Psychol.,* 1962, 18, 40-43.

Watts, Alan W. *The way of Zen.* New York: New American Library, 1959.

Watts, Alan W. *Nature, man and sex.* New York: New American Library, 1960.

Westwood, Gordon. *Society and the homosexual.* New York: Dutton, 1953.

Whitaker, Carl A., and Malone, Thomas A. *Roots of psychotherapy.* New York: McGraw-Hill, 1953.

White, Robert W. Motivation reconsidered: the concept of competence. *Psychol. Rev.,* 1959, 66, 297-333.

Whitehorn, John. Understanding psychotherapy. *Amer. J. Psychiat.,* 1955, 112, 328-333.

Whorf, Benjamin. *Language, thought, and reality.* New York: Wiley, 1956.

Whyte, L. L. *The unconscious before Freud.* New York: Basic Books, 1960.

Wiener, Norbert. *Cybernetics.* New York: Wiley, 1948.

Wilson, Robert A. To the end of sanity. *Independent,* November 1959, 4, 6.

Wolberg, Lewis R. *Medical hypnosis.* New York: Grune & Stratton, 1948, 2 vols.

Wolberg, Lewis R. *The technique of psychotherapy.* New York: Grune & Stratton, 1954.

Wolf, William. Wider horizons in psychotherapy. *Amer. J. Psychother.,* 1962, 16, 124-149.

Wolfenden, John, and others. *Report of the committee on homosexual offenses and prostitution.* London: Her Majesty's Stationery Office, 1957.

Wolfensberger, Wolf. The free will controversy. *Amer. Psychologist,* 1961, 16, 37-9.

Wolpe, Joseph. Learning versus lesions as the basis of neurotic behavior. *Amer. J. Psychiatry,* 1956, 112, 923-927.

Wolpe, Joseph. *Psychotherapy of reciprocal inhibition.* Stanford: Stanford University Press, 1958.

Wolpe, Joseph. The systematic desensitization treatment of neuroses. *J. Nerv. Mental Dis.,* 1961a, 132, 189-203.

Wolpe, Joseph. The prognosis in unpsychoanalysed recovery from neurosis. *Amer. J. Psychiat.,* 1961b, 117, 35-39.

Index

437